M̶O̶N̶T̶P̶E̶L̶I̶E̶R̶,̶ ̶V̶E̶R̶M̶O̶N̶T̶   P9-DGJ-847

WITHDRAWN

WITHDRAWN

THE KOREANS

AND

THEIR CULTURE

By

CORNELIUS OSGOOD

PROFESSOR OF ANTHROPOLOGY
YALE UNIVERSITY

THE RONALD PRESS COMPANY ⸱ NEW YORK

Copyright, 1951, by

THE RONALD PRESS COMPANY

———

All Rights Reserved

The text of this publication or any part
thereof may not be reproduced in any
manner whatsoever without permission in
writing from the publisher.

4

Library of Congress Catalog Number: 51-271

PRINTED IN THE UNITED STATES OF AMERICA

915.19
oo 82k
c.2

For my friend

PAUL FEJOS

21321

PREFACE

It may be said of Korea that there is no country of comparable significance concerning which so many people are ignorant. For hundreds of years the Koreans sought safety in complete isolation, developing unique customs and a distinctive way of life. Since the last quarter of the nineteenth century, however, they have suffered deeply in the discovery that a nation cannot sustain its independence if it will not share in the general development of civilization. Shocked by violent Japanese, Russian, and American occupations, the Koreans now struggle for the restoration of their liberty and national dignity. As that effort, with its far-reaching implications, can affect the whole world, it has seemed desirable that the characteristics of Korean culture and the circumstances which led to their development should be made available, particularly to those whose obligation is the welfare of the sorely beset Koreans.

The material presented falls into five Parts, each of which may be considered separately. The first consists of a study of a Korean farming village on the island of Kanghwa, chosen as typical of the thousands of such communities in which the great majority of Koreans live today. The information was recorded by observation and from local informants during the summer of 1947, with the assistance of two Korean students.

The second Part consists of a survey of the distinguishing features of the culture of the ruling upper class, largely concentrated in the capital about the beginning of the present century. This comparative material results from the critical analysis of information systematically culled over a period of years from scores of books and articles on Korea, references to which are given in footnotes.

The outline of Korean political history offered in the third Part rests primarily on the English rendering by Homer B. Hulbert of the *Tong Sa Kang Yo,* a Korean summary of the four ancient histories of the country, together with a synthesis of private manuscripts on the last Korean dynasty to which he or his translator, a native scholar specializing in that period, had access. Hulbert also used the history of Ma Tuan-lin in describing the early tribespeople of the region.

v

More accurate and extensive translations of the Korean histories which would be desirable do not exist, so the inevitable deficiencies of Hulbert's early efforts are admittedly shared. The record has been tempered, however, by comparisons with James S. Gale's *History of the Korean People,* with special studies of the Chinese dynastic annals, and with variant translations of Ma Tuan-lin. Footnote page references to Hulbert's *History of Korea* have been eliminated in both the third and fourth Parts of this study, since his account is chronologically presented and any desired correlation becomes reasonably simple without them.

The résumé of culture comprising the fourth Part of the volume likewise uses the work of Hulbert, to which data from many other writers have been added. It should be recognized that Hulbert, through his papers in the *Korean Repository,* his editing of the *Korea Review,* and the publication of his various books, contributed more to an understanding of Korean culture by the English-reading world than any other person of his time.

The final Part, dealing with modern Korea and the climactic events of 1950, results from a combination of a study of the commentaries on the contemporary period, plus personal observations and discussions with individuals directly involved.

Since it is inevitable that any writer, no matter how objective he attempts to be, introduces a personal factor in selecting and evaluating the data he uses, the critical reader will doubtless demand some indication of the writer's background. His focus on Korea has been sharpened from two directions. One was northwest America, where extended research on the aborigines and their relationship among circumpolar peoples to those of the Asiatic homeland in which they originated, proves more pertinent than would seem obvious because the Koreans themselves first came into their Peninsula from the area now known as Manchuria and Siberia. The second direction of approach was that of China, in which country a comparable community study was undertaken in 1938. This latter research, together with the intervening years spent in the teaching of the history and diffusion of Chinese culture, has had a most direct bearing on the understanding of a people who have borrowed so heavily from the "elder brother." Korean and Chinese bilingual colleagues and students have been depended upon both for interpretation in the field and for translation of textual sources.

The study which has resulted in this volume has been carried on as part of a research program of Yale University and its Peabody Museum of Natural History, with the generous financial assistance of The Viking Fund, Inc., of New York. Acknowledgment is also due the Department of State and the Department of the Army for co-operation in making it possible to conduct investigations in Korea at a period when each additional American visitor to that country added a strain to a complex administrative problem.

In Korea itself, numerous individuals contributed in large or small ways to the project. Lt. Gen. John R. Hodge, commanding the XXIV Corps, not only provided extraordinary freedom for unbiased investigation but also supported the undertaking with all necessary material assistance. Among other American officials who gave unusual help were Mr. Robert A. Kinney, Dr. H. H. Underwood, Mr. Younghill Kang, Miss Margit Harris, Capt. James D. Finkle, Mr. Leonard Bertsch, and Mr. Warren A. Gilbertson.

Of Korean friends, Dr. Kim Che-won, Director of the National Museum, was especially cooperative. It would likewise be remiss not to mention my gentle host for the summer of 1947, Kim Chung-sŏp, Abbot of Chŏndung Sa. Most significant for the research were my two student-collaborators, Kim Woo-sik and Han P'yo-ku. Their courage and devotion during the weeks that we lived and worked together on Kanghwa will always remain an inspiration.

For personal support in connection with the Korean project my thanks go to Mr. Edgar S. Furniss and to Mr. Dean Acheson. Mr. Younghill Kang, apart from other favors, has left me in his debt by critically reading the manuscript. My Chinese colleague, Professor Li An-che, provided me with his translations of pertinent sections of Ma Tuan-lin. I am also grateful for the editorial assistance of Mrs. Doris E. Irons. Credit is primarily due Jean Day Zallinger for the appearance of the maps and drawings in the text. Shirley P. Glaser and Rudolph F. Zallinger also assisted in their preparation. Among those individuals whose great influence takes on almost intangible meanings with the passing of time I must pay deference to Harriett Osgood. Finally, I wish to express my sincere gratitude for long years of encouragement and stimulation from my friend Paul Fejos to whom with humility I have dedicated this volume.

CORNELIUS OSGOOD

Yale University, January, 1951

CONTENTS

PART ONE

A Contemporary Korean Village

PART TWO

The Korean Capital and the Ruling Class

PART THREE

The Origins and Chronological Development of the Korean Nation

PART FOUR

A Résumé of the Cultural History of Korea

PART FIVE
Modern Korea

MAPS AND TEXT FIGURES

PLATES

In the descriptions of the plates, the following keys indicate the source of photographs: Author = Photograph taken by the author on Kanghwa Island in 1947, with negative number; Buk. = Photograph from *Bukkoku-ji Temple and Sekkutsu-an Cave;* C.K.Z. = from *Chōsen Koseki Zufu;* M.E.I. = from *Museum Exhibits Illustrated.*

THE ROMANIZATION OF KOREAN WORDS

This book uses, almost without exception, the McCune-Reischauer system, which has been adopted by various United States Government departments, including the Army Map Service. Vowels are pronounced as follows: *a* as in *father, e* like the *a* in *rate, i* as in *machine, o* as in *home, u* as in *rude, ae* like the *a* in *cat, o* like the *o* in *son, u* like the *u* in *put, oe* like German *ö*. Consonants are pronounced as in English except for *r*, which has a combined *l* and *r* quality. The sign ʻ indicates aspiration. Hyphens have been restricted to personal names, thus helping to distinguish them. Personal names have been spelled according to the owner's preference, when known.

Part One

A CONTEMPORARY KOREAN VILLAGE

1

INTRODUCTION

THE STUDY of human culture as an exacting technical procedure has been one of the most recent developments of the great
rise of science which has distinguished western civilization during the
past few hundred years. In fact, it was not until the advent of the
second World War that anthropology reached a maturity which
brought a general recognition of the tremendous importance of an
empirical knowledge of those complexities of human relations distinguishing one national group from another. Without such inter-
cultural understanding, any attempt to resolve the conflicts which
result from psychological, social, and political differences seems hope-
less. The procedure of the anthropologist is still experimental and
variable but it has gone far beyond the stage of casual observations
by the isolated individual with intellectual curiosity. How it may be
applied in the case of Korea is a pertinent question.

In a general sense, the anthropologist would like to know how and
why the Korean thinks and behaves as he does. To collect the necessary data requires a training which will enable the investigator to
perceive and record the culture which has attracted his attention. His
skill depends largely upon his familiarity with the methods of his
predecessors as well as upon his own experience in a variety of societies. All peoples have struggled to resolve certain basic problems
of human existence and they have worked out many ways of doing
so, some with greater effectiveness, and some with less. The more
one knows of these varieties of human experience, the more quickly
one discerns the similarities and the differences in a new cultural
scene. Thus the knowledge that the anthropologist brings with him
is the more essential factor in determining the thoroughness of his
research. The notion that a foreigner is always at a disadvantage
in understanding an exotic culture is a fallacy. Actually, probably
no culture is harder to comprehend than one's own because the pre-
requisite objectivity is gained only by a complex process of sophisti-

3

cating self-alienation. The native is lost in a confusion of inbred ideals, which, in serving to cushion the shocks of reality, blind him to the truth of his own behavior and of those like him. Whatever his education, the peculiarities of others will be more apparent.

In order to know all the data of Korean culture, theoretically one would have to be aware of the totality of the ideas and the behavior, including the material results therefrom, of each individual in the nation. Fortunately one need not eat a whole jar of kimch'i to become familiar with the quality of that Korean national dish. The sampling technique has proved one of the most important mechanisms of social science and it is by selecting a segment of a national culture for study that the anthropologist approaches the problem of understanding it. The unit which can be studied most effectively is the community or village. When a number of communities representing regional variations has been analyzed, together with a selection of larger towns and cities, as well as the ties that interrelate them, one will have moved far toward the understanding of the culture of the nation.

The procedure in studying the community is in itself also a sampling process, but one attempts to learn the ideas and behavior of as many individuals as possible. At least one should try to obtain representative data from members of all classes, ages, sexes, and other differentiable aggregates of the populace. And for the avid, one needs description in endless detail of everything from facial gestures which externalize an emotion to the intricacies of the weaving in a straw sandal. Inevitably, the anthropologist falls short of the goal, yet nonetheless may be richly rewarded for his effort.

Such an accumulation of information answers the question of the *how* in a culture but not the *why*. The latter problem is faced by determining the causes for particular ideas and behavior. Possibly one of the generally unrecognized contributions of anthropology has been the tacit acceptance of the theory of multiple causation in the macrocosmic social sphere. The modern anthropologist no longer seeks a single determining cause for a national culture but recognizes the complex interaction of many.

The causes will include the historical factor which is the extension of the impact of culture on personalities through time. People inherit most of their culture from the preceding generation. It is inculcated from their parents in earliest childhood and reinforced by their teachers whether formally in the classroom or through the casual contacts of interpersonal relations. From their first acts to the final disposition of their dead bodies, they are certainly influenced by their ancestors.

The natural environment is also a causative factor in the development or change of culture. If one source of food is destroyed or disappears, people to survive must seek out another. People are always adjusting to their environment, attempting religious controls when frustrated by the lack of technical skills, or perhaps constructing machines for refrigeration or for radiant heating when they are not.

Also there is the important cause of change which may be seen in the impact of one cultural group upon another, whether by the stimulus of diffused ideas or the introduction of physical forms. The idea that man had discovered a mechanism in which to fly stimulated countless millions of people who had not yet seen an airplane and on the other hand an English countryman, unaware of the diffusion of his vehicle, may ask if Ford automobiles are also used in the United States.

Perhaps most important, if less clear, are the effects which an individual may have on his society. An understanding of the impact of personality on culture involves the deeper limits of psychology and takes one into the spheres of psychoanalysis as well as general psychosomatic investigations. When we speak of great men we are generally referring to those who by some still uncertain process of origination have transformed their cultural increment into a force which changes those who follow after. Let their impact be strong enough and they will be honored as gods.

There are likewise other causative factors which aid in the explanation of the *why* of culture but we need not proliferate here. At the time of the American occupation of Korea no community study had ever been undertaken from the approach indicated above. What has been accomplished since constitutes the merest beginnings in the study of Korean national culture. As yet we can only hope to answer some of the *how,* possibly suggest an inkling of the *why.*

Korea, a country of approximately thirty million people is comprised, like China, almost entirely of small villages. They are tucked away in a myriad of little valleys, their fields of grain filling the open land between. There are some intervening plains but they too are dotted with clumps of thatch-roofed houses. Only the upper reaches of the hills and the mountain areas, especially in the northeast, appear still unoccupied.   Elsewhere as one follows the edge of the growing fields around some spur of rising land, one comes upon a group of houses, perhaps ten, perhaps many more.   It is in these little communities where a score to several hundred individuals live that one finds the basic Korean society.   Each village is an almost independent social unit and despite the political despotisms which so often overshadow the nation, they remain democratic.   Korean men are fond of traveling but they are apt to know other parts of the country better than adjacent villages.   They may meet their neighbors in the fields or district town but they seldom visit a near-by community except on some ceremonial occasion.   Certainly if one does not know the village, one cannot begin to comprehend Korean culture.

Villages vary somewhat in different parts of the Peninsula.   Least typical as a large group are those of the northeast, an area considered relatively wild throughout Korea's long history.   This was the region of uncouth tribespeople and deep forests.   Agricultural development was more difficult and the opportunities for cultural advance seemed always to lag behind other quarters of the country. But even the early Yi kings worried about the situation and sent teachers to establish better schools.   In our time, there are still differences, but the commonality of all Korean villages is unmistakable when they are compared, for example, with any Chinese or Japanese community.

A more subtle eye is required to catch obvious differences between the villages in other parts of the country, certain localizations excepted, of which the isolated island of Cheju is a unique example.   The fields are more verdant in the south and have a bamboo warmth.   The physical appearance of the people shows some variation and there are dialectic differences,* but taking the culture by and large, from a casual perusal it seems much less differentiated, say, than the variations within Italy, a country of similar size, population, and length of civilization.

Korea is essentially agricultural and about four fifths of the total population is engaged in producing crops from the land. One of the

* According to Younghill Kang, the dialects of Korea are all mutually intelligible except for that of Cheju Island. For the distribution of the seven distinct dialects and the per cent of Koreans speaking each, see *Summation*, August, 1946:83. Presumably the information was taken from the elaborate studies carried on by the Japanese.

Figure 1. Map of Korea Showing Provinces and Localities Mentioned in the Text

7

main exceptions as a way of gaining a livelihood is fishing and we find that many of the seashore villages, although by no means all, are occupied by fishermen. Even among the fishing families, however, one may expect to find some land under cultivation to augment their income from the sea.

Further, it is quickly obvious from the economic records that the typical Korean villager is primarily engaged in raising rice. The characteristic air view of the land in summer is that of a multitude of paddy mosaics in an infinite variety of shapes and shades of green, filling all the crevices in a jagged land of hills.

With these facts in mind, the anthropologist, to begin his studies, would logically seek out a village of rice farmers of perhaps two to three hundred population in an area with as nearly typical Korean culture as one may predicate from historical sources. Speculating on the most desirable Korean locality in which to begin research, the writer before visiting Korea came to the conclusion through study of the literature that any one of three regions would be satisfactory. One was the country around Kyŏngju, the capital of the ancient Silla dynasty in the southeast of the Peninsula. These are proud districts which have enjoyed more peace with dignity than any other part of the country. Their contribution to what we know as Korean culture is as rich as are their fertile rice fields. The principal disadvantage appears in that the province has been so far removed from the capital center during the past thousand years.

To avoid this weakness, if it proved essential to do so, the region rising to the east of the modern capital of Seoul was considered advantageous, being also almost the geographical center of the country.

Third of the choices was Kanghwa Island. Here prejudice entered in as one might say that no other part of the country is so symbolically Korean. It was on Kanghwa that Tan-gun, the traditional ancestor of all the people, came down to earth and built his altar on Mari San. This was the island to which the Koryŏ kings were accustomed to flee, holding it as the last free soil when the Mongol invaders controlled the rest of the land. Refuge and defense of the capitals for a millennium, it was on Kanghwa that the French and later the Americans fought in their frustrating attempts to bring the Hermit Kingdom into contact with the modern world and it was there that the contact was finally accomplished by the Japanese in the treaty of 1876.

Certainly the farmers of Kanghwa should be richly immersed in the culture of their nation. Yet an island seems a strange place to choose as typical of a continental civilization (Fig. 2, p. 15).

The considerations discussed have been largely theoretical. The anthropologists must also resolve practical difficulties and in the Korea of 1947, they were not lacking. An attempt to undertake independent research under the aegis of a military occupation should be avoided if possible for, though cooperation is generous and sincere, it can be even more confusing than the complications of operating as an alien in a country at war.

The acquisition of native collaborators, vehicles for transport, local currency, shelter, and a minimum of supplies were the specific problems. The more obvious difficulties were resolvable in the matter of days by a special order of the American Commanding General. During years of war, however, the rural roads, poor at best, had suffered and the torrential rains of the summer period often rendered them at least technically impassable. The housing shortage was as bad as in most of the war-disrupted world, and all of this in a country seething with political turmoil for which no one can be thanked. Still, even these complications can be accepted as professional hazards, and incidental.

The matter of acquiring native collaborators is a more important aspect of a short intensive research period. In such circumstances, one needs interested, courageous, and sophisticated co-workers and they prove rare in any society. Interpreters, in great demand by the occupation forces, had gained a bad name among the people because of the chicanery of some. Thus, ordinary interpreters were out of the question if one wished to lose oneself in the life of a village for a few months. The situation was resolvable by letting it be known that a few students of social science might be chosen for a period of rural research. Candidates appeared from strange occupations, men who had struggled under the most oppressive circumstances to gain knowledge prohibited by the Japanese rulers. They wished verification for what truth they had gained from short periods in the universities before the war and were enthusiastic about the opportunity to continue their social studies.

The decision on the locale in which to work was reached when it was ascertained that one of the best students was a native of Kanghwa and knew the local situation intimately, whereas a survey trip to southeast Korea had demonstrated practical difficulties of a serious nature in working so far from the capital. Inquiry also indicated the Kanghwa villages to be probably as typical of Korean culture as any to be found. Finally, on examination of the geographic factors one realizes that Kanghwa, although technically an island, actually comprises the western reaches of the central Kyŏnggi Province, being cut off from the mainland of which it is physiographically a part only by a narrow estuary of the Han River in taking a short cut from the capital to the sea.

Our first trip to visit the Kanghwa villages was memorable and had as its goal the selection of a community on which to concentrate, together with the not-so-simple problem of finding living quarters with space for writing to accommodate at least three people. My student's village was ruled out for three reasons. First, it was primarily a fishing village and we were seeking a settlement of typical rice growers; second, the housing shortage was extreme and we needed more space than squeezing someone out of some single room would allow; and third, we could not approach within miles of it in our borrowed vehicle.

A simple solution suggested itself. On southern Kanghwa is situated one of Korea's most famous Buddhist sites, the fortified monastery of Chŏndung Sa, nestled behind ancient stone walls in a pocket formed by three hills some hundreds of feet high (Pl. 1, p. 30). This relict of past glory was occupied only by the abbot, two priests, a nun, and a few lay servants. The great beauty of the spot had attracted the Japanese governors-general and some assistance had been given to modernize one wing of the main building into a delightful retreat consisting of two bedrooms and a glass-enclosed solarium looking out toward the sea.

We were courteously received by the abbot but it was clear that he wished no permanent guests and would consider no suggestions of renting his desirable suite to a strange American in such times as we had come. With reasonable pride he did ask us to visit the temples of the monastery. Now it so happens that living in a hinterland village of China before the war, the practice of Buddhism became an essential part of the process of inculcating the anthropologist into Chinese culture. That quality of the grotesque and exotic which appears in the later manifestations of the religion of the great Gautama had long disappeared in a respect for the most tolerant of the messiahs, and it is easy to pay obeisance when it can be freely offered. What passed between us before the benign figure of the Buddha is uncertain, but when we returned to the abbot's quarters to say farewell he said in his quiet voice that he would be happy to have the teacher and his students as his guests for as long as they wished to stay. In this manner we came to make our headquarters in the monastery of Chŏndŭng Sa.

From one of the monastery gates a path leads over a ridge and down at no great distance to the principal town in south Kanghwa. It is in itself a small place with a population of about 800 people. In it is the district school and the market place in which, on each fifth day, farmers and traders meet to supply each other's needs. Most important, the town is the bottom rung of the official ladder, the smallest place in which one finds police and paid political officers. The town thus is the point of contact between the democratic village units and the national government. This local center would be worth considerable attention in relating the community to the outside world.

Climbing from the monastery to the opposite gate one follows a path which, once through the guardian wall, twists downward almost to the level of the Yellow Sea lying clearly visible in the distance beyond the slope of Mari San. The pines have been trimmed of their lower branches and the grass grows thin beneath, with a wild flower here and there to give color to the scene (Pl. 2, p. 30).

Halfway down, a cluster of thatch roofs appear below, making a graying yellow border to the green rice fields spreading out beyond. This paddy land was reclaimed from the ocean many centuries ago when a stone embankment was built between the seashore hills in order to cut off the high engulfing tide. We wandered into the village from the hill path like dropping into another world. Not even a cart road connected this isolated settlement with the rest of the country. It seemed ideal for our purposes.

We soon encountered a young man with whom my Kanghwa student had gone to school. The formalities of introduction were undertaken and after some exchange of information we went to call on one of the principal men of the village. He received us with some anxiety but after establishing the family relationship of my companion, broke into smiles and invited us to the small room of his house which served for the entertainment of guests.

In due course, our general purpose of visiting the region was explained. This created some suspicion only allayed by the inbred Korean respect for scholars. Being at last convinced that our interests were not political and that our activities were wholly independent of any governmental authority, he answered some preliminary questions. We discovered that the village contained somewhat less than two hundred people, that almost all the families were nominally Confucianists, and that, except for one or two, the men were engaged in raising the rice which spread out in front of his house. Satisfied that no community could be more effectively the object of our study, we explained that we would like to participate in the life of the village for a few months. This suggestion was a surprise if not a shock and we talked on. It was agreed that the Americans had failed to understand fully the Koreans' problems and when it was pointed out that such information as we might come to have of the common people could be helpful, our host was suddenly pleased. It was the first time, he said, that he had known of anyone from the great nation across the sea to take a real interest in the problems of his countrymen.

During the course of the following week we established ourselves in the monastery, surveyed the general vicinity, and held long seminars on the procedure and methods of our research. The goal was to study one village as completely as possible, gradually extending our knowledge to include comparative data from the other communities in the same li (or ri), and at the same time to make a special analysis of the local town, particularly with reference to governmental, economic, and educational factors which served to tie together all the villages of the area. For these purposes, one student spent most of his time in the town while the other joined with me in the analysis of our primary village. Week after week passed by with a rich harvest of information, sometimes surprising my companion who had been born and raised in the vicinity. With the excitement of what we were learning, the days and nights seemed too short for the recording, comparing, and planning of our work. Wearily we strained our eyes as the kerosene in the little lamps burned low, three small lights in the Kanghwa hills that kept flickering after the temple gongs had been silenced and the villages had become dark in the sleeping valleys below.

Intimate and involved we became with the people after the passing of a month. In some measure we shared their tragedies and joys. We ate and drank with them, we laughed and we went to funerals, we shared their secrets, and sometimes we tried to save their lives. Before the summer was over we observed the outside world, by then almost forgotten, throw its mantle of fear over the peaceful valleys as the national police began to herd the young men of the villages into jail by the truckload. We learned what we would have been happier never to have known. Until the end of the memory, there will be no forgetting the silent nights on a village matang with gray-haired men sitting speechless, with the moonlight glistening in their pain-filled eyes.

In this survey of a Korean community it will not be possible to present the full measure of what we learned. Some of the information is too technical for appreciation except by the specialist in social science, and would probably confuse rather than further a general understanding. As might be expected, there are the perhaps inevitable deficiencies of an initial study, and certain subjects, such as the role of Buddhism, are lightly treated because they are regarded as being more tractable to deal with in a topical monograph. At best, we have merely sunk a shaft and tapped rich veins. Most of the precious metal must yet be dug.

Unless otherwise indicated or clearly obvious, the data offered should be accepted as applying specifically to one small village in southern Kanghwa. Some comparative material will be offered to extend the picture. Nevertheless, the intention is to present explicit and accurate descriptions of one locality. Also, there will probably be some glaring errors besides a few that do not glare. The difference in taste between a pickled turnip and the pickled daikon or oriental radish still baffles me. All things considered, if one comes to feel that a greater appreciation of Korean culture has been gained through our efforts, we shall be content and give haven to the hope that others will soon do better. And so to Kanghwa.

2

THE ISLAND OF KANGHWA

THE ISLAND of Kanghwa lies juxtaposed to the western shore of Kyŏnggi Province in central Korea just south of the point where the Peninsula begins to reach out into the Yellow Sea.[1]* It is separated from the mainland to the east by the secondary mouth of the Han River, a channel which narrows in places to about three hundred and fifty yards, a tortuous stretch of water easily whipped into fury by the force of tremendous tides which rise and fall between twenty and thirty feet, leaving rapids and whirlpools in their wake. To the north passes the main course of the Han, bending around the larger of the many islands adjacent to Kanghwa before emptying into the ocean.

Kanghwa, like most of Korea, has a rugged surface made up of innumerable hills and valleys. Few of the former are very high and few of the latter very broad. Nonetheless, the several mountains rising between fourteen and sixteen hundred feet take on a definite dignity in an island only about seventeen miles long and ten miles wide. According to the *Kanghwa Chi* or history of the island compiled by Chun Hun, there are fifty-one rivers and large brooks, thirty-three ponds, and seventeen "medicinal" springs pouring forth "water from heaven."

Pines are the most striking and plentiful trees of the island's forest cover, which on many of the hills has been thinned in the search for fuel. There are other varieties as well; common fruit trees such as the persimmon and pear. Occasionally in an ancestral garden one may find an arborvitae, or more rarely, some tamarisks with their feathery leaves. The oldest trees are protected and regarded with religious veneration. These ancient ones are particularly noticeable in the temple grounds where one is also likely to find comparative rarities such as the silver bell tree. Flowers are profuse in their sea-

---

* References to sources are grouped together at the end of each Part. See page 129 for the references for Part One.

son, the azaleas and rhododendrons perhaps making the greatest show. But there are many others, such as dogwood and roses, besides smaller wild flowers that twinkle under the pines on the hills. There is color enough on Kanghwa.

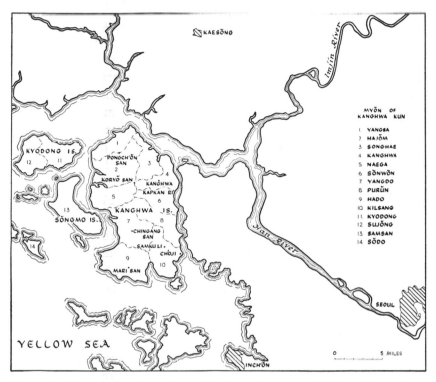

Figure 2. Map of Kanghwa Kun (District) Showing the Myŏn (Townships), Important Cities, and Mountains

Of wild animals, the largest and most decorative are the deer that go skittering through the hills, turning up their heels to the human intruders and warning the badgers and foxes that they too had better escape. Rabbits and weasels add to the number of four-footed things in the forests. Bird life is prolific. The long-legged birds such as the heron are a common sight in the rice fields and one needs only to walk along the roads to stir up the beautiful ring-necked pheasants. Sea birds swirl along the beaches and, in the migrating seasons, wild ducks and geese wing their way across the hills and valleys. There are numerous smaller birds to give life to the scene, as well as crawling creatures, snakes, and a plethora of pestiferous insects.

The story of Kanghwa begins with the legendary descent of Tangun attributed to the third millennium B.C. The forefather of Koreans is supposed to have built the two altars, one on Mari San in the south and the other on Pongch'ŏn Mountain, somewhat less than a thousand feet high, about twelve miles directly north of the first.

Even more impressive of age, however, are the dolmens or "table stones" built of great monoliths. A number of these are known on the island, the largest examined being one of three lying in the valley southeast of the above-mentioned Pongch'ŏn San and some three miles northwest of the capital city. A tremendous slab of stone, roughly eighteen by twenty-four feet in its maximum dimensions, rests five feet off the ground, supported by two more monoliths lying on their sides. Such constructions, widely spread over the ancient world, have been mostly associated with early cultures. In Korea they may well be later than in other areas but it would be difficult to believe them to have been constructed in our era (Pl. 3, p. 30).

The first recorded name of Kanghwa is Kappikoch'a and the name was changed to Hyŏlgu, or Cave Mouth, at some time during the Koguryŏ dynasty. In the middle of the eighth century under the Silla kings, Kanghwa was called Haegu, or Sea Mouth, but a few decades later the older name was revived with the special political designation of chin (fortress).

Early in the Koryŏ dynasty a hyŏn (prefectural) government was established in place of its chin status. In 1018, there were two political centers of the island, of which one was about three miles northwest of the present capital and the other on the southern slope of Mt. Chingang in the southwest. This situation apparently continued until 1232 when, during the Mongol invasions, the Korean capital was transferred from Songdo (Kaesŏng) to the island, whose status was then raised to a kun (district). There the rulers remained until 1270. In this period, the name Kang Do, or River Capital, was used as well as the present designation of Kanghwa, or Glory of the River. The latter term was a natural addition for it was during the royal occupation that many glorious undertakings were carried out.

Under the resident kings the present location for the island capital was apparently chosen and in 1233 an extensive outer wall enclosing 96,000 p'yong * of land was built around it. Pressed for protection

* A p'yong, or tsubo, is an area of 35.55 sq. ft. or 3.95 sq. yds. There are approximately 1,225 p'yong in an acre.

from the Mongols, at least some of the sixty to a hundred forts that form the ramparts around the edge of the island were also constructed. The need for increased agricultural development soon led to the erection of dikes in order to extend the rice fields into tidal lands and four of the present forty-one such engineering projects are recorded as having been put up in the decade following the year 1240.

In 1246, a large part of the capital burned, including the king's palace. Three years later he erected another inside the wall protecting the Chŏndung Sa Monastery as well as a detached residence on the south side of Mari San.

The famous wall of Chŏndung Sa with its four gates is known by the name of Samnang, or Three Sons. According to the story, it was built in one day by three children of Tan-gun, a truly singular feat as it is about a mile in length. Before the present "Temple of the Inherited Lamp" was erected within it, three other temples are said to have had their successive days and disappeared. Chŏndung Sa has also been, since the Koryŏ dynasty (918-1392), one of the five repositories of the national records. Buddhism has not greatly flourished since the last of the Koryŏ kings but there are still seven temples on the island, besides the ruins of at least ten more.

When the court returned to Songdo in 1270, they left four royal tombs including those of two kings, one on the slope of Chingang San and the other on Koryŏ San. This was not the last of Kanghwa as a royal residence, however, for most of the ruling family resided there during 1636 when the Manchu had the king besieged in Namhan fortress south of Seoul. The following year, the Manchu destroyed the Kanghwa capital and razed the walls, those now existing dating from reconstruction in 1676 and 1710. This was still not the end of Kanghwa's regal connections, for in 1831 the island became the birthplace of King Ch'ul-jong, the next to the last emperor of Korea.

In 1866, the French punitive expedition under Admiral Roze, angered by the execution of Christian priests, landed on Kanghwa. In the short course of their stay, they attempted to storm fortified Chŏndung Sa and were driven back with heavy casualties. In revenge, they sacked and burned the capital, leaving little but a great bronze bell and the Confucian temple to remind the people of the former glories of their city.

Again in 1871, troops of an American flotilla of war vessels, fired upon by one of the Kanghwa forts in fear of a second foreign attack, undertook a reprisal landing and defeated the unequally armed Koreans. With the end of the century and the development of new military methods, Kanghwa lost its importance as a guardian of the river and of the national capital.

Economically, Kanghwa has no great or distinctive significance for the nation, although besides rice and other grains, pottery and granite are important exports. Until modern times, the Han River was the route of communication with Seoul. Now there are antiquated buses on a gravel road which extends from the latter city northwest about thirty-five miles to the ferry crossing connecting with the village of Kapkan Ri, port of Kanghwa City which lies still another three miles inland. The journey is longer than it seems, especially in the rainy season when the road is often flooded. Also, a vehicle must wait on the tides to be barged across the fast water of the straits. In consequence, freight and the main flow of traffic proceed by a daily steamer plying between Kapkan Ri and Inch'ŏn, stopping at Ch'oji near the southeast corner of the island on its way. Inch'ŏn, the great eastern port of Korea, is connected to Seoul by railroad which makes this latter route far more dependable than any other.

Besides the road to Kanghwa City from Kapkan Ri, the most important highway runs some ten miles to connect the island capital with Samku Li,* or Three Roads Village, the principal town in the south, and by extension with the second ferry port of Ch'oji. Normally, there is a bus line on this route but since the war it has been periodically suspended. The north-south road actually comprises the eastern segment of a highway which loops around the island and provides adequate passage for an automobile except in the rainy season. There are numerous other roads orienting out from the capital, not to mention minor lanes which can almost imperceptibly disappear into narrowing rice dikes. Actually, in 1947, one saw little but pedestrian traffic on the highways. Occasionally an oxcart lumbered along, soon to turn off toward some hillside village. If there were any other motor vehicles on the island besides three or four government trucks and a few old buses, they remained effectively hidden.

Both telephone and telegraph lines connect the island with the mainland. The police seem to have the better of the two systems and with vigorous grinding of the generator, it is usually possible to shout

* Samku Li appears on the 1:50,000 maps of Korea as Onsuri.

from one headquarters to another. This indeed is a marvel considering the shortages of equipment and technicians with which the Koreans have been faced since the war.

Industries are few on Kanghwa. In ancient days, beautiful Koryŏ celadons were produced in its kilns. Today only the household jars are made, these varying in size from table utensils to tremendous kimch'i jars in which a man might hide like one of Ali Baba's thieves. One village near Samku Li is devoted wholly to such manufactures, which are trundled off in oxcarts to the ferry landing at Ch'oji. Near Kapkan Ri, there are also clay deposits from which bricks and tiles are fashioned.

Kanghwa has long been a source for granite and during most of this century a Japanese operated a quarry on the south shore of Hado Myŏn.* The best stone, however, comes from other islands. Gold mining on a small scale is carried on periodically, the sands being shoveled up and panned for colors. The income is probably relatively small.

A number of small weaving factories are spread around the island, with the center of production in the capital. These have produced cotton or silk cloth but not of the best quality. Famous mats are made in northern Kanghwa but this contribution has almost disappeared since the end of the royal regime to which the mats were supplied. So it was with the fine horses bred on Kanghwa long ago. Now this animal is scarcely to be seen except in a bridal cortege.

Ginseng, the supposedly aphrodisiacal elixir which Korea has for so many centuries supplied to China, can be found growing on Kanghwa, carefully protected by fences. Requiring six years to mature, the raising of this plant has been a traditional government monopoly. At a few places along the coast, salt is boiled from seawater in which it has been concentrated by the sun. For home consumption, there are iron smelters producing the metal heads of agricultural tools besides some other everyday necessities.

In the towns one sees small shops in which are sold endless varieties of merchandise imported from the mainland and ranging from medicinal drugs to simple knickknacks. There are a few carpenter shops largely engaged in supplying coffins. Most common are inns, restaurants, and teahouses, the latter in the larger places with their

* Hado appears on the 1:50,000 maps of Korea as Hwado, which seems to be an error.

complement of kisaeng, now descended to the role of familiar waitresses.

The government of Kanghwa fits into the national hierarchy of descending authority. The system would be simpler to comprehend were it not changed so frequently, but the general outlines can be made clear enough. Korea is politically divided into thirteen provinces plus the island of Cheju and each of the provinces is broken up into kuns, or districts (Fig. 1, p. 7). Kanghwa, including several of the larger off-shore islands, is all one kun. The kun, in turn comprises a series of myŏn, or townships, of which there are said to be currently fourteen in Kanghwa Kun. The ku, called locally purak, or community, is the next smallest unit of which there are 275 in Kanghwa Kun. Finally, there is the pan at the end of the political scheme and there are no less than 1,565 of these, or almost six for the average ku.

The finer aspects of this system were inaugurated by the Japanese and whatever its governmental virtues may be, there is some conflict with the simple sociological facts which must be explained. In the first place the villages, called tongni on Kanghwa, which are the obvious social units are no longer political unities at all. In the days of independence, aggregates of such villages formed li, which were subdivisions of the myŏn. The Japanese are said to have found the latter too large, and hence made the change. Politically, we shall of course accept the new system in our discussions, but in other cultural matters we shall adhere to the social realities.

The political head of Kanghwa Kun in 1947 was appointed by the Governor of Kyŏnggi Province, who in turn had been selected by the Korean Civil Administrator with the approval of the South Korea Interim Legislative Assembly, or at least that is the local official statement of the matter. Under the Japanese, just as the Provincial Governor appointed the first official of the kun, so the latter appointed the head man of the myŏn, or myŏn jang. Since the liberation, however, by proclamation of November 15, 1946, the myŏn jang are elected by one representative for each eighty of the population. The people think this is an improvement.

Just as in the case of the myŏn, the ku jang, instead of being appointed by the myŏn jang as was done under the Japanese, is now elected. One member of each household in the ku casts a secret ballot and there is no argument. Finally, we discover the pan jang elected by the same system as the ku jang.

A closer examination of the system in practice reveals some interesting facts. It should be noted that the office of the myŏn jang is the lowest in the political hierarchy to receive monetary support, including salaries, from the government. The ku jang, it is true, receives a share of the crops collected and passed on to the myŏn office but this is a nominal reward for his services which must be shared with the pan jang. Perhaps a more significant fact of the practice is that the elected pan jang must be validated in their position by the myŏn jang, even as his own appointments in the myŏn office are subject to the approval of the head of the kun. Finally, it seems that all of these officials hold office until they deem it desirable to retire or the people sufficiently object to them.

With extended observation, one notes that the pan jang do not seem to be very important individuals in the villages, often being too young to carry much weight with the family heads. This seems puzzling at first. Studying the political system historically, one finds that in the days of the empire, the li were said to be dominated by the "most intelligent" men in the area. In relative measure, this was true of the tongni, where the family heads concerned themselves democratically for the village welfare. In aggregate, the power of the farmers was tremendous, and as the early Yi kings clearly recognized, government existed for these people. Controls from the capital reached down so far and stopped. If under tyrants it came further, the masses writhed and revolted.

Thus the men who are village leaders of today see the jang as symbols of a new system, symbols of a centralized control, who lack any effective power. Distrustful, they vote their weaker representatives into office to act as intermediaries between the appointed political rulers and the hidden strength of the people. The crux of the opposing forces lies in the office of myŏn jang, who must please the higher officials and at the same time retain his contacts with the real leaders of the community. If he does not drink himself to death in his efforts to stabilize his social position, he is fortunate.

Even as described, the political organization would be simple if there were no more complications, but there are serious ones. One aspect of government, hitherto unmentioned, is that of the national police. Their hierarchy of internal controls roughly parallels the executive branch and is not subject to local discipline. The police chief of the kun in the Kanghwa capital is responsible through his superiors in the province to direction from Seoul. He passes his orders to his constabulary in their private quarters in the chief towns. His is a dangerous and unhappy position which again requires some historical reconstruction to understand.

As should be clear, when the Japanese were moved to annex Korea to their empire, the reaction of many of the Peninsula people was violent. Hatred burned and smoldered deep in the valleys and the fire of resentment was never really quenched. Obviously, most of the Korean police who accepted a position of enforcing the conqueror's regulations were looked upon as hardly less than traitors. The relationship between the native police and the villagers created a selective factor which undoubtedly led more sadistic individuals into the force than might otherwise have been expected and their experiences heightened such tendencies. By the time of the Second World War, the hardened brutality of the Korean national police was infamous throughout the East wherever they were used by their Japanese masters. Koreans imprisoned in their own country say that the Japanese were kind compared to these who served them.

When the liberation came in 1945, the people turned on the police and in some cases meted out vicious punishments that were extended to the innocent families of their victims. Korean culture engenders cruelty and the people at times break into uncontrolled fury. The police lost their jobs, but in the course of years, with experienced men needed for such positions, they learned to evade the weakening restrictions. Those who lost their positions in the north migrated south, and found a haven in the force. At least, so it was on Kanghwa.

Sympathy and human pity they needed but they received cold suspicion and hatred instead. And hatred they returned. When a police officer says that he will kill every "communist" on Kanghwa if it costs him his life, what does it mean? "Communist" has become a strange word in our time and it may refer to a political philosopher, a Russian spy, a member of any other political party, a labor organizer, a traitor to one's country, or someone who happens to be regarded as an enemy. On Kanghwa it seemed to mean just "any young man of a village." Sometimes my heart went out to the lonely ones drinking in their police box in order to escape the fear that out of the unfamiliar valleys would come the boys of the tongni with their sickles sharpened. And to my shame there were moments when I did not care.

There is still a third independent order of government officials in the kun. These are the representatives of the Department of Agriculture who are chiefly concerned with the problems of conservation and improvement. Three located in the myŏn office are assigned respectively to the problems of wet fields, dry fields, and fertilizers. A fourth is in charge of all the forests, both public and private, in the myŏn. He controls tree cutting and actively directs the program of reforestation, so essential for the winter fuel supply. This branch of the government service clearly represents one of the real contributions of the Japanese administration and although sometimes in conflict with individuals, is generally appreciated by the population. During the stress of war, sacrifices were made in the program, and for a period following the liberation controls were not enforced, with consequent damage. But since that time an obvious effort is being made to restore the system to its former effectiveness.

3

THE VILLAGE AND ITS ENVIRONS

SŎNDUP'O, the principal village on which our study centers, lies on the lower reaches of the southwest slope of Mt. Chŏngjok, which encloses within its three spurs the monastery of Chŏndung Sa. Sŏndup'o literally means "Boat prow port," a name which has hardly been descriptive for some centuries. The origin of the designation probably lies in the fact that the li of which it is a part, comprising eight or ten tongni, or villages, was first called Sŏndu Ri, or "Boat Prow Area," as most of the settlements were on the seashore and the little vessels lined up on the beaches would quickly suggest such a designation. Sŏndup'o, then a protected port, logically gained its name. Since the dike was built centuries ago, Sŏndup'o and several other villages of the li have become inland settlements with their residents looking out over the rice fields which have replaced the salt water tidal flats between them and Mari San (Pl. 4, p. 31).

Politically, Sŏndup'o consists of two pan. These, together with the four pan comprised in the two nearby villages, make up Sŏndu Ku, one of the nineteen ku of Kilsang Myŏn. Sociologically, Sŏndup'o may be regarded as one of the ten villages of Sŏndu Ri, itself one of the six areas of Kilsang Myŏn. Samku Li, the principal town of the myŏn, happens to belong in another li.

In Sŏndup'o there are 27 thatch-covered houses sheltering a population of 169 persons. The settlement is slightly smaller than the average village of the li, which contains altogether 332 houses and 2,147 people. The whole myŏn has 1,570 houses and a population of 9,300 of whom about 800 live in Samku Li.

Except for the boats and perhaps some piles of fishnets stored on the beach, the villages of Sŏndu Ri look much alike. It is the same with the people in them. Therefore a description of Sŏndup'o should serve to give a feeling of familiarity with the whole area.

The houses are not arranged in straight lines but dot the paths which seem to have existed from time immemorial, partly following valley contours and partly cutting across them. In any event, the orientation of the houses is not exacting although perhaps more doors open out at right angles to the lowland and sea than in any other direction.

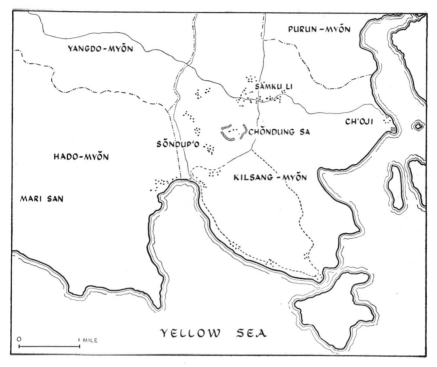

Figure 3. Map of Southern Kanghwa Island

The floor plans of the houses are of four general types: (1) rectangular, (2) L-shaped, (3) double L-shaped, and (4) U-shaped, or "open mouth." The cheapest and probably most primitive style is the rectangular but it is hardly of adequate size to accommodate an average family of six individuals. Even in Sŏndup'o there is only one such dwelling. The standard type of the region is the L-shaped building, which allows for at least three rooms with different functions (Pl. 5, p. 46). As a family grows economically more secure they will look forward to adding a complementary L-shaped structure thus giving, when observed superficially, the appearance of a square to the building. In Sŏndup'o there are fourteen of the L-shaped houses and ten more of the double-L variety. The remaining two dwellings are

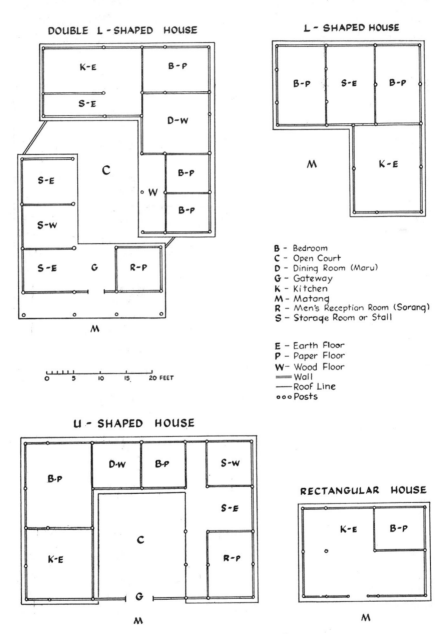

Figure 4. Plan of Village Houses

U-shaped. This latter pattern has been introduced only in the past ten years. Conservative residents say they are "inconvenient" or "ridiculous" as the ideal of the double L-shaped structure serves to set apart storage facilities from the living space proper, which the U-shaped house fails to do. Actually, this form is the common style of another part of the country and appears in Sŏndup'o because it has struck the fancy of certain individuals.

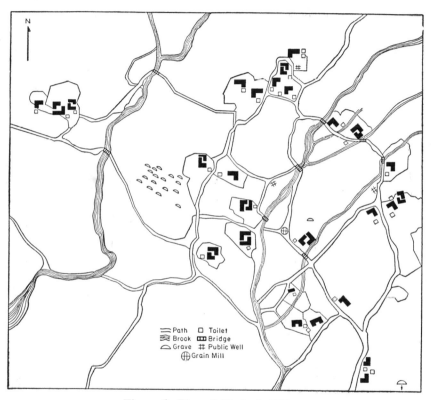

Figure 5. Plan of Sŏndup'o Village

Juxtaposed to each house is a walled garden with no outside opening, entrance being gained through the kitchen. The wall, usually of stones, is high enough to afford privacy and a sense of security which is not so complete, however, if the barrier is made only of sorghum stalks. One may expect to see vines covering the walls in summer and probably a few potted plants. In any event, both large and small pots will be in evidence, and if the family is well to do, in great numbers. A prosperous family will likely have a well in its kitchen garden which furnishes water both for drinking and washing. The garden is an area primarily for the women of the family and visiting males are not invited.

The kitchen differs from the other rooms of the house by having a lower floor of pressed dirt or clay. This feature is demanded for the stove, the flues of which run under the bedroom in order to heat it and finally converge into a separate round chimney of stone and clay, with a tile tube projecting from the top.

A greater appreciation of the kitchen can probably be gained by a description of a typical one of the better class. The room is about twelve feet wide from court to garden, a foot or two longer, and nearly nine feet high to the ridgepole. The walls are plastered with dike clay. The stove, on the right-hand side as one enters, is a rectangular stone and clay affair about seven feet long, two and a half feet wide, and sixteen inches high. Three large globular iron pots of differing sizes are sunk into it, each with a small fire pit beneath, shielded by an iron door. The largest pot, over two feet in diameter, is used for cooking grass for the ox or heating water for laundering. The other pots serve to prepare rice and other foods. The ironwork is imported to Kanghwa and the stove constructed by a skilled craftsman of the myŏn.

The ceiling projects down over the stove, providing a wall cabinet available from the main sleeping room which adjoins. On the far wall, on the left of the garden door, are open shelves containing four dining tray-tables—plus a smaller one either for a child or for special dishes. An upright cabinet for food faces the open shelves and several large kimch'i jars take up much of the intervening space. Porcelain dishes rest in an earthenware wash bowl and a slop jar for pigs' food stands near the stove. Small rings of straw of different sizes lean against the wall opposite to the stove—these are to keep the kimch'i jars off the floor in winter so that they will not freeze. A small hand brush for sweeping lies in the corner near a round rice straw cushion on which to sit. The quarter of the room on the left as one enters is partitioned off for pine branch fuel for the stove.

A further look around shows a hooked pine branch for pulling out coals from the stove into the little ditch in front of it, a small iron ash shovel, three gourds of different sizes, a rice scoop, a pot scouring brush, and a wooden cutting board. In one corner is a simple Chinese-type pot stove for an extra fire. Against the wall, at the far end of the stove, is a wood box for matches and some pine slivers with which to light a fire, together with a woven straw fan to stir the flame.

Figure 6. Hand Brush for Sweeping Floor

Besides these things there are trays and baskets and a shallow brass soup spoon hanging from a nail. On the right-hand corner of the stove rests a bundle of spice plant stems to keep the crickets away. Somehow, however, a cricket is apt to be chirping merrily when one looks at a Sŏndup'o kitchen.

The bedroom or paper floor room forming the corner of the house, so characteristic of Korea, has often been said to be of one standard size. This is believed by the people, but the accuracy of a ruler proves considerable variation in both length and breadth. The most distinctive thing is the floor, with layers of special paper placed on a smooth clay covering of the stone flues beneath. The oiled brown surface when in good condition glistens like the best linoleum.

Furnishings are at a minimum for there are no beds or chairs. A large wood cabinet is the essential addition, on top of which in the daytime is folded the mattress and covers used at night. About half the houses in Sŏndup'o also have paper on the walls but of a cheaper quality. One man had used many copies of the same edition of a Korean newspaper, each so it happened with a familiar picture of President Truman. In the corners of the room may be a pillow or two, an ashtray, or a bundle of clothing. On occasions the ancestor tablet is also in evidence. Shoes are always removed before entering the bedroom, which is private to the family.

Adjoining the paper floor room and extending out to form the other angle of the L is the maru or wood floor room of the house.* This is essentially the dining room. It is not heated by flues, as is the bedroom, and serves to receive the family guests. Ordinarily, the polished hardwood floor extends beyond the walls to form a narrow porch along one side of the court, a space "to come aboard," so to speak, as one removes his footwear. Again, furniture is at a minimum although there may be a cabinet, some wall hangings, a sizable mat on the floor, thin cushions, and a few ashtrays.

The three rooms described are the essential components of the typical Korean home. When needed, as is usually the case, additional paper floor rooms may be extended from the maru. These extra paper floor rooms have their own heating systems with fire boxes on one side and chimneys on the other.

In the double L-shaped house, the second part generally contains one or more wood floor rooms for storage purposes and some of dirt for giving space to fuel or to the family ox. At the angle of the turn in front, a passage will be left where otherwise a room might be. This is closed at night by a gate, sealing off the area within. On the far side of the gateway where the second L approaches the first, there may be a paper-floored room fixed up as the master's

---

* In some parts of Korea, as for instance in the Hamgyŏng Provinces, the term *maru* is used with the general sense of any floor. It is here used only for the special wood floor of the house and the adjoining veranda.

1. CHŎNDUNG TEMPLE IN THE SOUTH OF KANGHWA ISLAND

2. THE RICE FIELDS OF SŎNDUP'O

3. DOLMEN NEAR UN HWA VILLAGE IN HWANGHAE PROVINCE

4. VIEW ACROSS RICE FIELDS TOWARD SŎNDUP'O

study and private reception place for male guests. In any event, points of juncture of the two L's will be closed up with rocks, creating a private courtyard for the occupants within the walls.

It is obvious that the most significant factor determining the size of the village house is the number of paper floor rooms. In Sŏndup'o, seventeen homes have two, eight have three, one has four, and another has only one.

The matang is as characteristic of the Korean country house as is the maru or the paper floor room. This is a specially prepared area of smooth hardened clay almost as large as the building itself, in front of which it lies. It is on the matang that the people sit in summer, bringing out mats if they wish to stretch themselves. There grain is winnowed and vegetables dry, spread out beneath the sun. It is the man's workshop and his club. For half the year, social life centers on the hardened floor. There the little children play and old men spend their declining years. He who does not know the matang, will never understand Korea (Pl. 6, p. 46).

A few feet from each house stands a toilet shed, a small frame construction built square with posts at the corners and covered all over with thatch. An older type, being round, can be made of clay mortar and stones without using valuable timber. These have seldom been erected during the past fifteen years, however, and none survives in Sŏndup'o.

Close to the toilets of many of the houses is a pigsty with a sow and often suckling pigs. Adjoined to two houses are ox sheds although most of the oxen (nine in 1947, including one calf) in Sŏndup'o are sheltered in a section of the family living quarters. There are no horses in all of Sŏndu Ri. Chickens are common enough, however, for seventeen households have them in Sŏndup'o. Also, if one counts carefully he will find six dogs in the village, two of which belong to one man and are used for hunting. Four other families have a dog and the chances are that they will eat them.

Wandering about the village one observes that several rivulets wind down through it from the hills. In a number of places slabs of stone have been laid across these rivulets to form bridges connecting the narrow paths that edge the plots of cultivated fields between the houses. There are a number of public wells to which the girls come with jars on their heads to dip out the water with half a dried gourd (Pl. 7, p. 46). Only five of the houses have a private source of water in the kitchen garden.

Almost in the center of the village is a large grinding stone with a heavy stone cylinder which rolls around on top of it to crush the intervening grain. This machine is one of the few pieces of public property and any villager may bring his ox to mill his rice or barley (Pl. 8, p. 47).

Within the village limits we find three small patches of ground with the semiglobular mounds of green grass rising above them as though a plush carpet had been pushed up here and there by inserting forms beneath the turf. In one there is a memorial stone but the others are bare of such expensive markers. These cemeteries each belong to a specific clan and carry on an ancient pattern of placing the dead. Under Japanese influence, burial grounds have become restricted to nonagricultural land on the higher hillsides so that most of the people will ultimately be interred in the larger public resting places that now collectively serve a group of villages.

At the edge of the matang of one house there is a large tree and among its lowest branches there are the remnants of a wooden platform. The platform has not been used recently but represents the pleasant custom of building a resting place to catch the summer breeze and to look out over the beauty of the country. There are at least three other such relics in the village but the people say they have had little time for such relaxation in the recent years of war and turmoil. These primitive arboreal pavilions should not be confused with the watchtowers in the fields which one finds in less isolated sections of the country, where young men spend their evenings watching for passing birds of prey, both human and feathered. Sŏndup'o, without even a cart road to enter its precincts, suffers few visitors to disturb its peaceful ways.

The only other immobile constructions one sees in the surroundings are the dikes of the rice fields. These vary in size and form an endless variation of curves inevitably caressing the basic contours of the hills behind. These dikes are ancient for the most part and are seldom disturbed except for repairs or rebuilding, when an overburden of water washes a section away.

Considering the village as a whole, we see it as a group of independent thatch-covered homes, each within sight of some others a few score to a few hundred feet away. The aspect is one of openness and security in contrast to that of a Chinese village, where each house is wall-locked with the next, making a barrier against the outer bandit world. Overhanging trees, flowering vines, and fruitful fields of vegetables blend man's work into an idyllic scene, the village of Sŏndup'o.

To the first sight of a foreigner the people may look physically all the same except for the obvious characteristics accountable by age and sex. To the intimate, however, each villager appears unique with an individual personality showing in every motion, every glance of the face. The shrewd or open countenance, the kindly and the mean, the simple and the intelligent, they are all there, just as one sees them in his own community. Love and fear, like heartbreak and envy, come and go through the turn of days even as clouds linger for a while under the cliffs of Mari San. The diversity of emotion is more subtle than the variations of skin color ranging in shade like the clay slopes of denuded hills. Contrasts with other nations do appear in the people's collective behavior and even more strikingly in the clothes that they wear.

In most regions of the earth which are not tropical, costumes look different according to the season. There are also special occasions when individuals preen themselves for solemn ceremonies or gala affairs. Likewise age, sex, and class become criteria for distinctive dress, and so it is in Korea. Without being over-analytical, let us look at the people during the summer. There is a typical man standing on his matang. He wears a light cotton coat that looks like a pajama top and reaches to a little below his waistline, while the sleeves just cover his elbows. His full trousers are rolled up above his calves. There is something striking about these trousers: the low crotch drooping almost to the knees, which to a westerner at first glance may give the comical impression that the trousers are falling off. They are not, for they are supported by a belt. Over the coat is a vest with three pockets, like the western garment from which they were copied. All these articles are made of white cotton cloth. Our man is wearing rice straw sandals which cover little but the soles of his brown feet. His hair is clipped short. He is comfortably cool, he looks clean, and he thinks no costume could be more reasonable under the circumstances.

Other men about the village appear in similar costumes except for some of the younger ones who are wearing out the pants which they acquired during the war while working for the Japanese.

If we glance at the man's wife standing in the background under the eaves of the house, we first notice a white cotton skirt which falls loosely almost to her ankles. There is nothing strange about it. She also has a jacket coat of the same stuff but here is a Korean surprise. Her midriff is bare and the tips of her pendant breasts hang exposed to the air. From this we can infer that she is at least in her middle thirties, for a younger female would wear a longer skirt with its top edge bound over the slope of her breasts. On her feet the woman has sandals indistinguishable from those of her husband, and her long black hair is done up in a bun and held with a heavy rod-like pin of brass at the back of her head. The smaller silver one beside it is essentially an ornament and her only one. She may, however, use it to clean her ears, and it is stated in all seriousness that a woman may stick her husband's testes with it if his sexual vigor lags.

Either a little feminine or scientific curiosity will discover that the woman, unlike her husband, is wearing underclothes. The two unseen pieces are pants, again of the same white material, the innermost of peculiar cut leaving them open between the legs and ending in a pair of pennants with strings which cross behind the back and tie in front. The overpants are cut with a low crotch like the men's, are slit up the front and have tie-around strings attached to the loose corners. Both inner and over pants hang loosely to just below the calves of the legs.

The children one sees playing around the village are dressed with somewhat more variation and simplicity. Although most of the little girls wear a white skirt and jacket, some few have single-piece dresses in color, the style being the result of Japanese influence, in turn affected by the West. In summer, the boys are usually content with only a pair of short pants. Rarely do young ones of either sex wear anything on their feet in summer. One of the commonest variations in the dress of all individuals is the use of rubbers, introduced by the Japanese. These are of oriental style rather than western and follow the pattern of Chinese slippers. For these, men may substitute flat wood soles with a single strap over the top of the foot to hold them on.

The Koreans' modesty shows in their dress but it is not a false one. Men fishing in the lower reaches of the rice fields, which are flooded from the drainage of many little streams, do not hesitate to remove their clothing when wading through the water. They state that females avoid a place where such activities are going on but I have observed young women passing without averting their faces or showing any sign of constraint. Paralleling this situation, an older woman, naked to the waist, may be seen on a hot day flailing barley. If approached she will slip on her jacket but otherwise continues to work oblivious to the passerby.

Seasonal variations in costume are clearly differentiated, especially in the materials. Clothes for the spring and fall are made of a double thickness of cotton cloth and in winter a third costume is substituted, one which has a layer of cotton quilted in between the fabric. In these seasons, socks which come above the ankles, are always worn by both sexes. These socks are of double-thick cotton cloth, and are padded in winter. Men fasten the bottoms of their trousers legs over the tops of these socks with a ribbon but women (except for Buddhist nuns) do not. Everyone but babies wears wristlets during the coldest part of the winter. These are quilted cotton or silk tubes about eight inches long. Old people have white or gray ones while younger individuals use black. Straw sandals or rubbers remain the common footwear in all seasons.

A word must be said about the color of the Korean costume. Basically it is white for all sexes, seasons, and ages, as it has been since the Koreans copied the Chinese custom thousands of years ago. In village circles, only a bridal couple and small children on ceremonial occasions appear in gaudy hues. Girls and younger matrons may be seen in black or red skirts, especially in winter but also not infrequently in spring or fall. Unmarried men generally wear black in winter and occasionally a married man will choose gray for fall and spring.

Before the coming of the Japanese, the villagers wove their own cloth, hemp for summer and cotton for the other seasons, although silk was also substituted for the finer costumes. The Japanese managed to insinuate their machine-made cotton yard goods until today the home manufacture of cloth has been greatly reduced. The conquerors' last attempt toward change was the introduction of black socks, but these the Koreans resisted. Black is a color to wear on the head; on their feet they still wear white.

Finally we must look at the hats which, of all articles of Korean dress, have attracted the most attention from the outside world. Certainly, the black horsehair headdress of the Korean gentleman, looking like an inverted flowerpot with a broad brim, has a rightful claim to being one of the most distinctive articles of dress ever widely adopted by any people. Until the present century, such a hat was the privilege of the upper class but in recent decades it has been adopted by any man who could personally carry that dignity as a mark of his own success (Pl. 9, p. 62).

One should not ordinarily expect to see it in the village, however, as it was always a dress affair, put on for special occasions such as a visit or ceremonial gathering. Until the Japanese prohibited the custom, a Korean on assuming the role of manhood, through being married, did his hair up into a topknot, using a black band of woven horsehair to bind around his head. This piece the Korean gentleman wore even at home. On going for a walk he added the brimmed flowerpot, holding it in place by means of ribbons fastened beneath his chin. If caught in a sudden rain, he could unfold a conical-shaped waterproof paper cover to go over the top. In ancient days the straight hat brims were very wide, requiring delicacy of behavior to insure their safety. In the present century, by gradual reduction, they seldom extend more than a foot in diameter. Indeed, they are becoming altogether rare but are still commonplace compared to the almost nonexistent topknot.

The commonest hat which the villagers wear looks like a large conical basket of woven straw inverted upon the head. This generous cover protects one against the sun, or rain, or snow, forming a kind of parasol or umbrella so light that it can be pushed back off the head when not needed, to hang comfortably from the neck cord. If this hat is not available men may throw a piece of cloth over the head but generally they do not bother (Pl. 12, p. 79). In cold weather, women wear a quilted headband or perhaps a hood on the rare occasions when they leave the village.

4

THE SOCIAL ORGANIZATION OF THE VILLAGE

TO UNDERSTAND the Korean village we must examine the social organization of Sŏndup'o, which will tell us something about the distribution and relationships of the one hundred and sixty-nine individuals occupying the twenty-seven houses. First we must realize that the Korean system is patrilineal or, in other words, that the primary relationships are those which link males together through descending generations. No two persons are formally so closely related as a father and son. As in the United States, they bear the same surname which is passed on from generation to generation.

From our list of the families in all the houses we discover that, with one exception, the males living under one roof share a common name. Further, we find that all the people in the village bear one of twelve surnames so that besides the instance where two men of different names live in the same house, there are two homes occupied by people of the same name of Han, two by the name of Sim, three by Hyŏn, and thirteen by Li (also spelled Yi, I, and rarely, Rhee).

At first we might suppose that the individuals of the same surname all recognize a family relationship but it is not so. In general, only a few of Korean name groups such as those of Han and Yu are so unified. Others may be divided into scores of clans, each distinguished by a prefatory name indicating the place of traditional origin. For all of Korea, there are about eleven hundred clans and three hundred surnames. With this in mind, we learn that the Li of our village belong to three different clans. Ten of the Li households are linked as the Kyŏngju Li, tracing their descent to the old Silla capital, two others are Chŏnju Li, and one represents the clan of T'aean. Thus we have, in Sŏndup'o twenty-seven houses, twelve name groups and fourteen clans. Clearly, the Kyŏngju Li have a numerical dominance in occupying ten out of the twenty-seven houses and it is not surprising to learn that the founding of the village in some unknown century past is attributed to them.

37

To determine how characteristic this situation is for the area we can turn to our comparative data. We find in the whole li that thirteen is the average number of clans per village and that in only one case does a single clan exceed 50 per cent occupation of the houses, whereas in another village of twenty-two homes, no single clan occupies more than two. We can add, however, that the Kimhae Kim predominate in three of the villages so we might give them top position among the sixty-seven clans in the area as a whole. The presentation seems to involve considerable arithmetic but it puts an end to uncertainty concerning the matter.

Clans function in two important ways. They put a restriction on marriage for one thing, as they are strictly exogamous. A Kyŏngju Li male must not marry a Kyŏngju Li female. To do so would be incestuous, no matter how distant their actual blood relationship. This taboo does not hold for persons of the same name group if of a different clan, although some feeling of common origin is shared. Clans also serve as the integrating unit for ancestor worship.

Here we must pause for a brief discussion of this latter subject, which lies at the roots of Korean social organization and ideally determines the pattern of behavior for all the individuals in the state. To overlook it would be to lose one eye in perceiving Korean culture. In the sixth century B.C. Confucius formalized the system of values of which ancestor worship has become the manifest externalization, giving to his ethics a ritual of deep emotional significance. Ancestor worship became widely inculcated among the people of the Peninsula, over a thousand years ago, and however much a modern Korean may seem encrusted with other beliefs, hidden Confucian values will show up beneath a scratch.

Fundamental to the Confucian philosophy is the notion that a good life depends upon a knowledge and observance of the proper behavior between one individual and another. Five categories of interpersonal relations form the basis for instruction as to the duties and obligations involved. These relations are those (1) of parent and child, (2) of king and minister, (3) of husband and wife, (4) of elder brother and younger brother, and (5) of friend with friend. Ideally, the approach demands a mutual attitude of benevolence, high-mindedness, restraint, understanding, and faith. In practice it most obviously means that the highest respect must be paid by a son to his father. The dutiful son remains implicitly obedient through-

out his life. The parent, when he dies, becomes an object of worshipful veneration and for three years the son observes ritual mourning. To a lesser degree, younger generations of sons participate in
the obligations to their grandfathers until by extension they become
unbreakable links in the chain of the past. The most important
festivals of the year focus on the reinforcement of this system of which
the social matrix is the clan.

In a sense, the other relationships are merely special applications
of the father-son unity. A subject must give a filial response to his
king, a wife must remember that her one important role in life is to
be the physiological producer of the son—that next link in the chain
without which life becomes the bitter end, not only of self but of all
preceding and future time. The younger brother, at first, is but a
vice-son, a potential substitute should death strike down the elder.
The latter, after marriage has secured the lineage, gradually takes
over the role of father to his younger brothers, both its authority and
obligations. Even in the relationship of friend with friend the similarity of responsibilities may be seen.

In the clans lies the hidden strength of this social system, just as
though they were meshed steel rods buried in the concrete structure
of the family life. At its best, the clan is the source of invisible
security, at its worst it turns all eyes backward on the past, limiting
opportunity for complete individualism and demanding greater personal courage of him who would originate something new or change
the age-old customs. Few Koreans probably have not suffered a
passion for revolt at one time and another—subject, son, wife, and
younger brother. It is these repressions which, when they fully
break out, result in such sadistic fury and such an unconsolable turmoil of unconscious guilt.

Despite the great underlying significance of the clan system, it is
not the most important of the social mechanisms operating in the
everyday life of Sŏndup'o. That primal position belongs to the
family, which in this village is identical with the household group,
if one allows for individuals who are temporarily absent. The members of the households are bound to each other by blood, marriage,
or adoption, and share in the same economic, social, and ritual
privileges and duties.

Permitting a little more arithmetic, we find that eleven persons
are the most that live in a Sŏndup'o house and four the least, with an

average of 6.25. Taking the li as a whole, with its three hundred and thirty-two households, it is not surprising that we can discover the rare extremes of from only one to as many as twenty individuals occupying a single dwelling. But the average is 6.46, which demonstrates the typicalness of our village. The composition of the family in half the houses (14 of 27) comprises a husband and wife with their unmarried children, but in seven more there is also a son's wife and possibly grandchildren. Only in one case is there more than one son's wife living in his parents' home and this aberrancy becomes understandable when we note that the first son's wife is a widow.

The social pattern seems clear. The household basically comprises a nuclear family which in time becomes extended, for when the eldest son is of an age to be married, he brings his wife home to carry on the clan tradition in the same residence, even as his eldest son in turn will be expected to do. Ultimately the parents will die and be buried in the village cemetery, if the family is not one of the few to retain a private graveyard. Until that time comes, the parents remain in their home, cared for by their children.

In Sŏndup'o there are three households where the married couple have the husband's mother with them, and in one case his father's mother as well. There are also two homes where the wife's father resides. This latter situation may arise when a couple has a daughter but no sons. To escape the tragic consequences of family extinction, the traditional pattern is to adopt their daughter's husband. As a man does not wish to give up his own family affiliation, this solution may be difficult to attain, but the younger son of some poorer family may be persuaded to transfer his allegiance. In Sŏndup'o, it is now at least more common for a son-in-law to be taken in without adoption.

Except for the eldest son, the other children may be expected to leave the paternal home. Daughters will be married and go to live with their husbands of another clan. Younger sons face a more serious departure. They may receive assistance from their fathers and elder brothers but the solution will not be easy unless the family wealth stands well above the subsistence level, which is not frequent in a Korean village. Should there be sufficient family land to permit a division of it, then a younger son may receive a share including space in the village on which to build a house. This was obviously more frequent in times past, as is shown by the local grouping of households of the same clan. Now it is more likely that these sons drift away to the cities or wherever they may be absorbed into a wage-earning economy. For many, their first goal will be to obtain suffi-cient funds to purchase some land, for whether or not they ever revert to the life of a farmer, their hearts will beat happily only when they know that they can lie quietly on their own Korean earth.

Normally, as we have indicated, there are only two or three gener-ations occupying a village house. In Sŏndup'o, there is only one family with representatives of four generations living together, that with the husband's mother and grandmother mentioned before. This single instance makes 3.70 per cent of the total, of course, which compares closely with 4.81 per cent for the whole li. While we are playing with figures we might add a few more and be done. The statistically curious may have computed from what has been stated in a preceding paragraph that 25.92 per cent of the houses in Sŏndup'o contain two married couples, which is amazingly near to the figure of 26.20 per cent for the whole area. There are no in-stances of a home with three married couples but in the ten villages of the li there are a handful of them, comprising 3.91 per cent of the households, including three houses, or less than 1 per cent with four married couples. In two of these latter there are three married sons at home; in the other, two married grandsons.

Although we cannot say that most of the individuals born in the village stay in it, since the daughters and younger sons generally move out, most of the men who live in Sŏndup'o were born there. In fact, there are only three who were not. First there is the case of the son-in-law of old Ko who sits on his porch weaving rice straw sandals and mats. Old Ko is only fifty-one but he looks more, for his life has been hard. He had no sons and when his wife died she left him a daughter. The latter is married now to a man named Ch'oe who came from Ch'oji-li in the same myŏn of Kilsang. He did not change his name. Old Ko looks at his five grandchildren who do not bear his name and sometimes he is sad.

Mr. Yu moved to Sŏndup'o in 1944 from another village of the li. He had a rice field near by and it was more convenient to live as close as possible so he bought a vacant house at the far end of the settlement. There he lives with his wife and three daughters.

The third arrival came the same year as Yu but his history is much more unusual. He is seventy years old and, according to the story, has spent much of his life wandering, after losing his patrimony in early youth. He belongs to the T'aean Li clan and has no relatives in the village except the members of his own household. They came from north Korea and settled in Sŏndup'o because, as a fan maker, he could find the material for his trade growing along the great dike at the far end of the rice fields. Li owns no land and rents his house from the proceeds of his sale of fans. With him are his wife and daughter with the latter's two children, one of whom is a boy. The daughter's husband has gone away at present. If you live in the village, this old one will sell you a fan very cheap.

Just as the men can be expected to have been born in the village, so we may presume that the wives were not. If the community is not theoretically exogamous, it is practically so. Of the twenty-five living wives of family heads in Sŏndup'o, none was born there. However, 28 per cent came from the li and another 8 per cent from within the myŏn. An additional 56 per cent were born on Kanghwa which leaves only a final 8 per cent, or two women, from the mainland. One of these is the wife of the wandering Li. The other, Mrs. Sim, was born in Kaesŏng, the ancient Koryŏ capital to which city part of the Sim family removed some generations ago, where they are consequently useful in arranging marriages.

Being a small sample, the provenience of Sŏndup'o wives is not entirely consistent with that of the wives in the ten villages as a whole. In the 318 cases on which we could find satisfactory records, about 20 per cent of the women came from within the li, another 12 also from Kilsang Myŏn, 45 per cent more from the island, and 23 per cent were born on the mainland. The nearest point of consistency is the total figures for the myŏn, 36 per cent for Sŏndup'o and 32 for Sŏndu Ri. The difference shows up in the increase of off-islanders. This discrepancy may be largely explained by the fact that the dominant clan of one village originates in the nearest large town across the straits, whereas some of the fishing villages have long-standing connections in the mainland city of Inch'ŏn.

We should gain some conception of the age pattern of the village but this may be difficult to do without resorting again to figures. The number of years which one has lived, however, is a matter of much greater importance in Korea than it is in western culture, and we must consider the matter. Whether a person is chronologically older than another generally determines the formal pattern of respect shown and if there is a marked difference in years, gestures of consideration for that fact are mandatory. Descriptively, a man in the village may divide the years of life into ten-year periods, considering the first that of "infancy," individuals in the second as "boys and girls," and those between twenty and thirty as "young people." When villagers arrive at the decade between thirty and forty, he would refer to them as "steady people;" after forty, they are "old." The classical Chinese age units of twenty, forty, and sixty years gain no common recognition except that everyone knows that to reach the age of sixty is one of the greatest possible events in an individual life. To do so puts one almost in the category of the immortals. At the time of our study three persons of each sex in the village had attained this distinction. The oldest woman is seventy-six and the eldest man, seventy. This group of the Sŏndup'o community is somewhat lower than the 7.31 per cent of people over sixty in the whole li, of which 56 per cent are females. Half of the population are under twenty years of age (56.80 per cent in the village; 49.13 per cent in the li) according to the records, and this estimate can be somewhat increased because children who die at birth or shortly thereafter often do not appear on the official lists of the myŏn.

The diseases of which people die are many and no adequate account of them is available. In Samku Li, the myŏn town, there are two western-style doctors who operate clinics, dispensing medicines obtained from the capital. The older is a graduate of one of the country's few medical schools of recognized standing, whereas the younger has largely trained himself by a study of standard texts. There are also Chinese-style doctors who deal in the established pharmacopaeia inherited through centuries. Even the more intelligent Koreans of the country may resort to both traditions. Desperate is the search of the ignorant for solace from pain.

One of the clinicians who frequently sees patients from Sŏndup'o stated that many children die of tuberculosis. Adults seem to succumb largely to some uncertain malady of the stomach or intestines. This may be bacillary dysentery. Worms were mentioned. Diseases such as smallpox, typhoid, typhus, and cholera attack the population but vaccines have been available locally for some of these. There are sporadic cases of malaria while leprosy and venereal disease, although not unknown, are said to be relatively rare.

Besides the medical cures, the people also resort to lay practitioners with special reputations for curative powers. There are also many popular herbal remedies generally known to most persons. Castor oil, for example, is a simple physic procured from home-grown plants. The flower and top stem of opium poppies may be boiled and drunk when someone has diarrhea or dysentery. Some of the local practices seem much more novel. For instance, a fisherman says that for venereal disease he seeks out a live baby lizard about an inch and a half long and wraps it in the sticky underside of a soybean leaf. Folding over the ends of the leaf, he places this pastille on the back of his tongue, and swallows it without benefit of liquid. I contented myself with carefully checking on the fact that this treatment was not unique, but did not try it myself. But after all, perhaps a lizard accumulates penicillin from the soil. One way in which malaria is thought to be cured is by licking human excrement; another is to have the sufferer led around by a relative who shouts, "Buy malaria!" The clinicians recommend quinine.

The class structure of present-day Sŏndup'o has become rather amorphic, because of the disruptive effects of the Japanese conquest and the impact of many recent ideas. People will now say that there are no class distinctions, which statement becomes an important verbalization even if it does not represent the whole truth. To comprehend the situation, it will be advisable to examine the social conditions before the close of the Yi dynasty at the beginning of the twentieth century. At that time, two distinct classes predominated in the area. These were the Yangpan, or nobles, and the Sangnŏm, or commoners. The former did no work, wore horsehair hats, and lived off the labor of their tenants or each other. Their local power was great and sometimes absolute and they acted as intermediaries between the commoners and the government. Needless to say they held the important political offices and operated a system of nepotism which was classic in its proportions. The commoners, on the other hand, did most of the work for a fraction of the profits. Whether they suffered personally or were protected in their daily life depended largely on the individual character of their local lords. On the whole, they took the system for granted and got along, for they had known no other way for centuries.

Apart from these two main classes was a special group, the slaves. Until 1907, slaves could be either purchased from individuals who owned them or they could be acquired on occasions when individuals

wished to sell themselves into slavery.* This some did when hunger
stalked them or when the burden of normal social responsibilities became too onerous. In a sense, the position of a slave often was easier
than that of a freeman, providing one could accept psychologically
the loss of a nominal independence. Slaves did not have to worry
about their food supply nor, by and large, were they much abused.
They might be beaten but not killed, which sometimes proved half
the advantage over a commoner.

Slaves might be individuals of either sex or they could be held
as married couples. It is said that the latter, if having sold themselves, could ordinarily gain their freedom by giving in their place
a son or daughter of seventeen. This seems understandable, as a
youth could prove more valuable economically than an aging couple
with two stomachs to fill. A young female slave could expect a
marriage to be arranged for her by her master, who would choose
some male slave or a free beggar. In the latter case, however, a son
of the marriage could claim his freedom and generally fought for it
with success. Also, an owner might liberate a slave by tearing up
the legal record of the purchase. Occasionally this happened for
among all people there have always been some who will repudiate
the shameful indignity of man to man.

Besides these classes, there have traditionally been certain outcast
professions. The villagers have forgotten the classical seven which
originated in Chinese culture but they will provide a similar list of
their own. For example, we are told that meat sellers rank at the
bottom, even below the butchers, for whereas the latter must kill so
that men can eat, the seller has no such justification. Such rationali-
zation has a familiar homely touch.

Next to these comes the mutang, the female shamans or sorcerers.
The local explanation of their position is passed over with a story.
Once a king called a female shaman, or mutang, and a fortuneteller.
He had put a chestnut in his cheek and asked them what could be the
matter with his face. The mutang said that he had been attacked by
spirits and that she could cure him. The fortuneteller suggested that
the king had put something into his mouth. Hence mutang are low,

---

* That customs die hard is indicated by the fact that as late as May 27, 1946 an
ordinance (No. 70) was promulgated prohibiting the sale or contract for the sale of
females. *Summation,* May, 1946:24.

fortunetellers not, which may be a solace to Americans who spend so much money on them.

In the middle of the list of outcast professions stands the monk. He has that position because he does not marry—or did not until the Japanese arrived—and thus publicly contravenes the duty of every man to raise children that they may carry on his lineage and its worship.

Next comes the boatman because he is rough and immoral. More important, he does not know when he is going to die. How can one live properly if one does not prepare himself for this final ceremony toward which all life is focused?

Jailers and merchants may be added to complete the list but toward them the feeling is weaker, if more personal.

In the days of the old social classes, there is no satisfactory evidence that any Yangpan ever lived in Sŏndup'o, although some nobles still reside in other villages of the li. Also, slaves were rare or absent and as far as the despised professions go, only a few boatmen may have had their houses there. Therefore, informants speak truly when they say, thinking of the past social forms, that the villagers recognize no class distinctions among themselves.

In the less obvious technical sense, one may make out certain strata within Sŏndup'o. It might be burdening a sociological concept too much to call them classes in so small a community, but setting the matter of terms aside, any man will select the most important families from the others. Allowing a reasonable period of continuous residence in the village, wealth, particularly as it is reflected in the ownership of land, becomes a diagnostic criterion. Other factors would include the size and quality of house, the number of sons, the skill and energy of the female members, and particularly the education and intelligence of the men. On the other hand, within the scope of the present field work, it would be hard to justify more than a dual division and that in fairly arbitrary halves. The village people are basically too individualistic, too democratic, and too conscious of the turn of fortune over a few generations to divide into self-conscious segments at present. Rather, they find unity in themselves as village farmers overshadowed by a world of towns and cities with their politicians, tax collectors, and police.

Turning to the matter of interpersonal relations, we might begin our discussion with some consideration of the position of women.

5. HOUSE AND MATANG IN SŎNDUP·O

6. MEN AND BOYS ON MATANG OF SŎNDUP'O HOUSE

7. GIRLS AT PUBLIC WELL IN SŎNDUP'O

8. GRINDING BARLEY

It has already been indicated by direct statement and inferences that the theoretical position of the male is outstandingly predominant. In fact, the family may be thought of as a patriarchy. This in itself points to the fact that the woman has the inferior role. As a child she must obey everyone, including a brother. After her parents marry her to a man she has never seen, she must obey not only him but his mother as well. Only after she bears children herself does she acquire authority, and for status she must have a son. In time, when he brings home a wife, her controls are widened, and should her husband die before her she may achieve a supreme position in the household.

Let us examine these relationships a little more carefully on the basis of average interactions. As a child, a girl's dealings with her mother are apt to be on a sympathetic plane. Mothers usually love their children and little girls are sweet. The father is likely to be tolerantly affectionate to the little one but becomes more removed as she grows up. This may be an advantage if he has not a quiet disposition. With her brothers, she has childhood attachments and quarrels. She is sure to carry any younger member of the family on her back much of the time. Gradually, as she approaches the time of her first menstruation, she spends more and more of her waking hours at work. There is less leisure for communication and her interpersonal intercourse becomes largely restricted to her mother and close female relatives.

Then from the onset of catamenia until her menopause, or roughly from at least fourteen to forty, she will not ordinarily enter into a discussion with any man who is not of the household, and quite likely, will have little to say to her husband. For an American, it is almost unbelievable how uncommunicative she can be to the man with whom she lives. Should a neighborhood man ask her a simple direction while passing on a path, she may avert her head and give no answer. Nor will he be surprised at her avoidance. Once "old" in local parlance, she will become more social but the long years of reticence are not apt to result in much volubleness.

The normative pattern is, of course, subject to the fallacy of an application to every particular woman. There are exceptions where, without being over-verbal, a woman "wears the pants" in her own family. Lacking words, she may in rare instances even beat her beloved spouse over the head with an ironing stick. Usually, dominance is a psychological matter, where an accumulation of little fears is subtly brought to bear on those with whom one lives.

Even in ordinary situations, the theory of inferiority does not correspond completely with the practice. The wife has fairly definite control over the food that is eaten, over the clothing that is made, and over her babies and younger children. Also, she probably has the final word in the marriage of her daughters, which is a slight compensation for the lack of such responsibility with respect to her sons. Someone looking for her husband may come to the door and ask if the "outside master" is in. This is a tacit recognition of her position as "inside master"—which she may actually be called. Certainly she rules over her kitchen and the adjoining garden. When she goes abroad, she is secure from molestation and is always spoken to in the polite forms of speech. There are other factors in the role of the woman which will be made clearer as we proceed.

The relationship of father and son has an ambivalent quality. Although basically perhaps the most important, because to them the family and clan owe its continuance, it is not a union of familiarity and demonstrable affection. Custom dictates that a father be restrained in his attitude toward his successor and he often appears coldly distant, whatever his real feelings may be. The father also becomes the symbol of the disciplinarian and is apt to be a strict one in practice. The son must show utter respect regardless of how he really feels, and it would be strange if he did not often resent such a one-sided relationship. God only knows how many Korean sons must hate their fathers. As children they run to their mothers for relief and she is known as the "kind parent," he as the "stern" one. For the most part, the son must repress his animosity and it adds to the accumulation of repressions which sometimes explode in other directions.

The elder son must be shown respect by the younger, as well as by all his sisters. The common father orientation of all the sons seems to draw most of the sting, however. Some brothers like each other and some do not, but their sense of mutual responsibility almost certainly will be high. If they are nearly the same age, they will probably spend more time together than with anyone else. In true affection, brothers and sisters often become deeply attached and the girls will remain, except for a wife, the only women with whom a man can freely talk.

Another important relationship often occurs between a younger son and his elder brother's wife, who comes into the home when the former may be quite small. There is a saying in Korean that "an elder brother's wife is like a mother" and so it is, for this strange and exciting new member of the household is sure to take over many of the heavy chores, including the care of the younger children. Her young brother-in-law may well adore her. This close relationship will not be expected with a second son's wife, for she will probably be more distant than a sister to her husband's younger brother.

Male first cousins of the same clan almost certainly know each other and have a feeling of in-group status. One's mother's sister's children seem most removed of all the cousins. Indeed, one may never see them; they are most likely to live at the greatest distance from home, since both mothers would normally have left their place of origin. Next most distant are one's father's sister's children, as they are only once removed from the family home. Both these groups of cousins necessarily belong to another clan and the tie is only biological.

Grandparents notoriously spoil their grandchildren in Korea, as apparently they do almost everywhere on earth. Between them the gap of generations is sufficient to reduce all sense of conflict and competition. The old see the young as little fragments of immortality which they will leave behind (Pl. 10, p. 63). The young see the quiet aged ones as protector companions who will provide hidden sweets and toys. Common is the sight of a white-haired man sitting on the matang whittling out a present for his idolatrous grandson. Best of all, when paternal wrath becomes aroused grandfather can allay it by the unrelinquished authority of the patriarch. Finally, their role as teachers should not be forgotten. The old ones have the time and a veneration for learning. Given half a chance, they will pass on far more of their intimate knowledge, however rich it be, to their grandchildren than to their own first born. Unfortunately, grandparents do not always survive and children may have to depend on father's uncle for special favors, if he lives near by.

The role of Korean husband can almost be a lonely one. The culture which sets him up as lord and master of his little domain exacts the price of a certain isolation. From his parents he is removed by the necessities of respect and from his children by inevitable dominance. Even with his wife, his intimacy is largely periodic and sexual. He does not have an established and inherited pattern of discussing the details of his domestic, social, and economic problems with his wife. Typically, when decisions must be made he concludes them all alone and would be ashamed to ask his woman for advice. Such unilateral behavior often leads to sadness in the home, for what man's mind is equal to two, especially when the other is a woman's? For friendship, he will turn most often to individuals outside the formal barriers of house and clan.

Before continuing with a consideration of the external relationship of individuals, it may be timely to interpolate some account of the terms of address. Before the Japanese annexation, only boys received proper names. The first was that of the clan, the second, shared by all brothers, was that of the generation, and the third, the distinctive personal name. Since the generation names are taken in preordained order, it is thus possible for a Kim to determine his relative age group with reference to any other member of his clan. His actual age becomes a secondary matter in this respect and he gives or accepts deference according to his grade.

In olden times, girls received only nicknames such as "Small-baby," "Flat-face," or "Pretty." Since about 1910, they have usually been dignified by such appellations from poems as "Calm-integrity" or "Jade-princess." Nicknames are still given to girls but they are not used after marriage.

One of the functioning aspects of the name system is the practice of what is known technically as teknonymy. This means that after a married couple have a child, it is taboo to call them by their personal names, and that they must be spoken of as the father and mother of their child. If for example, the child is a daughter named "Calm-integrity," the parents will be referred to as "Calm-integrity's father" or "Calm-integrity's mother." This system gives the parents a raise in status by restricting the use of a personal given name to children, or more exactly, to those without children. It is characteristic of the region that the parents and grandparents are called after the name of their youngest descendant.

Personal names of parents are not only not used to their faces but are never mentioned in front of their children unless the speaker is a generation older than the individual referred to. This latter taboo is explained, at least in part, by the fact that the names of Yangpan were formerly not used, official titles replacing them. Thus the application of a personal name remains a symbol of lower-class status to which the common people and particularly their children have become extremely sensitive. To mention the given name of his father to a contemporary in Korea is one of the worst of possible insults.

Apart from parents and children, individuals address their fellow villagers of their grandfather's generation as grandfather or grandmother, those of their parents' generation as uncle or aunt, those of their own as elder or younger brother or sister. Descending generations, as has been indicated, will be called by the system of teknonymy, or if of preparental age, by their given names. Exceptions occur to the general rule in that the differentiations of "elder" and "younger" are given by males speaking to all male cousins, but only to female cousins of the male speaker's clan. Women speakers use the differentiations of "elder" and "younger" for women of the same generation, regardless of clan relationship, but not to any males. To one's immediate relatives of the ascendant generation, descriptive relationship terms are used.

Of interpersonal relationships outside the clan and family, the strongest is that of "friendship-brother." Such attachments may be established by married men even of fifty years of age, if they have not done so previously. Only one such relationship may be allowed, however. The arrangement arises when two men meet and find themselves mutually stimulated to an unusual degree, sharing the same ideas and values. If they decide on partnership, they need only ask a third party to witness their agreement over a bottle of wine. A person who becomes such a friend is said to be practically like a real brother—but not quite. In any event, he acts like a family member, wearing the hemp clothes of mourning whenever his partner does. Two women may form such a relationship as well as men.

Related to the "friendship-brother" association is its predecessor carried out by children. Two boys or two girls may pledge allegiance and mark the occasion by tattooing two tiny marks on the arm of each other, pricking the flesh with a needle and drawing through an inky thread. My old informant on whose arm I saw blue spots said his friend made them when he was about fourteen. He added that such childhood partnerships were soon forgotten and do not count. The practice seems to have largely disappeared but the idea lingers in my mind that much more could be learned about the custom.

Other interpersonal relations have a more casual significance, despite the formal procedures sometimes involved. Individuals do not talk about serious things to each other very much, or at least to those outside of the family. Even a casual visitor is received hospitably, however. When a friend calls he is invited into the master's study, or if this convenience is lacking, as is usual in the village, he is directed in summer into the maru, or to a paper floor room in winter. Unless he is more than a decade younger than his host he is offered the favored place—in the maru, that with his back to the kitchen garden; in the heated room, the one which is closest to the firebox. The visitor may be expected to refuse the place twice, his host to offer it three times. Finally the guest accepts and the host seats himself nearer the door. The favored location of the guest is known as the "lower" side—which might cause some confusion in English usage if not properly understood. Should there be a second guest he will be seated on either side of the first. A person looks down when showing respect or talking to an older individual. Only in anger will two persons stare into each other's eyes. The visitor may be offered tobacco held out in one hand with the other touching the inside of the extended arm above the wrist. This gesture is made to the elder, but should the recipient be the younger, he instead will make the gesture on accepting something. To be considered courteous, children should cup both hands side by side when receiving a gift. Under no conditions will a cigarette or other article be tossed to a guest, for such treatment is accorded only to a child.

When the time comes to eat, the guest may expect to be invited. The host will urge him to satisfy himself from the individual tray placed before him by a woman of the household but there is no order of waiting by guest or host. Both will give first attention to the devouring of the food with few interruptions for conversation. The guest, to indicate his pleasure, will simply smack his lips to emphasize the tastiness of the family cuisine.

Recently, because of food shortages in the area, families are most likely to eat at home. Nonetheless, the hospitality for which Koreans have long been famous is clearly obvious and even the alien stranger will not be turned aside if he makes the courteous approach. It is significant that no one will even close the door of his house if a person happens to be passing. To do so would be so much of an insult that one incident may be told as an illustration. Late one evening, after a session of drinking, a man was passing by the matang of his friend's home. The latter's wife, not perceiving him, happened to shut the gate for the night. Immediately enraged, he broke down the gate and it was some time before his feelings could be assuaged.

Social intercourse between a number of people of the same sex is more common than interpersonal meetings. If one man visits, others will gather, with the result that privacy is difficult to arrange. This may be a strain for the westerner but it seems perfectly natural to the Koreans whose work and play are largely a group affair. Besides the various ceremonial occasions which will be discussed later, there is one formal association of villagers which should be mentioned. This is the sangge, or burial society. Since it is linked to a common cemetery and set of funeral equipment, men from three villages belong to the same organization. Each member family contributes ten hops of rice to that of the deceased, to assist in the expenses of interment. This fund is gathered by two members of the society who are appointed by the chairman to collect it. Of the twenty-seven families in Sŏndup'o, only four do not belong to the organization as they are too poor to afford this insurance. When a death occurs in one of the latter households, their village neighbors theoretically may be expected to render them some assistance.

Most commonly of all, men work together. But before explaining their activities it will be necessary to discuss the general economic background of village life.

5

THE ECONOMIC LIFE OF THE VILLAGE

ALMOST all of the land in Sŏndup'o and its environs is private property. In fact, only the paths and the small patch of ground on which the stone mill stands can be considered public domain. If we add the cemetery which lies behind another village and is jointly controlled by three communities, we come to the end of our list of land not in the possession of some individual. There is the same dearth of public buildings and other appurtenances of a commune, although the funeral equipment may be said to belong collectively to the three villages sharing the cemetery. The stone mill remains as the one imposing object of village ownership. In the same category as the mill are two scales and a bushel measure which can be found in the home of the last person to use them. If these objects must be replaced or repaired, a collection is made from each house to provide the funds.

The wealth of Sŏndup'o lies chiefly in the rice fields which stretch out in front of it, together with a smaller amount of dry fields and forest land behind. We should be interested to know the ownership of these fertile paddies, each of a unique shape, and which collectively form themselves into a design that would make a patchwork quilt appear comparatively simple. The problem of ascertaining the land distribution is complicated and so illustrates the procedure of field work that it may be instructive to outline the investigation of this subject. The preliminary approach may be to inquire about the situation from one of the larger owners of the village when he is in a friendly and communicative mood. The probabilities are that, being acquisitive of property himself, he has a fairly accurate knowledge of the situation. Trying this, we find that our informant has even kept a record of the land owned by those in his half of the village, or pan, and can quickly estimate the position of the remaining families. At times, in his exposition, we note that he seems uncertain, as might be expected, and also his eyes change their focus when he accounts for his own holdings, which may be a natural reticence or something else. At best, the data need checking and we turn to the possibilities of the myŏn tax records. This proves to be an extensive undertaking and for weeks a student participant spends his time in copying the Japanese records of the village and in tracing the detailed map of the fields in the Sŏndup'o section. At last we have attained a mass of material which has the reliability of Japanese surveyors, so sophisticated in such matters that it is unlikely that any land holdings have been hidden.

Even after careful analysis, complications and sources of error seem unavoidable. First of all, the land office records, and particularly the map, are several years earlier than the time of our village study. Holdings may have changed. Further, if a villager works land a considerable distance away from Sŏndup'o or, even worse, has such ground which he rents to someone else, it will not show up in the results of our weeks of copying, for we obviously cannot afford to spend the time to collect such detailed records for the whole area. Then there is the potentiality of error in the extensive land office volumes, as well as in our translating, copying, and analysis.

What we learned in the village may be summarized as follows: seven of the families own enough land so they do not rent any, eleven families own some land but must rent more to gain sufficient food, six families rent all their land, and three out of the twenty-seven do no farming and are landless save for their houselots. To this was added the statement that no one in the village owned enough land to rent any to others. What did our search of the tax records show, allowing for a reasonable margin of error? Certainly there were three landless families. Of the six who were said to rent all their land, half owned small amounts of dry fields but we could understand informants overlooking these items as land-conscious owners think of their wealth essentially as vested in the valuable wet rice paddies. One of the households which both rents and owns seems to have acquired more land than it uses, but we were not able to ascertain detailed facts in the matter. Among the seven wealthiest families of land owners, we discover that our first-mentioned informant with the changing eyes not only has the fields that he claims, but also rents out a great many more. It is our turn for courteous appreciation, with possibly the slightest twinkle in our eyes. Another point which could be checked was that none of the men farms land farther away from home than that which lies in front of the neighboring village. Also, although holdings are typically broken up into separated plots, the distance between them is not great enough to cause any serious inconvenience or loss of time in moving from one to the other. These plots of ground, it may be added, range between 9 and 1,600 p'yong in size with the average near 520 p'yong.*

Besides the agricultural land, twelve of the families in Sŏndup'o own pieces of forest on the upland hills. No part of the latter area belongs to the village as a whole, but it is all under theoretical governmental supervision as far as cutting is concerned. Pine trees are the valued timber because the sappy wood has more resiliency than the oak or chestnut when used for house construction, its principal destination. Small branches serve as fuel, as do the grass and bushes which grow beneath them.

From the viewpoint of area, we are able to locate some 69,591 p'yong (roughly 57 acres) of land which is owned or used by the Sŏndup'o villagers. Of this ground, about 75 per cent is wet rice fields. We also ascertained that of the total amount, 30,967 p'yong is rented from absentee landlords and 28,973 p'yong utilized by Sŏndup'o owners themselves. The remaining 9,651 p'yong owned in Sŏndup'o is apparently mostly rented to outsiders, some to fellow villagers, but unfortunately the record is not clear on all of it.

Although isolated families make up the poorest group in the village, there is no indication that the larger the number of households in a clan, the wealthier they will be. In fact, the most affluent people seem to belong to families with not more than two clan houses. It is notable that the head of one of these possesses some 10,150 p'yong of the grand total of land owned by the villagers. The people say that a man gets stingier as he becomes richer.

Most of the absentee landlords live near by, but there are a few in the island capital and a couple more who reside in Inch'ŏn. Before the American occupation, rentals consisted of one half the produce, but since that time the return has been reduced to one third. At

---

* A p'yong, or tsubo, is an area of 35.55 sq. ft. or 3.95 sq. yds. There are approximately 1,225 p'yong to the acre. A study of Korean agriculture has shown that the average size of plot for the country as a whole is about one acre, but is only seven tenths of an acre for Kyŏnggi Province in which Kanghwa lies. The Sŏndup'o plots are unusually small, perhaps as are those on Kanghwa as a whole. Lee, 1936:101.

harvest time, the landlord's agent comes around to observe the threshing and to note the owner's share. Cash income for most Sŏndup'o people is negligible. For the many, after the grain taxes have been paid and seed set aside, there is not a satisfactory amount to feed the family. These are difficult days. Small amounts of cash in the village are hidden. For the one or two men who will accumulate much money during the year, the goal is usually to loan it out securely which is not too difficult to do at 5 to 10 per cent interest per month. Under the Japanese, the legal rate was theoretically $1\frac{1}{2}$ to 3 per cent.

The people would like to have more cash income because they must necessarily buy many things, such as iron tools and cotton goods for clothing. Every fifth day an open market is held in the myŏn town of Samku Li (Pl. 12, p. 79). If the prices are not cheaper than in the stores, at least it is an exciting event. Women are tempted by various household goods, children by candy, and most men if they get to town on market day would enjoy a drink of wine with their friends. The vendors generally set up temporary tables under cloth sun screens supported by poles, or sometimes lay out their goods on mats spread over the dusty earth. There are the brass merchants with their simple bowls and spoons, the yard goods sellers and the basket makers, besides many purveyors of foodstuffs, including those who ladle out bean or sesame oil. Prices have been so variable and constantly rising during the post-war inflation, that to quote them for any week would not be generally meaningful.[2] Everything seems to have become too expensive for the people of Sŏndup'o and they have unfortunately little to sell except young pigs which they cannot afford to eat.

During the course of the year, a few itinerant tradesmen visit Sŏndup'o on their regular rounds. Most familiar is the shoe repairer who comes almost every other month, on some unpredetermined day. He will fix any kind of leather goods and patch up rubbers as well. The other tradesmen generally come once during the year. The stone carver usually arrives in the fall. He roughens the millstones so that they will grind the grain more effectively, or he will build a whole new mill if needed. Then there is the man who mends and sells the individual Korean serving tables. These articles represent the finest woodworking one can find in the village and require the care of a skilled craftsman. The gourd repairer is another specialist who can cleverly sew up a cracked gourd with root line. One brings him the gourd and asks the price to fix it. One says the price is too high and the price comes down. The umbrella maker displays his wares in the rainy summer season. He also repairs as well as sells. After the harvest, a man with a motor-driven rice polisher may come to the village. Finally, there is the man who makes sieves and fixes up old ones. He likewise appears in summer since, as a side line, he hunts for snakes to sell for medicine in the city. What these itinerants do not mend, the villagers must care for themselves.

One of the most serious concerns of the farmers is the enforced collections of grain paid for at a nominal price. Under the Japanese, grain collections are stated to have amounted to 50 per cent of the rice and barley raised, but during the war it was often higher. One thing that is said in favor of the procedure, however, is that the collections were equitably made and the price was relatable, at least, to the general economy. The Japanese thoroughly understood the local agriculture and carried on their operations with high efficiency. They placed a heavy load on the farmer's capacities for production but they did not break his back. Their appreciation and need for his services made them harness his strength with the care given to a valuable beast of burden. When they levied grain to the limit under pressure of war demands, they nevertheless left a share of the crops in the district so that if too much hardship hit the people in the planting and preharvest periods, sufficient seed or food could be distributed to ward off disaster.

When the Americans arrived and removed all the Japanese officials, they also reduced the grain collections to 30 per cent. The farmers were delighted and their regard for the liberators reached a high point. Unfortunately, the good intentions of the United States officials seem to have been largely nullified through no fault of their own, unless one wishes to charge them with unreasonableness in undertaking so responsible a task without the essential competence to carry it out, an inevitable deficiency considering their lack of first-hand knowledge of oriental agriculture, to say nothing of their inability to communicate with the people with whom they had to deal.

The implementing of the new program was left to the local Korean officials, who by culture, temperament, and lack of personal experience were overwhelmed by the complications of the task. Starting with good will, they were soon sent orders that a specific amount of grain was expected from the collections. In order to hold their positions, the goal of making just apportionments was soon shifted by the seeming necessity of satisfying their superiors. As time went on, the bookkeepers, left without skilled Japanese guidance, faced a situation of confusion and frustration. The farmers were likewise in a turmoil. Some few managed to escape with a bare minimum of crop payments, while others lost practically everything. Naturally, the most influential, the most intelligent, and the richer generally suffered least, while the poorer and more ignorant starved. Black market prices rose higher and higher, things went from bad to worse, and graft and corruption, the twin Korean demons, no longer hid their putrid heads. In some cases, young American military officers in the districts commandeered grain and distributed it, cutting red tape at great personal risk. One does not have to speak a language to see that children are starving.

The people did not blame the Americans except for their ignorance. They saw them as taken in by the grafters and the age-old trickery of the official class, political descendants of the slave-holding Yangpan now freed from the obligation of even feeding the poor who raised their rice. Neither did they blame the mass of petty government employees with whom they came in contact, for in large measure the farmers understood their predicament and gave them sympathy. Orders simply came from the distant capital, seemingly reinforced by a great military power. That this was government for the people, the Korean farmers regarded as an illusion; and as for government by the people, that they considered but a dream.

The Americans, with willing hearts, tried to assuage the situation under the greatest difficulties. Some commodities have been distributed at controlled prices well below the market value. Kerosene, cloth, rubber shoes, matches, and laundry soap serve as examples. In midsummer, one pan of Sŏndup'o, or half the village, received three small packages of matches and a bar of soap for each of the fourteen households; also a yard of cloth and three pairs of rubber shoes for the pan collectively. To dispose of the latter items the pan jang marked four pieces of paper out of fourteen and the families held a lottery. The description of the scene was recounted with some humor but with no contempt. Village people sincerely appreciate a gesture of consideration, no matter how small.

Cash tax returns in Kilsang Myŏn for 1943, previous to the departure of the Japanese, showed roughly the following distribution of sources:

Tax on land	14%
Income tax	10
House tax	6
Tax on wine	62
Business tax	1
Tax on mines	5
Butchery tax	1
Wagon tax	1

Only the first three items are felt by any except two or three of the village people and one of the largest land owners paid a total of less than 600 wŏn (yen) in toto for 1946. That does not prove, however, that others did not pay more. At present, the tax situation has become so confused in the minds of the villagers that they do not understand it, a condition which is not unlike that suffered by some Americans at home. Neither could the students investigating the situation fully comprehend the matter in the time at their disposal.

Before turning to the means of earning income, a word may be said about inheritance. In practice, the eldest son inherits all of his father's property on the latter's death—the land, the house, and all of its appurtenances. If he has younger brothers he is expected to share some of his inheritance with them. Actually he may give them much, or little, or nothing. Often the situation is dictated by necessity, as he will be obliged to keep the household going and to support his mother and her younger children if any survive. When his younger brothers are old enough to marry he must, as the family head, assist them, and the degree to which he does so may depend on his economic ability as well as his good will. Each case varies in some degree. Should a man die, leaving only a wife, she inherits the property. A clever woman may then hire men to cultivate her fields or she may rent them. The lot of a widow, however, is almost sure to be hard.

For the Sŏndup'o villagers, gaining a livelihood depends almost entirely upon agriculture. The products raised, with a general indication of their growing periods in an average year, are shown in the accompanying chart. It should be noted that the months given correspond to those of the Korean or Chinese calendar, which is more variable than that of western culture. The first day of the Korean year 1947, for example, was January 22 in the United States. Without burdening the reader with the technicalities of a calendrical system, the full details of which can be easily found elsewhere, it may be pointed out that the Koreans regard the first three months of their year as spring, the second three as summer, and so on, thus being a season ahead of us, so to speak. This seems reason-

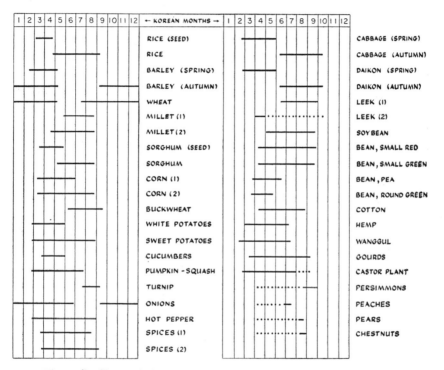

Figure 7. Chart of the Growing Period of Grains and Vegetables

able, since as their whole calendar lags behind that of the West, the growing season of most of their products begins in the first few months of their year, while their winter, which roughly corresponds to our autumn, proves least fruitful.

Some general idea of the annual cycle of activities may be gained by mentioning the high points of the yearly round. The first half of the first month is the New Year's holiday period during which the people work least. They visit friends and especially make calls of salutation on the old. Men play cards and boys fly kites or spin their tops. For the twenty days following, the farmers fertilize their dry fields with night soil and rake up leaves in the woods for fuel. Before the end of the second month, spring barley, white potatoes, hot peppers, and pumpkin seeds are sown. With the coming of the third month, the people go on to fertilize their rice fields, using oxen to plow them. They then plant a few of the best paddies as seed beds. By the middle of the fourth month it is time to transplant the rice seedlings into the waiting wet fields. This arduous labor continues for weeks. The fifth month is characterized by the harvest of barley as well as the hand cultivation of the rice fields. From the tenth of the sixth month, for a period of fifty days, the people must intermittently cut grass in the forest with which to mix ox and pig manure to make compost for the rice beds of the following year. The eighth month demands the most labor, which is put into weeding the rice fields. The ninth is the great harvest month when the rice is cut, carried home, and threshed. During the last three months, or winter of the year, people concentrate on nonagricultural activities. Men weave straw for the roofs which must be resurfaced regularly, make grass slippers, mats, bags, baskets, and various odds and ends. Women cook and sew as they do in other seasons. In many ways winter is the least arduous time and the one of greatest pleasure. The rice crop is in and there is no concern over food for the immediate future. The next thing to look forward to is the New Year's holidays.

Of all the crops, rice and barley are certainly the most important on Kanghwa Island and, for that matter, in Korea as a whole. Informants place them in a primary class by themselves. The reason for this is that rice, above all else, is the staple food while barley gains its importance by ripening four months earlier at a time when the people, having eaten up their store of rice, might otherwise starve.

The farmers of Sŏndup'o place in the second category of importance white potatoes, wheat, millet, beans, cabbage, the daikon (Japanese radish), hot peppers, and leeks. In a third group fall cucumbers, sweet potatoes, pumpkins, onions, sorghum, and spices, and finally, in the group of least significance, are corn, buckwheat, and turnips. This last item, apparently so greatly valued over much of Korea, seems largely to have been displaced in the Kanghwa economy by the daikon. Some carrots are also found on the island

9. OLD KOREAN ON HIS WAY TO TOWN

10. THE OLD AND THE YOUNG

but, although the people like its taste, the yield of this vegetable—which is called "China root"—is believed to be inadequate.

Certain fruits are common in the area, particularly the persimmon, as well as peaches and pears. Chestnut trees and a few walnut trees may also be mentioned.

Besides the food plants, the people raise some cotton, hemp which is also used for making clothing, a reed called wanggul from which the finer mats are made, and gourds. The luxuriant green gourd vines, with their great globular yellow fruit, may be seen in summer growing up over the roof of almost every house. The gourds, after being prepared, serve as the common water dippers as well as for kitchen bowls.

The fields may be divided into types according to the crops which are grown in them. By far the great majority constitute wet rice paddies. As has been noted, the best of these serve also as seed beds at the beginning of the growing season and a plot may be set aside here and there in which to plant the mat fiber, wanggul.

All the other fields are dry and are located around the houses on the higher ground which stretches back up the hills. Of these, the most important group is reserved for barley. During the hottest months after the harvest, the same areas may be filled with soybeans intermingled with transplanted sorghum. Smaller plots suffice for wheat and these too, after the grain has been reaped, will be planted with vegetables, usually small green beans and the small red ones. A separate section of ground contains cucumbers and another white potatoes. Both of these give way to the late-growing varieties of cabbage and daikon. Finally, there may be individual fields for the remaining plants such as millet, sweet potatoes, leeks, onions, and hemp. As for spices, corn, and buckwheat, they may be seen lining the edges of the paths. Cotton is planted in some available field only once every few years.

Probably nothing in the economy of the area can be considered as so fundamentally valuable as a thorough knowledge of how to grow rice. Words will not make up for the accumulated experience which sensitizes fingers to distinguish the weeds or strengthens the arm muscles into effective instruments for pulling the cultivator or sickle while the back is bent over to the sun and the mud oozes between one's toes. The process of rice cultivation can be described in some detail, however, with the hope that the theory may bring a greater realization of the activity in which so many of the Koreans spend so much of their lives.

During the second and third months, the farmers spread pig and ox compost over the paddies. With water about two inches deep on the surface, they hitch their sleek-haired oxen to the plows and slowly move twice across all the area of their fields.* Selecting for first attention a few of the most fertile paddies, generally to be found in the lower reaches of the valley, a man and his wife prepare them for seeding. The plowed surface is gone over with a heavy wooden rake drawn by the ox. The seed beds are then divided into strips about four feet wide by means of little ditch paths scooped out perhaps five inches deep by hand, or sometimes with a shovel. The workers spread the resulting dirt over the beds to smooth them, stroking the mud with their palms or using a wooden stick to make them level. Then the water which flows gently down from the paddy above is blocked off and the plot allowed to drain so that it may dry at least one day in the sun. The hot rays will kill the worms, the people say. Afterwards they allow the water to flow in again to a depth of a single inch. Then the seed is sown.

Good seed beds are important and if people do not have them, they may rent a special plot for the seeding season from a more fortunate neighbor. Also, if the beds lie on the higher land the people may not be able to allow the sun to kill the worms because if they drain them, more water may not be available at the crucial time. In some instances this deficiency may be repaired by raising water from lower levels. To do this, large wooden water scoops are slung under tripods and deftly maneuvered to spoon water onto higher ground.

There are actually three varieties of rice planted by the villagers. Besides the common "dry" rice planted in the wet fields, some few individuals set aside a marked-off plot for "glutinous" rice which is made into special rice cakes or wine. "Glutinous" dry field rice should also be mentioned, but scarcely anyone in Sŏndup'o plants it. This dry field rice provides flour for rice cakes but is not good for making wine.

The seed to be sown is first soaked in a large jar or barrel filled with water containing a 1½ per cent solution of salt. A raw egg dropped unbroken into the liquid will indicate by floating when there

---

* In this area, ploughing is done with one ox, whereas in north Korea, two oxen are frequently used. Lee, 1936:73.

is enough. Dirt, husks, and useless seed rise to the top to be removed in a bamboo strainer. Then the salty water is replaced by fresh and the clean seed allowed to soak overnight.

Early in the morning on a day near the beginning of the third month, a man loads seed into a rice straw bag and carries it on his packboard to the prepared plots. His wife accompanies him with more seed in a basket on her head. The seed is strewn by hand over the water on the beds with such skill that little settles in the paths. While the seed is growing, purchased fertilizer, called "money manure," is thrown over the young crop and every five days or so, weeds must be pulled out. The latter, known as "barnyard millet," require skill to distinguish them from the rice.

By transplanting time, in the middle of the fourth month, the water has usually disappeared from the seed beds. A man works with his wife, pulling each blade out between the thumb and first finger, grasping the rice close to the mud. These shoots are collected in the opposite hand until it is full, whereupon the little sheaves are tied with a piece of rice straw looped around the seedlings, then twisted and tucked under itself. Some energetic persons pick seedlings by using both hands alternately, building up two bundles at the same time without shifting the blades. Individual Stakhanovites, one might say.

The sheaves of seedlings are either carried directly to the growing fields, where they are spread around, or if water is available in the seed beds, they are left immersed for not more than two days. Women and children transport four or five sheaves in each hand, but a man will use his packboard and load up to a hundred and twenty sheaves horizontally in its basket attachment at one time.

Transplanting takes twenty days or more, depending on the adequacy of the water supply. It is an arduous task, for the seedlings from one p'yong of land will produce four handfuls of sheaves which in turn will spread out over twelve p'yong of growing fields, at least under the conservative system of planting. It must be remembered that the efficiency of rice cultivation varies according to the knowledge of the farmer and the local conditions.

Since the transplanting of the rice, as well as its cultivation and harvesting, is a cooperative affair, something should be said on the latter subject. Men who work cooperatively in the rice fields vary the size of their groups from two to fifteen, but six is most common.

Men usually enter into this relationship on the basis of village friend-ships and work for each other year after year. If a newcomer took up a residence in the village and asked someone to exchange services, he would probably accept. Although it might seem that the strong and willing worker would lose by such an arrangement with a slightly lazy neighbor, the difference is insignificant, for the pattern of work habits keeps everyone in much the same position of effort. It is not unusual for one individual to work longer for another indi-vidual, who has a larger acreage, than the latter can work for him. In this case, the man working longer is compensated by a standard daily wage, which in 1947 was 200 wŏn (yen). Women cooperating under the same arrangements with other women for work in the dry fields receive the same amount of adjustment compensation.

Until World War II, it was a normal pattern for a labor group also to comprise an orchestra whose instruments included a small drum, one of hourglass shape (changu), large and small brass cym-bals, and a flute. One man struck the cymbals in the morning and the party gathered together for breakfast, after which they marched out along the rice dikes with the musicians playing and the remainder of the party dancing. A man whose fields were being worked had to supply food for all his companions. Three times during the day, his wife was expected with a basket of lunch, and wine if it could be afforded. On these occasions, the men stopped their work to gather on the dikes to eat, then played music and smoked their pipes. The morning performance was duplicated on the way home, and, if en-thusiasm overcame their exhaustion, the playing and dancing con-tinued on into the evening. Since the war, this gay pattern of life has been discontinued because the Japanese confiscated the cymbals for their brass and the drums have gone to pieces. Besides, such pleasures are too expensive since the liberation. A wife must still bring out food for the workers, however.

In preparation for transplanting the rice, two special lines are stretched along the long sides of the field to be filled with seedlings. The field should have a little water on the surface, but water may be short. These lines have marks approximately eight inches apart. Then a cross line, handled by two boys or girls, is extended across the field, beginning with the eight-inch marks at one end. The men, as they move backwards down the paddy, can manage the string them-selves if children are not available. The workers line up each holding part of a bundle of seedlings in his left hand, palm-up, with the roots extending beyond the little finger. Each man draws out three seed-lings between the thumb and first two fingers of his right hand, inserting the roots in front of the line by using his second finger to punch a hole in the mud to half its length. The seedlings are placed about seven inches apart laterally, thus making almost a square of plants as the cross line is moved to the next eight-inch marker.

The villagers learned this system of transplanting, together with the manner of soaking seeds and laying out seed beds in approachable units with better drainage, under Japanese tutelage in the regime of Governor Ugaki, or during the decade between 1930 and 1940. The straight lines in the growing fields decrease damage during cultiva-tion, both from walking on and turning the soil. The reduction to three seedlings from the previous five or six eliminates crowding, for seedlings double, and the new stalks bear most of the rice. Actu-ally, many Koreans still plant five or six seedlings together, thus cutting down production by stunting the heavy bearing stalks. Near the end of the war, the custom of making a small furrow where the line crosses the field and of planting seedlings only two or three inches apart on the intervening ridges was recommended. This method allows more sun to strike the roots, thereby increasing the yield as much as one third. Also, cultivation is easier. Japanese instruction ended with the American occupation, by which time few farmers had learned the new procedure. In the old days, the people distributed their seedlings somewhat haphazardly.

As soon as the cooperative workers have transplanted all the rice, they continue as groups to undertake the cultivating by hand. For this labor, the group lines up at the opposite end of the field from which the transplanting was started, each man about ten plants apart from his neighbor. The farmer leans over from unbent knees, so as not to damage the plants, and strikes a blow with his cultivator into the mud of the row in front of him, pulling it up on a plant. With his left hand he picks out excess weeds and covers them under the next turn of mud from his cultivator. A second blow falls to the right and is also pulled up on the same plant. Two scoops of dirt are thus thrown on each clump of rice. He works back and forth across his section of ten plants, moving forward row by row over the cleaned area. His pattern of movement has been diagramed on the following page. Frogs and snakes run from the farmers but bloodsuckers sometimes bother them. About ten days after the first cultivation of the rice fields has been completed, the groups begin the same weeding procedure over again.

The third cultivation of the rice starts after another interval of about ten days, the individual owner undertaking this task by himself. This time no tool is used and, after being plucked, the weeds are simply pressed under the mud with the feet. There are fewer weeds, however, as by this period the rice itself is shading the mud in which they grow. Nonetheless, the individual weeding takes much longer and may last from ten to twenty-five days. Near the beginning of the eighth month, rice grains appear on the plants and for weeks following, weeds growing up with them are at last distinguishable by their lack of grains, although hard to differentiate otherwise. These weeds should be picked out.

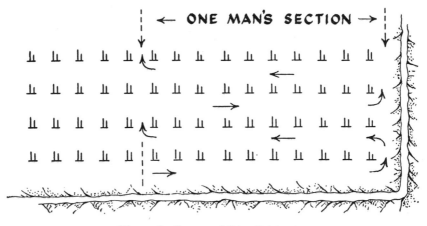

Figure 8. Pattern of Rice Cultivation

As the plants grow, the rice fields change in color from light green to dark, and become a golden yellow in the ninth month as the harvest time approaches. From the joy of cutting the grain, no one is excluded. The day before the reaping begins, the people put a fine edge on their sickles with small sharpening stones. The men work cooperatively but their womenfolk join in with children tagging along to assist where they can.

The cutting begins at any side of a field. A man usually grabs a handful of rice plants in the left hand with the thumb up and the palm toward him. Grass, when being cut, is usually held with the thumb down and the palm away from the body, and some people do the same in harvesting rice. Also, left-handed men have left-handed sickles and of course hold the grain with their right hands. Curiously, it might be added that even left-handed farmers use the iron cultivators with their right arms. The actual cutting of the rice is done by a pulling motion with the blade of the sickle about two inches above the mud, but the less the better. Skill is involved as the man leans over, his knees unbent as in previous activities in the paddy. The cut handful of grain is placed on the ground.

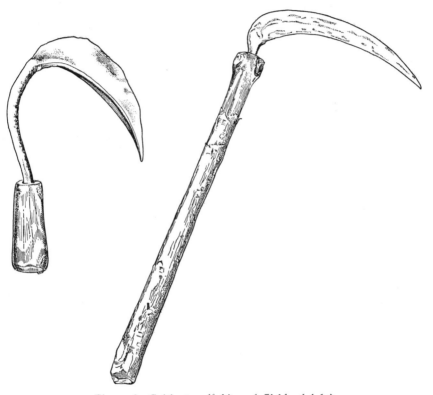

Figure 9. Cultivator (*left*) and Sickle (*right*)

Old men fall in behind the reapers and spread out the rice as thinly as possible in order that it may dry for three days, or longer if the weather is cloudy. Should rain actually fall, sheaves must be made immediately. Sheaves consist of "six handfuls" of grain tied together by taking a small group of blades, dividing them in two and twisting them against each other about a foot above the cut ends

of the "six handfuls." The two ends of the binding strands go around
the sheaf and are passed under each other as in tying a shoestring.
The free ends are then twisted and the twisted parts tucked upwards
under the binding encircling the sheaf. The sheaves are left where
they are tied. One old man takes one blade from each to keep count
of them and if the farmer is a tenant, the owner sends an agent to
gather the counting blades.

Most farmers stack the sheaves along the dikes, leaning four
bundles into each other as an anchor and then sloping the other
sheaves against them in pairs, alternating from side to side. A few
farmers put up a pair of tripods with an additional pole between them,
on which they hang the sheaves upside down by splitting the bundles
up to the place they have been tied. This dries the sheaves faster but
is more work. Once in sheaves the grain is left in the sun from three
to ten days. Finally the sheaves are carried home, men or oxen
bearing them on packboards.

Children go out to collect rice blades dropped on the fields during
the harvest and bring them to their parents. Usually they restrict
their efforts to the fields of their own families, but they may extend
their search. Roots of the rice plants remaining in the ground the
diligent farmer plows under before the ground freezes, but the less
assiduous leave them throughout the winter.

The sheaves are stacked circularly on one of the outer corners of
the matang with all heads toward the center. The man who places
them in position counts loudly as he does so. When the pile has
been completed, a specially woven conical thatch cover is placed on
top to keep the whole stack dry. At this time, the farmer will estimate his crop. Sixty to 100 sheaves, depending on the quality of the
grain, will produce 1,000 hops, or one sŏk, of unpolished rice.*

Threshing begins as soon as possible after the sheaves have been
stacked. First a fence is made all around the matang by stretching
large drying mats over poles or any convenient object which will
support them. A big wood mortar is laid on its side at one end of

* The Korean system for measuring grain is as follows:

10 sa	(pinches) = 1 hop
10 hop	(handfuls) = 1 toe
10 toe	(measures) = 1 mal
10 mal	(pecks or "bushels") = 1 sŏm or sŏk (bag)

A sŏk is 5.1 U. S. bushels. For the complexities of Korean mensuration, see
Hunt, 1896 and also the *Korean Repository,* Vol. 4 :1897 :332.

the matang, where the rice has been piled. One man takes off the conical thatch cover of the stack of sheaves and begins to throw them down. Another man, or sometimes two, begin to thresh the rice. This is done by winding a piece of rope twice around a sheaf just above its fastening, then twisting the rope a few times, and using it as a handle to swing the sheaf over the head and bring it down against the sides of the wood mortar, thus knocking off the grains of rice, which spread out over the matang. If the farmer is a tenant, an agent always watches this process because the advantage to the owner lies in having the rice well threshed. The farmer, on the other hand, will try to leave some grains in the straw which he piles up at one side of the matang. The agent inspects the straw but will probably be lenient, as his position will be more comfortable if he is on friendly terms with the farmer. By this means, a tenant may gain an extra hop of rice for himself when some old woman of the family sits cross-legged in a circle of mats and beats out the last grains. She will do this several days later, after the agent has departed, because it would not be polite to do so when it would make his oversight obvious. The straw itself is saved to use for a myriad of purposes.

The regularly threshed rice which spreads over the matang is drawn into a center pile with a solid wood rake. The hard surface of the matang is then swept with a broom to make sure that no grains have been lost. The next step is to winnow the harvest. To do this, a large clean rice straw mat is placed in the lee of the pile of threshed rice. The farmer takes up his woven winnowing tray, scoops it full of rice, and by holding it sidewise and using a sifting movement, slides the grain gradually off the edge. As the rice drops, the chaff blows off in the wind. Sometimes the wind is not strong enough to separate the chaff adequately, in which case another man must remedy the deficiency. This he accomplishes by a fan, which is simply a pliable piece of matting held at the ends in a vertical position, with its concave side facing the end of the winnowing tray. By vigorously moving the ends of the mat fan towards and away from each other, considerable draft is supplied. Such fanning is exhausting labor for which few women have the strength.

As the rice pile grows, the farmer periodically fans it with his winnowing tray, driving the excess chaff off the top. When the task is done the chaff is swept up to be burned and the rice scooped with the hands or a gourd into a 100-hop measure. Such a measure is always filled heaping for one's self or for the landlord but smoothed over if the grain is to be sold. Six of these measures of rice are then put into one of the straw bags in which the harvest is stored.

There is always some rice remaining in the cracks of the rough drying mat on which the winnowing has been done. To preserve the last grains, a man steps into the middle of the mat at one end and lifts up the two sides and kicks them, causing the rice to fall to the bottom. In this fashion he continues down the mat until the remnant rice has accumulated in a middle line. Then he lifts the two ends, bringing the grains into a pile. Finally, still standing on part of it, he lifts the mat and "jumps" the rice, catching it at that moment in a gourd. He will also measure these savings, so carefully sought, but they will amount to less than a single hop.

At the present time, the old method of threshing is being largely replaced through the introduction of a small footpower machine which has a revolving drum with staplelike appendages fastened all over it. One or two individuals, perhaps a man and his wife, pump the pedals, at the same time placing the heads of the sheaves against the spinning drum. The staples catch the grains and send them whirling onto the matang. There is also a rotary fan operated by foot pedals as an aid to winnowing. These laborsaving devices are said to have been introduced during the Ugaki regime in the thirties.

To finish the account, polishing of rice should be explained. This process the people may undertake periodically, whenever a supply of grain is needed for the kitchen. When polishing is to be done, the matang is first swept off and a large clean drying mat spread out upon it. Rice is dumped out of a bag onto the mat and spread about an inch thick with the solid wood rake. Then many little trenches are made with the corner of the rake, to increase the drying surfaces. Old men and children guard the grain from chickens or magpies as it dries. If a sudden rain intervenes, the ends of the mat are folded over, first in one direction and then the other, the whole package being quickly transferred into the house. Rice that has sunned all day is never put back into a bag while hot but rather is left to cool awhile in the evening.

The next day a mat is again put down on the matang and the large wood rice polisher placed upright in the center. This implement is constructed from a log about two feet in diameter. The lower section is perhaps two and a half feet high with a conical top containing radiating grooves ending in a rod projecting several feet upward. The upper section, of the same diameter, has a hole in the center slightly larger than the rod of the lower piece and its bottom is smoothly concave to match the convexity of the former. This section is placed on top of the other. The polisher is capped by a special basket with a hole in its center to allow it to fit over the rod. Into this basket the man or woman doing the polishing pours dried grain, which falls down along the rod as the top piece is turned, then rolls over and over on the corrugated surface of the lower part before spilling out onto the mat below. The farmer then winnows the milled rice, putting the grain into a round basket and saving the husks to stuff pillows or to use as fuel.

The final stage of the polishing consists of pounding the ground rice in a large stone or wood mortar, the latter being the same that was rolled over for use in threshing. Women hit the grain with a polelike wood pestle whereas men substitute a stone-headed hammer (Pl. 11, p. 78). A man can finish a portion of grain in about thirty blows but a woman will take forty to fifty with the pestle. The worker then removes the rice with a gourd scoop and replaces it in a round basket. Afterwards it is winnowed again, the last husks and the skins being saved for pig food. This final pounding and winnowing process may have to be repeated two or three times before all the skins come off. When a large quantity of rice has been polished, it may be kept in a great storage jar rather than in round baskets.

Instead of setting up the big wood polisher, people may make use of the public mill in the center of the village, bringing an ox along to turn it. Once hitched, he walks counterclockwise around the mill, making about four circumambulations a minute, while the attendant following with a flat stick keeps pushing the grain beneath the rough rolling stone that spews it out along the periphery (Pl. 8, p. 47). Some people prefer the wood polisher as it saves them from having to take their rice and equipment, as well as the ox, to the mill. Modern influences will probably do away with both practices as an itinerant with a kerosene-driven polisher is making it possible to do all of this work at one time.

A last word may be added about the yield of rice. Unpolished grain is saved for seed at the rate of 100 hops for every 120 p'yong of fields to be ultimately harvested. Each 120 p'yong may produce 1,500 hops of unpolished rice from this seed, or a return of fifteen times. This amounts to 12.5 hops per p'yong which, by polishing, is reduced one half. Some farmers estimate the yield of polished rice at 5 hops per p'yong, which is somewhat lower than the 6.25 computed above. Villagers have reason enough to keep their estimates low, however, which fact, together with the variability of season, fertilizer, supply, and location of the paddies, adds complications to such computations for an individual village, although they can be easily evened out by taking large-scale averages.

Although the reader may be somewhat weary of agricultural details, a few more paragraphs on the cultivation of barley, the second most important crop, are needed to balance the farming picture. Barley of two kinds, the spring and autumn, fills a large part of the available dry fields around the houses for at least part of the year and sometimes even rice fields receive a planting of the spring variety before serving their primary purpose. We might note that what Koreans call "autumn" barley, we would ordinarily term the "winter" variety, as it survives under the midwinter snow.

A few days before ploughing time, in the ninth month, ox and pig manure is carried by men or oxen in rice straw bags cut open at the seams and tied to the poles of the packboards, from which it is dumped in piles on various parts of the fields. Several days later, these piles are thoroughly scattered with a manure spreader, a scoop-shaped instrument woven from the sticklike stems of bush clover. Then the farmer plows the field with his ox while another man may break up the clumps of earth with a solid wood rake. Men always do the plowing and most of the fertilizing but other labor in the dry fields is carried on by the women, sometimes cooperating in groups.

Barley seed is selected exactly as is rice for seed and carried on the fields in the same way. A woman will probably sow the furrows, tossing the seed through an opening between her first and second fingers. The tops of the intervening ridges are then pulled over the seed with a rake.

When barley of either variety has grown about three inches high it must be fertilized. A woman brings night soil in a characteristic globular jar with two horizontal handles, carrying it on her head, while a man, if so engaged, takes a packpole to convey two full buckets at a time. The woman dishes out a little fertilizer for each plant with a gourd, while the man substitutes a urine ladle for this purpose. A gourd of approximately eight inches in diameter contains enough for all the barley plants in about six feet of a row. This fertilizing is generally done twice with a two-week interval, and then again in the spring.

Before the ground freezes, in the case of autumn barley, the earth must be pressed down beside the roots by walking astraddle of the rows. Everyone joins in doing this job except old men. The trampling is necessary, it is said, because the ground, after freezing, would otherwise heave when the sun shines on it, leaving the barley roots in a pocket of air which is bad for them. There is a saying that anyone who "steps" on barley in the winter will be rewarded by three bowls of wine. This may not come true, but the importance of the act is indicated.

The people harvest their barley in the spring in the same manner as they cut rice, but the grain is made into sheaves without being first spread out to dry. The farmers bring the latter home and pile them, not in a circle as with rice, but in parallel rows, one above another. To thresh barley, sheaves are laid with the tops facing each other in two parallel lines on the matang. Then a man or woman beats them with a flail. This simple instrument consists locally of a wood pole handle, perhaps five feet long, with a small rod through its end on which a shorter pole revolves. By making a circular movement with the hands holding the larger pole, the other piece turns a complete revolution which should end with its length evenly striking the rows of barley heads. The technique cannot be learned by reading alone.

When the threshing has been finished there are no more lines of sheaves left on the matang. All is in confusion. The straw is picked up with the hands, or less often with a pitchfork, leaving the grain and chaff on the hard clay. The straw serves as fuel or may be put into the ox stalls or pig pens to mix with manure. The barley is then winnowed and measured in the same way as is rice. Polishing likewise follows the routine used with rice, the only important difference being that some water is mixed with the grain to dampen it during the process.

Of the less important agricultural foods, one need not describe the details of their planting and care, especially since their cultivation, except for fertilizing, does not seem to differ greatly from that common in western culture. Most readers will have grown some radishes or beans themselves, or at least observed the process casually. During the last half of the tenth month such vegetables as radishes, cabbages, leeks, sweet potatoes, and white potatoes may be put into storage pits. The white potatoes will have been kept on the earth floor of the storage room in the house until then. Usually the men of each home dig a hole with a pick and shovel in the middle of a dry field. Such a pit is about three and a half feet wide, five feet long, and four feet deep, with the sides widened out so that the bottom is larger than the top opening. The hole is lined with rice straw and the vegetables are laid in, with alternating layers of rice straw. Rice husks are mixed with the straw surrounding the potatoes. When filled, pieces of wood are placed on top of the hole, then rice straw and a mound of dirt are added. A bunch of straw is left protruding to mark the storage pit, which will be opened to supply food for the New Year's feasts.

Fertilizers, so important in Korean agriculture, deserve special comment. Human excrement and urine are carefully preserved by farmers in the East because of the enriching effect of their high nitrogen content. Dipped from the toilets, these excreta are put in a mixing basin and ashes are added. This fertilizer, widely referred to as night soil, the farmers do not spread on the rice paddies but apply to the dry fields before they are plowed. Later, when individual plants must be treated, the excreta are applied in liquid form. The people have no prejudice against handling night soil nor does its use make the country smell unpleasantly, as do the cities when the "honey carts" pass by. One superstition does exist, however, which is that if anyone falls down inside a toilet shed, to say nothing of dropping into the basin beneath, he may not expect to live long.

Ox and pig manure has already been mentioned in the treatment of rice fields. The third type of fertilizer, locally referred to as "money manure," is acquired from government agencies. A considerable supply of ammonium sulphate has been available from northern Korea in past years but this source has not sufficed since the division of the country into Soviet and American spheres. Recent substitutes shipped in from abroad have begun to be used but not without difficulties. Ammonium nitrate many farmers do not like because if too much is spread at one time, it may "burn up" the crop. Tricalcium phosphate, the Koreans say, requires too much time.

Calcium superphosphate is also known in Korea. In any event, in Kilsang Myŏn the amount of commercial fertilizer available in 1947 was only a fraction of what was needed and crops were estimated at only 60 per cent of the potential output.*

Besides vegetable food, a limited amount of fish, fowl, eggs, and meat is consumed in Sŏndup'o. Meat eating occurs rarely except on ceremonial occasions, when some beef may be purchased in Samku Li. No one would think of killing an ox for food in the village, for these animals are regarded as members of the family, much as dogs may be in the United States. Indeed, it is sometimes said that people feed their oxen better than they do themselves. Certainly, in appearance, the oxen are a fine group of animals with friendly dispositions (Pl. 14, p. 95). Although only eight households in Sŏndup'o have oxen, it appears that seven others have a share in them for use. Three families without agricultural land do not need them and the rest borrow the oxen of fathers, uncles, brothers, or sons. Occasionally a man may rent his ox because of the problem of feeding it during the winter, but for this he only gets the ox fed plus a certain use of it. The man who rents the ox is not responsible if the ox should die, but any money that may accrue from selling the carcass must be paid to the owner. Difficulties over the sharing of oxen are sometimes a source of quarrels.

Ten families keep cows, of which two own a pair. Another two households each have a hog. There are numerous sucklings as well, which find their way to market as the villagers can rarely afford to eat them. The main value of these animals seems to lie in the fact that they supply manure.

Seventeen of the twenty-seven households have a few chickens, which supply a limited number of eggs as well as poultry dishes for feasts. As in the case of pigs, however, the villagers can rarely indulge themselves.

During the summer, one farmer acquired a white rabbit which he promised to eat in due time.

Besides the two hunting dogs kept by one young man, four other households each have a scrawny-looking cur. These are kept to eat

* In 1941, fertilizers imported into Korea were stated to have been in order of amount: ammonium nitrate, superphosphate, ammonium sulphate, and potassium sulphate. This was approximately the situation for 1947 but amounts varied according to province and ammonium sulphate became rare south of the 38th parallel. *Summation*, August, 1947 :55-56.

during three hot days of the year when the meat is regarded as having a special salutary effect. The dog is killed by strangling it with a rope thrown over the branch of a tree. The hair is then burned off and the carcass cut up and cooked. When a man has a feeling that he would enjoy eating some dog, he finds a person with a bitch and pups. For bringing the bitch some rice soup, he will be given one of the litter to raise.

Hunting dogs, which are expensive to acquire, prove their worth in winter by running down the deer that are numerous in the surrounding hills. The dogs bring the deer to bay and then kill them by biting their throats. The farmers themselves have no guns. The hunter then sells the deer meat for a considerable price and the blood for even more, as it is considered to have great tonic value. Horns, too, would bring a premium but the animals caught are said to be too young to have salable antlers. Hunting dogs also sometimes kill badgers and weasels, the skins of which are sold but only the meat of the former is eaten. At this point, it might be interpolated that none of the Sŏndup‘o people has a cat or other pet. One cat was observed in another village of the li, however.

During the warmer part of the year, some Sŏndup‘o men go fishing in the lower reaches of the rice fields, where the water accumulates before running out to sea. Fishing is a social affair involving group participation from the surrounding villages. The party starts when someone reports that fish seem plentiful; perhaps the word spreads around on market day. The next morning as many as seventy men and boys may be seen plunging through the water, about half of them naked and the others wearing abbreviated trousers. The fishing procedure consists of forming lines across a shallow estuary, each man with a conical basket trap in his hand which he thrusts down into the water in front of him every few steps. The men make these basket traps by weaving bush clover sticks into an openwork funnel about two and a half feet high and twenty inches in diameter at the larger end. The fisherman thrusts the basket down through the water into the mud with both hands. If he traps something he can usually feel it bumping against the sides. So he reaches through the hole in the upper end, which is just large enough for his arm, and swishes his hand around until he grabs the fish, at the same time giving a distinctive yell indicating success. The catch is either put into a mesh bag carried by a strap over the shoulder or spitted on to a cord fast-

11. WOMAN POUNDING GRAIN IN STONE MORTAR

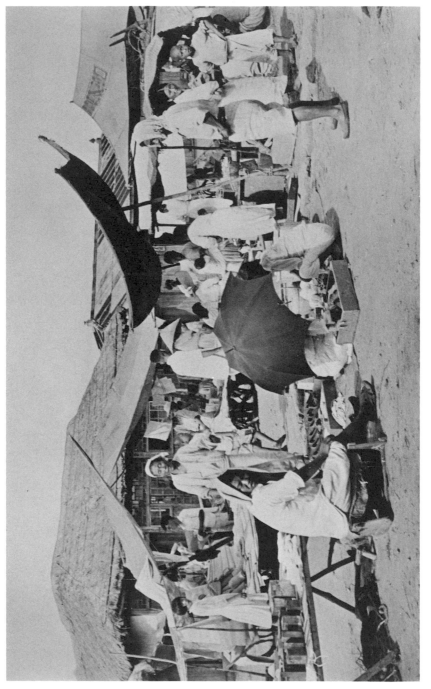

12. MARKET DAY IN SAMKU LI

ened around the waist. Most of the fishermen catch nothing after an hour or two of this sport but many trap a few and the luckiest may be seen with five or six hanging against his back. The fish vary in length up to about fifteen inches.

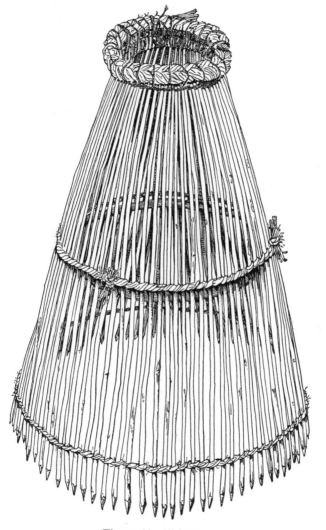

Figure 10. Fish Trap

Later in the season a group of men may dam up the water spreading out in the lower parts of the rice fields, so as to prevent the fish from escaping. A few men have triangular dipnets with which to collect small fry (Pl. 15, p. 110). On the same occasion, men grapple for eels by means of a pole with hooks on the end. Rarely, young boys may be seen fishing with a bamboo pole and a purchased hook on a line. All in all, fishing seems to provide more diversion than sustenance, which is perhaps equally needed during the long and hot summer days. At odd times women bring fish or an octopus to sell from the near-by villages along the coast but the market has not been good since incomes fell.

To conclude the discussion of food, there is the important matter of its preparation. Korean meals have a national distinction because of the combination of ethnic dishes which typically appear on the table, among which the outstanding ones are varieties of kimch'i. First, it may be instructive to list the main items of food served under the categories given by a native of Kanghwa.

A. Rice dishes
    1. Plain boiled rice
    2. Boiled rice with barley
    3. Boiled rice with beans
    4. Boiled rice with white potatoes
    5. Boiled rice with sorghum
    6. Boiled rice with millet
    7. Boiled rice with barley and white potatoes

B. Kimch'i
    1. Daikon kimch'i
        a. "Large cut"
        b. "Small cut"
        c. "Salty"
        d. "Very salty"
        e. "Pickled"
        f. "Summer"
    2. Cabbage kimch'i
    3. Cucumber kimch'i
        a. Cucumber
        b. "Salty"

C. Sungyung

D. Soups
    1. With soy sauce
        a. Chicken

   b. Fish
   c. Bean curd
   d. White potato
   e. Soybean sprouts
  2. With soybean mash
   a. Squash or pumpkin with vegetable tops
   b. "Very salty" daikon kimch'i
   c. "Salty" cucumber kimch'i
   d. Daikon from field thinning
  3. With hot pepper mash
   a. Bean curd
   b. Fish
   c. "Very salty" daikon kimch'i (rare)
   d. "Salty" cucumber kimch'i (rare)
  4. With kimch'i
   a. "Large cut" daikon kimch'i
   b. Cabbage kimch'i

E. Miscellaneous dishes
  1. Hot pepper mash
  2. Soy sauce
  3. Grilled fish
  4. Grilled dryfish
  5. Scrambled eggs
  6. Mountain vegetable

F. Special and Ceremonial Dishes
  1. White rice
  2. Beef soup
  3. Pork soup
  4. Seaweed soup
  5. Hot pepper mash
  6. Hot pepper powder with spices
  7. Grilled pork
  8. Grilled beef
  9. Fried bean curd
  10. Fried eggs with pumpkin or dryfish
  11. Chinese "Flower Bell" boiled
  12. Soy or small green bean sprouts boiled
  13. Cabbage kimch'i or pumpkin dipped in flour and water and fried
  14. Grilled fish
  15. Glutinous rice cake

16. Steamed rice cake
17. Yǒt
18. "Sweet wine"
19. Wine-spirits

Informants do not always agree whether breakfast or supper is the principal meal of the day and the latter opinion may result from some urban sophistication. Soup, which a housewife serves for breakfast and supper at the same time as the other dishes brought in on a tray, is distinctly a winter item of the menu. The others are not seasonal except as chance provides or ceremony demands. Sungyung, the inevitable concomitant of all regular meals, is brought in after the food has been eaten. People rarely drink wine or spirits with their meals but take them as aperitifs.

In eating, individuals ordinarily use a spoon for rice and to take up the liquid of soup or kimch'i. It is bad manners, however, to click the instrument against the teeth. Soup may likewise be drunk quite properly from the bowl and the same is true of kimch'i juice which should be sucked from the dish with the same elegant noise that accompanies the drinking of wine. Like the spoon and bowls, chopsticks are generally of brass, and serve to convey kimch'i and other substantial morsels to the mouth, most frequently at close range. These instruments should be held near the top for to grasp them close to their working ends is a sign that the user will have a bad wife or so young boys are told. Finally, it is not good taste to scratch the bowls with either spoon or chopsticks.

Women, with their daughters' help, prepare all meals at home. Rice, the most desired of all dishes, they wash three times in a large gourd, saving the water from the first washing for the pigs. Then water is put on the rice for the fourth time and shaken to make waves, following which the rice is ladled out with a sieve into another gourd. This process removes any stones which may have gotten in. To make certain, the remnants of rice in the first gourd are eased into a third and then back into the second. One does not expect stones in one's rice in Korea. The cook pours the cleaned rice into the iron cooking pot set into the stove, adding fresh water to the amount of 120 per cent. A fire is then made. When the pot boils, the woman takes off the lid and blows on the bubbles. From this time, the fire is allowed to die, the rice being left about ten minutes and then removed, ready to serve. If not immediately eaten, it keeps itself warm in an earthenware jar for a limited period. Rice, as one probably knows, cooks harder or softer according to the amount of water with it and it is amazing how particular some Koreans can be as to the ultimately satisfying texture.

When the cooked rice has been removed from the hot iron pot, some burned rice remains at the bottom. After some cold water is thrown in and mixed with these remnants, it will be served as sung-yung at the end of each meal.

Barley which is generally polished for the third time just before using, takes long to cook. Therefore, it is boiled for a while separately and is then mixed with the rice when the latter is put into the pot. Barley is said never to be eaten alone although very poor people may mix it with only white potatoes. A well-off man has no more than one-third barley with his rice and a rich man is above eating it at all. Barley thus becomes a social symbol, quite apart from its taste and nutritional value. To illustrate the point there is an old story about a Yangpan who one day went on a ship to make a short journey. He was offered rice and barley but said, "A Yangpan does not eat barley." So he got nothing. Unfortunately, the trip took longer than was expected. Being thoroughly hungry, he asked the cook what variety of barley he was serving. "Autumn barley," the cook answered. "Good," said the passenger, "Autumn barley a Yangpan will eat!" As may be seen from the list of dishes, rice may also be boiled with other grains and vegetables. The quantity of this food which a village farmer may consume for breakfast is tremendous.

Kimch'i is the Korean national dish. To the natives it smells good, to most foreigners it simply smells, which shows their provincialism. Besides the categories listed for Sŏndup'o, kimch'i can be given a threefold classification, to wit: "large cut" daikon kimch'i, "very salty" daikon kimch'i, and "cabbage" kimch'i. To some, these three types are regarded as basic. Also, a twofold grouping can be made by separating the pickled kimch'i from the unpickled.

To make daikon kimch'i, a woman picks the young radish-like tubers, and washes them well, after removing the tops which are tied together like roof thatch and hung under the ceiling to dry for soup. Then she cuts the tubers into slices on a board, one inch long for "large cut" and half that size for "small cut" kimch'i. The pieces are afterwards laid into large earthenware jars along with some onions. This dish is prepared in the fall and is eaten all during the winter by everyone, as a side dish to accompany their rice. The "salty" varieties are prepared much in the same manner, except that larger vegetables are used and more or less salt is added to each layer, depending on whether the "salty" or "very salty" kind is prepared at the time. "Salty" kimch'i are made in the tenth month and eaten during all other seasons, the salt preserving them as long as one's appetite will allow.

"Pickled" kimch'i requires the hand of an old mistress of the art. She cuts the daikon into strips about the size of a cigarette or perhaps a bit thicker. These are dried in the sun for a week, on a large grain-drying mat. When ready, the woman mixes these with soy sauce, leeks, onions, spices, and possibly peppers, placing the lot in a globular jar. These vegetables, except for the onions, are sliced; the latter are pounded into shreds with the butt of the knife. "Pickled" kimch'i is put up in the fall and may be eaten throughout the year by everyone. As for "summer" kimch'i, it may be made of turnips more often than daikon. The vegetables are washed and cut up into four or five pieces, the greens being treated the same way. These the maker puts into a globular jar with some salt and sliced hot peppers and leeks. If the cook can afford to splurge a little, she may add some salted shrimp caught locally in the fishing villages. The jar must be left in a warm place one day before the contents may be eaten. This kimch'i, made in the summer as the name implies, will keep only for a few days.

The villagers make two kinds of cabbage kimch'i, one in the winter and the other in summer, but they are not distinguished by name. A woman prepares the important winter type by first soaking large cabbages in salty water overnight, after which they are washed. This process is called "killing the cabbage" because the freshness is eliminated. At the same time, she slices washed daikon at an angle, thus providing oval pieces which are piled on top of one another and cut into strips. These strips the woman puts into a small jar with salt, hot pepper powder (enough to make the daikon look red), some ginger (purchased at the market), leeks, and shrimps. Then she mixes these ingredients. Having done so, she interlards the leaves of her soaked cabbages with this preparation, placing the finished product into a large earthenware jar. When all the cabbages are in, round stones are placed on top to hold them down. This kimch'i is made in the fall and eaten during the winter. The summer variety

follows the recipe for "summer" daikon kimch'i except that young
cabbages without the roots are washed and cut up, instead of turnips
or daikon. The Korean vegetable here referred to as cabbage is not
the round plant of the West, but is the elongated one with the leaves
turning outwards at the top, sometimes called Chinese cabbage.

The women prepare cucumber kimch'i by washing the vegetables,
then cutting small pieces off their ends, and slitting the sides in three
or four places. A wood water bucket is used for this preparation.
They then mix cut up hot peppers and leeks with smashed onions in
a shallow bowl. This material is then stuffed into the slits of the
cucumbers, after which they are placed in a jar of convenient size
to be left for forty-eight hours. The food is then ready to be eaten
and does not last long. The "salty" variety of cucumber kimch'i is
made without slitting the vegetable which is simply laid in the bottom
of a jar. Rough salt is spread over the top in a fairly thick layer,
then more layers of cucumbers and salt are added, a round stone being
placed on top to hold them down. Both varieties of cucumber kimch'i
are made in the summer but the "salty" kind will keep into the autumn
if a sufficient quantity has been prepared.

In concluding this somewhat extensive discourse on the preparation of the Korean national dish, a few general notes may be added.
Kimch'i is made on the wood floor room or maru, generally by the
oldest woman in the household because the greatest experience is
needed in judging the proportions of the ingredients. The kimch'i
jars are regularly covered with thick, coiled rice straw pads and the
contents, if "very salty" or "pickled," could presumably last indefinitely although no one had heard of such quantity being available
that it would last the year around. Despite the number of varieties
made in Sŏndup'o, there are even more known to the sophisticated
cooks of the capital who add rarer elements to the common fare.

Soups are all made with the second washing water of rice as a
base and have as the diagnostic ingredient such things as soy sauce,
soybean mash, hot pepper mash, or kimch'i. To the first three, more
substantial elements are added.

Of the miscellaneous dishes, first place is given to hot pepper mash.
To make it, a woman dries red peppers on a round rice straw mat or
shallow basket on the matang, a pretty sight to see. After about a
week of drying, she cuts the peppers in two with a pair of scissors
and then suns them a few days longer. Following this, the woman

beats them with a four-foot stick to knock off the seeds, but some still stick. A little more drying and the last of the seeds can be removed by winnowing. At this time, the peppers are pounded up in a wood or stone mortar and the powder is sifted through a pine-root sieve. The rough remnants serve for kimch'i or are occasionally put into soup. To make the mash from the pepper powder, the latter is mixed with soy sauce, sticky rice (ch'apssal) powder, and seasoning made from leeks, onions, and spices. This condiment is usually allowed to stand in a jar for about a year, although people may use it after two or three months. Some people making pepper mash add powdered dryfish (usually the mengtei) and ground-up roots of the balloon flower found in the hills (doraji: *Plotycodon grandiflorum*). Poor people may substitute powder made from sorghum or sticky millet (chichang) for that of rice.[3]

Soy sauce is made in the fall. A cook contrives this important item on the Korean menu by boiling soybeans until they are fully done and then pounding them, hot and wet, in a mortar. She continues by molding from this mash a truncated cone about eight or ten inches high and a foot in diameter, in the center of a large wood bowl. After this, the cone is put on a rice straw or pudul (a wild reed) mat laid out in the paper floor room. When the cone has dried fairly hard, two bunches of rice straw are wrapped around it, crossing at the top, and the cone is hung from the ceiling of the same room for several weeks, where it will ferment. About twenty such fermented cones are then put into a 500-hop rice straw bag and left all winter at the "upper" end of the paper floor room, away from the fire. In the spring, the woman will break the cones into several pieces and put them into a large earthenware jar, which is then filled with water. She adds salt, whole red peppers, and a few lumps of charcoal before leaving the jar in the sun for several days. Pieces of moldy soybean cone will float on top and the liquid will become black. This liquid, finally ladled out with a gourd and boiled, is the soybean sauce, while the remaining contents of the jar is soybean mash.

Soybeans, one of the most important elements in the diet, are also treated in other ways. They may be simply soaked overnight in fresh water and then cooked with rice, at a ratio of about one part to three of rice. Such a dish is eaten at intervals throughout the year.

Sometimes the raw unsoaked beans are burned at the bottom of the iron pot, which makes them jump. The cook bites the beans from time to time to determine when they are done. If satisfied, she takes them out with a gourd and grinds them up, afterward sieving the meal. This powder is used on rice cakes and children like to sprinkle it on ordinary boiled rice. They also enjoy eating the part of the bean meal which does not go through the sieve.

Another way of fixing soybeans is to soak them overnight and then grind them with water. The ground liquid meal is afterwards put through a sieve, the remaining part being boiled and eaten. The milky liquid is also boiled, then strained through a hemp bag into a shallow bowl. The curds remain in the bag to form a cake which may be cut and dipped into soy sauce to eat, or sometimes fried in seed oil.

As a last comment on the illustrious soybean, it should be stated that they can be germinated before being eaten. To do this, a woman spreads out the raw beans on a serving table and picks out any that have been damaged by worms. The others she washes in a small jar at the well. Then she adds clean water and a little rice straw with a few sticks at the top to make a temporary strainer so that she can change the water each day for about a week. She keeps the jar in the "upper" part of the paper floor room in summer, but if the preparation is being carried on in winter, she will place the jar in the "lower" or warmer end, wrapping it in a thin quilted Korean mattress. In a week's time, the bean sprouts should grow about four inches. The beans are then taken out and the sprouts cut off to be made into soup or to be pickled. Small green beans may be treated in the same way.

Fish or meat is usually grilled over hot coals in a little pot stove. A cook scrambles eggs and steams them in a dish on top of a rice pot after the water has boiled down, while frying can be accomplished by using the top of the iron pot upside down.

Of special dishes, perhaps the most important is yŏt, which is regarded as candy and is a strong favorite of the children for whom it is primarily made. Married women prepare it, especially at New Year's time, by wetting barley and allowing it to germinate in a basket for about ten days. The resulting material they grind to a powder and mix in a ratio of one to three parts of boiled rice, then heat it with water. They are careful not to overheat the mixture, lest it turn bitter. The thick part is spooned off, leaving behind a liquid which is boiled until it begins to candy. This is yŏt, which is generally eaten by dipping rice cakes into it. Also at New Year's, cakes are always made by mixing soybean powder with liquid yŏt. What is called "sweet wine" is simply a nonalcoholic mixture of liquid yŏt with the residue which is previously spooned off.

Years ago, the people in Sŏndup'o had some honey from the combs of wild bees but the bees flew away and they have had none since. No domesticated bees are kept in the area but there are some apiaries in the neighboring myŏn. Corn, or maize, is regarded as a kind of secondary food and is mostly eaten by children. Generally the ears of corn are steamed on top of the rice pot. They are not sweet but children like them, sometimes taking the kernels off with their thumbs. Corn is not fed to animals but the cobs are thrown to the pigs after the children have finished. Corn stalks may also be given to the pigs or to an ox, but most of them are burned as fuel.

Of more exotic foods in the village there are, for example, crickets which may be boiled whole and mixed with soy sauce as a special dish for children and babies in the fall. This dish is said to keep them from drooling. Crickets, incidentally, are still a favorite delicacy of the upper class in the capital. When silkworms are available, they are given to children as nourishment, after being boiled and the thread drawn off by old women. The children like them.

The villagers drink water at any time and think well water superior to any other except that from springs, which is regarded as having medicinal qualities. No woman is allowed to wash her menstrual band near a well or the well will dry up. Hot water is sometimes enjoyed for lunch in winter but not at other times and tea is nonexistent in the villages, although it has been introduced into the cities and towns through Japanese influence.

The fondness of the Koreans for wine and spirits has been proverbial from time immemorial and the Sŏndup'o villagers drink three kinds as follows:

1. T'akju, or turbid wine—a light wine slightly stronger than beer.
2. Yakju, or medicinal wine—a stronger variety of t'akju.
3. Soju, or burning wine—a strong spirit which burns the stomach.

The Japanese took over the production of alcoholic beverages as an important income-producing monopoly, but since the American occupation, private production for home consumption is permitted.

Villagers, however, make only the lighter varieties, purchasing the strong spirit in the market.*

Old women make the wine on the maru in summer or in the paper floor room in winter, generally just previous to the ceremony in which it will be used. To prepare t'akju, they grind wheat roughly in a stone mortar and then sift it. After the white flour has been removed, they mix the wheat skins with a little water and make them into a cake which is allowed to ferment about twenty days in a warm place. After fermentation has occurred, the woman breaks the cake into pieces about the size of marbles and mingles these with boiled rice in the proportion of two parts of rice to one of wheat. More water is added and the mixture is allowed to ferment for another eight days. The resultant mash is spooned into a sieve and cold water to one third its volume is passed through the mash. This final liquid is t'akju.

Yakju is obtained in almost the same way. The difference lies only in the quantity of water used and in the method of passing it through the mash. The mash is put into a jar after which a little water, perhaps 10 per cent by volume, is poured in on top and whished around the upper edges, cleaning them, then soaking down through the mash. After this, a special tubelike strainer a few inches in diameter is sunk into the mash, with its top edge remaining above the surface of the mixture. The liquid seeps through the walls of the strainer into a clear pool. This yakju is then dipped out.

Liquor is expected to be served at funerals, at marriages, at sixty-first birthdays, at any old man's birthday, at ceremonial festivals, and when cooperative workers go to the rice fields. T'akju is poured into a semiglobular bowl four inches in diameter. This bowl is passed around, men sitting on their heels to drink. Yakju appears in a slightly smaller bowl, while strong soju is presented in a wine cup. Only married men and old women over fifty-five are expected to participate, but this is an ideal. Young men also drink, turning their backs to their elders so as not to give offense. A younger woman may also take a taste. A little kimch'i is generally eaten at

---

* In commercial production the alcoholic content of t'akju is expected to be 10 per cent or less, of yakju, 15 per cent or less, of soju, 25 per cent or less. *Summation*, Nov., 1947:194. It is an interesting commentary on the post-liberation Korean liquor industry that in an examination of 370 samples of whiskey, brandy, and distilled spirit, 96 contained the poisonous methyl alcohol. *Ibid.*, Nov., 1945:199.

the same time, a sort of hors d'oeuvre. The drinking takes place on the maru in summer, or in a paper floor room in winter. Men sometimes drink extensively, in which case they are expected to retire and sleep off the effects. Ideally, at least, drinking too much does not lead to disturbances and women do not become intoxicated at all. In practice, the results are sometimes different. In Samku Li, for example, there was a curious little coterie of three old ladies who were said to become very tipsy almost every afternoon. That, however, is an example of the looseness of town life from the villager's point of view and he would never admit that a woman in his own community might get drunk: such behavior is considered much too bad. Of course there is the question of defining an excess of drinking and sometimes one may argue that a man is not intoxicated if he can still move an arm.

In concluding our consideration of economic production, a few plants should be mentioned that do not provide food. Cotton, for example, is planted in some dry field about once in three years, to supply padding for clothes and mattresses. An area of a hundred p'yong is said to be sufficient for a family of six. The cotton should be frequently cultivated to produce a good yield. Women and old men pick the cotton and remove the seeds by hand. Seeds, incidentally, are supplied, as in the case of most vegetables, by anyone in the village who happens to have some. There is no direct repayment but some courtesy may be expected in exchange.

Castor plants, previously mentioned with reference to their oil, are grown in most villages of the li at the edges of the fields. The fruit is mashed in a mortar and then boiled to render the oil which women use on their hair, as well as to dispense for constipation.

Tobacco, like liquor, was a Japanese monopoly and the farmers were forbidden to grow it unless under license. Raising tobacco privately is still forbidden and the farmers resent this. In some villages, if one knows where to look, a few patches may be found to fill the old man's pipe. Tobacco is never chewed but most males use pipes, as do some old women as well. Cigarettes are too expensive for a villager to purchase but are greatly appreciated.[4]

Opium, the farmers say, was sold in Inch'ŏn under the Japanese administration. They add that no one ever smoked in Sŏndup'o, although a man died there in the twenties from overdosing himself. Apart from the fact that negative information on opium is often unreliable, there are in the area no obvious signs of use discernible to an experienced smoker.[5]

None of the famous ginseng root supplied to the Chinese market for centuries as an elixir restoring male potency is grown in the Sŏndup'o area, but a few fields may be seen in neighboring myŏn.

Finally, it may be added that one of the wealthiest family heads in Sŏndup'o had recently started a salt manufactory on the coast near by, which represented a considerable investment. Within a few months, he had over a 60 per cent return on his capital, however. The method of making salt is to plow the salt flats when the tide is ebbing for the month. The mud is then allowed to dry for several days. In a lower corner of the area, a space about fifteen feet on a side is dug out and surrounded with a low dike. Sea water is run over the plowed flats from the upper parts down into this basin, from which the salt-filled water is then scooped up and boiled in a large iron tank until the water has been evaporated. One of the large costs derives from the fact that eighty bundles of pine branches are needed for the fire to boil one tankful of brine.

6

THE LIFE OF THE INDIVIDUAL

IN KOREAN culture, the birth of an individual is not as socially significant as his death. At a birth the focus of attention is not on the child but directed to the parents, whose status is markedly changed. They have proved themselves in a society which demands a continuation of the lineage as the most meaningful function of personal existence. Only by having a child do they become adult. Contrariwise, the infant at birth is hardly more than a biological organism. If it dies, it will receive scarcely more deference than any other animal. If it lives, only through a long course of learning and ceremonies will it obtain the position of a recognized personality. Parenthood and a continuing line of descendants are the goals which, when clearly established, bring recognition and honor in the departure from life. Still, to die, one must first be born and we should know the process.

In the poorer households of the village, a pregnant wife usually continues to work up until the time of her childbirth pains. If the family can afford the expense, certain medicines believed to improve her strength may be given her during the last three months. In the case of a first confinement, the husband's father not uncommonly sends his pregnant daughter-in-law to her father's home so that, as it is said, she will not be "shy." Generally, however, the mother-in-law takes charge and some old woman of experience may be invited in to help, for which service a small gift is later made. The husband will also be present at the birth and may be expected to assist if his mother is dead. There are no doctors or professional midwives in the villages of Sŏndu Ri.

When labor pains set in, it is not unusual for a woman to crawl around on her knees, groaning. Then when the baby is about to appear she lies on her back, with her legs outstretched. Once delivered, the umbilical cord is cut with a pair of common scissors and the end tied with thread, then cauterized.

The baby is believed to cry out in order to start breathing, but if it does not, an old woman may hold it upside down and strike it. One informant stated that he saw one woman bump a newborn baby's head on a rice basket, which may be a variant technique if the observation was accurate. The infant, after being washed in warm water, is given to the mother, who feeds it immediately, as well as whenever it cries thereafter. The husband takes the afterbirth, mixes it with rice husks, and burns it on the cleaned matang. As soon as possible, three small piles of red clay are placed outside the door or gate of the house, two next to the posts and one in front of these. This indicates a birth has occurred in the family and bars all visitors for three days, after which the clay piles are expected to be removed. Actually, they are generally allowed to disintegrate, being casually kicked away. There is no ceremony of any kind during this period of household privacy.

The infant will be treated the same way whether it is a boy or a girl, although the birth of a male child makes everyone especially happy. The real concern, however, is directed to the mother, for her importance to the family as a potential bearer of descendants seems paramount. Should she die, there is little love for the newborn infant and small hope of its survival. If a woman is strong and has had an easy parturition, she may return to her household duties within three days, but generally she rests for ten.

After the child has been born, an ordinary letter announcing that fact is sent to the mother's parents and within the first three days the oldest man in the clan gives a boy his regular name, which is derived from records. It rarely happens that a woman gives birth to twins. Such an event is not appreciated, as the people make an unfavorable comparison to multiple births among animals. The mother will attempt to rear them, however, but her efforts are not likely to succeed because they are not strong, or so it is said. In one case where both twins died, even years afterward the father looked out the window when his wife recalled their birth. He seemed to be slightly ashamed. No instances of infanticide for any reason could be found among the people of Sŏndu Ri. An account of the killing of a child by an unmarried mother in Seoul, however, did appear in newspaper reports during the period just preceding our study. Needless to say, if infanticide did occur in any of the villages, it might be extremely difficult to discover.

The ceremonial life of each child begins at the end of the first three weeks, when relatives and intimate friends are invited to the house. The invitations are sent orally and the guests bring gifts, generally consisting of a small amount of money in an ordinary mailing envelope. These are presented without comment to the father by men and to the mother by women. The parents, on their part, serve glutinous rice cakes, kimch'i, liquid yŏt, and if possible, yakju or t'akju on the maru (summer) or in the paper floor room (winter) to the arriving guests. The baby may be viewed but only informally on this occasion. The people talk awhile and then say "Goodbye," the parents thereupon presenting them with a few rice cakes wrapped up in paper, a gesture which also may be extended to all families in the neighborhood. There is no ceremonial bowing, the affair being considered as an ordinary party. Exactly the same performance takes place for the child, whether boy or girl, on its hundredth day.

On the first anniversary, a more elaborate party is given. The procedure remains much the same except that on this occasion the baby, in special costume, is formally introduced to the relatives and guests. For the ceremony, a male infant wears light blue trousers and a peach-colored jacket with the lower half of the sleeves brightly banded in broad stripes of red, dark blue, and green. Over this coat rests a dark blue vest with three red buttons down the front. On his head perches a special type of hat, black in color, with the characters for "long life" and "fortune" embroidered or painted in gold on the sides. Two black ribbons hang down the back from this elaborate headgear. If it can be afforded, the clothing will be made of silk. The female costume will probably include a peach-colored skirt and a yellow jacket with colored bands. No hat is worn, but some decoration may be added to the hair.

The infant is placed in front of a food table on which various objects have been scattered. These will include, in the case of a boy, a writing brush, coins, pieces of threads indicating long life, and possibly other things. For a girl, a needle and various appropriate articles will be added. What the baby grasps in his hands is believed to indicate the course of his future fortune. Even if not taken seriously, the people watch and laugh. Afterwards they are given rice cakes and food, as on the previous visits. When departing, wrapped-up dainties are brought to each guest on a tray by a girl of the house and the visitor deposits some money in its place. For some

13. KOREAN WITH LOADED PACKBOARD

14. AN OLD MAN WITH HIS LONG PIPE AND HIS OX

days, all the cash collected during the anniversary ceremony, as well as on the previous parties for the child, is put into one envelope in the baby's pocket where anyone may see. This money, which has been donated as a gesture, is never associated with the wealth of the giver and, since the envelopes are not opened until after guests depart, one need not know how much has come from whom. The parents either save the cash which has been presented for the child or else buy something for it such as clothing. It is possible that the money may be used to have a photograph taken.

The function of these parties for an infant is to rejoice in the continuation of the family. Girls are included as being essential to the process, even though their role will be played in another clan.

After the baby has been introduced to society, it settles down to the slow process of learning the customs and manners of the community. Toilet training begins by placing the baby on a jar early in the morning. The mother says "sh . . ." and touches the genitals to suggest urination, or says "ung-ga" to encourage defecation. The baby may just wiggle its nose. No great pressure is put on the child, for people in the villages are not strict about these matters. Children a few years old, however, are slapped on the buttocks with the hand for relieving themselves in the paper floor rooms, the maru, or the kitchen. Elsewhere, an inadvertent conversion of space to toilet purposes is apt to create only amusement.

Normally, a child nurses for two years although occasionally a youngster over three times that old may be seen drinking at his mother's breast, with no embarrassment to either. Babies are always fed when they cry. The arrival of the second-born tends to force the first-born to ordinary feeding, as the milk will be needed for the second. Sometimes there is conflict, and it is not rare to see a baby fighting off an older competitor for possession of both of its mother's breasts. To wean a child, a woman simply pushes it away, but when this is not effective she sometimes puts a little pepper on her nipples. If she is short of milk, rice "milk," consisting of water in which rice has been stirred, will be substituted, but a baby soon begins to eat well-cooked cereal, first fed to it a few grains at a time on a spoon. It is tragic, however, when a mother dies soon after childbirth for, unless a wet nurse happens by chance to be available, the little thing may literally starve to death. A can of powdered milk supplied by the research worker will bring rewards to all concerned.

When a child begins to eat by himself, he is given a boiled ear of corn or white potato on which to chew between meals. A raw daikon soaked in salt water also serves effectively as a pacifier. Sometimes a child will suck his thumb and no one seems to care. One oddment is the occasional practice of tying a coin over a baby's navel to prevent it from bulging, a condition which is viewed as ugly.

A mother may sing to an infant to put it to sleep but formal lullabies do not seem to be common. She generally simply repeats the word "sleep" over and over again, often alternating it with a variant term to supply a rhythm. A baby spends much of the time on its mother's back or on the back of an older sister or even brother, when sisters are lacking. The infant is held in position by placing a broad cloth band around its buttocks and lower back, the band then being fastened over the stomach of the carrier. The child soon becomes accustomed to this position and, despite the irregular movement, will sleep with its head dangling in any direction (Pl. 7, p. 46).

As it grows older, the village child learns to play with the other young ones in the community, using mud and water and sticks and stones to make things in imitation of adult activities. Dolls or toys are few although not entirely absent. Grandfather may cut some rice straw stalks, fitting one inside another ingeniously to construct a human figure that waves its arms when one moves the inner straw up and down. Perhaps he will buy his grandchild a rubber ball when he goes to market. More than likely, he can be persuaded to fashion a bow and arrow for a boy to shoot during the fall, after the harvest is in. When other amusement pales, little boys and girls may play at hide-and-seek or make string figures. Boys fashion whistles from poplar bark or make pinwheels from paper, a bamboo pin, and a piece of sorghum stalk. These latter toys girls like to run with too, if they can persuade a brother to construct one for them.

A favorite activity of the boys is to continue to kick into the air with the instep a small "bird" made by fastening a coin into a piece of light paper, and cutting the excess covering into small strips. A good performer can do it over a hundred times without letting the "bird" hit the ground. One of the earliest games that children learn to play consists of making a circle on the matang with a knife and then adding a large number of cuts inside it, in one of which a piece of grass is hidden by one player while the others turn their backs. Each of the others then takes turns in digging up the cuts, and he who finds the grass is the winner. Even more common is the old hand game in which two players simultaneously throw a hand toward each other, either with two fingers spread (scissors), with palm open (cloth), or as a closed fist (stone). "Scissors" win over "cloth," "cloth" over "stone," and "stone" over "scissors." A more complex variant consists of taking five steps away from the starting point for winning with "scissors," ten for winning with "cloth," and twenty by "stone." The first to go thirty or forty steps out and back wins. The hand game, called "tossing" in Korean, is often used to determine the preferential order of commencing other games and sports.

A game which was probably introduced by the Japanese during the last ten years is started by the winner of a hand game drawing a circle about two feet in diameter on the matang. From this circle he bats out a small stick about three inches long with a two-foot one. The other player may catch the little stick or miss it. In either case, he attempts to throw it back into the circle from the point at which he obtains it. If he succeeds, he becomes the "guardian" of the circle who alone can win points. If, when the stick is thrown back, the guardian of the circle can bat it out, or if the little stick lands outside the circle, of its own accord, its distance from the circle is measured with the two-foot bat as a unit. Each unit gives the "guardian" one point. Boys play this game much more commonly than girls and a boy does not play it with a girl.

Boys also play a kind of soccer, using a rice straw ball about eight inches in diameter. A pair of sizable stones is placed six feet apart at each end of the matang or unused dry field. The boys divide into teams, with the side to kick first being determined by the hand game. The object is to drive the ball between the pair of rocks representing goal posts of the opposing side. To accomplish this wins one point, which is expressed as the losers "eating one point." Fouls are made by a player on either side touching the ball with his hands or kicking offside intentionally at his own corners of the field. A foul gives a free kick from the place of touching or going offside. One boy chosen as guardian of the goal may use his hands, however. The game generally continues until the players are tired and one side is way ahead.

In the evening, koni or changgi, which may be called the Korean parallels to checkers and chess, may be played, but changgi is almost exclusively played by grown men. More games and sports are seasonal and some exclusively pertain to certain periods. Boys swim in the summer and skate on the frozen rice fields in winter, using simple triangular blocks of wood with a piece of sharpened steel set into the bottom of each. A boy may sometimes convert a pair of skates into a kind of sled by nailing them onto the ends of a short board. This he sits on, pushing himself along with a pair of spikes set into wood handles. Boys also spin tops on the ice.

The New Year's holiday is a special time for ceremonial recreations, of which kite flying is probably the most celebrated. Boys make kites on the first day of the year and fly them for two weeks. These kites have certain characters written on them. On the fifteenth of the month, when the kites are high in the air, they are cut loose, and this is expected to keep any evil away. Kite flying is taboo at other times. During the same period, girls and women undertake the national ceremony of jumping each other up from the ends of teeter-totters. This performance is exclusively limited to females and to the New Year's holiday.

A stick game called yut, not to be confused with the candy, or yŏt, proves extremely popular during the long evenings of the first month, and older men play cards. The old custom of villages fighting each other with stones disappeared about fifty years ago but until the fall of the Yi dynasty, in 1910, combat with clubs between communities was encouraged as a kind of military practice. Before passing from the New Year's holidays, it might be noted that on the last night of the year, small children are advised not to close their eyes lest their eyebrows turn white. Sooner or later the small ones do fall asleep, of course, and then their older brothers and sisters dust wheat flour on the sleepers' eyebrows, much to everyone's merriment in the morning.

Another of the famous holiday sports of the Koreans is swinging. Women, girls, and boys engage in this activity on the fifth day of the fifth month. Ropes are suspended from any available large tree and the women and children whirl up and down. When queried for an explanation for this concentration on swinging, old men in Sŏndup'o say that it is done to keep mosquitoes away in the coming rainy season. Boys and men also wrestle on the same day and there may be intervillage bouts between the best of the sport.

Gambling proves to be a common vice among the Koreans. During the winter holidays, particularly, men gamble when playing yut or cards and the habit can sometimes become disastrous, especially among the richer men of a community. Boys acquire the gambling fever when groups of them rake grass in the hills. They bet their accumulated piles of grass by calling the toss of a rake.

Among quieter pastimes, one finds the people telling riddles and stories during the evening. The former may be illustrated by a single example. What is it that the more it is whittled, the larger it becomes? Stories told in the paper floor room on long winter evenings or in the cool of the matang in summer seem to fall into three general types. First come humorous tales which are more often than not of a scatological character. Excrement is a commonplace of the Korean village and women listen with as little embarrassment as do men. The second type might be said to comprise stories told for the edification of young men. The third group consists of biographical accounts of famous historical characters. Before giving an example of the village tales, it may be mentioned for any to whom it has not been obvious that what becomes larger the more that it is whittled is a hole.

A typical example of the humorous village story is that of a rather stupid young man who had to make a formal call with his uncle on a friend, following the decease of the latter's father. Not knowing how to act, he asked his uncle to instruct him and the latter said simply to do exactly as he did himself. Now when they arrived at the friend's house, the uncle, being an unusually tall man, bumped his head on the gate cover as they went in. The nephew following him, seeing this, but being short, stepped back, and taking a run jumped up and hit his head also. They went inside and after bowing to the ancestral tablet, the uncle bowed to the host. As he did so he accidentally broke wind. When the nephew tried to imitate him, he could not. He kept on trying, however, with the result that he defecated instead. The uncle was so disgusted that he took him home.

A more celebrated example of this characteristic type of humor which is considered instructive to young men, but is usually expurgated for the English reader, is the story of the two brothers and the gourds. Once there were two brothers, of whom the elder was a kindly man, but the younger mean. One day a swallow fell to the ground from its nest on the ridgepole of the elder brother's house and broke its leg. The elder brother was sorry for the bird and put its leg in splints. When the leg had healed, the bird flew away to south of the Yangtze River and reported what had happened to the King of the Swallows. The King, being impressed by such kindness, sent two gourd seeds to the elder brother when the bird returned in the spring. The elder brother planted them in due time and there was a fine crop of beautiful yellow gourds on the roof. When the day came to prepare them for use, the elder brother and his wife brought them into the house and sawed them in half on the maru. To their great surprise, each was full of gold. Thus the elder brother became suddenly wealthy.

His younger brother, learning the story, went back to his own home and finding a swallow in its nest on the ridgepole, pulled it out and broke one of its legs. Then he put splints on it so that it would heal. When the bird was well, it too flew off to the King of the Swallows and reported what had taken place, and again the King sent gourd seeds. The younger brother was delighted and even more enthusiastic when a tremendous crop of gourds grew over the roof. He could hardly wait until they were ripe to saw them. At last he and his wife set to work on the maru. The first gourd they opened was full of excrement. The couple went on cutting more, desperately looking for gold, but there was nothing but excrement. Unable to stop their feverish search, the house became so full of ordure that it collapsed on top of them.

The old village woman telling this to her grandsons used to add, "You must not be jealous about things; you must not be cruel!"

Formal education among the villagers has changed greatly during the lifetime of family heads, as a result of Japanese influence. In the old days before 1910, learning in the classical tradition was instilled at home and the farmers who benefited were few indeed. Some elder members of the family who knew characters gathered the children into one room to teach them, the boys studying Chinese texts as well as ŏnmun, the Korean syllabary, while for the girls, the latter was considered quite sufficient. From the viewpoint of modern pedagogy, the methods of instruction as well as the content of the learning were archaic. Among the few wealthier families, it was not uncommon for a teacher to be hired and sometimes a group of households contributed collectively to his meager salary, sending their children to him. One household supplied a school room as an additional gesture. The saving grace in this system was the extreme respect paid to learning under Confucian values. Limited as the system may have been in opportunities, the truly gifted student was highly regarded. Such a rare one might sometimes be encouraged to continue his studies and, on passing the national examinations, rise to prominence in the kingdom and thereby bring glory to the whole area. In any event, the relation between a student and his teacher was a most important one. A Korean may say in illustration, "A father and mother are the parents who bring me up while a teacher is the parent who educates me." Even the teacher's wife is called "teacher-mother" and one may talk to her in confidence about one's personal life. In the end, a true student should go to pay respect at the death festivals of both his teacher and his teacher's wife.

About 1911, the English Episcopalian Mission on Kanghwa Island started a school in Kilsang Myŏn which at least one boy in Sŏndup'o attended to obvious advantage. In May, 1920, the first public primary school opened in Samku Li under Japanese supervision and it has been operating ever since. Theoretically, every child in Sŏndup'o between the ages of six and twelve attends, although only fourteen are said to have been graduated up to 1947. Two of these have been able to continue their education in Seoul. Literacy is definitely increasing, but of the twenty-seven family heads, only six are said by their peers to be able to read and write both the Chinese and ŏnmun characters, which is the classical standard.

The school in Samku Li which the children of Sŏndup'o attend had 1,323 students in 1947 under the tutelage of a principal, six teachers, and eleven assistant teachers. Since 1920, there have been only 1,963 graduates of which 458 have been girls. The teachers, except for two assistants, are men, none of whom attended college. But all of the teachers except seven assistants were graduated from class-A (five year) middle schools. Of the latter assistants, the five men were graduated from class-B (three year) middle schools and the two women from a girls' (four year) high school.

The curriculum consists of social studies (including Korean history, world geography, and morals), arithmetic, general science,

Korean language (reading and writing), physical education, music, art, domestic science, and agriculture. Classes commence at nine in the morning and are held in forty-minute sessions with ten-minute recess periods intervening until about noon. School convenes again at one for the afternoon period. There are six grades, and all boys and girls of the upper half practice agriculture in the afternoon while the lower grades continue classes.

The school occupies 950 p'yong of land, an additional 800 p'yong of fields being available for agricultural practice. The building itself has twenty classrooms, almost everyone with a blackboard. In them are 320 double desks and 650 single chairs. A sizable playground adjoining the building contains some exercise apparatus such as ladders and parallel bars. Under the Japanese, the school had chemical laboratory equipment but since the liberation this has been mostly broken and the chemicals have been used up. Formerly, there was a rigid inspection of the school once during each of the terms but since these functions have been taken over by Koreans, there is some indication that such investigations are less exacting and suffering from a period of readjustment. A private doctor makes a health examination once a year, however, and inoculations are given to students if such diseases as cholera and typhus are spreading.

The school has a motto: "Love." In 1947 all the primary schools of the province had three slogans in addition: these were (1) the development of patriotism, (2) the development of scientific education (in place of paying so much attention to Tan-gun and Ki-ja, the Korean culture heroes), and (3) the development of the body. In addition, the Samku Li teachers have three more precepts: (1) to strive for the independence of the country, (2) to come closer to the students through love and example, and (3) to teach through the union of wisdom, morals, and health.

The school year begins on the first of the ninth month and continues to the seventh month with vacations between terms and several holiday celebrations of which the Memorial Day for the Invention of Ŏnmun Characters on the ninth of the tenth month, the Opening of Heaven Day (Tan-gun's birthday) on the third of the eleventh month, and the Memorial Day of the Independence Movement of 1919 on the first of March are typical examples. The Samku Li school, like other public institutions, is operated by the

Department of Education of the province and is financially supported by the government, with assistance from the School Support Association. Teachers' salaries are modest, it being presumed, as apparently is the case in most parts of the world, that the satisfaction of undertaking such an important duty as educating the youth of the land compensates one for concomitant material hardships. In any event, the teachers dwell less on their own problems than on the need for enlargement of the greatly overcrowded school, some millions of wŏn (yen) being needed for the purpose. Under the Japanese, there was a special school tax based on income, but this has been discontinued. Some of the myŏn officials hope that the funds can be gained by the people's contribution, believing that the villagers will have confidence in doing so. The farmers themselves speak of nothing so consistently as the desirability of improving the educational facilities. Although claiming to be willing to contribute, they show indubitable suspicion of the grafting proclivities of public officials.

Besides the class-A primary school in Samku Li, there is one class-B (four year) primary school in one of the coast villages of Sŏndu Ri. This school has a modern building and four teachers, making it possible for the younger children of the locality to begin their education at a time when it would be too far to walk to Samku Li. This institution had its origin in a one-teacher school in a neighboring village where each family paid ten hops of rice each year for each child. This was the teacher's salary.

Kanghwa Island is considered fortunate to have in its capital two schools above the primary grade. One of these is an agricultural school and the other, a girls' high school. The individuals in Sŏndup'o who would like to attend them cannot afford to, but at least they represent a hope that some day there may be a middle school in the south of the island. Until that time comes, they will continue to work in the village and look forward with some trepidation to their oncoming marriages.

Marriage under the old Korean system was almost as certain as death. A youth might escape it by becoming a monk but that was unlikely, and in recent times no bar to taking a wife. He is impressed with the fact that he must have children as a sacred duty to his family and that, indeed, he will be only a boy in the community until he does so. The role of wife and mother is, if anything, even more inevitable for the daughter in the family. Affection or love as a preliminary relationship has nothing to do with the choice of a spouse. In fact, the young couple has little or nothing to say in the matter, as it is arranged by their parents. So it has been for centuries and change comes slowly in the villages.

Ideally, a boy is expected to marry at the age of twenty, which is only eighteen or nineteen according to the system of counting in western culture. Koreans, like the Chinese, are accorded the age of one at birth and become a year older each New Year's day. Hence a child born on the last day of the year is two years old within twenty-four hours of his birth. In theory, the bride will be twenty also. Actually, the practice by no means always fits the theory, for various reasons. The most important factor is the health of the prospective bridegroom's mother, if the boy to be married is the eldest son. If the mother is not strong, she may need a daughter-in-law in the home to help with the household duties and in this case a marriage may be arranged when the son is about seventeen (Korean age). In that event the bride will most likely be older than he, as a competent girl will be all the more needed.

From the records of 386 living married couples in Sŏndu Ri, 12.17 per cent are the same age and in 15.28 per cent of the cases, the wives are older. Of the remaining 72.55 per cent of marriages with younger wives, the most or 10.62 per cent are two years the husband's junior; the next largest group of wives, comprising 9.33 per cent, are three years younger, and the third, of 8.54 per cent, one year younger. The extreme range of relative ages of wives is from sixteen years older to twenty-three years younger. It should be remembered, however, that these figures include the cases of second marriages as well as initial ones.*

The parents of a son or of a daughter may initiate an engagement, but the most essential case is that of a father arranging for the marriage of his eldest son. To take a specific instance, one of the village farmers asked his clan relatives in another locality to look around for some suitable candidates. According to his statement, no factors of preferential mating on the basis of relationship were involved. It

---

* Interesting as a check on the general validity of such data for Korea, the results of a study of 5,000 wives gave 76 per cent of the husbands as older (against 72.55 per cent in Sŏndu Ri) and 5 per cent of the wives as more than two years older (against 6.21 per cent in Sŏndu Ri). Sixteen was the average age at which these women married. Van Buskirk, 1931:157.

was simply required that the girl must not, of course, belong to the same clan. When a few potential brides had been singled out, he went to call on the fathers, his relatives introducing him after providing such information about the families as they could. The most important qualification considered was the education of the families. There was no direct talk about money, although the education of the children implies the wealth of the family. Neither side would wish to marry beneath itself so agreement becomes a matter of relative equality in educational standing. In no case did the prospective father-in-law actually see the potential bride. He did, however, arrange for the introduction of a female go-between to investigate the girl herself—her manners, appearance, and education.

No final decision was made at the time. The father returned home and discussed the whole matter with his son. Since this parent is one of the most educated men of the village with modern views, he offered his son the opportunity to see the chosen girl before they proceeded with the engagement. He was greatly relieved when the son relinquished this privilege out of deference to his parent. The father then returned to the house of the girl with a paper, bearing the date and time of his son's birth. This paper is a formal document folded an odd number of times (never an even number) and inserted into a split stem of bush clover which is fastened from one end to the other, making a loop of red and blue strings. This document, wrapped in cloth, was presented to the girl's father and he, having accepted it, thus formally sanctioned the engagement.

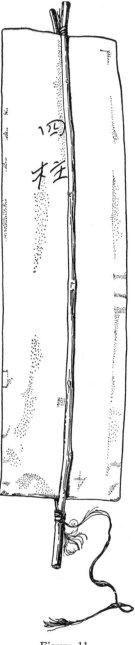

Figure 11.
Engagement Document

In the following days both fathers consulted fortunetellers, each being presented with a number of lucky days on which the marriage could take place, as told from the birthdates of the children involved. These dates were exchanged by the fathers and if they happened to agree it was particularly fortunate. In cases when a common date is not found after protracted effort, the boy's father may be expected to have the predominant role in the final decision. In these days, a man can weary of deference to fortunetellers if their good offices become too much of a nuisance.

On some occasions, especially with girls or younger sons, a father may be too busy, or for some other reason not care to make the initial contacts with the family of a prospective spouse. In such cases, a female go-between may visit the home of potential parents-in-law under the guise of selling needles, thread, bride's face powder, or such things, taking the opportunity to learn what she can. Actually, women in general seem to have a highly developed tendency for matchmaking and spend much time promoting engagements by all kinds of indirection. Even nuns like to put their hand in when the opportunity suggests itself. Whatever be the influence of women, however, the formal decision in the case of the marriage of a son remains the father's prerogative.

Between the time of the engagement and the marriage, a bridegroom may view his prospective bride but this modern privilege is seldom taken advantage of, it is said. The two families may exchange visits but even this intercourse depends upon the proximity of the homes to each other. When a girl is informed of her engagement, if she is a well-trained daughter she accepts the matter with at least external equanimity. If she has a dominant personality, she may have exerted considerable influence on the household before the formal document has been accepted. In last resort she may refuse to marry but this would be truly exceptional, although some signs of independence are increasing with education. Ordinarily she is helpless and ignorant. Since her first menstruation, which is a tightly kept secret among the women of the household, she has been forewarned of the inevitable day when she is to assume the role of a woman in a strange man's house, to serve him and his mother with obedience. Such a prospect can be both exciting and fearsome.

The night before her marriage, the bride has her hair done up at the back of her neck, any hairs which are too short to stay in place being pulled out. Her face will be heavily powdered for the ceremony and she will be dressed in a special coat and skirt provided by her future husband's family.

The bridegroom, on the day before the marriage ceremony is to take place, goes to his bride's village in the company of his nearest male relative except his father, who remains at home. The bridegroom rides on a horse hired with an attendant, for the occasion. The relative walks, carrying a lacquer box. The girl's father has arranged for a place for them to stay in another house. That evening the relative conveys the lacquer box to the bride's home and presents it to her father. He places it on a rice cake, prepared beforehand, and opens it. The box contains a skirt and coat for the bride. These articles are taken to the bride's room. One amusing feature of the presentation occurs in the traditional play of a young boy of the bride's family who waits surreptitiously to rub charcoal on the face of the bridegroom's relative when he delivers the lacquer box.

About eight or nine o'clock on the following morning the bridegroom mounts the horse and ceremonially rides to the house of his bride. This is done regardless of how short the distance may be. He is expected, of course, and the family has laid rice straw mats from the gate to the maru. The bridegroom wears a special hat, small and decorated in red and green, on the back of his head with a heavy pin or silver bar placed horizontally below it. When he dismounts, the attendant holding the horse hands him a wood "duck." * The bridegroom takes the "duck" and carries it to a table on the matang which is backed by a screen. At that instant, anyone in the bride's family snatches it up and takes it inside the house. The faster this is done, the better, for the "duck" is the symbol of conjugal faithfulness. The bridegroom bows three times before the empty table.

So important ceremonially is bowing that some description of that act should be interpolated at this point. Korean bowing may

* My informants state this ceremonial bird is a duck, although the goose, believed to be monogamous, is the classical marriage symbol in both Korean and Chinese cultures. The duck is likewise a common emblem of conjugal affection, however.

be made up of two elements, the "half" bow and the "full" bow. To make the "half" bow, a man bends his knees slightly with the arms stretched downwards and the palms of the hands facing in toward the legs at a level about halfway between the knees and the feet. The hands do not touch each other and the head is inclined downward. For the "full" bow, a man places the palms of the hands flat on the floor as he drops first onto the left knee and then onto the right. He then brings his nose down almost touching the floor but not quite. One remains in that position for the time required to take a long deep breath. Then the man raises his head and right knee, and continues to rise to his feet, his hands leaving the floor with his left knee. In the worship of ancestors, the ceremonial gesture consists of five bows beginning with a "half" bow and alternating with "full" bows, thus including two of the latter. For other occasions "half" bows or "full" bows are used separately. A woman's "half" bow varies only in that the palms of both hands face only the right knee, and in the "full" bow, neither knees nor head touch the floor, but the left knee is bent more than the right.

To return to the bridegroom, he stands before the empty table and makes three "half" bows. The boys of the neighborhood then guide the bridegroom from the matang to the maru, where he sits on a mat facing the gate through which he has come. The bride is brought in immediately by women attendants. The bridegroom stands up, still facing the door, and the bride faces him, but looking down. Each bows to the other, the bride slightly in advance of the groom. Her bow is peculiar to the occasion and starts by her placing her right hand on top of her left, palms down, in horizontal position at eye level. Then she goes down, first squatting, then on her knees, and finally leans toward the groom, her hands still in the original position. Her partner performs one "full" bow. They then sit facing each other, the bridegroom with his legs crossed, and the bride with one knee up as befits the inferior. Some woman of the family brings a bottle of yakju, a bowl, and some jujube fruit on a small table. She pours wine into the bowl and gives it to the bridegroom who drinks part and hands it back. The woman afterwards passes the bowl to the bride who swallows the remainder of the wine. This procedure is repeated three times after which the new wife gets up without bowing and retires to her room. The jujubes are generally left untouched.

This whole performance has been attended by guests who have arrived early. A representative of each visiting household brings an unwrapped gift of money, or sometimes of food, which is given to the parents as assistance in defraying the cost of the wedding. As usual, a man presents his gift to the father and a woman to the mother, both recipients making note of the amount as it is expected that at least an equivalent sum will be returned on the occasion of attending a wedding at the home of the giver. Almost all the guests are friends of the bride's family, except for the groom's relative and possibly some other males of his clan who have made the journey if it is not too distant.

During the wedding day a bride must neither smile nor speak. If she smiles, she may expect to have only girls as children. After the bride has retired, the groom goes and bows once to his father-in-law and once to his mother-in-law. Then a dinner is served, the bride-groom eating alone on the maru, with all the guests watching. He will probably not be very hungry and in any event he will leave some food which is taken to his wife to eat in private. She may not be very hungry either. There will almost certainly be some singing, the usual accompaniment of drinking wine. All in all, the ceremony may take three or four hours and the newly married couple must then face the journey home.

When the feast has been finished, the bridegroom leaves the house and mounts on his hired horse led by the attendant. The bride follows in an enclosed chair rented for the occasion, with her father walking beside her. Porters carry boxes of clothing, household furnishings, and food which the young wife is bringing to her new home (Pl. 13, p. 94). The procession continues on its journey which may require several hours, or rarely, a couple of days. A village farmer will hardly discuss a marriage procession without reference to the common story of the bride, typically shy, who could not stand the inevitable bouncing of the trip and urinated in her palanquin.

When the marriage procession reaches the house of the bridegroom's father, the new wife follows her husband inside and goes to his room after bowing once to her father-in-law and once to her mother-in-law in the same fashion as she did to her husband. She shuts the door of the room which may have been freshly papered and waits.

Guests and relatives in the village gather and a feast is served at which vermicelli is substituted for rice. There is sure to be wine. The bride's father is supplied with a room, either in his son-in-law's home or in another house. After sunset, when the festivities have quieted down, the bridegroom goes to his wife, who has been waiting with mixed anticipations, doing nothing. The women of the family gather in an adjoining room trying to observe what will happen, sometimes poking holes through the paper to catch a better view.

What does happen depends upon the personalities of the newly married couple. The women seldom tell but in one case it was reported that the bridegroom was so bashful that he did not touch his bride but sat sidewise until the watchers, tiring, went away. In another instance, a less bashful groom tried to untie the ribbons of the bride, but she pushed him away. He talked to her persuasively and finally she allowed him to help her remove her dress. The watchers saw nothing more, for the newlyweds blew out the lamp as they inevitably do on such occasions. There was no conversation for the girl will not speak on her bridal day.

The sexual life of the Korean couple may not be presumed to be very rich or even adequate, relative to any standard except that of conceiving children. Sex education has no formal place in the child's life and although sex occupies a major place in youthful discussion, it is not shared between males and females. Indeed, repression appears to be one of the dominant characteristics of marital relationships, at least from the formal point of view. The Korean farmer seems to pride himself publicly on his disregard of the sexual appeal of his wife, however much he may attempt to compensate for this attitude in private.

On the day after the wedding night, the bridegroom must feast his friends who come to call. The people who came with the bridal procession go home. For the first three days the bride enjoys a sort of honeymoon, and except for bowing to her parents-in-law each morning, does not share in any of the obligations of being a housewife. On the third day after the wedding night, the bridegroom must return to the house of his father-in-law and formally bow to his wife's parents. His wife, on the other hand, does not have to return for a visit at any special time. When her honeymoon is over, she starts working under the guidance of her hus-

15. FISHING IN FLOODED RICE FIELDS

16. FISHING BOAT WITH NETS DRYING

band's mother. Ideally, the latter should be generous in her demands at first as the girl will not be accustomed to undertaking
duties in the strange house. Soon, however, she assumes a full
burden of daily activities and fortunate she is if her mother-in-law
is understanding and kind. If not, even her husband cannot protect
her from abuse.

About a fortnight after the wedding, a special marriage certificate obtained from the myŏn office is signed by the bride and groom
as well as his parents. It will also be signed by the girl's parents
when someone takes it to them. This certificate is usually kept by
the bridegroom's father. If they can be afforded, the bridegroom
may present the girl with a pair of gold or silver engraved wedding
rings which are both worn on the third finger of the left hand. The
husband's father actually buys them and generally they do not fit
so the girl wraps the rings with thread to make them smaller. These
rings may be included with the coat and skirt in the lacquer box,
in which case the bride puts them on when she reaches her husband's
home. More often, if she ever acquires such jewelry, it will be
after settling down with her husband, and perhaps a great many
years later.

The daily activities of the couple begin early in the morning,
both getting up a little before sunrise in summer. While the woman
prepares breakfast, perhaps a bowl of white potatoes and barley
with side dishes of kimch'i and hot pepper mash, the man goes out
to inspect his rice fields. His concern will be chiefly over the condition of the dikes, for sometimes in a sudden surfeit of water they
break, carrying part of the precious crop and soil into the plot below.
After eating, he will go to the paddies to work, and his wife, after
tending the younger children, may engage in weeding the dry fields.
She will also prepare her family's lunch, perhaps carrying it out on
the dikes for the men to eat.

Afterwards she may take clothes to the stream to wash them,
beating the garments on a stone with a flat-sided stick. Starch is
made of rice flour paste, balls of which are dissolved in water and the
white clothes dipped in and rinsed. Then she hangs her wash on
a line in the shade, for the sun would shrink the material. Before
the pieces have completely dried, she folds them, piles them up, and
wraps them in a clean cloth, afterwards treading on the bundle to
stretch its contents. Later she perhaps begins to iron by beating

Figure 12.
Laundry Stick

the starched cloth on a stone ironing block in the kitchen garden, pounding away with a pair of round sticks in the characteristic rhythm so distinctive of Korea. This is the famous night sound heard by every traveler in the cities but, bothered by the darkness, the villagers do their ironing only in the daytime.

When her husband comes home she feeds him and then herself, cleans the kitchen, and settles down to do some of the many odd tasks around the house. Her good man may talk to his friends on the matang and wish that he had more leisure.

A winter day varies from the summer in that the work is not so strenuous, especially for the man. The days are shorter and one rises with the sun. The woman goes her usual round, with the sewing of clothes making up for the lack of agricultural labor. The man may cut grass in the hills if there is no snow or he may stay at home and make various implements of wood or straw. In any event, he is more likely to stay up later in the evening to gossip with his friends while his wife gathers with the women of the family.

In the course of a year the wife may expect to become pregnant. This will probably please her, if not for the excitement and joy of having a child, then because of the increase in status which she will gain as a mother. Thus the cycle of life completes itself.

With the passing of years it sometimes happens that a man seeks the company of a woman who is not his wife. Of course, he may go to town and drink wine in the house of a kisaeng, but this is a luxury much too expensive for the average farmer. The traditional source of extramarital relationship is between a man and a widow. Such liaisons are apparently rare but they do occur and if conducted with restraint, survive considerable gossip. Even less often, a man may contrive an affair with an unmarried girl. Knowledge of contraception in the village is slight. Some women regard the drinking of cold water, or urination immediately after intercourse, as having contraceptive value and there is the general belief that impregnation is least likely to occur at periods closest to menstruation. Should a woman conceive out of wedlock, she may attempt abortion with drugs purchased from the "Chinese" doctors by her lover. If unsuccessful, she will try to keep the matter a secret but everyone is said to know in time. A widow is sure to tell her most intimate friends and an unmarried girl will inform her mother. The latter inevitably becomes excited but keeps the matter to herself as much as possible in order to lessen the unfavorable comments. An illegitimate child is registered as the father's and he is always found out, but the mother raises the infant. An unmarried mother may only expect to be married off in the city or to some very poor man in a distant locality who will accept the circumstances. Were it not for such implications of hardship, the girl would be punished enough by the social ostracism and intolerant gossip in her own community. Traditionally, married women are said to find outlets for extra-marital relations by visiting priests in the temples. Historically, this seems to have been true but in the recent period there is little reason to believe that such a statement is correct.

Concubinage has long been an accepted custom in Korea and still exists in the villages of Sŏndu Ri among the oldest people. The practice is clearly dying out and less intimate informants sometimes deny its existence. Among the 332 families in the area, there are eight instances. Five of the villages contain no concubines and there is no indication of more than one concubine in a single family. Concubines were acquired for two reasons. The first, and only really acceptable one, was to supply children in the case that a wife was barren. For a wife to suggest that her husband take another woman under such circumstances has been long regarded as a noble gesture for which the wife is respected. Respected or not, it usually brought personal sorrow to the wife, for the husband by common report paid little attention to her afterwards. The second reason for a man to adopt a concubine was simply to satisfy himself. In either case, a separate room had to be made available for the new woman. Depending on the personalities involved, more or less difficulties followed. Theoretically, the wife held the superior position but if the concubine had a dominant disposition as well as the support of the head of the house, she might easily overshadow her predecessor. More complications arose over the position of the concubine's sons, if she had any. Even under Japanese rule, such children were placed at a public disadvantage and found it difficult to enter the secondary schools. The position of such boys, much worse under the Korean dynasties, probably takes the most prominent place in the romantic literature of the kingdom. The secret of being a concubine's son is now kept from all but one's most intimate friends if one escapes from the local scene.

To grow old in Korea has some advantage, for age is respected. Once a woman passes the menopause, which is no secret, she becomes somewhat sexless in the eyes of the population and may do much as she pleases within the restrictions of lifelong habit. The old man, too, receives a special share of consideration with all the young people of the area respectfully calling him "grandfather." The important thing is to have sons and grandchildren. If the old couple has a living son residing in the house which he will inherit, and if there are a number of grandsons playing about, the ancient ones who enjoy good health will probably be happy enough. A reasonable leisure will be theirs and the satisfaction of reflecting on lives with the principal goals achieved. For them, only death lies ahead, but they have little fear. To become one with the ancestors they have worshipped for decades is a proper conclusion to the pains of the world and they are certain that in the unbroken and endless chain of clan obeisance they will not be forgotten. Thus they prepare for their decease.

7

DEATH AND RELIGION

CHILDREN who know that a parent is about to die gather in his room. They recognize death when it comes by the lack of breath, the absence of pulse, and by the turn of the eyeballs showing white. The women wail loudly and all in the village who hear them understand that someone has gone to his ancestors. Immediately after the death, some close male relative goes outside and performs the ceremony of the "Invitation to the soul." The person first places a tray with rice, dryfish, and plain water on the matang in front of the door. Then he climbs up onto the roof by way of the stone wall and shouts three times that Mr. So-and-so of Such-and-such clan is dead. With each pronouncement, the relative waves a coat belonging to the deceased. In this fashion, the soul of the dead is asked to depart from the house, but as the farmer explaining the matter added with a laugh, "Sometimes the soul does not go." If death occurs in the dark of night, the announcement may be made from the top of the large wooden grain mill, in order that the speaker will not risk his neck climbing up onto the roof.

After the "Invitation to the soul," the women of the family unfasten their hair and weep loudly in the room with the deceased, the men joining in but with restraint. This first-night wake conducted by the relatives at least serves, according to an informant, to keep the people from being afraid.

Soon the women begin to sew together mourning clothes from hemp cloth stored for such an occasion. The son orders the coffin to be made by a carpenter, possibly from hardwood boards which have been accumulated in anticipation of the death. The box is roughly rectangular but slightly narrower at one end than at the other. On the top is written "The Coffin of the late Mr. So-and-so of the Such-and-such clan." Rich families may afford a lacquered coffin for the head of the house but the majority must be satisfied with a box of common poplar wood put together on the matang and polished with hen's eggs. The poorest cannot even afford this and will be carried off to the cemetery in a rice straw bag on a plank.

Two days following the death, the unwashed body of the dead man, dressed in his best garments with special paper shoes, is tied in seven places with hemp rope as he lies stretched out on his back with his hands, palms down, on his pelvis. The tyings are correlated with the seven stars of the Constellation of the Bear, which Koreans consider lucky. Relatives place the body on a plank which rests on two wood pillows in the lower end of the room, which is to say, the most honored position nearest the fire. Then they add a folding screen in front.

When the coffin has been completed, men bring it into the room where the dead man rests and, lifting him by the feet and shoulders, tuck him into it on a loose mattress of dike grass. More grass is added over the body and the flat cover is fastened down with slanting pegs.

As soon as the women have completed the mourning clothes, the family gives a death feast, collectively making the five-part ceremonial bow before the body of the deceased. The son will determine the day for the funeral and obtain a permit for it from the myŏn office. The feast may be prepared for the day following that on which the person dies, and the interment occur on the next, or third day, as the Koreans count it. If more time is required, the burial may be delayed up to a week but must take place on an odd day, that is the fifth or seventh including the date of death. The third day is most common, however.

On the morning of the funeral, the son sends several young men to dig the grave. If, as is usual, this is to be in the community cemetery, the boys choose a sunny place with as few roots and stones as possible so as not to make their labor more arduous than necessary. Formerly, when there were less restrictions on burials, a geomancer would have been consulted to determine a lucky location but this ancient custom has almost disappeared.

When the people are ready to proceed to the cemetery the coffin is conveyed to the back of the maru and a food offering including t'akju is placed before it, to be eaten by the members of the burial society. All the family bow ceremoniously and collectively in farewell.

Members of the burial society bring the funeral equipment into the village from the thatch-covered shelter on the hillside, which is similar to a toilet shed. The equipment consists of a covered wood platform supported by two parallel carrying poles, all painted in several colors, together with decorations of red and blue cloth. There is also a hand bell. After the farewell on the maru, the coffin is taken out to the matang and placed on this hearse, which is then raised by twelve men of the burial society, six on each side. Another man takes the bell and climbs onto the front of the coffin carrier.

The funeral procession begins with a man walking in front carrying a flag on which the dead man's name has been painted by his son. The hearse follows and the rider rings his bell, singing a verse of the funeral song. When he finishes, the bearers repeat the same verse. Then the rider rings his bell and sings another verse, the same process being continued throughout the journey. Behind the coffin follow the men of the deceased's family, then the women, then other relatives and friends.

When the cemetery has been reached, the hearse is put down crosswise at the lower end of the open grave. Men slip lines under each end of the coffin and thus carry it over the hole, lowering it down, and pulling out the ropes when it is at rest. The foot of the coffin slopes downhill: there is no other orientation. Finally, boys take the distinctive Korean shovel with a rope attached to each side of the blade and fill in the grave, one holding the handle, numerous others the ropes. The filling process proceeds apace and when the ground is smooth again, food offerings are laid out below the place and the relatives bow ceremoniously. After this the boys take up the shovel again and pile all the remaining earth into a mound over the grave. No subsequent additions are made to this simple monument unless sudden heavy rains should wash it down. The members of the burial society take the funeral equipment apart and replace the pieces in the near-by shed. The family returns home to put a folded paper, with the name and date of the death of the deceased on the outside, against the ancestor tablet at the back of the maru. Should a photograph of the dead person be available, it will be added. A food offering is made once more and the family collectively bow in obeisance for the fourth time. That is the end of the funeral.

The expenses of the interment are in part directly borne by the family, in part by the collections of the burial society, and in part by gifts of relatives and friends. The gifts may consist of either food or money, the latter generally being presented by men and the former by women. People offer their contributions to the principal person of the family of the same sex, either on their arrival or at their convenience, and sometimes even after the funeral but that is rare. Money is not wrapped and a record of it is kept so that the favor may be reciprocated when an analogous occasion arises. At least an equal return will be expected. Should the amount be less, there will be disappointment but the matter is not one about which a person will gossip. Gift giving at death is essential, for there is no preparation for such an expensive emergency except the participation in the burial society and the acquisition of hemp cloth and possibly coffin wood, which have been previously mentioned.

The description of the funeral given above applies to the male head of a family with sons. In theory, an adult woman's obsequies should be the same, but they may be less elaborate. Children and young people under twenty years of age can be expected to be buried in a mat without formalities. Interment is usually in the graveyard but may be on the nearer hillside, especially in the case of babies. On the other hand, a few of the richest clans still have private cemeteries adjoining their homes and in one there is a stone monument in front of a perfect hemispherical mound of bright green grass. People in Sŏndup'o have heard of cremation and there may have been a case or two in the area, perhaps as the result of Japanese influence, but they do not remember them.

The mourning clothes of the immediate family of a deceased parent consist of coarse hemp cloth purposely sewn in rough fashion to indicate grief on the part of both the makers and the wearers. To hide his sorrow a man has a special hemp hat, and more rarely, a conical reed headdress, large like the common rain hats, may still be seen. The special piece to cover the face has gone, however. A man also wears a rice straw belt and carries a short bamboo cane if it is his father who has died or a plain wood one if he has lost his mother. He also puts special straw sandals on his feet with the fibers wrapped with bits of white cloth, the mourning color.

Women also acquire similarly made sandals and fasten a rice straw rope around the head. These ropes, formerly fashioned from arrowroot instead of rice straw, as was also the man's belt, are specially twisted clockwise in the making, which is opposite to the normal procedure in manufacturing lines. Women likewise place a square of hemp cloth on top of their heads and a white ribbon in their hair. No other color is permissible in their dress.

Except for the men's hats and canes, the mourning clothes are taken off after the funeral and are not put on again except at the annual ceremony for the deceased in the following two years, thus making a total of three occasions. Then the hemp cloth is taken apart and put away until the next occasion of a death among the adults of the family. Men's mourning hats are burned at the end of the regular mourning period in which they are worn. On the whole, other external signs of sorrow disappear fairly soon in the villages, as work and time inevitably close the wound. It is not unusual, however, to hear the wail of a widow for her lost husband suddenly break forth from a thatch-covered house. Wailing in the area conforms to either of two established kinds, one known as the Kaesŏng type, the other as that of Seoul. The latter is a wail with a strong inbreathing at the end. It is done three times, followed by a pause. The Kaesŏng style is a continuous cry, varying in emphasis and tone and very sad to hear. It is the preferred form in Sŏndup'o. For the first two years after a man's death, rice, soup, and wine, if possible, are placed before the ancestor tablet on the first and fifteenth day of each month and the wife or daughter wails. Then they remove the food and eat it.

Following the decease of a spouse, a widower may remarry at any time. A widow, on the other hand, must wait two years and it may earn her respect if she never takes another husband, a true deprivation if she is young. Of the 2,147 people in Sŏndu Ri, 153 or 7.12 per cent have lost their partners. Only 39 are widowers, however, compared to 114 widows, which indicates the greater ease and potentialities which a man has in starting a new nuclear family.

The principal ceremonial occasions of the year have a direct connection with mourning. The New Year's feast, for example, is essentially a ceremony in honor of the last three generations of deceased direct male antecedents, including their wives. It is held on the first day of the first month at the house of the eldest member of the common lineage. In a formal sense, only men of the clan gather, but women may come to help in the preparation of the food.

The proceedings vary from simple to complex according to family wealth and custom, but a typical case of a fairly well to do village clan should serve as an illustration.

A table is placed in front of a cabinet with the ancestor tablet in it. Women put rows of ceremonial dishes with high pedestal bases containing food on this table. The rear line of offerings should comprise harvest grains; in front of the grains are fish, meats, fruits, polished nuts, and other items according to taste and opportunity. There is also a brass bowl on the table and a pair of brass chopsticks, the latter being extended between the two food dishes at the left rear. The women who have prepared the service then retire, leaving the room empty while the male members congregate in another.

The ceremony commences when the eldest son of the three honored generations enters, followed by his male relatives. A woman of the family stands at the door with a serving table. Everyone is quiet. The eldest son opens the cabinet with the ancestor tablet and takes the table from the woman and places it in front of the cabinet. On the table are a bowl of rice, a bowl of soup, a bottle of soju, besides a cup and brass chopsticks and spoon. The son takes off the covers of the bowls and adds a little of the rice to the soup as a symbol of eating. Then he returns to the left end of the line of men facing the table and they all make a full ceremonial bow which requires twenty to twenty-five seconds.

Once again the son approaches the table, adding a second spoonful of rice to the soup, after which he picks up the chopsticks stretched between the two left rear ceremonial food dishes and taps each one twice against a brass bowl cover to call the spirits of the ancestors, before replacing these implements between the third and fourth food dishes. After doing this, he returns to the line of his relatives and they bow again.

For the third time the eldest son goes forward, at this point substituting for the soup a bowl of cold water which the woman serving brings. He puts a spoonful of rice into the water. Then he taps each chopstick twice again and rests them between the fifth and sixth food dishes, returning for the last bow, after which everyone quietly retires, leaving the door shut behind them for a few minutes.

With respectful mien, the eldest son re-enters the room, followed by the others, and each takes a piece of food from the table. He

pours a cup of wine, sips it, and passes the cup to the next eldest
male of the family who drinks a little and hands it on according to
seniority. All are squatting on their heels during this part of the
procedure. Then all arise to their feet and retire, for the ceremony
is over.

The men make a breakfast of the ritual food and wine, which is
removed by the women and served to them on the usual individual
tables. Once again they chew and suck audibly. In theory all
should afterwards go to the graves of the ancestors and perform
the whole ceremony over again with food on a mat in front of the
burial mound, but some may prefer to spend their day in a more
carefree manner. The eldest son will perform the ritual in any
event. For an outsider to stand and watch such a ceremony at the
cemetery will be considered impolite although poor children may
do so in the expectation that some share of the food offering will
come their way. The eldest son may gratify them. When he
returns home he will, at sunset, close the cabinet containing the ancestor tablet.

The above procedure varies somewhat from those on the mid-
night of the first and second anniversary of an ancestor's decease,
called "small death" and "great death" respectively. On the fifteenth
of the first month there is a repetition of the New Year's ceremony,
and again on the fifteenth of the eighth month, although the latter
occasion is considered less important.

Between the first and the fifteenth day of the first month each
child in the village must sometime visit every house in Sŏndup'o
where there is an adult man as family head, and bow to him. If
the old man of a family has died within two years, his tablet will
still be up, and to this the child must bow. The head man answers
this respect by saying a word which means "yes" but is only ad-
dressed to infants. More rewarding, he should then offer the child
chestnuts, dried persimmons, and some coins—a few pennies, so
to speak.

Generally in the tenth month, on some convenient day after the
harvest has been taken in, there is a feast for the collective ancestors
antecedent to the three generations to which so much attention is
paid on other occasions. This celebration also varies with the clan
and is performed in the village of the eldest son, which means much
moving around. In Sŏndup'o, for example, sixteen of twenty-seven

households, representing only six of the fifteen lineages, have their ancestral feasts in their own village, while the rest must go elsewhere.

Except for ancestral worship and the study of the classics by boys learning the Chinese characters, the present-day impact of Confucianism on the villages of Sŏndu Ri seems to be limited to the subtle, if almost ubiquitous, influence of this ethical system on the Korean personality, an influence which has made itself felt over many centuries. It so permeates the society, however, that it appears indestructible in the face of any direct opposition, although in the present cycle of change it is certainly weakening under pressure of western culture. There are no Confucian temples in Sŏndu Ri but there is a famous one in the Kanghwa capital. Also, certain villages in the province gain recognition for their outstanding adherence to the principles of that great Chinese.

Spirit worship, the oldest of Korean religious patterns, still obtains some deferential recognition from the farming populace despite various efforts to stamp it out, the most recent being that by the Japanese. Again, the external manifestations may be prohibited under penalty, but once the pressure of punishments is lifted, the ancient ideas produce behavior that education alone can eliminate. Korean animism seems to focalize on some half a dozen conglomerations or groups of spirits. There are those, for example, which cluster around the house and are attached to its parts or juxtaposed constructions. There are the spirits of old trees, the spirits of mountains and other elements of the terrain, and the spirits of water and the sea. Finally, there are the more personal spirits which may be divided into two principal categories, the heroes of heaven, ranging from deities to the immortalized great whom time has hallowed, and unnamed uncertain spirits of the unhappy dead who haunt dark places to find both vengeance and escape by preying on the careless villager.

By and large, the present population of Sŏndu Ri show little interest in most of these spirits most of the time. Their attitude may be partly influenced by the fact that in this period of history they have more realistic fears for their personal happiness and security. Also, during the Japanese regime, the educational level of the younger generations was unquestionably raised. Under such circumstances, the acquisition of controlled information becomes

most difficult for the research worker and a true measure of the sub-
tleties of Korean religious life must be deferred until more extended
studies are available.

Probably the most obvious aspect of spirit worship in Sŏndup'o
appears in connection with the building of a house. After the
ground has been smoothed and the clay matang has been constructed,
the carpenters raise the corner posts on stone socles set into pounded
clay. When the roof is to be added, all the men in the village gather
to set the ridgepole, the heaviest piece of the building. Rice cakes,
t'akju, cooked pork, and dried fish are prepared for the occasion.
When the beam goes up, the oldest woman of the household rubs
her palms together and chants, "Please Grandfather and Grandmother of the ridgepole, bless us with full fortune and long life and
also many sons!" This appeal she repeats several times while
throwing wine or food at the ridgepole. More food and wine are
placed under the beam for several hours to please the spirit who is
expected to protect the house. The date is painted on or cut into
the ridgepole and at the end nearest the center of the dwelling are
characters which state "The Dragon goes up to heaven," while at
the opposite end is the complementary phrase "The Tortoise sits
down on the floor." These inscriptions imply that the roof should
prove strong and the foundation solid. The workers eat the feast
that has been prepared.

The people observe a similar ceremony when the stone wall
around the kitchen garden is being put up, a protective spirit being
urged to keep out sickness and other misfortunes, just as the wall
itself bars more material intrusions. There is a variety of black
snake about five feet long and with a yellow belly that the people
consider as the embodiment of both the ridgepole and garden wall
spirits. Should this snake enter a house, the occupants treat it
with respect. People simply keep away from it and only children
become frightened. Under no circumstances may this species of
reptile be killed.

No spirit could be found which is definitely attributed to the
stove, as in China, but there is one associated with the toilet shed.
This creature, which the people correlate with the superstructure
and not with the cesspool beneath, has a somewhat malevolent
character, unlike the other spirits of the home. One indication of

this lies in the belief that anyone falling onto the floor of the shed will die. From historical sources, other spirits of the house can be inferred but were not substantiated in the village of Sŏndup'o.

Spirits of ancient trees are widely respected over Korea and it is stated that anyone cutting into a tree that is over three hundred years old will die. The spirit which so protects the venerable growth is not in itself a source of good or evil, and one has the feeling that the people's attitude is a carry-over from their generally Confucian admiration of things deep-rooted in the past. Trees of great age are more characteristic of monastery grounds than of villages so they are generally removed from the immediate purview of the farmer.

Mountains, like trees, command the respect of the people and the spirits of the innumerable surrounding hills are regarded as of a superior order. The embodiment of the mountain spirit is the tiger and it is said that if a bad man climbs the heights, the tiger will eat him. Apparently, either the taboo is effective or there are no evil people in Sŏndu Ri for no one is reported to have been eaten recently. The fact that Kanghwa Island is a part of Korea which is not inhabited by real tigers may also somewhat affect the situation. In general, the islanders do like to climb, it may be added, and it is not unusual on reaching the top of some outstanding peak to find a couple of farmers resting in pensive appreciation of the awe-inspiring view.

Passes in the hills where a trail breaks through from one valley village to another have special spirit guardians and it is common to discover a small mound of pebbles near the height, each pebble brought by some traveler out of deference to the potential protector. Pieces of cloth—the fragments of clothing of those who have come and gone—may be seen in a near-by tree, apparently left behind as a symbol that the spirit may also keep any misfortune from following them. It becomes obvious from the size and condition of the piles that such protective mechanisms have become the indulgence of the few.

One spirit of the terrain is that of the house site. A small offering to this spirit may be found in the corner of the kitchen garden under a conical straw cover. It does not always prove easy for a visiting male to break through the privacy of a kitchen garden, and especially one which contains such a shrine forbidden by the

Japanese rulers, but photographic evidence verifies that they still exist in Sŏndu Ri.

Another category comprises the spirits of the sea or any body of water, including even a marsh. It is natura! that in Sŏndu Ri more concern with such spirits occurs among the people of the coastal villages. A colorful ceremony takes place in each of the fishing communities during the second month, when the boats first go out after the winter period of holidays and weaving of nets (Pl. 16, p. 111). The boats are drawn up on the beach, with gangplanks extending down to the shore, and preparations are made to sail on the ebb flow of the tide five days before the middle-month height of water. Three expensive silk flags bedeck each craft. Two square ones about three feet on a side stand across from each other in the stern. One has a black and yellow tiger outlined in black ink on a red field, the other contains a brick-red horse and a black general with a raised sword in light blue, also outlined with black ink, on a yellow field. Between them flies a red pennant about eighteen inches wide at the mast and ten feet long, with the name of the boat in black ink.

At the beginning of the ceremony, the captains of all the boats fasten one side of their barrel drums to the mainmasts and beat on them at the same time, first slowly and then gradually faster and faster. This tattoo they roll out three times in succession to call the spirits. Whether the latter attend or not, all the children in the village come running. After the drumming, one of the mates in each boat throws a little t'akju and some pinches of rice cake and dryfish into the water. Then the captain and crew sit aft and pass a bowl of t'akju among them, taking drinks in the order of their rank, from captain down.

While this is going on, one of the mates from each boat takes the rice cake jar—which is distinguished by the holes in its bottom for steaming—some dryfish and a bottle of wine, and goes ashore to a special shrine over which he throws a small amount of his food and liquor as an offering. When he returns to his boat, the children are waiting and he gives each one a handful from the rice cake jar. If any is left after each child has been served, he must distribute that to them also. In this fashion, every child receives rice cakes from each boat.

About this time the boat owner comes out of his house and walks down to his vessel, his pants rolled down below his navel and his belly pushed out in pride. In one hand he carries his long pipe, in the other a fan. Behind him follow sons and daughters bearing wine, tobacco, and his steel cash box. The crew of the boat descend to meet him, conveying on board the articles which have been brought by his children. If the tide covers the lower end of the gangplank, the cook may carry him across the water, while the crew follow him on board.

Then the anchor is weighed, the rudder put down, and the sails raised. As soon as the shore has been left behind, a circular pine raft about five feet in diameter is dropped overboard, to be towed some twenty to thirty feet astern. This raft bears a four-foot mast made from sorghum stalks, on the top of which is tied an eight-inch ball of cotton previously soaked in bean seed oil and set afire as the raft is floated. While this flaming torch is being towed, the members of the crew play music until they are tired, using drums, small and large cymbals, and a wood and reed whistle with a brass end. It is believed by the people that the raft which remains blazing the longest will indicate the ship that will catch the most fish during the voyage.

The boats on their outbound journey sail about seven hours, if favored by a good wind, to a particular uninhabited island. At that place, a small calf which has been transported on the vessel is taken ashore. There they kill it with an ax as a sacrifice to the sea spirit.[6]

Of the more personalized spirits recognized by the Koreans, the figures called changsŭng, commonly referred to by western writers as road idols, have attracted the most attention (Pl. 18, p. 127). These carved wooden posts have almost disappeared during the twentieth century and there is none remaining in the region of Sŏndu Ri. Only a decade and a half ago, however, a pair stood near the beach on the path between two fishing villages and several informants remembered them well. These posts were made of pine, the tops being carved into faces with rectangular pieces attached as ears. Most of the columns had been painted red but the hats and eyebrows were blue. There were also touches of white and characters had been written in black on both front and rear of the columns, one of which was crooked like the pine tree from which it came. The posts stood up eight to ten feet tall, one larger than the other. The larger one bore on the front the legend "Great General under Heaven," the smaller, "Woman General on the Earth." On the back sides of the

17. MADONNA OF THE SORGHUM

18. CHANGSŬNG OR "ROAD IDOL" IN SOUTH KYŎNGSANG
PROVINCE

posts were written the dates of their construction—dates which have been forgotten.

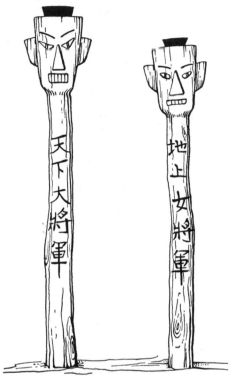

Figure 13. Sketch of Changsŭng or "Road Idols"

The primary function of these posts is said to have been to protect a village from evil spirits. People bowed in passing and children were afraid of them, especially at night. On a certain day early in the second month, men who owned fishing boats carried a tray of rice cakes, t'akju, and dryfish to the figures. They pinched off pieces of the food and threw them with the wine against the posts, saying as they did so, "Please make it possible for me to catch many fish!" Then they returned home.

Less distinctive spirits inhabit Korea in large numbers, although perhaps they are becoming more and more nebulous with the passing of time. Among them are the spirits of the recent dead. The funeral bell is rung to scare them away, but informants state they may return despite such prophylactic measures. Some persons claim not to be afraid of these disembodied souls.

Intimately connected with the collective spirit world are the mutang or female shamans, the high priestesses of the formalized cult of spirit worship which has survived from primitive prehistoric days. At least one mutang lives in the town of Samku Li and has her private temple in which she will establish helpful, or at least informative, communication with her spirit associates for a fee consistent with one's ability to pay. In this way one may circumvent malevolent spirits causing disease or other difficulties, or perhaps get in touch with a relative who has recently departed from the world of more ordinary conversations. Shamans pay obeisance to innumerable spirit deities among whom, it might be mentioned, is the General Ma Won of the previously described fishing boat flag, a famous warrior of the early Chinese Han dynasty. Five other mutang are reported as practicing in Kilsang Myŏn as well as one p'ansu, or blind man, as a male shaman. But as far as could be ascertained, there are no professionals in the villages of Sŏndu Ri.

The religious participation of the people of Sŏndup'o itself, apart from periodic worship at the ancestor tablets, proves uncertain and irregular. There is no formal study of Confucianism and there are no avowed Buddhists and, according to one opinion, few if any in the whole li. This, of course, does not prevent a crowd of people, particularly women and children, from attending the important annual feasts at the temple of Chŏndung.

Christianity, which has had a remarkable impact on Korea, has made itself felt in the local scene since the beginning of the century. The largest village of Sŏndu Ri, that adjacent to Sŏndup'o, has its own brick Methodist Episcopal church of which some hundred of the local residents are members. Another of the smaller communities along the coast also has a little frame church of the same denomination to which most of the eighty-four villagers belong. One Methodist lives in Sŏndup'o and he attends the town church in Samku Li, where there are another hundred communicants.

Even older in the district is the Episcopal Church, which has an imposing edifice in Samku Li. According to the priest, there are about a thousand communicants on Kanghwa Island, about half of whom reside in the six myŏn of the southern part under his ministrations. Nearly three hundred members live in Kilsang Myŏn and two thirds of these in Samku Li. Only four reside in Sŏndu Ri—two in a seacoast village and two in Sŏndup'o.

It is clear that Christianity has had little effect on Sŏndup'o which must be described as a Confucian village, if it is marked by any formal religious belief at all. As for the two of the ten communities in the li which do have a large proportion of followers of the western faith, the influence of Christian ideals and ethics strikes the sophisticated observer immediately. The women, who have gained a position of new respect and dignity, face one with quiet assurance despite the ingrained modesty intrinsic to the culture (Pl. 17, p. 126). A welcome from the head of the household brings not only the men of the family to the reception room, but also the women, sitting comfortably together if somewhat shyly. There is something about both house and people that provokes a sense of unusual cleanliness, perhaps that which someone has said is next to godliness. More flowers appear to be growing in the gardens and one is aware of love. There is at least an illusion of social gains and strengthened personalities. The Koreans have suffered long for their faith, they had some devoted leaders, and it does not seem prejudiced to say that at least for those in Kilsang Myŏn the reward has been more spiritual than material.

REFERENCES TO SOURCES FOR PART ONE

[1] The best references in English for the history and description of Kanghwa are Trollope (1901), Landis (1897), and Hamilton (1904:282-95). I have also used a Korean work, the *History of Kanghwa* by Chun Hun (1931).

[2] For data and tables showing price fluctuations in common commodities during the post-liberation years, see *Summation,* June, 1946:50-53 and *Ibid.,* January, 1948:20-32.

[3] My notes being incomplete on the manufacture of pepper mash, the data presented have been expanded through the kindness of Koreans living in New York.

[4] For data on the monopoly products, tobacco, ginseng, and salt, see *Summation,* June, 1946:57-61.

[5] For data on opium production, see *Summation,* March, 1946:11-13.

[6] For some interesting comparative data on ceremonies connected with boats, see Underwood, 1934:28-37.

Part Two

THE KOREAN CAPITAL AND THE RULING CLASS

8

THE KOREAN CAPITAL AND THE RULING CLASS

TO UNDERSTAND Korea as a whole, one needs to be able to correlate the basic village culture, such as we have seen in Sŏndup'o, with that of the city. Urban culture was distinguished by the behavior and values of the Yangpan class and especially of the officials and wealthy men among them. These individuals concentrated in the capital, where their lives represented a glittering intensification of the arts and manners of Korean society. Even in the metropolis they were a minority dominating the tens of thousands who had either gathered in their service or were caught like night-flying insects in the brilliant glare of the culture center. These Yangpan determined the measure of personal liberty for the people and the reward for one's labor. Sometimes they chose between peace and war; more often they decided whether an ordinary man might live or die. In returning to the country, either for political service or in failure, they created an impact great or small on the local communities and at the same time gave these valley villages a sense of somehow sharing in the complex national structure.

Since the countryman always lags behind in following a change in the behavior of his rich and respected city cousin, the Korean village of today is still more in step with Seoul, the royal city, than it is with a capital dominated by aliens. Thus to synchronize comparisons one must turn to the records of the period between the advent of numerous European observers and the overthrow of Korean independence, or, roughly, that score of years between 1885 and 1905. Fortunately, these are the decades which produced numerous descriptions of the Yangpan in the Korean capital by travelers and missionaries. The westerners were surprised by the strange customs and consequently recorded them with reasonable objectivity. From their accounts we can put together a picture of the life which to the simple Korean symbolized the power and the glory of his national culture.

To consider first the Yangpan class as a whole, which comprised perhaps 10 per cent of the total population, we discover that it may be divided into such groups as the royal line with the title of prince running out collaterally in the fourth generation, then the families holding high official office, and finally the remainder of the nobility distinguished only by being either rich or poor. The class situation was not completely static, however, for not only did commoners become ennobled because of exceptional distinction, but a so-called chungin or "half and half" group developed as a result of irregular marriages. This middle group, "neither ox nor horse" in native parlance, was numerically small and not clearly distinguishable culturally from the upper class despite the fact that in theory only some of the lower official positions such as secretaryships and those of translators of Chinese were open to its members.

The Yangpan showed themselves in their pride, using the low forms of speech to the commoners and demanding the high forms in return. They ordered the average man around at will, not allowing him to sit or even smoke a pipe in their presence without permission. It is the customs of these Yangpan which we must examine in order to understand their political organization and their general way of life.[1]*

Seoul at the end of the nineteenth century was a city of somewhat over two hundred thousand population, crowded within and overflowing its seven miles of ancient walls.[2] The king was nominally an absolute monarch with complete power over his subjects. As is usually the case with a ruler who inherits such a position, he was practically a prisoner of court tradition and prevented as an august personage from any realistic contacts outside the confines of his palace. The effective government of the country rested in the hands of an official group, the leaders of which surrounded the king with a constant pressure of influence, largely spent in securing for themselves a continuation of their personal prestige and power. At the top of the hierarchy, beneath the king, was a prime minister who, together with a minister of the right and a minister of the left, comprised the final authority in an elaborately expanded officialdom.[3] Independent of them, however, was the office of the censor, which reviewed decisions with the obligation of pointing out mistakes and issuing warnings of resultant dangers, even to the king himself.

* The references to sources for Part Two will be found on pages 152-54.

The principal business of government was directed through six ministries, the names of which can be translated as interior, law, ceremonies, finance, war, and industries. Each ministry was headed by an officer appointed by the king with advice of his three primary ministers, who kept a close personal watch on the departmental activities. Interior was most important for the reason that the local government was controlled through it, both directly and by the listing of nominees for the majority of official positions. It was this ministry which directed the national examinations through which for a thousand years individuals rose to preferment in the political system. The law ministry, as its name implies, dealt with legal matters, both the enactment of regulations and their enforcement, the police bureau being subsidiary to it in the latter respect. The ministry of ceremonies staged the elaborate ceremonial affairs which, in an oriental monarchy like the Korean, involved tremendous preparations and a degree of precision unequaled in any other division of the government. Such displays gained their importance not only from the near sacred quality with which long tradition endowed them, but because of the direct impression which they enabled the world of officialdom to make on the general public. The finance ministry collected the taxes and had charge of such correlated activities as taking the census. The duties of the ministry of war were equally obvious. The last and least important of the ministries, that of industry, was not so much concerned with production as a person in the industrial nations of the west might think, but was rather more of a department of public works with responsibility for the care of roads and government buildings, besides supplying such paraphernalia as a ceremonially disposed officialdom required.

This pattern of political organization, with all its subsidiary functionaries, was carried over to the provinces and on down to the prefectures where each local dignitary had his miniature cabinet appointed from the lower rung of officials known as ajŏn who were the actual negotiators between the mass of the farming population and the officials. Thus one sees a traditionally established system based on a division between a well-defined ruling group on the one hand and the majority of the people on the other.

From casual observation, the homes of the Yangpan class in the capital would not have struck one as greatly different from those of the country farmer. The culture did not encourage the construction of minor palaces for the nobility and the houses were all single-story dwellings, primarily, it would seem, because of the necessity for not violating the isolation of the women's courtyards. From a second floor, it would have been difficult to avoid seeing women, and to gaze on the face of an upper-class lady would destroy her social position. Even as it was, when a roof needed repair, notice had to be sent to one's neighbors for the women to protect themselves against possible, if unintentional, damage.[4] The roof, most often made of tiles in the case of the Yangpan's house, was one of the obvious marks of the class.[5]

The basic plan of the Yangpan house was the hollow square with a central court. Not all homes conformed to this design, but it was so characteristic of the capital that it is widely known over Korea as the Seoul type. The house, as typical of all, was measured in a standard unit, or kan, roughly eight to nine feet square with each room being from one to four units in size.[6] Besides this primary structure, additional courtyards for servants and retainers might be juxtaposed, their size and number depending on the wealth and ostentation of the family with the total establishment in some cases measuring up to two hundred kan.[7] Except for the tile roof, the materials were essentially the same as those used in the average farm village, including the common oiled- or thin-paper windows.[8] When building a house, the wealthy official might well substitute larger stones covering the flues of his radiant heating system. These would provide a more even temperature to the floor and, since he could afford more fuel, a certain measure of increased comfort in winter was his.[9] Also, the quality of the wood and paper used for floor and walls might have a manifest elegance among the upper class. Some walls were covered with quilted silk and the house furnishings of the rich were clearly distinguishable by their costliness.[10]

Most notable among the class-differentiated aspects of the houses was the even sharper separation of the male and female quarters than is found among the common people. The reception room for men, or sarang, was the normal, if not the almost required, adjunct of the gentleman's home, rather than a rarity. There he entertained his male friends and if he had a large following, it became something of a private clubroom for his intimates, who rarely entered other sections of the house. In consequence, the woman's quarters, or anpang, proved a place of almost complete isolation and were protected by law even from legal search, thereby in unusual instances supplying sanctuary for a criminal until he could be enticed outside.[11]

The most obvious contrast in Korean buildings, however, appears in the palaces and Buddhist monasteries of the country, where elaborate paintings and carving add splendor to the complex roof construction which is the essential artistic component of the architecture (Pl. 20, p. 143). For an individual to copy such forms in a private residence would have been a sacrilege. He had to square his house posts rather than leave them round and even the use of paint was prohibited, except for symbolic figures on the walls.[12] Although the imposing roofs of palace and religious buildings gave them magnitude, most of these constructions were not of more than one story, in the functional sense of normal occupation on superimposed levels. The same was true of the great gates of the capital, which may have a house on top of the arch. In fact, the guild headquarters have been reported as the only native two-story buildings, except for the palace, to have been erected in the capital.[13] In concluding these remarks on the various edifices of the upper class, the summer houses or pavilions of the rich should be mentioned (Pl. 19, p. 142). These were usually small buildings put up in some scenic surrounding to which friends could resort for an outing, such contacts with natural beauty being close to the hearts of most Koreans, whether wealthy or poor.[14] Few of the ordinary buildings of Korea are very old, as the material disintegrates in time and must be restored—which is no great undertaking. A curious custom of the country was that when a house had well caught on fire, it was generally allowed to burn up, for to quench the blaze would antagonize the fire-spirit who would then vent his spite more furiously on the neighbors. They simply climbed upon their roofs and waved pieces of clothing toward the flames to scare him away.[15]

Certainly one of the most obvious differences between the upper class and the mass of the people appeared in the dress. A gentleman of wealth and position wore a long flowing gown with full sleeves of generous proportions over his other clothing, or sometimes several of these robes, one on top of another, the increased bulk of the costume being compensated for by the sheerness of the material from which it was sewn. High rank and the number of tunics were correlated, some bearing embroidered insignia—a stork or phoenix for civil officers, and an oriental unicorn, a lion, or a tiger for the military leaders (Pl. 23, p. 174).[16]   There were no buttons, the gown being held in place by a belt from which were suspended pouches and fan.   As might be expected, the quality of cloth varied according to the owner's purse.   In general, silk was practically restricted to the Yangpan class, both men and women wearing it, whereas the common people had to be content with hemp—sometimes called grass cloth— or cotton.   Rarest of all were winter garments made from innumerable pieces of the yellow fur which grows only at the throat of the sable.   This material rich Koreans admired so much that they spent large sums to obtain it.[17]

In the color of clothing, Korean children took honors for variety and brightness of hue, quite irrespective of class.   Among adults, however, it was the upper-class women and particularly the officials who had the opportunity to dress themselves in gaudy array.   Government officers wore red, green, or blue, sometimes in combination, with the sleeves contrasting in color to the remainder of the garment, or perhaps with a gown of scarlet over one of blue creating moving harmonies of purple.   The magistrate in his violet robe stood out from his guard who appeared in soldier's blue, while the king might be seen wearing a brilliant scarlet dress and his queen, a yellow silk jacket above a long flowing blue skirt.[18]

Shoes also pointed to the class status of the wearer.   Whereas the common person put on footwear of woven straw, hemp twine, twisted paper, or wood, the Yangpan men, ladies, and children appeared in a low shoe of Chinese style, upturned at the toe.   These articles of dress were manufactured by shoemakers working at home and were not the product of factories.   The material was stiff oxhide which readily chafed the feet if heavy socks were not worn.   One might order them in different colors, such as black or blue, the popular fashion shifting from time to time.   Also, one could choose between wood soles and leather bottoms studded with nails.[19]   Besides these common shoes of the wealthy, special short cloth or felt boots were worn when in attendance at the court.   The style of these was also of Chinese origin.[20]

A slightly more subtle difference between the classes showed in the hats worn by the men.   The gentleman's regular head covering was that most distinctive Korean headdress, with a crown in the form of a truncated cone and a wide straight brim, the whole finely woven and sometimes resting on a stepped pyramidal inner hat of the same material sandwiched in between the brimmed top piece and the headband, which was tightly bound around the temples on coming of age and was not taken off thereafter. Such a hat would not survive anything but gentle treatment and consequently was the mark of a man not engaged in physical labor, at least at the time. In theory, the inner piece, or kwagŏ, was a badge and privilege of a man who had taken certain examinations and was in this sense a scholar. In the latter years of the kingdom, however, the attainment of scholastic honors was so debased that the kwagŏ was worn by many who did not deserve to do so. The quality of these hats themselves also varied. The finest might be discerned as being made of woven silk on a bamboo frame, the next of split bamboo so delicately woven as to be hard to distinguish from the other, and finally the least expensive and most common variety was contrived of woven horsehair.

Generally, these hats were lacquered black, but some of the split bamboo ones were yellow. Besides the distinction of quality, the hats of the higher officials were not flat on top but rounded, with a silver ornament, such as a crane, added to the crown. Also, wealthy individuals, instead of using plain ribbons with which to tie on the hat, substituted strings of amber or tortoise-shell beads.[21] For court dress, as in the case of shoes, a change was made. Men removed the kwagŏ as well as the brimmed top piece and put on a headdress somewhat similar in form to the kwagŏ but with two heavy outer wings appended. The higher the rank of the wearer, the thicker these appendages. These wings supposedly symbolized ears attentive to the words of majesty. The king's hat also had wings but the latter pointed upwards, rather than out, perhaps to indicate that authority for him lay only heavenward. Besides the hats mentioned there were other varieties of ceremonial distinction as well as more or less elaborate skullcaps, generally made of horsehair, for use inside the house.[22]

Another unusual article of dress which, if not limited to the Yangpan class, was at least more commonly worn by elderly noblemen, appeared as a loosely woven cooling frame of split bamboo or wisteria fiber in the shape of a vest. This construction was placed next to the skin to hold away cloth garments in very hot weather, thus allowing for a cooling evaporation of perspiration without that dampening of the clothes which later might result in a chill. Long cuffs of the same material or of horsehair for the lower arms were also available.[23]

Although elaborate jewelry was not a characteristic of Korean culture, some pins and clasps were worn. It was the ambition of an average woman to own a solid silver rod ornament for her hair while rich ladies might have them in gold. In his topknot, held by a net of horsehair or glazed thread, a nobleman also wore a pin, usually favoring silver because this metal was believed to have the power to frighten evil spirits.[24] Since these pins, unlike those of the women, were light in weight, one did not need to be rich to acquire them. Men of wealth, however, did distinguish themselves by hanging expensive watches and fans to their belts and officials wore flat sashes a few inches wide decorated with ornaments according to rank.[25] Also, attached to their headbands at a point behind the ears, nobles wore perforated disk-shaped buttons of smooth white jade, smooth gold, carved gold, carved white jade, or tortoise shell, corresponding respectively to five descending ranks. The members of the royal family had these insignia in smooth green jade.[26]

The fans also had an important function for the upper class in serving to screen the face while in a public place. Actually, a gentleman had a special face screen to hold over the lower part of his face but a fan was a more convenient substitute.[27] Most women in the capital, when they passed through the streets, wore special green silk jackets thrown over their heads and drew them across their faces when men approached, quite likely turning their heads aside as well. Women of the upper class often could be detected when their heads were exposed by the relative simplicity with which they did up their hair, as compared with the common style of adding switches to enlarge the size of the coiffure.[28]

Generally members of the Yangpan class did not walk on the street but used various conveyances, the most common of which was the sedan chair. This was usually a box about three feet square and four feet high, swung between two poles. The passenger squatted inside on the floor in such elegance as the owner of the vehicle cared to afford. Sedan chairs, besides being owned privately, could be rented at stands like taxicabs. There was a special type for women only, which was more tightly enclosed by curtains and had certain decorations of brass as well as ribbon streamers to warn the curious away. Sedan chairs were ordinarily borne by two men, one in front and the other behind, but the highest officials used four carriers. This was an exclusive privilege which resulted in a much more comfortable ride. Sedan chairs served for traveling over the countryside and at a much faster speed than one could expect by journeying on a Korean pony.[29] Actually, for a nobleman to ride horseback was not very practical because he was by custom forced to perch himself on an extraordinarily high saddle—presumably a compensation for the smallness of the animal— where he would be safeguarded by a retainer walking on each side, as well as by another retainer leading the horse. Mounting a donkey was traditionally a privilege of officials. It may be added that no commoner was allowed to ride in any fashion in the presence of a member of the upper class unless he was on his wedding journey or was going to his grave.[30]

One of the most peculiar means of locomotion in Korea was the unicycle, consisting of a chair perched above a single nail-studded wheel about two and one half feet in diameter. A pole extended in front and behind from beneath the seat. One man pushed and another pulled while several others supported the sides to avert a possible catastrophe. This monowheel chair was the special privilege, also, of officials of a certain rank.[31] Some rich men had pleasure boats in which to entertain parties of guests but these craft seem to have been largely limited to the Han River near the capital.[32] In contrast, for the great majority of the Korean populace, walking was the only way to go from one place to another although occasionally people might be seen riding in oxcarts or on ponies.

One of the most important differences between the Korean classes was that the rich had unlimited leisure. A certain amount of this time was spent in such a classical activity as archery. Many gentlemen had practice targets in their gardens and used their compound bows of oxhorn with amazing skill. Public competitions with royal awards were held at certain seasons. One eyewitness reports seeing experts make bull's-eyes with the iron-tipped reed shafts at two hundred yards and even hit a target at three hundred.[33]

Hunting with hawks was another pastime of the wealthy man. Pheasants, so common in Korea, were the usual game but bustards, ducks, cranes, and rabbits also fell prey to the hawk. The hawk, hooded and with a small bell around its neck, was carried on the heavy gauntlet of one of the two falconers required to care for the bird. The hawk was starved before the hunt and also deprived of sleep, besides being teased into viciousness. One curious part of its training was that after the kill, the hawk did not return to the wrist but perched on the back of the retrieving dog until they were joined by the hunters.[34]

The men also spent considerable time playing those games of skill which are the Korean counterparts of chess, backgammon, and checkers, as well as lounging around and gossiping with friends. Eating likewise became a major pastime. These aspects of behavior, however, did not distinguish the Yangpan from the commoner so much by kind as by degree. The former simply had more time and food, making it possible for meals to be extended for hours, the rich man gormandizing in relative silence on meat and other expensive dishes which were seldom if ever seen on the farmer's table.[35] When not eating, the Korean gentleman was apt to be smoking his pipe, an implement sometimes so lengthy that a servant was required to light it as the owner could not himself reach the bowl when the stem was in his mouth. Such effeteness among the upper class was also shown in the more common custom requiring that a gentleman carry nothing, not even a book which he was studying.[36]

One of the most interesting characteristics of the social life of upper-class men was their enjoyment of female entertainers at dinner parties as some measure of compensation for their isolation from their own wives with whom it would have been both gauche and embarrassing to sit down to a meal. These entertainers were known as kisaeng, and like their sister geisha in Japan, were trained from childhood for their profession. Originally a royal prerogative for the development of court dancers, private schools were later established, the most famous being said to be those of the Province of P'yŏngan. Pretty girls were purchased at the age of from eight to ten from poor families, the parents perhaps hoping that their daughters' lives might be happier without the inevitable drudgery which would otherwise follow. And, of course, the parents were aware of both immediate and possible future pecuniary gain for themselves. The sacrifice made by the girl was primarily that of losing normal class status to become part of a special group in which her descendants, having only limited civil rights, were more the losers than herself.

The education of the kisaeng consisted of an extended course of study in dancing, singing, and the playing of musical instruments. She was also carefully instructed in manners so as to be a combination of gracious hostess and serving girl. The schooling likewise included a general education, the students learning to read and to write as well

19. PAVILION IN THE KYŎNG POK PALACE, SEOUL

20. INTERIOR OF SŎKWANG TEMPLE. SOUTH HAMGYŎNG PROVINCE

as to recite poetry and to tell entertaining stories. One result was
that the kisaeng thus formed the most cultivated group of women in
Korea, a few gaining fame for their brilliance and beauty while the
average probably enjoyed life more than the ordinary Korean wife.

These dancing girls were also distinguished by the richness of
their dress, gorgeous silk costumes being characteristic of their profession. They used much cosmetics, put up their hair in elaborate
coiffures, and wore distinctive little caps. Perhaps their greatest privilege was freedom of movement. Only they among Korean women
would pass along a crowded thoroughfare without turning their eyes
in shame from men. Even more, they could smile where they pleased
without fear of molestation for, whatever their formal position, their
personal status was one in which their beauty was not repaid by any
traditional disrespect for their sex or profession.

The formal dancing for which the kisaeng were primarily trained
varied from elaborate ballet-like performances given at the court to the
more abstract or formal expressions at private parties. In either case,
movement and gesture were standardized, a fine performance being
gauged by a degree of gracefulness only recognizable to the connoisseur. Two eyewitness accounts of the special palace dances may
prove illuminating.

In the grounds before us appeared a pretty boat with wide spread sails, in
which were seated some gaily dressed girls. Others now appeared, dancing
to slow native music, a stately figure almost in minuet fashion, with waving
of flowing sleeves and banners. They were evidently the spirits of the wind,
and the boat was waiting the favoring breeze. The music grew quicker, while
faster and faster stepped the dancers, more and more swiftly fanning the sails
with sleeves, skirts, and scarfs, till at last the boat slowly moved forward, and
with its attendants moved out of sight. When the boat had been thus grace-
fully fanned away, a couple of mammoth lotus plants were brought out, with
great closed blossoms seen among the leaves. Following them came a pair of
gigantic storks, extremely well simulated. The birds came forward slowly,
advancing, retreating, sideling, mincing, waving their heads and long bills
about, all in tune to the music, wavering and uncertain, yet evidently with
some definite, not to be resisted, purpose in mind. At length, after long hesi-
tation, one of them plucked up courage and gave a vigorous peck at a lotus
bud, which forthwith burst open and released a pretty little child, who had
been curled up at its heart. The other stork, with similar good fortune, discovered another little one.[37]

A description of a dress rehearsal for a palace festival in about
1903 conveys an even more vivid impression to the senses.

From the dais where my host was sitting the dance was radiant with colour. There were eighteen performers, grouped in three equal divisions, and, as the streaming sunshine played upon the shimmering surface of their dresses, the lithe and graceful figures of the dancers floated in the brilliant reflection of a sea of sparkling light. The dance was almost without motion, so slowly were its fantastic figures developed. Never once were their arms dropped from their horizontal position, nor did the size and weight of their headdresses appear to fatigue the little women. Very slowly, the seated band gave forth the air. Very slowly, the dancers moved in the open space before us, their arms upraised, their gauze and silken draperies clustering round them, their hair piled high, and held in its curious shape by many jewelled and enamelled pins, which sparkled in the sunshine. The air was solemn; and, as if the movement were ceremonial, their voices rose and fell in a lingering harmony of passionate expression. At times, the three sets came together, the hues of the silken skirts blending in one vivid blaze of barbaric splendour. Then, as another movement succeeded, the eighteen figures broke apart and, poised upon their toes, in stately and measured unison circled round the floor, their arms rising and falling, their bodies bending and swaying, in dreamy undulation.

The dance epitomised the poetry and grace of human motion. The dainty attitudes of the performers had a gentle delicacy which was delightful. The long silken robes revealed a singular grace of deportment, and one looked upon dancers who were clothed from head to foot, not naked, brazen and unashamed, like those of our own burlesque, with infinite relief and infinite satisfaction. There was power and purpose in their movements; artistic subtlety in their poses. Their flowing robes emphasised the simplicity of their gestures; the pallor of their faces was unconcealed; their glances were timid; their manner modest. The strange eerie notes of the curious instruments, the fluctuating cadence of the song, the gliding motion of the dancers, the dazzling sheen of the silks, the vivid colours of the skirts, the flush of flesh beneath the silken shouldercoats, appealed to one silently and signally, stirring the emotions with an enthusiasm which was irrepressible.

The fascinating figures approached softly, smoothly sliding; and, as they glided slowly forward, the song of the music welled into passionate lamentation. The character of the dance changed. No longer advancing, the dancers moved in time to the beating of the drums; rotating circles of colour, their arms swaying, their bodies swinging backwards and forwards, as their retreating footsteps took them from us. The little figures seemed unconscious of their art; the musicians ignorant of the qualities of their wailing. Nevertheless, the masterly restraint of the band, the conception, skill and execution of the dancers, made up a triumph of technique.[38]

Apart from the court performances, kisaeng were available in their own establishments or could be engaged for entertainments elsewhere. The members of this profession were definitely not prostitutes although some became so in practice through personal weakness or inclination. The expected culmination of the kisaeng's career was to become the concubine of some wealthy man.[39]

Upper-class women certainly enjoyed no concomitant pleasure to match that of the men, and were far more restricted in their behavior and actions than their sisters of lower status. The higher the rank, the greater the seclusion, it would seem, for the ladies of the palace are said to have lived practically like nuns. At an age from about ten to twelve, girls were kept apart from the boys of the household and from that time on the males of the family could see them only under limited conditions. Even a husband talked little to his wife, but always used the polite forms of speech in addressing her as in speaking to any lady. This was not a class distinction, however, the much appreciated kisaeng being the only group excepted from this general rule of formality.[40]

Apart from managing the house, the Yangpan's wife spent part of her time in sewing and embroidery. She typically played some musical instrument, most likely the harp. Rolling dice provided a favorite amusement indulged in almost exclusively by women of the upper class, whereas, on the other hand, the Yangpan group looked upon playing cards as vulgar. Women of high social position also might spend some of their time in teaching the girls of the family. When living in the country or when the opportunity offered, they could engage without loss of dignity in certain economic pursuits such as tending silkworms and making the cloth for which they supplied the thread. Such profitable activities extended to caring for bees and taking care of fruit trees or even making straw sandals. When forced by circumstances, an upper-class woman might convert a street corner of her house into a shop but only one which sold wine. The lady herself would not appear in it, however, the visible operations being left to a female servant or slave.[41]

Although most of the lady's life was spent in seclusion in the house over which she ruled as mistress, she sometimes left her restricted domain to visit family friends. She would not walk on the street in daylight to do this but took a sedan chair from courtyard to courtyard, the bearers retiring while she made her entrance and exit from the conveyance. On such journeys, it was always known in her household to what place she had departed and a slave girl or female servant ran along beside her.[42]

At night, curiously enough, ladies walked through the streets under the most extraordinary circumstances, as the thoroughfares of the whole city were turned over to them alone, except for blind men and officials. This situation came about after dark when the fire beacons converging on the capital brought the evening message that the kingdom was secure and peaceful. Word being conveyed to the palace, the royal band played appropriate music, the great bell was rung, and the guards closed the gates of the city. This occurred usually between eight and nine o'clock, but earlier in the short days of winter. From that time until one in the morning, women were free to walk abroad, and any man found on the streets apart from those mentioned above as specially exempt, was subject, if caught by the patrols, to imprisonment and severe flogging. The women carried paper lanterns as they strolled, but in even so little light they protected their faces with their silk jackets. This evening promenading gave to the women their greatest pleasure, gossiping in groups as they walked, and for some few supplied opportunities for forbidden rendezvous.[43]

For high officials, the nights became the busiest period of the twenty-four hours, since the Korean king held court late into the morning, surrounded by his ministers and palace eunuchs. These latter individuals were acquired as boys from poor families for the royal service. In theory, they were given the best possible education and were expected to serve the monarch with unselfish devotion, exercising a restrained and dispassionate influence over the activities of the august ruler. The effect of the eunuchs apparently in practice proved much the opposite, for they are described as more often illiterate parasites devoted primarily to the purpose of enriching themselves. Curiously, these eunuchs married and carried on a continuum of eunuch families by adopting boys reduced to the same physical disability as themselves.[44]

The great importance of family and clan held for all the Korean people irrespective of class and condition, but for political and social reasons more emphasis was given to status by the Yangpan group. Active allegiance to a political party was almost inevitable, since these latter organizations were primarily alliances established between powerful families controlling most of the land and the farmers who cultivated it. Family records were kept over many generations and it was inevitable that sons to inherit the positions of power and prestige were a first requirement. Therefore, although the life pattern of the individual is parallel in both classes, notable emphases appear in that of the Yangpan, as we shall see.

As a child, the eldest son of a nobleman undoubtedly enjoyed certain privileges in anticipation of his inheritance. But since these things may also have been compensated for by the special attitudes of both his contemporaries and parents, any marked differences at an early age beyond those of general economic and educational advantages do not distinguish him from his poorer cousin. On assuming the adult role at marriage, however, his methods of dealing with his personal situation diverged somewhat from those of a young man of the lower class.

Custom demanded that a few days after his marriage (at which time he had first seen his wife) he assume an attitude and manner of behavior indicative of his disregard for the female sex. Since the chances of his being enamored of his bride to a degree sufficient to compete successfully with the attractions available to a rich young Korean man were small, the connubial relationship frequently became reduced to the minimum of social and sexual intercourse. Even as in the less common cases, when his personal dissatisfaction with the lady was replete, he could not divorce his wife without great difficulty as she was protected in her position by the noble family from which she came. Thus we find that divorce was largely, although not exclusively, limited to the lower class.[45]

On the other hand, the taking of concubines by rich husbands was a commonplace and, in the event that a son was not born to the legal wife within a reasonable period, it became an almost inevitable procedure on the part of a Yangpan of distinguished family. This step appears to have been more of ego gratification than a social necessity, however, since except for the unusual circumstance of the concubine's son being registered as that of the legal wife, the child's position was not one which permitted him to inherit the wealth and position of the father. The latter normally resolved the family problem before his death by adopting a ·son of noble blood from some less fortunate branch of the house. This was a requirement of the culture, since concubines were always found among women of the lower class, not infrequently being taken from the group of educated and beautiful kisaeng. The Yangpan normally set up his concubine in an establishment entirely separate from his wife, not simply in another room under the same roof. Such relationships were often happy and of

long standing. Thus we find in the frequency of the practice, as well
as in the manner of disposing of the women, an obvious difference
between the two classes in the matter of conjugal relations.[46]

The remarriage of widows is culturally unacceptable in Korean
tradition. Among the common people, however, it becomes a practical necessity in most cases for a widow to take a second husband,
and after a more or less lengthy wait she has apparently remarried
when possible. For the upper-class woman this was not so and she
was expected to spend the remainder of her life in mourning a man
for whom, as likely as not, she had had little personal regard. This
proved difficult either for reasons of temperament or because of the
advances of men from whom she was not able to protect herself.
Ideally, if she committed suicide to preserve her reputation, she was
greatly admired but it must be presumed that the majority of widows
found satisfaction in other ways, such as becoming the mistresses of
men of their choice. For widowers, there were apparently no more
restrictions on remarriage among the nobles than with the average
man.[47]

As has already been made clear from our study of the village, much
of Korean culture focuses on the individual's departure from life.
This is true irrespective of class, but the ceremonial elaboration among
the nobility was clearly perceptible and it rose to extravagant proportions in the ruling family. The celebration on the completion of sixty
years of life serves as an example. Although observed in some degree
by all Koreans achieving such an age, in the case of the king or queen
it meant a public holiday. A special session was held for the granting
of degrees, gifts were provided for the soldiers, and a general amnesty
was ordered for those in jail. The nobles, on the other hand, offered
presents to the ruler and performed the ceremonial bows expected
of the occasion, while the common people paid obeisance before a
picture of the royal person.[48]

The elaboration of ceremony for members of the upper class
showed itself nowhere clearer than in connection with funerals. Although the common people tried to follow the same ritual pattern, the
demands of their daily labor and their lack of money enforced a relative simplicity in the rural customs which varied somewhat according
to the locality. The ideal formal procedure at the death of a married
person has long been available in a Korean text on the subject, en-

titled *Funeral Rites of Adults.*[49]. The ordinary farmer could not read such a work and few perhaps knew of its existence. Therefore, it is not strange that the procedure was reduced in complexity and that sometimes specific acts were not only misunderstood but given contrary explanations. Members of the upper class, on the other hand, not content with carrying out the ritual in completeness, attempted to outdo each other in the extravagance of the performance.

One of the notable traits of Yangpan funeral rites was the delay between the time at which the deceased was sealed into his pine-wood coffin and the day on which the interment took place, a period not infrequently of three months to a year. This extension was required because so much preparation for the final obsequies was demanded that the arrangements could be concluded no sooner, some families financially ruining themselves in the undertaking. Commoners usually buried their dead within three to five days unless prevented by frozen ground, which by such chance caused a functionally unrelated similarity in behavior between the two classes.[50]

An emphasis on the use of geomancers or p'ansu by the Yangpan families in selecting grave sites should be mentioned as an upper-class characteristic, for although such advice was not infrequently sought by commoners the process was in the latter cases relatively short and inexpensive. Where wealth and time were available, however, these practitioners could go to extravagant lengths in determining the exact location for a grave, so that good fortune might be assured for the family. To add to the complications, should it seem that some bad luck befell the family after the burial, the whole process might be started over again and the deceased removed to a more satisfactory site, needless to say, all at considerable additional cost.[51]

The major expenditure, however, resulted from the price of the funeral itself. As might be expected, the extremes of elaboration were reached on the death of a member of the ruling family, the ceremony for a king having been estimated to cost the equivalent of a half million dollars and that for a prince or princess at least a hundred thousand. Several eyewitness accounts of processions to the grave serve to give an idea of what could be expected.

As usual with the upper class, the parade took place in the dark since the effect was the more staggering. First appeared flame bearers to light the elaborate torches, eight to ten feet high and a foot and a half in diameter, which were placed along the sides of the street. Following in the blaze of fire walked soldiers, some bearing silken flags and others wooden paddles to symbolize their role in keeping back the tens of thousands of spectators. After them, on fine horses, came the mayor of the city and master of ceremonies, followed by a series of sedan chairs bearing the significant material symbols of the deceased's life such as books, musical instruments, swords, decorations, and so on. Each of the chairs was in charge of a man assumed to be one of the historians of the achievements of the deceased. Next in the procession came men bearing large silken banners ten feet long and four feet wide hanging from cross poles, at the ends of which were bells and lanterns. These banners of white silk, with black or red characters embroidered on them, each represented the respect of one of the Korean guilds. Behind these followed forty-eight men carrying poles to which were attached long paper scrolls, each inscribed with a poem written by a famous scholar as a eulogy to the deceased. More banners preceded a chair containing incense with its burner, followed by a band playing music, then a large umbrella or canopy—red if the deceased were a king—preceding a sedan chair for the "spirit" of the dead, and again a band with more music.

One of the most striking features of the parade was four men wearing masks about three feet wide, each having a double pair of bulging eyes and a grinning mouth with projecting teeth. These maskers, intended to frighten away evil spirits, were dragged along, each on a heavy cart, by other men. After the maskers followed six great horses about ten feet high made of wood and bamboo covered with paper and painted in pairs—two white, two brown, and two gray. Four of the horses had saddles, the other two being held in reserve, so to speak. The horses were pulled to the grave on carts by men in white mourning clothes. The animals were later burned at the grave, to provide the deceased with transportation to the afterworld.

Largest of all the elements of the funeral procession were the biers which bore the coffin. There were two of these pavilions on heavy frameworks, the one in front being about half the size of the other. The smaller served to convey the coffin at places such as gates and steep inclines where the size of the other made movement unsafe. Also, it was believed that by having two biers, evil spirits might be outwitted since they would assume the body to be in the first, where it usually was not. The large bier was supported by two lateral poles forty feet long and seventeen cross poles twenty-two feet in length, interwoven with flat, padded hemp ropes. It was carried on the shoulders of one hundred and ninety bearers. Besides these, an additional two hundred and seventy men held on to ropes extending in front and behind to secure passage up and down inclines. For the small bier, one hundred and eight bearers and one hundred and fifty men on the ropes sufficed. The pavilion enclosing the coffin was covered with brocaded silks and colored gauzes which, with the gaudy painted decorations on both wood and silk, gave the whole a striking effect on the eyes of the spectators. At the front of the funeral car walked a man, and at the rear another, each ringing a bell to aid the bearers to keep in step.

Coming after the biers, besides military guards, was a peculiar feature consisting of a blue cloth fence inside of which certain palace women rode to the grave on ponies, thus protected from the glances of the onlookers. Then followed eunuchs on horses, more men bearing banners, the chief mourner—perhaps the succeeding king in a sedan chair borne by thirty-six men—and a myriad of officials, first civil and then military, according to rank, in chairs or on horseback.[52] Such a funeral procession, as may readily be understood, was an extraordinary and infrequent event. The wealthy nobles, however, achieved displays which if meager by comparison were still magnificent pageants of the night as compared to the funerals of the common people.

Finally, we find differences in the graveyards of the upper and lower classes. The final resting places of the latter were most commonly marked only by flattened hemispheres eight to ten feet in diameter and two to three feet high, the coffins sharing a common burial area with numerous others of the family or community. A royal tomb, on the other hand, occupied the whole south side of a carefully chosen hill and no other burial was permitted within a radius of about three miles. The mound was of imposing size and covered with carefully attended green grass. At the rear and sides, a grove of pine trees grew up to frame the scene (Pl. 21, p. 158).

One plain stone was placed beside the royal grave and another buried beneath it for permanent record. At the sides facing each other were erected life-size figures of attendant priests, horses, sheep, or sometimes other animals. To these, an altar, a stone railing, and a memorial arch were usually added.   Although the grave of the ordinary noble certainly did not reach the proportions of that of a ruler, elaborate settings and care, as well as ornamentation in stone, were characteristic of the Yangpan class, the mounds themselves reaching fifteen to twenty feet in diameter.[53]

In general, the mourning customs were also more rigorously attended to by the members of the upper class, in part, it may be presumed, by reason of their greater devotion to Confucianism on which system of ethics the behavior was patterned.   Indeed, the regard for a dead ancestor was so great that a wealthy family always faced the danger that villains might steal an ancestor's remains and hold them for ransom.   This crime, a capital offense, was more common in Korea than the kidnaping of living persons, and if the criminal was not apprehended he was almost certainly paid to release the parental remnants even though the cost proved a catastrophe to the family fortunes.[54]

Besides the upper-class emphasis on Confucianism, from the negative point of view there was probably also less attention to either Shamanism or Buddhism than existed among the common people.   It was also true that the large-scale conversions to Christianity took place among members of the lower class.

REFERENCES TO SOURCES FOR PART TWO

[1] For general statements on the Korean class situation, see Oppert, 1880:107-8; Griffis, 1894:238; Gilmore, 1892:111, 114; *Korean Repository,* 1896: Vol. 3:497-98; *Korea Review,* 1901: Vol. 1:211-12; Allen, 1908:80, 82; Moose, 1911:103; Longford, 1911:33-38; Sands, 1930:135; Oliver, 1944:29. (Source references are listed in order of date of first editions, e.g. Griffis, 1882 precedes Gilmore, 1892).

[2] Bishop, 1905: Vol. 1:34; *Official Guide,* 1913:271.

[3] Hulbert, 1906:47 ff.

[4] Lowell, 1886:187; Morse, 1897:3-4.

[5] Oppert, 1880:137; Griffis, 1894:262; Gilmore, 1892:121; Hulbert, 1906:244; Eckardt, 1929:40.

[6] Gilmore, 1892:97; Hulbert, 1906:242; Eckardt, 1929:14-15; Wagner, 1931:73.

[7] Gilmore, 1892:97; Hulbert, 1906:245; Wagner, 1931:71, 73.

[8] Oppert, 1880:139; Griffis, 1894:265.

[9] Lowell, 1886:271; Wagner, 1931:72.

[10] Wagner, 1931:74; Eckardt, 1929:164.

[11] Griffis, 1894:245, 266; Hulbert, 1906:246; Underwood, 1908:5; Longford, 1911:253.

[12] Lowell, 1886:293; Hulbert, 1906:250; Eckardt, 1929:41.

[13] Allen, 1908:105.

[14] Griffis, 1894:266.

[15] Underwood, 1908:85; Moose, 1911:71.

[16] Oppert, 1880:123-24; Griffis, 1894:273; Lowell, 1886:321; Gilmore, 1892:146; Savage-Landor, 1895:56; Wagner, 1931:66.

[17] Oppert, 1880:125; Griffis, 1894:273; Lowell, 1886:324; Gilmore, 1892:148; Savage-Landor, 1895:56, 60; Hulbert, 1906:23; Wagner, 1931:66.

[18] Griffis, 1894:274; Lowell, 1886:321; Gilmore, 1892:146; Miln, 1895:60; Tayler, 1904:53; Underwood, 1904:89.

[19] Oppert, 1880:124; Griffis, 1894:276, Lowell, 1886:327; Gilmore, 1892:145; Savage-Landor, 1895:54-55; Moose, 1911:98, 141; Wagner, 1931:69.

[20] Oppert, 1880:124; Lowell, 1886:329; Gilmore, 1892:144.

[21] Oppert, 1880:126; Lowell, 1886:335; Gilmore, 1892:139; Jennings, 1904:149-67.

[22] Griffis, 1894:273; Lowell, 1886:339; Gilmore, 1892:140; Savage-Landor, 1895:56; Jennings, 1904:149-67.

[23] Carles, 1888:107; Gilmore, 1892:147; Bergman, 1938:33.

[24] Griffis, 1894:271, 274; Gilmore, 1892:138; Underwood, 1904:167; Hulbert, 1906:386.

[25] Griffis, 1894:275; Gilmore, 1892:132, 148.

[26] Jennings, 1904:150-51.

[27] Lowell, 1886:326, 331; Gilmore, 1892:116.

[28] Gilmore, 1892:96; Savage-Landor, 1895:65; Hamilton, 1904:36-37, 42; Tayler, 1904:53; Moose, 1911:118.

[29] Oppert, 1880:145; Lowell, 1886:49; Carles, 1888:61; Gilmore, 1892:104, 132, 280; Tayler, 1904:75; Hulbert, 1906:263-64; Underwood, 1908:49.

[30] Tayler, 1904:13; Allen, 1908:80, 82, 91, 141.

[31] Gilmore, 1892:170; Savage-Landor, 1895:107; Hulbert, 1906:266.

[32] Griffis, 1894:196.

[33] Griffis, 1894:293; Culin, 1895:63-65; Sands, 1930:141.

[34] Griffis, 1894:294; Sands, 1930:140; Bergman, 1935:110.

[35] Oppert, 1880:142; Griffis, 1894:269, 295; Culin, 1895:79ff; Miln, 1895:168; Savage-Landor, 1895:89.

[36] Gilmore, 1892:112, 118; Van Buskirk, 1931:118.

[37] Underwood, 1904:94.

[38] Hamilton, 1904:50-52. Also see Allen, 1896:383-86; Tayler, 1904:41; and Allen, 1908:125.

[39] Griffis, 1894:290-91; Lowell, 1886:345; Gilmore, 1892:142, 178; Miln, 1895:154; Hamilton, 1904:47-50; Hulbert, 1906:357; Allen, 1908:126; Sands, 1930:133; Wagner, 1931:88; Bergman, 1938:215-16.

[40] Griffis, 1894:244-45; Gilmore, 1892:107, 157; Hulbert, 1906:350; Sands, 1930:133.

[41] Griffis, 1894:295; Culin, 1895:78-79; Savage-Landor, 1895:89; Hamilton, 1904:43; Hulbert, 1906:354, 370.

[42] Dallet, 1874:cxviii; Oppert, 1880:132; Griffis, 1894:245; Hamilton, 1904:42; Tayler, 1904:14; Hulbert, 1906:350-52; McKenzie, 1908:29.

[43] Oppert, 1880:132; Griffis, 1894:250; Lowell, 1886:227; Carles, 1888:87; Gilmore, 1892:57, 103; Cavendish, 1894:22; Savage-Landor, 1895:42, 65; Hamilton, 1904:39; Tayler, 1904:46; Underwood, 1904:3; Allen, 1908:79; McKenzie, 1908:30; Longford, 1911:46; Bergman, 1938:35.

[44] Dallet, 1874:xxviii; Allen, 1908:127; Sands, 1930:132.

[45] Griffis, 1894:251; Savage-Landor, 1895:159; Hamilton, 1904:108; Hulbert, 1906:368; Kang, 1931:33.

[46] Oppert, 1880:131; Miln, 895:81; Savage-Landor, 1895:154; Hamilton, 1904: 109; Hulbert, 1906:369; Moose, 1911:104; Bergman, 1938:55-56.

[47] Dallet, 1874:cxxviii; Griffis, 1894:254-55; Moose, 1911:77; Bergman, 1938:56

[48] Griffis, 1894:296; Bergman, 1938:98-100.

[49] Translated in Ross, 1891:320-52.

[50] Miln, 1895:242; Underwood, 1908:96, 98; Allen, 1908:142; Moose, 1911:172, 179.

[51] Griffis, 1894:278; Hulbert, 1906:441-44; Underwood, 1908:98; Moose, 1911: 178; Clark, 1932:113; Bergman, 1938:94.

[52] There is some inconsistency among authorities, essentially disregarded in the summary given, on the procedure of various elements of royal funeral processions but none as to their elaborateness. Underwood, 1904:204ff; Hulbert, 1906:437-41; Miller, 1927:15-29; Bergman, 1938:94-95.

[53] Griffis, 1894:279; Gilmore, 1892:179, 181; Savage-Landor, 1895:120; Hulbert, 1906:451, 454; Moose, 1911:180.

[54] Hulbert, 1906:455.

Part Three

THE ORIGINS AND CHRONOLOGICAL DEVELOP-
MENT OF THE KOREAN NATION

9

INTRODUCTION

IN OUR consideration of the Koreans, so far, we have surveyed the culture of a typical village and then gone on to review the life of the upper class in the capital. To pursue our subject further we must turn back in time to discover what may be inferred about the origins of the Koreans. We can first trace the growth of their political unity, using it as a design on which later to embroider the historical flowering of their culture. Our first problem is that of drawing the outline in true perspective.

Since through education and the mass military movements of recent wars we have become increasingly conscious of the oneness of our world, it would seem provincial not to emphasize the Korean development as part of the common heritage of mankind and one which parallels our own. We should recognize that Koreans are men and women who, even if they are somewhat distant cousins in the human family, are no longer strangers. To start from common ground, it will be necessary to consider the rise of civilization as a whole in order to relate Koreans to it. If a swiftly penciled sketch will be permitted, we can attempt this briefly.

In a few areas of the world where circumstances facilitated satisfying the needs of life, some individuals long years ago found the leisure necessary to invent the implements and to control the natural resources which made possible sedentary societies with populations rising into the tens of thousands. Having achieved that measure of economic complexity, the people struggled to adapt their social organization to the mass pressures of urban life. Certain families grew in power and wealth, which in part they devoted to the creation of new luxuries and in part to suppressing all competitors. Those who could not protect themselves were either crushed or forced to the limitless frontiers, accepting physical burdens in preference to the intangible strains of social conflict. Other men, however, turned towards the excitement and wonders of the metropolis, and rising above the misery and maladjustment, these centers flourished and the people multiplied. The rich rewarded their gods, while the priests of the newly organized religions fostered the arts and engaged in speculations to enhance their swelling prestige. It was no longer possible for such numbers of men and women to know each other personally and the rulers grew apart as a class, enmeshing the satellite towns and villages in their power while pushing the unsubmitting border tribes farther and farther away with ever-expanding pressure. That same pressure, however, also sent with it the stimulus of new inventions and new ideas, sometimes to root in virgin territory with such strength as to make the resultant culture far surpass that of the area in which it originated. In this way the focal centers of civilization sometimes shifted. Wars and revolutions, motivated by avarice or desperation, marked the passing years. Each new set of leaders destroyed themselves in conquest or lost their governmental virility through having too little intercourse with the masses of the people. The process repeated itself relentlessly, greater and more overwhelming in each era—and still goes on.

Treating of this situation more specifically, we find that the first great independent centers of civilization sprang up in three general regions. The earliest seems to have risen in the borderlands of the Near East and Africa, where the Tigris, the Euphrates, and the Nile flooded the land into rich fertility. From similar natural advantages another such district flowered in far Asia, creating a great cultural center in the Yellow River basin of North China. Completely isolated from the others, the Mayas developed a third civilization in the cities of Central America, marvelous in its architecture and with a unique hieroglyphic writing preserved in stone. This culture rose in the middle of the last millennium of the pre-Christian era, about fifteen hundred years after the Chinese who, in turn, lagged about as much behind the people of the Near East.

Until a few centuries ago, the history of civilization was but the growth and movement of the diverse cultural impacts of these three centers. The heritage of Europe extends in unbroken lineage from the first city states of Ur and Babylon, down through the empires of Greece and Rome to those of Spain and England. China, with its parallel development, was almost a world apart until, in the thirteenth century, the Mongols under their great khans staggered the Medi-

21. TOMB OF KING SŎNG-JONG (r. 1470-1495) NEAR SEOUL

22. GREAT KYŎNGJU BELL CAST IN 773 A.D.

terranean civilization into an awareness of the East. The meeting of
the peoples was measured more by death and destruction, however,
than by an exchange of culture. Interaction was predestined nonetheless, and two hundred years later Europeans returned the attack
with ships sailing under the more effective banners of trade and religion. When by chance the unknown western hemisphere loomed
up to block the voyagers, its Spanish conquerors almost annihilated
the civilization which they found, thus eliminating one contestant
from direct cultural competition. China, self-satisfied with its own
greatness and blindly ignorant of the world, attempted to avoid the
danger by closing its ports to the troublesome "western barbarians."
This reaction was perhaps symbolic of the pattern of oriental civilization, for during three thousand years its center of culture has been immobile and defensively cooperative as compared with the moving
vortex of the aggressive and competitive West.

Little by little, knowledge and wealth were sucked out of the East
until, combined with superior technical skills of the West, the barriers were broken down. By the nineteenth century, Europe dominated the world and no doors were barred to its people, who passed
through them with overbearing pride and special privilege. Significantly, Korea proved to be the last of the oriental nations to submit.
In fact, only during the lifetime of contemporaries did Korea feel the
force of western culture, and that for the most part indirectly through
Japan.

From this background, we can see that the development of Korean
culture lies wholly within the orbit of the oriental focal center. For a
time, we can dispense with thinking of the other centers while we
direct our attention to the origins of this hermit nation as a star in
the eastern firmament.

Man lived in the Yellow River basin of China at least half a million years ago. Perhaps he came there from some part of central
Asia, a member of the first human family. Archeologists, so far, have
given us little information on the earlier periods but we do know that
culture and the population increased very slowly. Nonetheless, it
seems certain that only a few hundred centuries before our time
there were sufficient people to have scattered all over Asia, and that
some were pushing across the northern straits into the unpopulated
expanses of the American continents. Others turned south from

their northeast course and moved into the peninsula we know as
Korea. This migration may have been delayed, as it was not easy to
cross over the mountain barriers and to permeate one of the most
hilly regions to be found. Cold in winter, and with heavy summer
rains pouring down to seas either without harbors or torn by tides of
tremendous ebb and flow, Korea tested the strength of those who
sought shelter in her valleys.

As more people came from the bleak Manchurian plain, some men
in the search for fruitful lands crossed the narrow Korean Strait to
the islands of Japan. Whether they proved to be their first inhabitants is an open question, as the hairy Ainu may have descended from
Sakhalin or come through the Korean Peninsula before them. In
any case, the basic population of both Korea and Japan was almost
certainly built up by successive small migrations from northeast Asia,
over a period quite possibly exceeding fifty thousand years. Probably
towards the end of this period another migration infiltrated Japan, a
people sailing their small boats to the Ryukyus from the south. It
was this strain that seems to have given the distinctive physical
characteristics to the Japanese. To what extent they also landed on
the mainland is unknown but some students account for physical distinctions among the Koreans by assuming these southerners also
penetrated the Peninsula in numbers. If so, the effect was minimal
compared with that it had on the island empire. Before the beginning of recorded history, therefore, we can imagine the Korean
Peninsula sparsely populated by a few thousand people, mostly Mon-
goloids from the cold northeast section of Asia. We can guess that
these first Koreans lived as separate tribal groups occupying the eight
or ten principal river valleys.

The Koreans have a story that in the twenty-fourth century B.C.
the son of the Creator, being somewhat bored, offered to turn a bear
and a tiger into human beings if they would eat of certain plants and
remain in the dark for three weeks. The tiger, becoming restless, did
not last out the ordeal, but the bear, having we suppose a hibernating
nature, changed into a woman. The master of this metamorphosis
was attracted to this female and she bore a grandson of the Creator
known to posterity as Tan-gun. This Tan-gun, the Koreans tell us,
built an altar on Mari San, the famous mountain of Kanghwa Island,
and ruled over the people for twelve hundred years, teaching them
agriculture and other civilized accomplishments.

Whatever one wishes to think of the general validity of this tale, it has several points of particular interest. First of all, it presents all the Koreans as the descendants of bears, an idea perhaps somewhat distasteful and unnatural to members of modern western society. To the people of that northern cultural zone from which, for geographical reasons, we presume the Koreans to have come, this would not be so. Even to the present day, they have failed to adopt that arbitrary distinction of the West which sets man apart from all other animals as the one unique and superior creation. To them, bears are a very powerful and respected kind of "people," despite their physical differences and lack of communicable speech habits. If one insists on rejecting this notion, at least it should be further evidence that the Koreans in tolerating it are probably related to their northern neighbors doing likewise.

A second point of interest in the Tan-gun myth stems from the possibility that it refers to an actual leader of the people who, as a late-comer, had previously lived in contact with the city states of the Yellow River valley which were developing in his time. Whether the date, correlating with that of the legendary Chinese Emperor Yao, may not be of somewhat exaggerated antiquity is of minor importance. Considering the epochal advances which we know were taking place in China, Korea seems to be too close not to have received one memorable bearer of the new marvels of human behavior. Such an impact, however, whether it came earlier or later, is a fundamental fact in understanding the Koreans, for even to the present day one finds their culture interlocking ancient Chinese customs with those of less known northern lands.

Going on from this period for which we eventually must seek enlightenment from archeological research, we reach one of somewhat more historical reliability. About b.c. 1200, the Shang dynasty was coming to an end in China. The eastern cultural center had already reached great heights and then fallen into a term of decadence. The last Shang emperor, Chou Hsin, never learned that the power and glory of his ancestors depended on their interest in directing the people toward new triumphs of creative activity. He was tired of the people except for his dancing girls, and obviously half bored even with them, for he devoted his mind to developing perverse amusements that would have fascinated the most degenerate of the Caesars. When his three principal ministers warned him that the misery of his empire might overwhelm him, he either had them killed or had them lodged in prison. They were correct in their predictions and he was overcome.

According to the record, one of these ministers, a relative named Chi Tzu, who had been released from jail by the admiring new ruler Wu Wang, felt that his honor would not permit of shifting his loyalty to the new Chou dynasty. He was given the opportunity to migrate with a large number of personal followers. The Koreans say that this Chi Tzu, whose name they pronounce Ki-ja, came to Korea and lies buried in the northern part of their country. Since a number of cities claim his grave, there is some doubt on that score, a trivial concern in itself, but one which leads to a geographical and historical problem deserving some clarification.

As school children, we learn to think of a nation as a group of people under one government sharing a definite geographic area. Thus, although periods of wars make us realize the temporary character of boundaries and national states, the colorful political maps are easier to remember than the complex changes from which they result. Today we see Korea, perhaps printed in red, occupying a peninsula hundreds of miles long jutting down like some Florida from the northeast Asiatic mainland. Actually, as a reference for the period from Ki-ja's time until almost a thousand years ago, such a map would be extremely misleading. There was no recognizable unity except for the excessively rugged character of the land which extended to a lessening degree into what we now call Manchuria. The people lived in valley groups, each group disregarding the authority of the other. The Chinese designated several of them by name before any maps were ever made and referred vaguely to the area nearest themselves by road as Chaohsien which, with some poetic license, has been translated as "Land of the Morning Calm." This loosely defined territory contained in ancient times the southeastern part of Manchuria including the Liaotung Peninsula. Ki-ja and his retinue may have gone no farther than this latter region.

Such a conclusion would hardly be more acceptable to Koreans than a hypothesis that Moses did not cross the Red Sea would be to the orthodox Jews. Ki-ja, save for the less substantial Tan-gun, is the first personality of Korean history and his role as a bearer of culture is unequaled. Whether he himself reached districts which are part of present Korea is incidental to the fact that an important influx of Chinese knowledge and customs reached the northeast part of the Peninsula about a thousand years B.C. Unfortunately, the development of the country during that period is only vaguely documented and archeological investigations have barely begun.

If we attempt to comprehend Korea in the time of Confucius, who was born in B.C. 551, we also find our data almost wholly by inference. Civilization, as distinguished by a knowledge of writing, was still limited to relatively small areas in the world, although it was expanding rapidly from the Near East. The kings of Babylon, of Crete, of Egypt—all had passed the zenith of their power and Greece was rising to her Golden Age. The Indus cities of Mohenjo-daro and Harappa had crumbled, the Aryan Vedic culture had pushed into India many centuries before, and Buddha had just been born. The Maya in Central America stood on the threshold of their great development. China was experiencing a burst of intellectual life and her influence on Korea must have been rising, while Japan remained a region of barbarians, probably still gaining some increment of population from the Peninsula.

At this point it may be instructive to consider the physical geography of Korea with respect to the natural facilities for the overland movements of people. The whole country is a succession of hills laid out in a pattern suggesting the skeleton of a giant resting on his right side with his skull smashed into Manchuria. The arms and ribs and legs form innumerable mountain ranges which, even though only a few thousand feet high at the most, must have proved discouraging barriers to the migrant. For example, we see in the northwest that the area of the provinces of P'yŏngan and the adjacent half of Hwanghae is a natural watershed which, if one succeeded in entering from the Manchurian plain, required more effort to leave in any other direction. A push to the south, however, brought one into the Imjin River valley. The road down the Peninsula then opened more easily into the valleys of the Han, the Kum, the Sŏmjin, and the Naktong. Turning up the east coast, one soon met the tail of the mountain spine which leaves only a narrow strip of isolated shoreland all the way to the north of the thirty-ninth parallel near the modern city of Wŏnsan. The northeast of Korea, comprising the Hamgyŏng Provinces which include about one quarter of the land area of the country, is, and has been since the time of Ki-ja, the least developed section of all. Colder, less fertile, and with higher mountains, it is the only quarter

Figure 14. Map of the Physical Geography of Korea Showing the Principal Rivers
and the Location of Early Culture Groups

of the Peninsula in which a high civilization has at no time centered.

During the first half millennium B.C., the heart of Korean culture was certainly in the northwest, where the cultural pulsations from the Yellow River valley flowed through the trade routes of southern Manchuria with increasing strength. As this outpost prospered, it in turn sent its influences onward, affecting the tribes in the south. At this time they had reached the stage of allying themselves into small federations, the chief among which were those of Mahan, Pyŏnhan, and Chinhan. Mahan, concentrating in the Ch'ungch'ŏng Provinces which are closest to the Chaohsien area, seems to have been dominant among the three, quite likely as a result of the greater stimulus provided by the more advanced neighbors to the north.

Towards the end of the third century B.C. a series of events took place in China which probably had more effect on Korea than anything since the fall of the Shang dynasty. History was repeating itself. The Chou dynasty, which had followed the Shang, began rapidly to disintegrate in B.C. 255 and by B.C. 221, the Ch'in were in complete control, for one of the shortest but most epochal periods that China has known. It was at this time that China became a truly unified empire. This development involved so many revolutionary changes that the people could not stand the burden and the Ch'in fell to the Han dynasty in B.C. 206. Among the undertakings carried on by the great Ch'in emperor, Shih Huang-ti, two were most important for Korea. Deciding that the Chinese should take worshipful eyes from off the past, and perhaps look up to him, the ruler in B.C. 213 ordered the destruction of nearly all of the books in the Empire. This extravagant act caused numerous intellectuals to seek a refuge in which to carry on their scholarly devotions. It seems certain that some of them reached Korea. At approximately the same time, Shih Huang-ti had set out to complete the boundary fortifications of his empire into a single great wall. This project, often considered preeminent among the wonders of the world, so decimated the families of the common people that they too sought escape through emigration, thereby creating a population pressure which influenced Korea.*

Part of the immigrants to the Peninsula came by sea, so that not only did the northwest region feel the impact but also the incipient

---

* Mass migrations of more than 10,000 persons from the old Chinese states of Yen, Ch'in, Chao, and Ch'i have been reported for the period about B.C. 200. Slawik, 1933 :5.

kingdoms to the south. For some reason not altogether apparent, Chinese incursions into the southeast of Korea were particularly notable at this time, bringing a sophistication which was probably responsible not only for stimulating the great rise of culture which was to follow in that area but also for creating the link of friendship with China which so long gave political strength to the descendants of the Chinhan.

10

THE THREE KINGDOMS AND THE
ASCENDANCY OF SILLA

AFTER THE RISE of the Chinese Han dynasty in B.C. 206, the recording of events in the Korean Peninsula so increased that our search through the twilight of tradition is suddenly given historical illumination, just as a city sparkles into incandescent life at the beginning of evening. In following the course of political and social development up to the present time, we should realize that the brightness of historical knowledge may actually blind one to the culture of a people. The glare of the metropolis darkens the surrounding countryside and even the narrow streets and crowded alleyways of the city itself lie black at the base of the lamp. The story is one of courts and kings, of the great men and their ideals, and we shall have to remember that it always overshadows the lives of the common people, the millions who bear the burdens of civilization and whose voice is small.

In the year B.C. 193, the dynasty founded by Ki-ja came to an end in northwest Korea.* Ki-jun, the forty-first ruler, was deposed by the treachery of Wi-man, a native of Liaotung. Wi-man had been a lieutenant of a Chinese general who, after being appointed governor of southern Manchuria, revolted against the Han emperor but was defeated and fled northward. Wi-man, with some of his followers, escaped to the east across the Yalu River, where he was given sanctuary as a border guard for the forces of Ki-jun. Soon afterwards, however, by means of a ruse, Wi-man occupied the capital at

---

* The basic data in this and the following section have been drawn largely from Hulbert's *History of Korea,* a translation of the *Tong Sa Kang Yo,* a Korean summary of the four ancient histories of the country, together with his synthesis of private manuscripts on the last Korean dynasty. Comparative reference to this source will prove easy because of its chronological arrangement. Also of great importance are the comments on Korea which exist in the various dynastic histories of China beginning with that of the Early Han (B.C. 206-25 A.D.). These, with information from other Chinese sources, have been summarized by Parker (Parker, 1890a; Parker, 1890b).

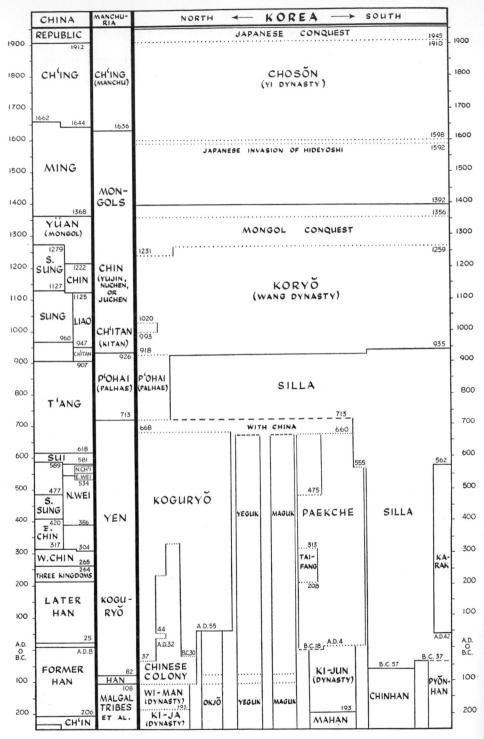

Figure 15. Chronological Chart of Korean History

P'yŏngyang, Ki-jun barely escaping by sea with the treasure of the court and his personal following. To what happened to Ki-jun, we shall return later.

The interesting thing about the records of Wi-man is the recognition of his ability to win support from the surrounding tribes, since that fact in itself indicates the political situation of the country. It is apparent that the preceding dynasty of Ki-ja was essentially a city state, a small center of developed culture existing in an area of less civilized native groups, more or less under centralized control according to the abilities of the particular P'yŏngyang ruler. Information on these tribal populations is limited and of those for which we have names, only a few are significantly described or have continuity through time.

The local population, we presume, was largely made up of people who apparently extended south into what is now Kyŏnggi Province, and there probably had contact with the less civilized Ma people, or in Korean, Maguk (Fig. 14, p. 164). East of the Maguk lived the Yeguk. These two, it is believed, may have together been characterized as the barbarian Yemak in the earliest Chinese commentaries. North of the Yeguk, in the area corresponding to the present Hamgyŏng Provinces, were the Okjŏ. Of the groups affecting northwest Korea these are the most important which had their homeland south of the Yalu and Tumen rivers. To the north were the Manchurian tribes such as the Puyu, Suksin (Yilou), Yujin (Nuchen), Kitan (Kedan, Kuran, Ch'itan), Palhae (Palha, P'ohai), and Malgal, though these are but a few of the many which change their names and locale, and merge or disappear with the passing of time.

Wi-man was undoubtedly more at home with these tribes than Ki-jun could have been. Although personally successful, by the time his grandson Ugu succeeded him as king, the Han empire had gained the strength to turn her attention to the Manchurian region which Wi-man had united under his control from the Korean capital. The Chinese had no particular reason to like the dynasty which had overthrown that of Ki-ja. Furthermore, they were irritated by interference with their overland trade route to south Korea. Therefore they started military operations and laid claim to the whole of ancient Chaohsien. The local population apparently had not entirely forgotten Wi-man's treachery, for when the Chinese armies besieged P'yŏngyang, Ugu was assassinated and the gates of the city were thrown open to the invaders. Thus in B.C. 108, northwest Korea lost its independence to its great neighbor.

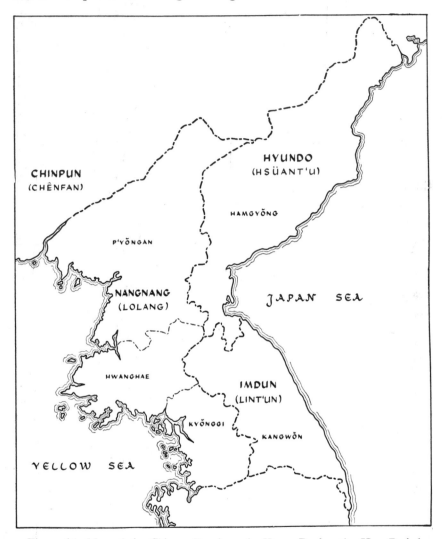

Figure 16. Map of the Chinese Provinces in Korea During the Han Period

We know little enough of the rule of the Chinese except that they divided this area, which they called Chaohsien, into four prefectures recorded in Korean history as Nangnang (Lolang),* Imdun (Lint'un), Hyundo (Hsüant'u), and Chinpun (Chênfan). Nang-

* The Chinese equivalents of the Korean terms are given in parentheses.

nang roughly corresponded to the present provinces of P'yŏngan, Hwanghae, and Kyŏnggi; Imdun to Kangwŏn; Hyundo to Hamgyŏng; while Chinpun represented the part of Manchuria bordering modern Korea to the west. Prefects governed these major administrative units, which in turn were broken up into districts (hsien) with headmen, called ling or ch'ang depending on the size of these divisions, a large one having more than 10,000 families. Nangnang, for example, is reported in Early Han times to have been divided into 25 districts with 62,812 families and a population of 406,748.* Several districts might be combined into a command post (tu-wei-pu) and Nangnang had two of these for a while. Twenty-five years after the conquest, the Chinese reduced the original four prefectures into two, uniting Nangnang and Imdun into Tongpu, and Hyundo and Chinpun into Pyŏngju.

Such procedure was in keeping with the political organization of the empire-making Chinese court, the boundaries representing an ideal more than the realities of unified control. Actually by B.C. 82, most of the area of Chinpun and Imdun had been relinquished to non-Chinese rulers. In B.C. 80, Hyundo suffered heavy territorial losses and even the focal prefecture of Nangnang was seriously diminished by B.C. 30.[1]† The Chinese officials in many areas were probably willing to allow the local people to manage their own affairs—if the officials actually appeared on the scene at all. At least, as we shall see, kingdoms could not only attain complete autonomy within the area but could also rise up to challenge the power of China itself. This brings us to the origin of Koguryŏ, one of the great dynasties of Korea.

Usually, the longer a ruling line survives, the more do traditions surround its origin, and Koguryŏ is no exception. Almost certainly the ancestors of the Koguryŏ kings came south into Korea from the region of the Amur River or its tributaries, where they were known as the Puyu people. In this they do not seem unlike most other Koreans. According to one story, a son of Tan-gun, the first culture hero of the Peninsula, was the founder of Puyu. This has the characteristics of a myth and we need not complicate the account by repeating the even less probable parts of the tale.

* It is not certain whether non-Chinese are included in these figures; also, the population data for the prefectures during the various periods are uncertain for other reasons. Slawik, 1933:9.

† The references to sources for Part Three will be found on page 210.

In the period when the Chinese had succeeded to power in P'yŏngyang, Ha-bu-ru was king of the east Puyu. He had a grandson named Chu-mong who for various reasons did not get along with his own people and decided to seek his fortune in the south. Taking three friends with him and acquiring some others on the way, he went to Cholbon in Tongpu.* There he is said to have married the daughter of the king, a title which we can take as a rather grandiose expression for the chief of the local population.

The establishment of Chu-mong at Cholbon took place in B.C. 37. Whatever power the Chinese had over the region must have disintegrated since their conquest eighty years earlier because Chu-mong, by absorption and conquest, in the course of the next few decades, brought the surrounding tribes including the Okjŏ under control, and was pressing the Manchurian groups beyond the Yalu, near which river he set up a permanent capital. Thus began one of the famous Three Kingdoms of Korea which were to dominate the Peninsula for a thousand years, and ultimately consolidate the people into a single nation. Before going further with Koguryŏ we must consider the formation of the others.

To understand changes in southern Korea we return to Ki-jun, who was driven from his rule of the northwest by Wi-man in B.C. 193. Ki-jun escaped from his capital at P'yŏngyang by boat, sailing down the Taedong River and then along the coast southward, past the modern provinces of Hwanghae, Kyŏnggi, and Ch'ungch'ŏng, until he came to the Kum River at the northern border of what is now Chŏlla. In that region lived a numerous group of semi-independent

---

* The location of a capital at Cholbon (Chulbon), which Hulbert says is the modern Sŏngch'ŏn, may be reasonably questioned (Fig. 1, p. 7). The Sekino Commission reports Cholbon to be on the right bank of the Hun (T'ung Chia) River, historically known as the Fei Liu River, between Tunghwa and Huanjen. Hulbert adds that the capital was moved to Whanto (Ch'osan) where it remained until 208 A.D. Apparently Kim Pu-sik, the great historian of the twelfth century, could not determine the site of the first Koguryŏ capital. Gale, following Japanese archeologists of the Sekino Commission, concludes that the Koguryŏ kings had three capitals, the first and principal of which was established in B.C. 37 at Kuknaisung, across the Yalu a little below the mouth of the Kangkai (Kanggye, Tongno) River. On the basis of its identification with the modern town of T'ung Kou by the Korean historian Ch'ae Nam-sun, however, this site appears to be above the mouth of the Kanggye River, just below Chian. Gale goes on to say that in 209 A.D. the Koguryŏ king moved some forty miles south-south-west to Whanto. In 234 A.D. (Hulbert says the following decade), the Koguryŏ capital was established at P'yŏngyang where it remained until about 335. It was then returned to Kuknaisung until 427. For approximately the last two hundred years of the dynasty, the Koguryŏ capital was almost continuously at P'yŏngyang. Hulbert, 1905: Vol. 1:38, 43, 57-59, 63; Gale, 1925:5-6, 28, 51.

tribes or clans which had apparently never been brought under the control of any one chieftain. These people must have known of the civilization in northwest Korea, however, and held its accomplishments in respect, perhaps even acknowledging its theoretical sovereignty. In any event, the refugee ruler seems to have been well received and was able to establish himself as king at Iksan, at which place he died the same year (Fig. 1, p. 7).

These people whom Ki-jun and his descendants united into a kingdom occupied the present provinces of Ch'ungch'ŏng and northern Chŏlla and were known by the collective name of Mahan. To the south of them was another aggregate of tribes called Pyŏnhan, while to the east in what we now term Kyŏngsang Province a third federation existed, which is recorded as the Chinhan. These last two were apparently more closely related than either was to the Mahan (Fig. 14, p. 164).

The cultural contributions of the Ki-jun dynasty while uniting the fifty-four districts of the Mahan must have been considerable, and the new political organization seems to have set a pattern for southern Korea. The prestige of the Mahan kings was great, for their neighbors paid them nominal tribute even after their power had waned. By the time Ki-hak, the ninth successor of Ki-jun, had come to the throne, the Mahan court had become too self-content to be concerned with aggression. Two years before, a small kingdom called Paekche had been permitted to develop on the northern edge of the Mahan territory. Ki-hak showed the same weakness which had brought about the downfall of his ancestor Ki-jun at P'yŏngyang. By 4 A.D., Paekche had so grown in strength that Mahan fell an easy prey and was absorbed into the new state. Thus the long line of kings descending from Ki-ja, ruling first in the north from B.C. 1122 to B.C. 193, and then in the south from B.C. 193 to 4 A.D., came finally to an end.

The downfall of Mahan is more than a parallel to that of the Ki-ja dynasty in the northwest, for just as the overthrown were personally related, so, we shall see, were their successors. We will remember that King Chu-mong, who founded the Koguryŏ dynasty, married the daughter of the ruler of Cholbon as a step on his road to power. According to the story, he had also left a wife and a son behind him when he set out from his original home. In due course that son grew up and, like Theseus, sought out his father. In the meantime, however, Chu-mong had acquired two more sons named On-jo and Pi-ryu. Their position was made embarrassingly insecure by the arrival of their elder brother and they decided to seek their fortunes elsewhere.

Pi-ryu, the elder of the two, went to the locality of the now famous port of Inch'ŏn, where he established a settlement. On-jo went to the district of Chiksan near the northern border of Ch'ungch'ŏng where he was given land by the king of Mahan. This was in B.C. 18. Pi-ryu did not like the region around Inch'ŏn, so he rejoined his brother. They did not have such an easy time of it at first because of the raiding of various tribespeople. They are said to have been attacked not only by the Yemak and Okjŏ but also by roving groups from beyond the Yalu such as the Malgal and Suksin, who skirted the more powerful civilized centers. After the Malgal besieged On-jo's capital in B.C. 10 and almost defeated him, several fortresses were constructed but these were pulled down by the raiders the next year. On-jo decided to move to a safer place and he chose Namhan, a site about twenty miles southeast from the modern capital of Seoul. There he built a town and enclosed it with a wall.

It is easy to understand that, as the years passed in organizing the people of Kyŏnggi Province, On-jo believed a larger scope was needed for his abilities. Perhaps he tired of absorbing the blows from the north which might otherwise have descended on Mahan. Probably he viewed the Mahan rulers as decadent and soon to be overrun from the east if he did not take power himself. For whatever reasons he gave himself, he put an end to the Ki-jun dynasty and coalesced his own rule with theirs, thus bringing about another of the Three Kingdoms into which Korea was so long divided. Paekche, founded in B.C. 18, was destined to dominate the western half of south Korea for over six hundred years.

Having considered the origin of two of the Three Kingdoms, we can now give attention to the foundation of the other, of which possibly On-jo was already afraid when he took over Mahan. As previously mentioned, at the time Ki-jun became king of Mahan there were already two neighboring federations of tribes called Chinhan and Pyŏnhan. Although their boundaries were never defined, it is certain the Chinhan centered in Kyŏngsang Province with the Pyŏnhan probably to the south or west.

眞歲卯十六阿事松中眞副司光

23. PORTRAIT BY KIM CHIN-YŎ (1719)

24. MURAL PAINTINGS FROM THE KOGURYŎ TOMB OF THE TWO PILLARS IN SOUTH P'YŎNGAN PROVINCE

A tradition too curious to be overlooked states that during the disruptions of the Chinese Ch'in dynasty (B.C. 221-206), thousands of refugees settled in the Chinhan country, having been directed there by the Mahan, through whose territory they presumably passed. Our knowledge of Chinese emigration during this period leads us to accept this tradition. Such a movement also helps us to understand the remarkable growth of civilization in that part of Korea which we might expect to be most backward. The Chinese would have had a great influence on the tribespeople but we must point out that the name Chinhan, as shown by the written character, has no relation to the Chinese dynasty of the period.

From one influence and another, six of the most important Chinhan chiefs came together in B.C. 57 and formed a kingdom, placing a boy by the name of Pak Hyuk-ku-se on the throne. As in similar cases, there is an impossible tale of the supernatural origin of the boy king and of his bride whom he married five years after his accession. But the writers of the first histories of the dynasty, with an amazing urbanity for their time, themselves advise readers to be skeptical of such events. The capital of the Silla Kingdom, by which name it is known to posterity, although not adopted until over five hundred years later, was located where now stands the city of Kyŏngju, about fifty-five miles north of Pusan.

Apparently there were the usual disturbances from surrounding tribes, including sea raiders from Japan, for it is noted that in B.C. 48 the attacks from the islands stopped for a while. A wall twelve miles long was built around the capital in B.C. 37 and during the same year Pyŏnhan was absorbed, apparently by peaceful agreement. The notable thing about Silla, in contrast to the other two of the Three Kingdoms, is that its development was not characterized by internal strife.

Having now seen the foundation of all of the Three Kingdoms, Silla in B.C. 57, Koguryŏ in B.C. 37, and Paekche in B.C. 18, we can briefly treat the political history of each one during the first millennium of our times.* We should not forget, however, that although during this period these were the dominant states in Korea, they can-

* The Chinese equivalents and variants for the names of the three Korean kingdoms are (1) Silla: Hsin-lo, Sinlo, Shinra; (2) Koguryŏ: Kao-chü-li, Kao-keu-li; (3) Paekche: Po-chi, Peh-tai; the Japanese equivalents are (1) Silla: Shiragi; (2) Koguryŏ: Kokurai; (3) Paekche: Kudara or Hiakusai.

not be conceived of as simply dividing the Peninsula between them. Minor kingdoms were permitted to exist and ran their course. Also, much of the population remained in tribal groups, particularly in the northeast, and it is questionable whether boundaries representing a realistic control by the Three Kingdoms ever touched each other for more than a few miles.

We can begin our survey by a consideration of Paekche. The position of Paekche, lying more or less between Silla and Koguryŏ, created a difficulty in itself. Paekche seemed particularly to resent her cultured neighbor to the east and sometimes attacked her, although conflicts were minor for the first few hundred years. Later, when Paekche became involved in fighting the warlike Koguryŏ, Silla frequently came to Paekche's assistance, service for which little appreciation seems ever to have been shown. Paekche turned against Silla again and again and finally set out to destroy her with the help of Koguryŏ. What happened we shall see.

Although the available data on the kingdom of Paekche are less than those for the other two, the outline of events is clear enough. In the year 63 A.D., the last of the Mahan tribes which had never submitted to Paekche voluntarily joined Silla. This apparently was accepted as an understandable action by the Paekche king, but somehow his efforts to discuss the matter were rebuffed. Annoyed, he sent out his forces in 68 A.D. and captured a frontier town in Silla territory. Nine years later Silla responded by annihilating the Paekche garrison. Paekche then seemed willing to let Silla alone for a century, while consolidating the internal control of the kingdom.

By 168 A.D., we find Paekche once again starting border warfare with Silla and this time with more success, as the latter kingdom was apparently only in a position to send a letter asking for the return of the captives taken and pointing out the advantages of peace. Later there was trouble with China, whose forces reconquered the Han River area of the old Nangnang prefecture in about 208, giving it the name of Taifang. Chinese authority, wedged in between Paekche and Koguryŏ, survived to some degree throughout the century. The Chinese, in final desperation, attacked Paekche in 313 but were disastrously defeated. Paekche and Koguryŏ then divided up the last of the Chinese-held territory between them.[2]

Things seem to have gone along fairly peacefully until the middle of the fourth century. During the intervening years all three of the kingdoms had developed in culture and population, expanding their political organization over the intervening areas. About the year 360, Koguryŏ built a fortress not far from the Paekche capital of Namhan, some seventeen miles southeast of the modern Seoul, using it as a point of vantage for raids on Paekche villages. Paekche re-acted by sending an army against this fortress and in a surprise at-tack defeated its large garrison. The victory spurred Paekche on to an even greater revenge, and shortly afterwards a large force made a concentrated attack against Koguryŏ, laying siege to the capital at P'yŏngyang. Although the city was not taken, the Koguryŏ king was killed by an arrow. This success seems to have affected the Paekche people in various ways. It elated the court and the king moved his capital north across the Han River to a point near Seoul. Some people, however, were disturbed for many abandoned the country for the peace and protection of Silla. One thing is certain, Koguryŏ became a bitter enemy and for years the border warfare continued with a severe defeat being suffered by Paekche in 392. Paekche, worried over the state of affairs, sent one of the king's sons to Japan, probably to establish an alliance which would bring assistance when needed. This reaching beyond Korea for foreign support came to a climax shortly afterwards when the Paekche king, following the lead of Koguryŏ, accepted the custom of investiture by the emperor of China in 415. This was actually the expression of an international alliance under forms distinctive to the East, where mu-tual obligations of autonomous states were recognized in the political sphere without ignoring ceremonially the cultural superiority of one of the contracting parties.[3] The situation soon became complicated, however, by the fact that China itself was not united at this period and, whereas Koguryŏ in 420 came to terms with the Northern Wei whose territory was nearer theirs, Paekche in 435 shifted her al-liance to the Southern Sung Liu Sung dynasty which held the ter-ritory across the Yellow Sea.

In 455, Koguryŏ saw in the death of a king an advantageous time to attack Paekche, but Silla responded by sending troops to the lat-ter's aid. Although saving the situation for the moment, this action only complicated matters and for a period all of the Three Kingdoms were fighting each other. Things had scarcely quieted down on a military level when Paekche tried to turn Koguryŏ's Chinese ally against her. This only embittered Koguryŏ into deciding to defeat

Paekche for once and for all. Paekche sent to Silla for aid, but before it arrived the Paekche capital near Seoul had been burned and the king killed by the Koguryŏ army, which then retired with thousands of prisoners. Paekche never really recovered from this blow, which fell in the year 475. The new king withdrew all of his people south of the Han River and established a capital where the present city of Kongju is now located in South Ch'ungch'ŏng Province.

This move took the court out of striking distance of Koguryŏ for some years and there was a period of peace. It is interesting to note that in 477 tribute was sent to the Paekche court from the culturally isolated island of Cheju, which lies off the south coast of Korea. For reasons which are not clear, the Paekche capital was moved to Puyŏ, a short distance to the southwest, in the year 540. Perhaps it was because pressure from the north was again increasing for we know that Koguryŏ, with the aid of such tribes as the Yemak and Malgal, attacked Paekche in 547. Silla and her allies came to Paekche's assistance and disaster was averted. Somehow Paekche could not keep peace with Silla either, and war broke out between them in 555, with the result that Paekche was forced to give up a large slice of territory bordering Silla.

For half a century, Paekche avoided major difficulties. Ultimately, however, she began to intrigue with Silla to get the Sui dynasty, which in 589 had united China, to turn on Koguryŏ. This political maneuver succeeded and in 598 China began to attack. The war that resulted removed the danger to Paekche for twenty more years. By 620, however, Koguryŏ had started border warfare in the south again. Instead of Paekche uniting with Silla, Paekche attacked her as she had done so often before, and soon all three kingdoms were carrying on forays against each other. Although all three kingdoms had established relations with the new T'ang dynasty in China, no Chinese help was forthcoming for any of them. The emperor had seen the preceding Sui dynasty fall because of costly wars against Korea and was not anxious to make the same mistake himself. He told them all to stop fighting and then let matters take their course.

Intermittent attacks on Silla by Paekche and Koguryŏ were still being conducted in 642, when Paekche decided to stop communications between Silla and China. Detaining the ambassadors was a mistake, for China was offended by this unceremonious act and thereafter was strongly prejudiced in favor of Silla. When she told Paekche and Koguryŏ to leave Silla alone, only Paekche stopped and China sent an army against Koguryŏ. The result was inconclusive and by 655 Paekche and Koguryŏ, now afraid of Silla's rising power, again took up the conflict against her. China once more declared war, for which she made long and careful preparations.

The Paekche court had become corrupt and Silla decided that the day had arrived for a decisive effort against her. This time China sent a fleet across the Yellow Sea and Paekche was caught in a pincers. By bad misjudgment, the Chinese were allowed to land and the Silla forces to break through the passes before either was attacked. The Paekche king and his army moved from the capital, then at Sŏch'ŏn on the seacoast, to Kongju where he was finally captured. When defeat came the women of the court at Puyŏ are said to have jumped from a nearby precipice into the Kum River, an act since famed in Korean songs and literature. The king, with thousands of his followers, was carried off to China, thus ending the Paekche dynasty in the year 660.

We can now review the history of Koguryŏ, which we should remember was founded by Chu-mong in B.C. 37. The problems implicit in the location of Koguryŏ were quite different from those of either Paekche or Silla. Koguryŏ was almost surrounded by tribespeople and those to the north were constantly a threat. The Koguryŏ were merely one among them in the beginning and only survived by keeping alive the skills of war. Furthermore, the Koguryŏ had the Chinese on her western border, so she was constantly influenced by the rise and fall of empires in that quarter. That she stood firm for so many centuries is an amazing tribute to the strength and courage of the Korean people.

As with Paekche, the first few hundred years of Koguryŏ history were apparently a period of consolidation. The absorption of the Okjŏ begun in B.C. 27 was formally completed in 55 A.D., although the extent of control over the whole of modern Hamgyŏng Province is uncertain. Koguryŏ also expanded into southern Manchuria, and for about the first two hundred years of the Christian era the capital was close to the Yalu River. As early as 27 A.D., the Chinese were resenting Koguryŏ incursions and sent an army to repress them. The Koreans fought behind their walls, however, until the Chinese retired in discouragement. Growing stronger, the Koguryŏ even captured the Chinese capital near P'yŏngyang and held it between 32 and 44 A.D.[4] By the second half of the century, the Koguryŏ were building border forts in western Liaotung, having recovered all the land lost to China. With their military power increasing, the Koreans pushed farther north. In the middle of the second century we find Koguryŏ, with the help of Yemak, still making encroachments on the Chinese territory (Fig. 15, p. 168).

Political conditions had been deteriorating in the Yellow Empire, and after the fall of the Han dynasty many refugees sought safety in Korea. In the second quarter of the third century, after an interim of peace, the confidence of the Koguryŏ king was so great that he dared to attack China and Silla at the same time. Much to his surprise, his forces were not only checked by Silla but the Chinese, having defeated him in battle, were finally thrown back only after the king had been chased into the wilds of his own country. Having learned his lesson, a peace was made with Silla which remained unbroken for a hundred years. The court was also moved south to P'yŏngyang, because a residence close to the Yalu was no longer considered safe.

Most significant for Koguryŏ was the rise of the Yen dynasty in Manchuria during the fourth century. China tried to suppress this powerful group in 320 and called Koguryŏ to her aid. The allies were forced to retire, however, and the Koreans found themselves with a dangerous enemy on their borders. When, in 333, the Yen decided on war against China, they felt it necessary to reduce the threat from the rear and first defeated the Koguryŏ who had been building forts along the Yalu. The Yen forced the Koguryŏ king to take up residence in that area so they could keep a watch on him.

The result of this situation was that Koguryŏ was compelled to look for expansion in the south, which led to the conflicts with Paekche previously described and a definite victory over that kingdom in 392. Koguryŏ tried to placate the Yen, but without success, for the latter captured the principal border fortresses again and carried off a large number of captives. In trying to equalize the danger in the north, Koguryŏ accepted the custom of investiture from the Chinese in 413, first bowing to the Eastern Chin emperor and transferring obeisance to the Northern Wei in 420. The problem of the Yen was disposed of by the Chinese who drove their ruler to seek sanctuary in P'yŏngyang, where he was put to death in 436.

In the middle of the fifth century, Koguryŏ began to have difficulties with Silla. First a Koguryŏ general was killed by mistake by officers of a Silla border post. Then, when Koguryŏ attacked Paekche in 455, Silla came to the latter's assistance, with the results already described.

An interesting note during this period, when Koguryŏ was attempting to keep on good terms with China, was the rather extraordinary refusal of the Koguryŏ king in the year 466 to give his daughter to become a wife of the Wei emperor. He told the Wei ambassadors that she had died, which was a transparent falsehood. Apart from the unrevealed personal elements in the action, it makes clear that Koguryŏ was no cringing dependency of her great neighbor. A few years later, the same Koguryŏ king inflicted the terrible defeat on Paekche which started the latter on her downward course.

The middle of the sixth century was characterized by another attack on Paekche. The growing power of Silla was a disturbing thing to Koguryŏ and in 586 the capital was again moved north near the Yalu River. When the Chinese Sui dynasty came to power in 581, Koguryŏ had little confidence in her own diplomacy but accepted investiture the year following. The Sui had been prejudiced in favor of Silla who, with Paekche, proceeded to persuade the Sui to make war against the northern Kingdom. China having declared herself, little Koguryŏ decided that the only hope lay in attack. With her Malgal allies, she proceeded to send her army all the way across the Liao River, conquering the towns on the way. One can imagine that the great Sui emperor who had succeeded in uniting China was shocked. He also sent a large army against Koguryŏ but unexpected difficulties were encountered which, as they have great significance for the successful isolation of the Peninsula, had better be explained.

For China to defeat the Korean people, armies had to be sent either across the Yellow Sea or by land across southern Manchuria. The sea route was unusually precarious because of the difficulties of navigation in approaching the Korean shore, with its innumerable islands and tremendous tides. On the other hand, the plains of southern Manchuria were a desolate frozen expanse in winter with no natural source of supplies for a large army, and in summer a region almost impassable because of heavy rains. To cross these plains even in spring or fall was liable to result in leaving an army stranded on alien soil where it could be starved and cut to pieces almost at will.

The Sui court recognized the difficulty and began to prepare for the overland campaign, amassing possibly the largest military force the world had ever seen. Koguryŏ was frightened and tried to make peace but the Sui emperor would accept no compromise. By 612, the Chinese were ready and Koguryŏ, with the courage of death, dared to oppose the great onslaught, even on the banks of the Liao. Then, driven back to their own country, they fought on from inside their walled cities. One great Chinese army was ambushed in making a march on the capital at P'yŏngyang and, if the records are correct, suffered losses running into the hundreds of thousands.* In any event, the outcome was one of the great military defeats of history. The fortresses could not be taken and insurrections at home caused the Chinese to give up the siege. In fact, it is clear that this costly campaign caused the Sui dynasty to lose the throne of China.

Koguryŏ nursed its wounds and soon turned to attack Paekche and Silla, now traditional enemies. The latter called on China for help, but the T'ang dynasty had learned a lesson from the experience of her predecessors and bided her time. It is said that Koguryŏ built a wall across the northern part of her kingdom but this is uncertain. It is a significant mark of respect that China was afraid of her. The situation had to be faced by the T'ang, however, and after combining with Silla to dispose of Paekche in 660, orders were given to attack Koguryŏ. This time, the latter country was caught between the Chinese already in the field with strong allies to the south, and armies moving in from Manchuria. Notwithstanding such difficulties, the Koguryŏ soldiers battled on until their skillful warrior king died, leaving sons who betrayed each other. Thus in 668 came the end of the Koguryŏ dynasty, with many of her people taken captive to China. Silla, the last of the Three Kingdoms, was left in a position of dominance in the Peninsula.

Returning to review the history of Silla, we find a nation in which intellectual values and the effort toward the internal development of the country seemed to have gained priority over the arts of war and conquest. For a long period after their inauguration in

* These results are supported by Chinese as well as Korean records. Parker, 1890a :195-96.

B.C. 57, the Silla kings were generous to their neighbors as is instanced by their refusal to take advantage of the disintegration of the Mahan dynasty in the period preceding its overthrow by Paekche. Silla tolerated her neighbors, often gave them assistance, and provided a refuge for thousands who fled from the disasters of war. For the hundreds of years in which Silla concentrated her efforts on the development of her rich natural resources and their defense, the kingdom was strong. The history of the first centuries is largely but references to her efforts at self-protection. The reason for this attitude was in part because of her geographical location. Relative to Koguryŏ and Paekche, Silla held an almost isolated position, surrounded by sea or mountains. Unlike the others, her watchful eye was turned seaward, from which direction came the Japanese pirates who periodically plundered Korea throughout history.

The piratical attacks from the east were clearly not those of an organized nation but of the tribal Japanese who occupied the opposite shores of the strait separating them from the mainland by about a hundred miles of sea. The large intervening island of Tsushima appears to have been a dependency of Silla and was periodically given aid by that country until it came under Japanese domination around the middle of the first millennium of our era. It is a poor land and in that sense to a degree secure against robbery. Silla, on the other hand, was a kingdom of fertile fields, of rich mines, and villages ripe for looting. The Silla people knew this and they feared the sudden destruction which might at any time whirl upon them from the sea.

Silla was also attacked by others. Mention is made of driving back the Nangnang people about 5 A.D., Paekche in 77, and Karak in 91. Karak was an independent kingdom southwest of Silla, founded in 42 A.D. Its territory embraced an area along the coast which would include the modern cities of Pusan and Chinju and extended inland almost to Taegu, with a few satellite dependencies even beyond this region. It is a commentary on Silla that she permitted such a political entity to exist as it did for almost five hundred years, finally absorbing it by 562. Silla also had contact from an early period with Cheju (Quelpart) Island, where the isolated kingdom of T'amna existed traditionally as a dependency of Paekche.

We have mentioned the border warfare with Paekche, starting in 168 A.D. This seems to have been a time of relative weakness for

Silla, but she soon recovered strength and in the first quarter of the third century destroyed a settlement which Japanese pirates had made on the mainland besides turning back attacks from various Korean tribes. In 249, we find record of an envoy from the Japanese kingdom. He was intentionally insulted by the general who received him and immediately returned home only to come back with a large military force. According to the Silla histories, war was avoided but not without bitterness.

By the fourth century, Silla had extended her borders as far as the neighborhood of modern Ch'unch'ŏn, northeast of Seoul. Paekche and Koguryŏ were also unifying control over their respective areas during this period but, in coming into conflict with each other, were less concerned about Silla. Silla, however, still had her Japanese problem. At one time, when efforts were being made for conciliation, it is reported that a daughter of one of Silla's highest officials was sent to become the Japanese queen. Later, in 344, a royal princess was requested but this Silla refused and the Japanese attacked, only to be defeated.

We should take note of the fact that the Japanese records make much of the defeat of Silla by a Japanese queen in the beginning of the third century. Unfortunately, Japanese history for the period is, in general, scarcely credible and is especially unreliable with respect to dates. Notwithstanding, it is clear that Silla suffered setbacks from the hands of the Japanese, whose reports of her victories are probably only fact written down with too much exaggeration and too little objectivity.

By the fifth century, Silla, although still subject to Japanese raids, was stronger internally. There is no sign of any devastating defeat which had stemmed her progress. The abundant harvests of the southern Korean valleys attracted settlers by the thousands from other parts of the Peninsula and undoubtedly some from China as well.

We should recall that Koguryŏ became more militant toward her southern neighbors in the second half of the fifth century and that Silla went to Paekche's aid, only to become embroiled in hostilities with both. Military strength was becoming more of a necessity for Silla and we find that she developed a navy as a defense against the Japanese. That her campaigns were now more than simply defensive ones can be seen in her conquest of little Ullŭng (Dagalet)

Island, which lies almost a hundred miles off the central east coast of Korea. This undertaking in 512 was a symbolic act which greatly impressed the people of Silla. The expansion to the southwest, which embraced the Karak kingdom, followed and Silla started on a more complex pattern of international diplomacy.

An outstanding situation which developed in the first quarter of the sixth century was the controlling influence of monks on political affairs in Silla. Although such influence was only sporadic, it is interesting as a forecast of conditions which in later dynasties were sometimes to rock the political stability of all Korea. Also in this century, we again find Silla going to the aid of Paekche and ultimately gaining a bordering section of her territory when Paekche attacked her.

Silla's cultural affinity for China and her emphasis on diplomacy in implementing her traditional defensive foreign policy gave her a natural advantage among the Three Kingdoms in dealing with their great continental neighbor. When the Sui again united China in 589, after some four hundred years of internal strife, Silla was quick to establish a firm relationship and to take advantage of it. With Paekche's help, they persuaded the Chinese that Koguryŏ was a menace to the peace of all nations, with the results which have been outlined in recounting the history of Koguryŏ. The Sui exhausted themselves, thereby allowing both Koguryŏ and Paekche to turn on Silla. The latter had to put diplomacy to work again, this time with the T'ang which was to prove a much greater dynasty than the Sui. The T'ang emperor who had come to the throne in 618 moved cautiously. One notable thing that concerned him was that in 632 a Silla queen undertook to rule for the first time in Korean history. Her sister followed her as the second queen and a revolt against her failed.

When the T'ang emperor died in 649, Paekche decided it was an opportunity to invade Silla. Silla responded in kind and called on China for help. The final result was the end of Paekche in the year 660, the deposed king being forced to serve wine to his conquerors. Silla's position in the matter was that she had no territorial aggression in mind, a point of view which seems consistent with her history. China therefore assumed control of the territory. Rebellions occurred, however, and the Silla forces proved more adept in subduing their fellow Koreans than did the Chinese. Besides, the latter were determined to take the opportunity to settle matters with Koguryŏ, since they could attack that state from two sides. Thus we find a Silla army besieging the northern capital of P'yŏngyang in the year 662. Proceedings were delayed by more uprisings undertaken in Paekche with the help of the Japanese. These were put down, however, and the Chinese appointed the brother of the last Paekche king as governor, making him and the king of Silla swear to peace on the blood of a white horse. By 665, full attention could be given to Koguryŏ again, and that kingdom was brought down in defeat in 668.

From the Chinese point of view, the larger part of the Peninsula had come under their direct control, but Silla took the position that it should be hers, taking care, however, not to contradict China in a verbal issue. Actually, it would seem that China had gained her real goal in destroying the threat of the warlike Koguryŏ and withdrew most of her troops. The next year, however, an ambassador of Silla was thrown into jail and by 672, China sent a large army to castigate the little kingdom for its ambition. Much to their surprise, they were abruptly stopped in their tracks and the T'ang called on the Malgal for assistance. This time the Silla army was driven back and the king asked for peace, which was not granted. He then, it would seem for the first time in history, called upon Koreans as Koreans to turn back the outsiders, offering amnesty to the revolting groups in Paekche. After a series of diplomatic maneuvers the T'ang and their allies attacked again, and this time were soundly defeated.

This seemed to be enough of direct conflict for the Chinese, who were heading toward difficulties within their own court. As a last expedient, they tried establishing along the Yalu a border kingdom known as "Latter Koguryŏ" but this artificial creation lasted only five years, ending in 682. By that time Silla already had established an auxiliary northern capital in Kangwŏn Province and had gained control of all the Peninsula south of the Taedong River which flows past P'yŏngyang.

The next fifty years were good ones for Silla. She set out by dividing the country into nine provinces and 450 prefectures. There was a redistribution of land, and regular salaries were given to administrative officials. Diplomatically, she went ahead by exchanging envoys with the Japanese and re-established harmonious relations with the Chinese court, then under an interim usurper, the Empress Wu. It has been suggested, and it is by no means unlikely, that

Silla already had established intercourse with the West through Arab voyagers, although the records for such connections are not definitive until 846.

An important political event was the founding, in 713, of the Kingdom of Palhae (P'ohai) in the northern part of the Peninsula, in the region of Myohyang Mountain. This new kingdom resulted from a coalition of Koguryŏ, Puyu, and Okjŏ peoples, under the leadership of the Malgal. Palhae rose as a power so rapidly that she had a foothold on the Shantung Peninsula of China by 734. This may possibly have affected the decision of the Chinese in the following year to recognize, at his investiture, the rule of the Silla king over all land south of the Taedong, a belated acknowledgment of the reality during the previous half century.

The last two hundred years of the Silla Kingdom was a period of decadence and disintegration. By the beginning of the ninth century, revolts were becoming commonplace and the kings, well on their way to impotence, were engrossed in the luxury of the court. Robber bands sprang up over the country, two of which were to threaten the dynasty. One of these was led by a man named Kyŏn-hwŏn who at one time proclaimed himself King of Southern Silla. Another was Kung-ye, who led a larger group in the north in 896, and in 905 founded the Kingdom of Majin. A few years later the court of Silla was existing only because it did not collapse by itself. Even the people of the capital were mocking their rulers.

The successor of Kung-ye was Wang-gŏn who established his capital at Songdo, the modern Kaesŏng, about fifty miles northwest of Seoul. He was one of Korea's greatest men, the founder of the Koryŏ Wang dynasty which was recognized by the King of Silla in 918. Kyŏn-hwŏn, on the other hand, was as cruel as Wang-gŏn was good. Fighting both Koryŏ and Silla, he made up for his defeat by the former by laying siege to the capital of the latter. Before help could be brought from Wang-gŏn, Kyŏn-hwŏn had caused the Silla king to commit suicide, had raped the queen, and had turned the palace women over to his troops. Then, loaded with treasure, he retreated southward. This was the final blow for Silla and although still another king was supported by Wang-gŏn, he finally accepted that ruler's abdication in the year 935. Thus, after 992 years, the last of the Three Kingdoms gave over to another line which was to establish the first Korean kingdom truly uniting the whole Peninsula.

11

UNITED KOREA

WANG-GŎN, the founder of the Koryŏ dynasty which was to last from 918 until 1392, was the lieutenant and later the leading general of the bandit leader Kung-ye who set himself up as King of Majin, a vague and transitory kingdom with its capital near the modern Ch'unch'ŏn in Kangwŏn Province. Kung-ye, who had at least re-established some morale and order among the Korean people, had the misfortune to lose his mind, becoming a homicidal maniac who killed his sons, tortured his wife, and imagined himself endowed with supernatural powers. Wang-gŏn avoided the problem as much as possible by leading armies in the field and occupying himself as governor of Songdo, the modern Kaesŏng, in Kyŏnggi Province. The courtiers and other officers who feared for their lives, finally forced him to supersede Kung-ye.

Wang-gŏn removed the capital to Songdo in 917, where, in the following year, he was acknowledged as King of Koryŏ by Silla. His strength was effective as is shown by the quick succession in which other autonomous states recognized his sovereignty. He made treaties with the most powerful groups of the northern border, and the King of T'amna on Cheju Island sent an envoy in 926. Little Ullŭng Island also sent presents soon afterwards. Wang-gŏn hoped to move his court to P'yŏngyang, a city which he revered as the most ancient capital of Korea, but this plan was set aside through an unfavorable interpretation of omens.

Wang-gŏn was one of those rare men whose political distinctions are unblemished by serious weaknesses of personal character. His courtesy to the last king of Silla is only matched by the protection and comfort he gave to his greatest opponent in arms when defeated. By 936 Wang-gŏn was master of all of Korea and recognized by the Chinese emperor. When he died, six years later, the government was well ordered and he left behind him ten rules for the guidance of his heirs. Among these was the advice not to make friends with the Kitan (Ch'itan), a powerful Manchurian group which had betrayed and overcome the Palhae in 926, not to marry a woman from the south where the Koryŏ kings could not be sure of loyalty, and not to build more monasteries, although recognizing Buddhism as the state religion.

As so often is the case, sons are not the equals of great fathers and Wang-gŏn's two successors were often in trouble. Curiously, the reaction to the advice about wives led the second king of Koryŏ to marry his sister and this practice became the characteristic custom of the dynasty. Also, instead of moderation in support of Buddhism, monks were soon running the government through their hold over the king. This domination by religious groups was another outstanding feature of the Koryŏ period which, although it was responsible for outstanding achievements in art and architecture, brought political confusion and crushing extravagance to burden the people of the Peninsula. Fortunately, the last quarter of the century was a period of reforms but the extraordinary development of military power by the Kitan in the north threatened Koryŏ's security, and war began in 993.

Koryŏ could not withstand the attacks of the Kitan and the king was forced to accept investiture from them. This led to deterioration in the court but not long after the eleventh century had begun, war flared up again. At first the Kitan had the best of it and the king was forced to flee southwards to save his life, the Kitan burning the palaces of Songdo in 1011. Then the fortunes of war changed and the Koreans, by fine generalship, won back all their territory in the following year. The Kitan continued their attacks, however, building a bridge across the Yalu River in 1015, but a few years later suffered a great defeat. By 1020, the Kitan had enough of the Koreans and turned their interests elsewhere, entering into a period of normal diplomatic relations with Koryŏ.

From this point on, the strength of Koryŏ rose. Shortly after 1032, relations were broken off with the Kitan because they would not destroy their bridge over the Yalu. In retaliation, a defensive wall was constructed all the way across the Peninsula, obviously a tremendous undertaking. In this connection it might be noted that Wang-gŏn, a hundred years earlier, is said to have had a defensive wall built across the northern border of Hamgyŏng Province.

In 1056, the arrival of an envoy from Japan is noted. Buddhism was regaining its hold upon the government and extravagant sums were expended for its advancement. Gifts, however, were also coming from all quarters, from the tribes of the north, from Japan, and from the island of Tsushima. Even the Kitan were persuaded to break down their bridge over the Yalu although it was not finally destroyed until 1088. The Sung emperor sent an envoy asking help against the Kitan in 1077. The envoy was so overloaded with presents in Songdo that he could not carry them away so he sold them, for which act the Koreans regarded him with contempt. Following the dictates of a prophecy for success, a second capital was founded at Seoul, although no palace was constructed there until 1104.

In the year 1114, an event occurred north of the border which brought a period of relative peace to Korea. This was the revolt of the Yujin against the Kitan and the establishing of the Chin kingdom by the brilliant Yujin leader. This was the beginning of that famous Golden Horde which conquered the Kitan in 1124 and northern China before two additional years had passed. Fortunately for Korea, relations with the Chin had not been jeopardized by any Koryŏ aid to the Kitan and, except for losing the provinces beyond the Yalu, she did not suffer while the Chin were engaged in overthrowing the Liao dynasty.

On the other hand, the benefits of peace were principally utilized for the priests, who again became the power behind the throne. The Koryŏ court lived for luxury and the people suffered. By 1165 there was trouble on the border because Chin settlers crossed the Yalu, but they were thrown back. A few years later there was a revolt on Cheju Island. Things went from bad to worse until 1196, when there was a move toward reform and the crown prince was banished to Kanghwa Island and the king's brother put on the throne.

This did not help very much, for there were more revolts including a rising of the slaves. Remnant groups of the Kitan were also raiding over north Korea, and the general who had disposed of the crown prince likewise removed the king to Kanghwa in 1214. This was a sad time for Korea and the beginning of the worst period in her history.

The opening of the thirteenth century saw the rise of Mongol power which was to spread fear throughout the civilized world. In

25. GREEN LANDSCAPE BY SONG MIN-GO
(SEVENTEENTH CENTURY)

26. LADY RIDING ON HORSEBACK BY YŎN TŎK-HI
(EIGHTEENTH CENTURY)

獰猛歷于説此逢魃土東海
老黃公
于今改尾橫行者誰識八中
此類同
甲午南昌

27. FIERCE TIGER BY SIM SA-JŎNG (DATED 1774)

28. PAIR OF MAGPIES WITH A GROUP OF CATS (ARTIST UNCERTAIN)

1208, Genghis Khan had declared his imperial intentions and in the following decade was fighting the Kitan, among others. Koryŏ had given the Mongols some aid when the Kitan were being driven over her borders and stood in a favorable position for an alliance. Blind to the real situation, however, and seduced by their own sense of cultural superiority, the Koreans spoiled their opportunity. When a Mongol envoy came to the capital at Songdo under the most friendly circumstances, the court was shocked by his fur clothing and desire to shake hands with the king. They gave him valuable presents and persuaded him to leave the country.

When an even less attractive emissary appeared in 1221, demanding contributions for the great khan, the Koreans built a wall along their northern border. Within ten years, relations had disintegrated to such a degree that the Mongols were attacking. Their methods were far more barbaric than anything Korea had ever experienced, the soldiers looting and killing at will. Instead of attempting to meet the situation realistically, the Koryŏ king fled to Kanghwa in 1232. The following year he added another wall to the defenses of that island and also constructed a palace there in 1234. The Mongols insisted that he return to Songdo but he would not, so they raped and burned at pleasure. By 1238, the people of Korea were in wretched condition and many, following the pattern of the king, fled to the islands, which were safe because the Mongols had no boats.

An interregnum in the Mongol Empire beginning in 1240 provided a short period of relative quiet but by 1253 the Mongols invaded the country more ruthlessly than ever before.

The king finally came to the mainland from Kanghwa and promised to return to Songdo, but then procrastinated. Another Mongol general was sent to deal with the recalcitrant ruler and he proved more brutal than any of his predecessors, killing countless numbers of the people and carrying into captivity according to the record over 200,000 Koreans. The intransigent king died in 1259, after having finally sent the crown prince to the Mongol court. The palaces on Kanghwa were destroyed by imperial order and the power of the Koryŏ kings had become a fiction.

A few years after Kublai Khan inherited the Mongol Empire in 1260, he began to make contact with Japan. Several envoys were sent over a period of years, but were given a poor reception.

Preparations for invasion were therefore begun in 1273 and 300 boats were ordered to be built by the Koreans, themselves almost in starving condition. Finally, an attack was made in three times that many vessels with a force of about 40,000 men, over one third of which were men of the Peninsula. The inadequacy of the expedition was realized soon after the boats landed. In returning to the mainland, however, the fleet was caught by a storm and about 13,000 men were lost.

Unaccustomed to resistance, Kublai sent another envoy to Japan. He was killed. Preparations for a much larger invasion were then undertaken and in 1282 the attack was made. But once again a storm destroyed the fleet, costing the lives of over 100,000 men including some 8,000 Koreans. The disaster was so great that Kublai gave up his ambitions to conquer Japan.

From fifty years of Mongol occupation the Koreans had inherited little save misery. The Koryŏ kings were forced to marry Mongol women, who naturally refused to be subservient in the Confucian tradition. For the interests of the Korean people no one seemed to care. One queen engaged herself in shipping off young women to China, apparently without the slightest consideration of the particular circumstances. Even the daughters of officials were not immune. The court operated on the most luxurious scale for which money could be found and, according to the Korean records, the life was one of continued debauchery.

By the last half of the fourteenth century, Mongol power was on the wane. Rebellions began in China and the reaction left Korea abandoned to its own resources, which were in a state of complete disorganization. Marauders from Manchuria, known as the "Red Head Robbers," swept down into the Peninsula capturing Songdo in 1361, the king escaping to establish residence in the south. In the struggle for self-preservation, the Korean armies found leadership once again and the "Red Heads" were destroyed. By 1364, however, the Mongols sent an army across the border because the Korean court had refused to accept the emperor's replacement of the Koryŏ king by one of the latter's relatives. Fear of the Mongols was great and the Korean force sent against them was defeated. The Koryŏ troops reconsolidated, nonetheless, and at the next engagement, which began at

Chŏngju in northern P'yŏngan, the Mongols were annihilated by General Yi T'ae-jo. This was the end of the Mongol scourge, as the Ming dynasty came to power in Peking in 1368. For the next few years, it was the Yujin who again became the enemy on the northern border.

Besides all the other troubles since the coming of the Mongols to Korea, there was one more which has been passed over in our survey of the period. This was the piracy of the Japanese. While the Mongols were devouring the Peninsula internally, the Japanese were biting at the edges. These attacks were not undertaken by any responsible national government in the island empire but by countless freebooters who developed sea raiding as a way of life, much as the Vikings did at a slightly earlier time. Their depredations rose to a point of significance for Korea about 1223 and continued for a hundred and fifty years thereafter. Korea, first distracted and then torn apart by the Mongols, offered no serious challenge, and by the last half of the fourteenth century the pirates kept even the corrupt court in fear for its safety. In 1360 such a bold raid was made on Kanghwa—the island that the boatless Mongols could not broach—that the king moved to Hanyang, the modern Seoul, in part because it seemed a more defensible residence than Songdo, although an extra wall had already been built around that capital as a safeguard against the Japanese. The move did not suffice for, in 1373, the pirates sailed their little boats up the Han River and burned Hanyang to the ground.

Previous to this, in 1368, the Japanese court had sent a friendly embassy to the Koryŏ court which had rejected this overture with such contempt that it caused a revolt among some peaceable Japanese who for many years had been allowed to live at the southern end of the Peninsula. Envoys were now sent to the Japanese court protesting piracy, and the report was returned that the government was trying to suppress the pirates. Notwithstanding, the raiders were harassing the west coast years afterwards, and as late as 1379 are said to have killed a thousand men on Kanghwa. On the other hand, we find that the Japanese ruler sent some troops the year following to help combat the pirates as concrete evidence of his sincerity. It was General Yi T'ae-jo, however, who won the blessings of the people by his efforts. In addition to fighting the "Red Heads," the Mongols, and the Yujin, he devoted himself to clearing out the sea raiders and developing defenses against them.

The last chapter of the Koryŏ dynasty was written when the king decided to invade Manchuria and challenge the power of the Ming dynasty. No act could show better how abysmal was the ignorance of the sovereign not only about the power of his opponents but also of the sad condition of his own country and its people. Or perhaps, considering the debased life he led, he did not care. He spent his time hunting in the company of harlots and concubines dressed in men's clothes, the whole party helping themselves to whatever they pleased which the people still had. In 1384, he had moved the capital back to Songdo, and his courtiers, weary of such expensive shifts in residence, had burned their Hanyang homes so that they would be unable to return. Nonetheless, in 1388 the king had a wall built around Hanyang, where he sent all the women of the court and their children, and commanded his generals to cross the Yalu. When Yi T'ae-jo reached an island in the river, he and his soldiers decided to turn back from this mad venture. The last Koryŏ king, even whose legitimacy was doubtful, was caught helpless and was ordered to live in retirement on Kanghwa. An adopted son was put on the throne, and Yi T'ae-jo proceeded to put the kingdom in order. But before the new king was recognized by the Ming court, which had withdrawn their troops sent to oppose the expected Koryŏ attack, he handed over the throne to the people's general, who established the Yi dynasty in 1392.

After considering the matter, the Ming emperor was pleased to grant investiture to the new king and approved the name of Chaohsien (Chosŏn) for Korea—which has reference to the northeastern position of the Peninsula as the land toward which the Chinese first see the dawn. Yi T'ae-jo chose Hanyang (Seoul) as the capital of Korea and so it remains until the present. Around the city he built a wall nine and a half miles in circumference. Piracy had been reduced to a satisfactory level, and envoys were received from the Ryukyu Islands and from Japan. In the interest of the latter he designated three ports in the south as ones in which trade might be carried on. The Yujin who had occupied the distant part of Hamgyŏng were absorbed diplomatically and the Peninsula began to develop as an organized and productive nation.

When King Yi T'ae-jo retired in 1399, he was succeeded by his eldest son who is notable for crushing a rising tendency toward feudalism by demanding that all officials disband their retainers. After reigning a year, however, he gave up the throne to his popular brother Tae-jong, who became one of Korea's greatest kings. Tae-jong was so concerned with the cause of justice for the people that he not only took land held by the religious orders and distributed it but also allowed direct appeal to the throne by anyone who was denied justice by the courts. He also banished the crown prince for dissoluteness. Finally, Tae-jong followed the precedent of his father in retiring while his advice would still be available, and in 1419 placed on the throne his fourth son, Se-jong, who proved a worthy successor.

The following year the Japanese pirates began their depredations again. Korea had gained such strength by this time that a punitive expedition was sent against Tsushima and Japanese coastal villages. This enterprise proved a dubious success, however. In 1432, border tribes in the north caused trouble but these were defeated. The unsettled state of affairs in Manchuria had caused some immigration of Chinese into Hamgyŏng Province. This gave concern to the government and Korean settlers were sent from the south to offset this influence. Again, Yujin raiders had to be set back in 1436. Better relations were established with the Japanese, however, including agreements for trade with Tsushima and permission for Japanese to live in Pusan and two other southern ports.

There was much cultural progress under the Confucianist king, Se-jong, but his death in 1450 led to a struggle for power. His son, weakened by excessive mourning, reigned only two years and the boy who succeeded him was murdered. Nonetheless, the successor who had usurped the throne worked for the good of the country and before he retired in 1469 had established peaceable relations with the border tribes, the Yujin had sworn allegiance to Korea, and diplomatic relations had been recognized with the Ryukyu Islands. His successes were in part due to the consideration which he showed for the army.

The new king, Ye-jong, held the throne only a year, after which his mother became regent during the childhood of the cousin who succeeded him. For twenty years, the Confucianist tradition of responsible rule continued and it was obvious that the condition of the people had greatly improved. There was some warfare but it did not reach serious proportions. The Yujin had been raiding China and the emperor called on Korea to make them stop. This was done and the grateful emperor sent gifts. Also, in 1491 and 1492, there were fights with the tribes on the Hamgyŏng border, but the Koreans were uniformly successful.

A break in the established tradition of the Yi dynasty occurred in 1494, when a prince who was primarily interested in dancing girls came to the throne. This would probably have been tolerated if he had not taken to killing off the officials who were more concerned with the welfare of the country. At last, in 1506, he was banished to the island of Kyodong which lies west of Kanghwa.

His successor was Chŏng-jong who, in a thirty-eight-year reign, brought Korea to what was perhaps the highest point of culture in its history. The major political event was an uprising of the Japanese settlers in the south. There seems to have been considerable justification for their action, as the Korean prefects of the districts had been oppressing them. In any event, the attack of retaliation which they instigated from Tsushima resulted in the thorough defeat of the Japanese force in 1512. Because of this affair, diplomatic relations practically ceased until 1572, although trade was begun again in 1548.

When Chŏng-jong died in 1544, his son and successor carried out his mourning to such an extreme that he might be said to have died of grief within a year. This was the apogee of the period of strictest Confucian morality and some reaction might be expected. The change was conditioned by the fact that the queen mother became regent and fell under the influence of monks. Buddhism had practically ceased as a political influence during the previous reign and made but slight gains before the regency ended in 1554 when the new king became twenty-one.

During the following thirty years there was some fighting with Japanese pirates, who met with one of their greatest defeats in Chŏlla Province in 1556. Official relations with Japan, however, were re-established in 1572 at the request of the latter country. The Japanese were again given the privilege of residing in Korea, but only at Pusan. As usual, tribes from across the border were driven off but the army had been allowed to become weak. Conscription, introduced in 1553, was a sign of lowered morale and probably contributed to it at the same time. Most important, there seemed to be little need for the military and consequently little opportunity for prestige in that profession under the Confucian values. Politically, the most significant development was the formation of a party system, really an organization of four cliques, each gathered around a group of great families which, as they developed, were to plague the Yi dynasty until its fall.

We now come to a decade in Korean history which, next to the invasion of the Mongols, was the most devastating its people have known. As is from time to time the case in practically all countries, a man whose abilities were almost equal to his insatiable lust for conquest now came to power in Japan. This was Hideyoshi, whose military leadership had enabled him to become Shogun. He knew that without continued war his great army would disintegrate and, blinded by conceit and ignorance, was intent on ruling the world which for him was symbolically China. In 1587, he asked that Korean envoys be sent to him but the king refused. The cultured Koreans were accustomed to receive ambassadors, not to supply them on demand. A second request was answered by agreeing to do so if Hideyoshi would capture and send back some Korean renegades who had been leading Japanese pirates on their raiding expeditions. This Hideyoshi did, at the same time excusing his government of responsibility for their actions, whereupon the king received the envoy who presented him with the first musket to reach Korea. Three Koreans were sent to Japan in 1590 where they spent a year ineffectively. They returned with a Japanese bearing a message from Hideyoshi, asking Korea to join with Japan in an attack on China. The Korean court was shocked by such a proposal. The Ming rulers had not been aggressive, but, rather had contributed the best of Chinese culture to Korea and even the people venerated the greatness of the Middle Kingdom. The Korean king not only refused but also admonished Hideyoshi for harboring such an idea. This was all the latter needed to conclude his final preparations for the invasion of the Peninsula.

In the spring of 1592, the great army of the Japanese landed in Pusan from thousands of boats. The Korean garrison fought hopelessly to the last man. Hesitating hardly at all, the two attacking generals, Kato and Konishi, started a race up the several roads to Seoul. Resistance was practically nonexistent. The Koreans were unprepared and frightened by the new weapons which the Japanese had recently learned how to make from the European traders at Nagasaki. The natives were also scared by the hideous war masks worn by the invaders. The combination proved too much for their courage and they fled.

The Korean king, hearing of the turn of affairs, dashed madly to Songdo. Konishi raced up the road from Taegu and occupied Seoul only eighteen days after arriving on the Peninsula. Kato was on his heels, having taken a longer road. There they rested, which was perhaps a necessity, but it gave some time to the Koreans to reorganize. The king retreated in fear to P'yŏngyang. He was in a desperate state of mind and could not decide whether to escape across the Yalu or go to Hamgyŏng, but finally chose the latter. His lack of strength in this crucial period was unfortunate for his people who needed leadership.

The Korean generals took advantage of the Japanese relaxation in Seoul by preparing to stop the invasion at the Imjin River, between Songdo and the capital. The invaders had no boats but cleverly tricked the Koreans into pursuing them across the river, then turned on them and gained possession of the means of crossing. A similar attack brought the Japanese safely across the Taedong when the Koreans, more foolhardy than thoughtful, forded the river and then in defeat indicated the crossing in their rush to escape. P'yŏngyang fell into Japanese hands with little effort.

The war was not wholly one-sided, however. The great Admiral Yi Sun-sin sailed against the reinforcing fleets of the Japanese and destroyed them. Hideyoshi's dream of conquering China was actually smashed by those brilliant victories. Also, the Koreans were turning to guerrilla warfare and administered severe setbacks to the Japanese, particularly in Chŏlla Province.

The Korean king begged aid of China but help was slow in coming. The Ming emperor was inclined to be disinterested. When he finally sent troops, they were defeated at P'yŏngyang. This spurred the Ming to action and a great army was assembled. But instead of attacking, a long truce was made while envoys were sent to the Ming court. In the meantime, the Korean guerrillas had made the whole country unsafe for the Japanese outside the cities, and their supplies were dwindling. The Koreans even attacked Kyŏngju, using newly invented mortars. Their methods were so effective that it has been suggested, and probably correctly, that the Koreans would ultimately have profited more if the Chinese troops had not supported them at all.

At the end of the year, however, Chinese and Koreans attacked in the north, surrounding P'yŏngyang. From this predicament the Japanese were allowed to escape, apparently by bribing the Chinese. Falling back on Seoul they decided to defend that capital and, in order to safeguard themselves from treason, butchered a large part of the populace. Seoul was brought under siege a few months after the Japanese evacuated P'yŏngyang, the Koreans having contrived to build a suspension bridge over the half-frozen Imjin River. The invaders again apparently bought their escape, moving south with sufficient leisure to violate one of the royal tombs on the way. Before the end of 1593, the Japanese were pocketed in the south and the king had returned to his capital.

For four years an informal truce was observed. Some of the Japanese left the army and married Korean women. Konishi returned to Japan in 1596, to explain things to Hideyoshi. Also during this period, trickery and jealousy caused the reduction of Admiral Yi to the ranks, while military action seems to have been frustrated by the presence of the Chinese and a weak court. Hideyoshi was angered by the state of affairs and, after killing the Chinese ambassadors who came to arrange peace, proceeded on a second invasion at the beginning of the year 1597.

This threat aroused the Koreans, who again sent for aid from China and reinstated Admiral Yi, but unfortunately too late for him to prevent the landing of another Japanese fleet, half the size of the first. This time the campaign was not so easy for the invaders. Although they won a victory at Namwŏn in southern Chŏlla, they were turned back a few miles from Seoul where they were faced with a great Chinese army sent by the Ming emperor, still smarting from the treatment of his ambassadors. Retiring, the Japanese moved south through Kyŏngsang Province, where they committed one of the greatest evils with which posterity can charge them by burning Kyŏngju, the ancient capital of the Silla Kingdom. Embittered by defeat, Hideyoshi had ordered his army to cut off the ears and noses of all Koreans killed or captured. These trophies were pickled and sent to Japan, where they were built into a great mound near Kyoto.

The year 1598 found the Japanese bottled up in the fortress of Ulsan and Hideyoshi died. Once more, the invaders seemed to have bribed their way out and were able to set sail for home. This time Admiral Yi was waiting for vengeance, and although he himself was killed in the engagement, it was not before he had brought disaster to the Japanese fleet.

The recovery from the destructive invasion of the Japanese was slow. The principal cities of Korea had been occupied and many of them had been burned as well as looted. The large Chinese armies were a burden to the country although, when the last of them were to be withdrawn, at the king's request eight thousand were left to guard the southern provinces.

Within ten years of the end of the invasion, having had a change in rulers, the Japanese were attempting to re-establish relations with Korea on a friendly basis. A mission was sent from Korea which accomplished the return of some three thousand Korean captives. There were countless others, however, who were not repatriated and became, with the treasure of Korea's ancient capitals, part of the heritage of Japan. By 1609, negotiations had progressed to the point that Pusan was again officially opened to Japanese trade.

Internally, the Peninsula was suffering from the shock of Hideyoshi's invasions. Although we find the Korean army capable of turning back the wild tribes on the border of Hamgyŏng, as it had so often done before, the political situation in the capital was in bad hands. The ruler did not stop at murder to secure himself, and the selling of official positions was introduced as a means of gaining income for the court. In 1622, there was a revolt and the king deposed, but other uprisings followed, which if they did not succeed, hardly contributed to the stability of the country. Some reforms were accomplished, of which the most notable was the recognition of concubines' sons as candidates for government offices.

If the Koreans might have restored distinction to the dynasty in the first half of the seventeenth century, circumstances beyond their control impeded the chance. To the north, the star of the Manchu was on the rise and the power of their arms was threatening China. In 1619, the Ming emperor had asked for help and a Korean army had been sent against the Northerners, only to be defeated. The Manchu leader seemed to understand the obligation of the Koreans toward the Ming dynasty, which had overburdened its strength by sending great forces into the Peninsula to rid it of the Japanese. Korean renegades plotted to make the Manchu invade the country, however, and in 1627 they did so.

The people suffered terribly, as the Manchu troops were hardly less ruthless than their Mongol allies who were with them. The king fled to Kanghwa where he was forced to make a treaty. All things considered, the situation would have been bettered if the Korean leaders could have brought themselves to recognize the inevitable course of Manchu success. They could not however, and their tremendous respect for the Ming, together with their almost snobbish contempt for the relatively uncultured Manchu, left them psychologically incapacitated for any acceptable relationship with the latter. They could not contain their disgust for the conquerors and even went so far as to ill-treat their ambassadors.

In 1626, the Koreans had completed a great wall around Namhan, the ancient Paekche capital seventeen miles southeast of Seoul, and for two years after the Manchu invasion they continued to develop defensive measures, establishing a naval base on Kyodong Island west of Kanghwa. This policy annoyed the Manchu, who would not tolerate a potential threat from the rear. Crossing the Yalu in 1636, they reached Seoul before the king had been given sufficient warning to escape to Kanghwa. He, therefore, undertook to defend Namhan, which the Manchu besieged, ravishing the country in the meantime. The Koreans held out for weeks, but after their food supplies had come to an end and the Manchu had captured the crown prince and other members of the ruling family on Kanghwa, they capitulated. Save for two members who were sacrificed as symbols of Korean obstinacy in favoring the Ming dynasty, the court suffered little in the way of physical abuse. The Manchu sovereignty was admitted and the troops departed, leaving a broken and miserable population wherever they had been. The Manchu established themselves in the Chinese capital in 1644 and the embittered Korean king whose opposition had cost his country so much survived only five years longer.

One of the principal results of the three great invasions by Mongols, Japanese, and Manchu was to turn the natural isolation of a peninsular nation into a positive political policy. Korea had suffered enough from the hands of outsiders and wanted no more of them. In a world which was advancing culturally by leaps and bounds, isolationism was particularly unfortunate when there was little strength of leadership within the country. The Yi dynasty, which like others began with strength, was weakening. The people were forgotten and the court corrupted by quarrels over succession and personal power. For seventy-five years the country was plagued with famines, revolts, and political dissension before a strong king came to the throne.

During this period we might note several occurrences of interest. In 1653, a group of Dutch sailors on a ship bound for Nagasaki was wrecked on Cheju Island. Except for a Christian priest with the Japanese army of Konishi, himself a convert, these were the first Europeans of record to live in Korea and return to their native land. One of them, Hendrik Hamel, has provided us with an interesting account of his thirteen-year captivity, a sojourn, however, which hardly proved profitable to anyone at the time.[5]

After the Korean king died in 1659, the political cliques which have been mentioned as having been formed previous to the Japanese invasion were reconstituted into four groups, the Namin, Soron, Noron, and Sŏbuk. The struggles in which they engaged to gain power added to the confusion of the period and to the weakness of the rulers. In 1684, there was an uprising of the people resulting from fear of another invasion which had been falsely rumored. Rougher elements, known as the "knife gang," took as their avowed purposes the killing of noblemen, the violation of women, and the stealing of personal property. Whatever else may be said of such activities, the dissatisfaction of the people with the government appears obvious. Another reflection of the insecurity of the times was the construction in 1711 of the mountain fortress of Pukhan behind the capital city of Seoul.

A period of improvement was brought about by King Yŏng-jong, who ruled from 1724 to 1777. Although he came to the throne under somewhat dubious circumstances and years later killed his own son, the crown prince, by sealing him into a coffin, his reign was characterized by many reforms. Also, during his reign the Noron political party came so firmly into power that it was never relinquished while the Yi dynasty lasted. This caused revolts by the Soron group which were firmly put down. In 1767, a census was taken which showed a population of a little over seven million and an increase of eight hundred thousand since the census of 1657.* One of the results concomitant with the rise in numbers of people was the increase in periods of famine following years of poor harvest. The most extraordinary act of King Yŏng-jong occurred when, as an old man of eighty-nine, he issued a proclamation formally protecting the lower class against serfdom under the nobles. This move, which took place about 1773, met with little opposition because it opposed the practice rather than the theory of class relations under the Confucian system.

The introduction of Christianity, beginning about 1776 through contacts of the Korean Embassy at the Chinese court, was destined to have considerable political significance. Within ten years of the first conversions, action against those accepting the new faith was undertaken by proclamation, but it was not until 1791 that punishments were invoked. The opposition to Christianity came largely from a general fear of foreign influence as well as from the seeming intolerance of a religion which, not content with asserting its own values, attacked the age-old Confucian ceremonies showing respect for one's ancestors.

The political history of Korea in the nineteenth century is essentially that of reaction to the pressure of modern nations, first resistance to any encroachment on her isolation, then dissension over how much contact should be allowed and with whom. Ignorance of the world, the penalty of protecting a culture behind an iron curtain, proved the downfall of Korea's diplomacy in the struggle for international recognition. The last kings of the Yi dynasty were not strong characters and, much of the time, control was vested in regent mothers or uncles and was fought for by queens. Graft and corruption permeated the whole political system, while torture and murder were commonplace methods of securing an advantage. Famine and

* According to Lee, 1936:40-41, the census was first taken in Korea in 1404. He provides us with the data for the following table.

Year	Households	Population
1404	174,132	360,929
1648	441,321	1,531,401
1678	1,342,428	5,246,972
1717	1,560,561	6,846,568
1757	1,773,289	7,304,232
1807	1,775,404	7,566,406
1852	1,588,870	6,918,826
1904	1,420,299	5,665,128

cholera periodically scourged the land and once, during the first half of the century, for nine successive years. The people of the villages suffered to the point of revolt.

In the year 1796, the British warship *Providence* under Captain W. R. Broughton touched at Pusan, and in 1816 Captain Basil Hall commanding the *Lyra,* together with Captain Murray Maxwell of the *Alceste,* visited the west coast making overtures for the opening of trade, but without result. The Reverend Charles Gutzlaff, traveling on board the British East India Company's *Lord Amherst,* also made periodic contacts with Koreans on the coast of Chŏlla Province during July and August, 1832, offering gifts of religious literature, potatoes, and various other items.[6] Shortly afterwards, three French priests entered the country in disguise but all were executed in 1839 after refusing to leave. Eight years later, however, when two French gunboats were wrecked on the Korean coast, the crews were well treated and assisted to leave the Peninsula. The Koreans simply wanted to have nothing to do with foreigners and referred all representatives to the Chinese court as a means of avoiding them. Consequently, when Peking fell to the French and British in 1860, the shock was terrific and the Korean court was in a state of mind which would have made a rapprochement possible. The European powers were otherwise occupied and the opportunity passed. It was in this year, however, that China gave Russia full title to the Ussuri Province which includes the Pacific coast north of Korea with about eleven miles of boundary along the Tumen River.

One reaction to the awareness of foreigners and their proselytizing was the rise in 1864 of a Messianic religious cult in Kyŏngsang Province, known as the Tonghak or Eastern Sect in contrast to the Western Sect, a name given to the Roman Catholics. This group, which was highly chauvinistic, stirred up the conservative Confucian court as much as did the Christians and although it was savagely repressed, it survived to affect significantly political action during the remainder of the century. It was the same year that the king died after a fourteen-year reign. The dowager queen, by quick action, managed to put a prince of her own choice on the throne. Her influence was superseded within a year by the new king's father, Prince Tae-wŏn, one of the dominant characters of the Yi dynasty. Whatever his strength, time proved that he made three errors of judgment. These were his opposition to establishing relations with foreign coun-

tries, his utter antagonism to Christianity, and his choosing as a wife
for his son a woman who had the ability to become his most successful
opponent.

The year 1866 is an extraordinary one for Korea. Up until that
time, contact with Europeans had been sporadic. Suddenly, the ships
of many nations began to anchor on her coasts, each trying to establish relations with the Koreans on one basis or another. But all were
refused, with various results. First a Russian gunboat visited Wŏnsan on the east coast and asked that trade be allowed between the
two countries. The matter was disposed of at Seoul by replying
that the request would have to be referred to Peking. The Russians
went away. Shortly afterwards, nine of the twelve European priests
of the Catholic church who had been proselytizing secretly in the
country were put to death in an attempt to stamp out foreign influence. During the summer, however, an American sailing vessel was
wrecked on the coast of Hwanghae Province and the crew was well
treated, being aided to reach China, a fact which shows that the
Koreans were quite willing to distinguish accidental visitors from
those they regarded as intruders. A second American ship, the
General Sherman, with a company of adventurers set on trade or
plunder, forced their craft up the flooded Taedong River near P'yŏngyang, where it grounded. This caused a local reaction and all were
killed. The same summer, Ernest Oppert, an American citizen sailing under the flag of the North German Confederation, visited the
coast. Because of his attempt to rob a royal tomb in the following
year, avowedly to force the court to come to terms with the outside
world, Oppert became the *bête noire* of most of the historical accounts
of the period written in English.

Of most significance was the punitive and unauthorized expedition of the French fleet which came from Shanghai under Admiral
Roze because of the killing of the priests. The French took their
boats up the Han River to Seoul, throwing the court into a severe
fright. Instead of taking advantage of their position, the French
sailed away. The Koreans immediately prepared to repel any repetition of such an event and when larger elements of the French fleet
arrived, the conflict was restricted to Kanghwa. The French captured the principal town with little effort, looting it of its treasures.
Then they made the mistake of attempting to storm the fortress
monastery of Chŏndung Sa, eleven miles to the south, with only

eighty men. Their defeat was a stinging one, so the French burned the capital of the island in revenge and departed.

Nothing could have injured the prestige of western nations more than the conduct of Admiral Roze. The Koreans regarded the whole affair as proof of their strength against the outside world, and in retaliation for the French actions, increased the persecution against the native Christians. Three months after the French expedition, an American naval vessel anchored off the coast of Hwanghae Province to inquire into the destruction of the *General Sherman* and the death of those aboard her. As was usual, the Korean officials told the foreigners to go away, which advice was followed for lack of other alternatives within the scope of their orders. Another naval vessel on the same mission reached the mouth of the Taedong River but, after doing a little surveying and receiving the local account of the *General Sherman* tragedy, it also departed without causing any further disturbance.

The third American expedition took place in the spring of 1871, in a squadron of small naval vessels. Wholly unequipped by training or personality to conduct negotiations in the time-consuming manner of the Korean court, the commander sent a survey boat up the estuary of the Han River which separates Kanghwa from the mainland. As might be expected, the boat was fired upon. The consequence was a punitive expedition which resulted in the capture of five forts and the death of hundreds of people, among whom were three Americans. The squadron then departed, having accomplished no more than the French. Although the Americans were not repulsed, as the French had been, they left an impression that did not enhance the Korean's respect for either the westerner's strength or his wisdom.

The Japanese, having a more realistic approach to the Korean situation, sent an envoy named Hanabusa to the Korean court about the beginning of 1872. By personal skill he ingratiated himself with the queen who had been gaining power since the recent coming of age of her spouse, but his main goal of establishing regular diplomatic relations was frustrated by the regent, Prince Tae-wŏn. When in the early fall of 1875 a Japanese survey party was mistaken for French or Americans and was fired upon at the mouth of the Han River, the Japanese made an issue of the matter, and returned with a military force at the beginning of 1876. The faction in Japan favor-

29. GROUP OF CARP BY CHO SŎK-CHIN (1853-1920)

30. STONE CAVE SHRINE (SŎKKULAM) BUILT IN 752 A.D. ON T'O HAM MOUNTAIN IN NORTH

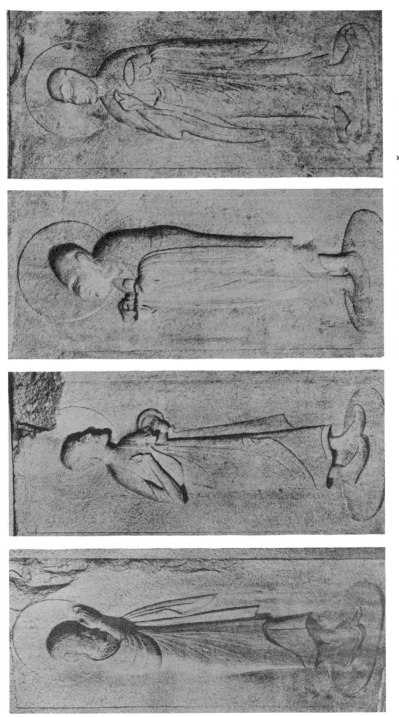

31. BUDDHIST DISCIPLES (ARHATS) IN THE STONE CAVE SHRINE (SŎKKULAM)

32. HEAD OF AVALOKITESVARA IN THE STONE CAVE SHRINE

ing peace had predominated, however, and instead of shooting, the Japanese approached matters through negotiation.

During the preceding year, the Koreans had come to some realization of the changing world. China had just opened up the neutral area across the Yalu in Manchuria to colonization and had advised the hermit nation to recognize the dangers intrinsic in her policy of isolation. Also, Hanabusa had opened the eyes of important persons to the meaning of international diplomacy. Thus, for various reasons, the Koreans gave in and on February 27, 1876, a treaty was ratified on Kanghwa Island between Korea and Japan. However, it was not until three years later that Hanabusa, as the first Japanese minister, took up residence in Seoul.

From this time on, there was always an active progressive group in the Peninsula. The year 1880 marked the end of serious persecutions of Christians, and commissions were sent to Japan and China the following year to learn what they could of world affairs.

The ex-regent Prince Tae-wŏn, who had withdrawn into semi-retirement about 1873, had been merely waiting to find a way to restore himself to power. In 1881, one conspiracy was nipped in the bud, but the following year a revolt brought about his restoration. His hated enemy, the queen, escaped only in disguise on the back of a member of the guard. The revolt was said to have been caused by the queen's relatives of the Min family, who mixed sand with the soldiers' rice to increase financial profits from feeding the army, which was being drilled by a Japanese officer. In the uprising, some Japanese were killed and Japan sent troops and a demand for indemnity. Consequent to this action, China sent about three thousand soldiers, who encamped around the capital. On orders from home, the Chinese general invited Prince Tae-wŏn, the actual ruler, aboard a Chinese ship and once there, had him carried off to China. The queen, who had been generally thought to have been killed, was then brought back to the palace and things went on about as before with the queen's family becoming more and more conservative and the progressives shifting to the Japanese.

The year 1883 was notable because treaties were ratified with the United States and, a few months later, with Germany and Great Britain. These were brought about on the advice of the Chinese statesman Li Hung-chang, who saw them as a counterbalance to Japanese influence. At the end of 1884, with the obvious connivance

of the Japanese, progressives attempted to murder one of the dominant members of the Min family and then took over the palace. The
Chinese gave military backing to the Koreans who shortly afterwards
retook the palace. During the conflict which ensued, the Japanese
legation guard fought their way out of Seoul in orderly fashion,
taking the minister and Japanese civilians with them. As was inevitable, the Japanese returned with troops and demanded an indemnity. The proceedings were not wholly unreasonable and the
Koreans promised to make restitution. Under the Tientsin agreement of April, 1885, the Chinese and Japanese both promised to
evacuate their military forces. Before the year ended Korea had also
concluded a treaty with Russia and by the spring of 1886, one with
France. Thus, in ten years, diplomatic relations had been established
with the principal nations with interests in northeast Asia.

From the opening of Korea into the world of international politics,
the history of the country becomes essentially one of struggles
between the great nations for power. The people of the Peninsula
suffered from taxes, bribery, epidemics, and warfare. Uprisings
occurred when their patience was exhausted but they had no effective
representatives at court. There is much evidence to prove that the
king and the queen were sympathetic at heart, but neither had the
personal greatness to overcome their ignorance or the whirlpool of
intrigue into which they were tossed.

In 1894, the Tonghak revolted in the south and 1,500 Chinese
troops were brought in to suppress them. This action broke an
agreement with the Japanese that neither country would send a
military force without informing the other. Consequently, the Japanese also sent troops and a war between the two nations was started
on Korean soil. On July 29, the Japanese defeated the Chinese at
Asan and on August 15, drove them north out of P'yŏngyang. Two
days later a Chinese naval squadron was badly punished near the
mouth of the Yalu River. The war continued on Chinese territory
and ended in a Japanese victory, the latter nation gaining Formosa,
among other advantages, by the Treaty of Shimonoseki in 1895.

At the very beginning of the war, the Japanese had taken the
palace, whose occupants had been under Chinese influence. Reforms
were insisted upon which seemed only reasonable from the point of
view of general world standards. The Japanese promised to safeguard Korea's independence. Inouye, the Japanese representative,

was a reasonable man and the troops were as well behaved as could be expected. Another rising of the Tonghak was effectively suppressed.

Unfortunately, the success of the war shifted strength in Japan to the militant party which had less tolerance for the slow course of educating Korean officialdom, and Miura was sent to replace Inouye. This man lost all the advantages his country had gained in Korea by directing a revolt against the palace, during which the queen was intentionally killed. For this act Miura was tried at Hiroshima with his subordinates. Although he was not convicted for the actual murder, it was clear that he had overstepped his authority.

Following the murder of his queen, the king was practically a prisoner in his palace for four months. Then he escaped to the protection of the Russian embassy, where he lived for a year until a new palace had been built for him. This move inevitably shifted the major influence from Japan to Russia. The conduct of Waeber, the Russian minister, during this period was exemplary but, as so often happens with success, the nation holding power became aggressive. Russia recalled her admirable representative and started on a policy which, as with China, was certain to lead to war.

For a period of about seven years events moved on without major conflict and with many local improvements, if but minor in character. In 1896, an Independence Club was formed which for a brief period became the voice of the people. The next year, the Korean king became emperor in a move to equalize Korea's position between the three great powers surrounding her. Foreign interest expanded, the Americans gaining some economic advantages as well as conducting one of the most successful undertakings in the history of Christian missions, while the Russians and Japanese sparred for political dominance. Japan's proceedings were defensively cautious but when the Russians began operating a timber concession south of the Yalu in a highhanded manner, the competition between the two became inflamed.

In February, 1904, Japan declared war on Russia. Except for an engagement of naval vessels near Chemulpo (Inch'ŏn) and some minor engagements on the east coast and near the Yalu River, the decisive battles were fought outside Korean territory. Korea, her independence guaranteed, as it was so many times before, was forced into the position of being Japan's ally.

As she had been in her war against China, Japan was the victor. In the flush of military success, again she lost her toleration in dealing with Korea. In 1905, the Peninsula was obliged to accept Ito as resident-general and the end of independence was near at hand. Two years later, the king was forced to abdicate in favor of his son, an act which stirred up a patriotic revolt among the people. But there was no turning back. With diplomatic acceptance of the accomplished fact, England and the United States acknowledged Japan's intention to incorporate Korea within her empire, which was done on August 10, 1910. Thus fell the Yi dynasty, after a rule of five hundred and eighteen years.

That it is wrong for one nation to take freedom away from another seems to be unquestioned in the minds of those who respect liberty and the self-determination of peoples. If the Koreans did lag behind other nations in the cultural developments of the past century, it is not evident that they have gained more under the Japanese than they would have if the nations which had guaranteed to respect the freedom of Korea had done so. Change is often a painful process and though the Koreans have suffered, the Japanese period did not prove wholly without benefits.

The policy of expansion undertaken by Japan was not satisfied by her annexation of Korea, and led to a chain of events resulting in the attack on the United States in 1941, thus commencing a war which was to bring crushing defeat to the island empire for the first time in her history. In 1945, the first atomic bomb fell on Hiroshima—where Miura had gone unconvicted of the murder of a Korean queen. Then on August 15 came Japan's surrender followed by the occupation of Korea by the forces of the United States and the Soviet Union, splitting the country into two areas of control at the thirty-eighth parallel. We will return to these events after considering the historical development of Korean culture.

REFERENCES TO SOURCES FOR PART THREE

[1] Slawik, 1933:5-6.

[2] Slawik, 1933:6.

[3] For an illuminating account of Korea's political relationship to China, see Nelson, 1945.

[4] Slawik, 1933:6.

[5] Hamel, 1918.

[6] Broughton, 1804:322-65, 379, 390, 393; McLeod, 1817:38-47; Hall, 1818:1-57; Griffis, 1894:354, 359.

Part Four

A RÉSUMÉ OF THE CULTURAL HISTORY OF KOREA

12

THE EARLY CULTURES

IF ONE IS to give depth to an understanding of the culture of a nation, it is necessary to seek out the data which will reveal how the ancestors of the people lived from the earliest times. Then, by considering the changes which have taken place from century to century as a result both of internal developments and of borrowings through outside contacts, we can estimate the age and meaning of particular traits. One thereby avoids the naïveté of attributing equal importance to features which are observable in a society at a given time, for it seems generally true that what is old in a culture bears a psychological value often too deeply imbedded in the entire national character to strike one as obvious.

We can begin with a survey of the cultural information on Korea before the end of the Ki-ja dynasty in B.C. 193, realizing that such data must be regarded with the proper skepticism due any accounts of venerable age. Then we can present the customs of the various groups living in the Korean Peninsula around the first century B.C. In several areas, the culture had reached a distinctly higher level than would characterize the region as a whole, and it may be profitable to take up these localized developments individually, following with commentaries on the less civilized tribes. Although they perhaps refer to a slightly later date, some of the records of people who lived just beyond the borders of the Tumen and Yalu rivers should be included. These records are a part of the larger cultural domain of the period which, though it has since been narrowed, remains the source land of the contemporary civilization. Once having gained a view of these cultures at the time of the earliest historical records, we can follow this integration and development through the period of the Three Kingdoms up to the present day.*

* The sources of information on the cultural history of Korea embody a tremendous literature, especially when one takes cognizance of the fact that much of Korean culture stems from Chinese customs which should also be carefully examined to comprehend the total development. For this brief study of the historical culture,

The first prehistoric colonists from the north almost certainly brought with them the art of making tailored skin clothing, and continued to hunt deer to provide the material for their winter garments as well as for some of their food. Fish may have been even more important in the diet, for there are many varieties in the rivers and along the Korean coast. The new inhabitants shared the berries with the bears and kept a sharp lookout for the tigers which still occupy the less hospitable parts of the country. It is more than likely that they made their winter homes by digging a few feet into the ground and roofing the hole with sod laid on a dome of poles. We do not know for how many centuries the descendants of these pioneers sat around their pine branch fires, working with implements of wood and stone, without any appreciable change in their way of life. In technical achievements, probably a thousand of their years would seem more similar than ten of ours do now.

In the story of Tan-gun there is the intimation that agriculture was introduced into Korea more than four millennia ago. In so far as an anthropologist may judge, this is a reasonable hypothesis. Millet, a hardy grain, seems to have been cultivated in China during the early Neolithic period and could have been carried around into the mountain peninsula before kings began to rule in Babylon. Whether or not Tan-gun was a real person, indicating the earliest cultural influence from the Yellow River basin (as has been previously suggested), he has become a quasi-religious figure in Korea today, a kind of national hero whose miraculous birth is taught to school children. Although he obviously failed to repress the Koreans' fondness for drinking, dancing, and singing, as he is supposed to have done, he remains an important symbol of cultural impetus in Korean history. Clearly, that impact must have been minimal at first. It is important to remember that the Koreans speak a language as different from Chinese as is French and that the people still show conspicuous contrasts in temperament, being no more like their

considerable data have been taken from the translation of the *Tong Sa Kang Yo* (Hulbert, 1905), from the early descriptions of Korea extracted from the Chinese dynastic histories (Parker, 1890 a and b), and from the *Institutional History of Ma Tuan-lin* presented to the Mongol emperor in 1319 (Li An-che, 1948). Tribal maps prepared from the *Tung Shih Kang Mu* (*Outline History of the East*, 1915) have also been available through the assistance of Professor Li An-che. Innumerable page references to the above sources have not been made in the text. For students enjoying scholarly pursuits, a personal reading of these basic sources will be essential. However, footnote references have been included to the many and various volumes consulted for special aspects of Korean cultural history.

neighbors in this respect than the Irish are like the typical Englishman. We can believe that at first they accepted from China what seemed good, often refashioning the gift, but also sometimes violently rejecting that which was too alien to their native ways.

By the time of the Ki ja dynasty (n.c. 1122-193), the increment must have greatly increased. Many things have been attributed to Ki-ja and his followers and to do so probably became a habit among classical historians. To be dubious in certain cases is not to detract from the great significance of foreign contributions in this early period. Rice, the primary food of Koreans to this day, was one of them. Barley, the next most valuable item in their present diet, and which is said by some to have been domesticated in the Chinese province of Shantung, was also introduced, as well as the less appreciated wheat. Such grains must certainly have come from China as these basic foods would hardly have been independently domesticated in an adjoining area.

Ki-ja is supposed to have started the custom of wearing the tremendously broad-brimmed hats so distinctive of Koreans. According to the story he did this to stop the brawling among the people, on the assumption that they would hesitate to risk such a large, fragile, and costly headdress.* The recognition of the emotional make-up of the Korean national character, with its tendency toward excessive rowdyism under certain conditions, is interesting but there is about the same likelihood that the Ki-ja immigrants invented the hats as there is that Ki-ja had long lines of willows planted in P'yŏng-yang, which supposedly was his capital.

Large numbers of horses needed for the army are reported to have been bred during the early part of the Ki-ja dynasty. These animals were probably the ancestral stock of the peculiarly small and ungainly beasts for which Korea has long been known among nations of the East. Comparable in size to the Shetland pony, they are much stronger and of a temperament not unlike the Koreans themselves, who made their distinctive hats from the animal's hair.

In the eighth century, war vessels are said to have been built. One does not have a sense of Korea as a seafaring nation, and unfavorable comments on their boatbuilding are frequent, despite historical instances brilliantly demonstrating the opposite. The contra-

* Gale records a tradition that these broad-brimmed hats were first made of clay, "wide as the moon, and as fragile as an eggshell porcelain." Gale, 1924:136.

dictions in part seem to result from confusing a comparative view
with the more localized one. Japan to the east, being completely
surrounded by water, was colonized by voyagers and many of its
people have lived on the sea ever since, fishing or raiding hundreds
of miles from their native villages. The Koreans, contrariwise, are
a mainland group whose traditional ties are with the hills and river
valleys and, more indirectly, with the horse-using tribes of Manchuria. Even China had the advantage of great rivers and a long
coast with harbors facing to the open sea. Although not the greatest
sailors, the Chinese built large ships and carried on a considerable
trade with Indonesia.

The Koreans, on the other hand, came out to the sea from their
valleys and found it treacherous. The east coast has few good
harbors and the great stretches to the north have always been inhabited by the people with the least cultural advantages. They
caught enough fish near the shore and were content. On the west
coast, facing the Yellow Sea, the extreme tides of from twenty to
thirty feet make navigation a special art. From days immemorial
the Koreans must have picked fish and all sorts of edible sea life from
the tidal flats. With time, they used boats more and more and
became adept in handling small craft in the precarious water which
rushes twice daily between the countless small islands, then bores its
way many miles up the rivers only to turn and almost suck them dry.
It is unlikely that the Koreans would have developed a predilection
for sea journeys far from home, but they were masters of offshore
tidal sailing and it is not for nothing that their rulers have been
called "King of the Ten Thousand Isles."

Like Moses, Ki-ja is believed to have set up a code of laws.
Murder was to be punished in the manner by which it had been inflicted, and those who had committed theft or adultery were to be
enslaved. Following the ancient Chinese system, land was to be
divided into squares of nine equal parts, with the produce of the
center reserved for the government. Obviously the group that introduced such changes must have had a more complex political and
social life than the common people.

The first solar eclipse mentioned in Korean history was that of
B.C. 722. Most people are interested in such celestial phenomena
and the Koreans became particularly so. The impetus was certainly
given by astronomical knowledge from China but these northerners,

perhaps because of their disproportionate concern with the religious significance of such things, came to preface their traditions with such observations. It proves helpful to the historian that they did, for by listing the sequence of such events they were ultimately to provide the means for a modern calendrical correlation with their records. Clearly, China was important to the ruling group and it is stated that in B.C. 670 a mission was sent to that country.

Although Ki-ja has been charged with introducing sorcery, this would have been like carrying spice to the Moluccas. The records indicate an effort in the eighth century to curtail sorcery by which a reference is probably meant to the Shamanism dominant among the aborigines of northeast Asia and of northwest America. Sophisticated Chinese might have demanded the greater restraints of geomancy and similar divinations. For the Koreans, Shamanism is still an essence of their culture which was distilled in the subarctic night thousands of years before they even reached the Peninsula. If they were not of the people who originated the practice, it is at least unlikely that any others ever developed it to such complexity.

The greatest contribution credited to Ki-ja is writing, the prime criterion of civilization. The early date of its introduction has not been proved, but significantly related information has become available since most of the sources on early Korean history were printed. Excavations in China have supplied visible evidence, in the form of inscribed oracle bones, that writing was in use in the Yellow River area before Ki-ja was born. This discovery was not a surprise, but did change historical hypothesis to fact. It would seem most reasonable to believe that Ki-ja, the great minister, or some of his followers were familiar with the technique of utilizing these primitive Chinese characters. Therefore, if we accept the immigration to Korea we can hardly think that they forgot this priceless invention on their travels.

The real point, of course, is how much the introduction of this writing would signify. Its primary use was of a religious nature. As a practical method of communication for the people at large the characters certainly would have meant little or nothing. Quite possibly, even if writing was introduced at so early a date, the art may have been lost, only to be restored at a much later period. In any event, whenever this particular connection with China came, it established a cultural pipe line which has supplied fuel for the intel-

lectual fires of Korean thinking until this day. Undoubtedly it took
some time to build them up, but they were glowing brightly before
Caesar set foot on the English isles.

The diffusion from the Yellow River culture centers, as important
as it was, must not be overrated merely because of our greater historical knowledge of China. To do so is a common fallacy in working from the known to the unknown. Also, we have been speaking
of effects upon Korea as though they pertained to the whole country
at a certain period, when actually we should recognize limiting factors even in the northwest part. The processes of dissemination are
slow, especially if one does not lose sight of the poorest villages.

Rice, for example, is said not to have reached the larger population groups in the south of the Peninsula until the first century B.C.
and there are still sections of Korea where, for one reason or another,
people do not grow it. Slavery moved southwards about the same
time but only as a punishment for murder, meanwhile practically
dying out as a custom in the north for a few hundred years.

From this period on, we can locate our data more specifically although still without the benefit of the many archeological studies
which should ultimately illuminate the earlier centuries. We can begin with the culture of the Chinhan which, we should remember,
centered in the provinces of Kyŏngsang comprising the southeastern
quarter of the Peninsula before the rise of the Kingdom of Silla in
B.C. 57 (Fig. 15, p. 168). Agriculture, it would seem, had already
long been practiced in this area, although we have reason to believe
that rice growing was a relatively recent innovation which gave a
strong economic impetus to the rising civilization. It is stated that
mulberry trees grew plentifully and that the production of silk and
the making of cloth were commonplace activities. We know the people had horses and cattle, which were both ridden and used as beasts
of burden. Another important factor in the economics of the area was
the development of mining, which supplied various metals to neighboring peoples including the Japanese. Iron was used as a medium of
exchange, just like coins. Behavior had become formalized as is indicated by the statement that two persons meeting on a path would
step aside, each insisting that the other pass first. The behavior between the sexes was also prescribed and ceremonies accompanying
marriage and death were carefully observed. It is said that when a
corpse was to be buried, men followed it to the grave waving feathers

in the air thereby to aid the soul on its journey to the hereafter. Head flattening, a widespread deformation common to China and Manchuria, occurred among the Chinhan by placing an infant's head against a stone. Tattooing was practiced by at least some of the people of both sexes. As most of the Koreans, the Chinhan group is said to have been fond of dancing and music. Specifically mentioned in the latter connection are a harplike instrument and a metal tube which, when struck, vibrated wires stretched inside it. Finally, it may be added that the Chinhan had the reputation of being good foot soldiers.

The neighboring Pyŏnhan people are reported to have spoken the same language and to have been similar in culture to the Chinhan except that they were more severe in the punishments which they meted out. They are specifically mentioned as being tall, wearing clean clothing, tattooing their bodies and having beautiful hair. It is also recorded that the ovens in their houses were to the left of the door which, to interpret the Chinese manner of speaking, would mean to the right of the door as one looked in.

What we know of the Mahan tribes which occupied the southwest quarter of the Peninsula would lead us to believe that they were somewhat less sophisticated in their manners than were the Chinhan. Their country was divided into fifty-four valley districts, in some of which lived more than ten thousand families, while the total area contained over a hundred thousand. This would indicate a population at least four to five times the latter number, which may be an exaggeration. Each of these districts was ruled by two military leaders, one of higher rank than the other. Their earth houses were semisubterranean, like a tomb, being entered from the roof which was covered with thatch. When building these houses, young men would sometimes pull pieces of wood by means of a line fastened under the skin of the back near the shoulders, yelling to show their bravery. There were no walled towns, a development apparently limited to the northwestern part of the Peninsula.

The Mahan were agricultural and, like the Chinhan, produced silk but apparently did not value it highly. Hemp and flax are specifically mentioned. They also raised fowls with tails about five feet long, a type of bird which has survived in Japan, and it is said that they had chestnuts as large as pears. These people rode neither oxen nor horses. In personality, the Mahan people are described as fierce, speaking in a loud or vehement voice, and not bowing or using any similar gesture on meeting. Their manners accorded no distinction of address to individuals on the basis of either age or sex. Cloth robes and sandals comprised the dress and the hair was done up on top of the head. Pearls were used to decorate the ears, neck, and garments. In the southern part of their country, tattooing was common. The Mahan seem to have had little regard for either gold or silver.

Religious ceremonies were held in the early summer (5th month) and also following the harvest (10th month) at which times there were singing and dancing, rhythms being made, it is said, by treading the ground. Large amounts of intoxicating liquor were consumed on these occasions. Spirit worship was practiced, apparently under the leadership of a district religious officer who during his performance rang bells and beat on iron drums, both hung from tall poles. The Mahan likewise had special buildings (Sut'u), seemingly as a part of their religious culture, in which refugees were protected.

After the unification of the Mahan under Ki-jun and his successors, beginning in B.C. 193, the ruling group in the capital at Iksan must have reflected the higher culture of P'yŏngyang from which they came, but the impact on the populace could have been only extremely slight for a long period. As has been previously pointed out, it is essential to recognize that the culture of the courts is distinct from that of the common people.

If we now turn to the northwest we find the court culture of the Ki-ja dynasty was on an extremely sophisticated plane, as contact with China was of long standing. Although Wi-man, who overthrew Ki-jun, perhaps enjoyed less urbanity in his life of conquest, he had come from the state of Yen in the intervening region of Manchuria, still closer to China, and certainly knew of the accomplishments of the Yellow Empire. After the downfall of his grandson Ugu in B.C. 108, northwest Korea became part of the Han Empire and the viceroys of the great Wu-ti were Chinese. They were guarded by legions equipped with the best that the wealth of the East could afford. The Chinese capital in Korea was a walled city with palaces and officials of various grades. The courtiers wore skullcaps and silk garments decorated with silver and gold ornaments. Their food was richly various and their whole lives were characterized by luxury ending in extravagant funeral ceremonies for which lacquer work, silks, and precious jewelry had been accumulated in preparation. When a great man died he was buried in a tomb of wood or brick and one or more persons were generally buried with him. The tomb was covered with a mound and the grave surrounded by pine and cedar trees. From the Chinese point of view this capital, which symbolized the whole Peninsular culture, was the source of fine horses, red jade, famous pearls, blue squirrels, and beautiful women.*

Needless to say, the share of the people was small and we know less about them than we do about their neighbors who were not overshadowed by such complexities of civilization. Our records are naturally in Chinese from the hands of the literate upper class. They speak of the local Nangnang people as fierce and violent and, as always in Korea, fond of drinking and singing. They also put them down as licentious and immoral, stating that both sexes occupied a single room at night with implied opportunities for adultery which was punished, however, if discovered. This commentary, whether biased or not, indicates the ideals of behavior held by the authors.

Agriculture in the northern part of the Peninsula appears to have been limited by environmental conditions, even as it is today, and the Nangnang people are depicted as frugal in their diet. They liked clean clothes, however, and the men impressed observers by the fact that they ran much of the time when traveling. Also, when they bowed, they did so with one leg extended behind them. Thieving is said to have been common; according to the law, what was taken had to be restored twelvefold. When criminals were apprehended by the government, they were not only killed but also deprived of the privilege of burial, and their families were enslaved as well. A daughter was married in her own home, removing to her husband's family residence only after the birth of her first child. If her husband died, she became the wife of her husband's brother. The people worshipped spirits and held a special ceremony in the fall (10th month) of the year. Stars and a cave god are mentioned as among

---

* Unsurpassed archeological descriptions of some of the tombs of officials of the Chinese colony near P'yŏngyang have been published by the Japanese (e.g., Harada, 1930; Koidzumi and Sawa, 1934). Unfortunately, the effect of their police system tended to suppress historical interpretations, or at least those recognizing Korean participation in the culture. It may be well to note that the Chinese term for this colony, Lolang (Korean Nangnang and Japanese Rakuro), was also that of the whole geographic area as well as its population, which was certainly not Chinese.

their deities. Before engaging in battle, an ox was killed and examined for omens. The people were warlike, having for weapons
swords, spears, and bows and arrows. To the sophisticated courtier
or Chinese, these people seemed a tough lot and no doubt they were.
They were even accused of corrupting the Yemak and simpler tribes
beyond the immediate periphery of the culture center, a charge which
seems to echo wherever civilization spreads.

The people collectively called Yemak (Wei-Mai) by the Chinese,
and distinguished as the Ye people, or Yeguk, and Ma people, or
Maguk, in the Korean annals, occupied a territory approximately
coterminous with the present province of Kangwŏn (Fig. 14, p. 164).
The principal settlement of the Ma (Mai, Meh) was near the modern
city of Ch'unch'ŏn in the Yellow Sea drainage basin while that of the
Ye (Wei, Hwei, Hui) was at Kangnŭng on the east coast of the Peninsula. The cultural records distinguish the Ye more specifically but
it is assumed that the two groups were related and similar. The
early writers regarded them as a simple and credulous people who
were an easy prey to their neighbors. The records state that in B.C.
128 some 280,000 of these people, reacting to such attacks, followed
their tribal chief who led them to take up residence in Liaotung.
The number is probably an exaggeration. As originally known, they
were not given to fighting like the more northerly tribes which
habitually came into conflict with one another; they nevertheless
were apparently forced to defend themselves against the same pressure of expanding populations. It is noted that although they ordinarily rode their small horses, they fought on foot, a statement which
implies that fighting in chariots or on horseback had become an expected part of the art of war from the point of view of more civilized
peoples. They had spears twenty to thirty feet long carried by several
men and a distinctive bow made of paktal wood which became more
widely attributed to the Nangnang people, who copied it from them.

The Yemak were agricultural, worked oxen, and knew the use
of hemp and silk although perhaps not weaving these materials until
a later period. They have been called modest and unassuming, however, and did not show any high regard for the jewels or finery of
their richer Nangnang neighbors to whom they considered themselves
similar in language, customs, and origin. Both sexes wore garments
with folded collars and men had a silver flower decoration. To the
Chinese they sold colored skins of a spotted fish which they obtained

33. TERRACE OF PULKUK TEMPLE IN NORTH KYŎNGSANG PROVINCE

34. SARIRA STUPA AT PULKUK TEMPLE IN NORTH
KYŎNGSANG PROVINCE

35. BRONZE STATUE OF VAIROCANA-BUDDHA, PULKUK TEMPLE,
IN NORTH KYŎNGSANG PROVINCE

36. GOLD CROWN FROM KYŎNGJU, SILLA PERIOD

from the Japan Sea. Also, tribute was collected from them in the form of grass cloth, horses, and fruit. Their houses, undoubtedly simple, were abandoned on the death of an important member of the family. Of their social organization we know little except that marriage was not allowed between individuals of the same name and that certain offenses were punished by a fine of a horse or cow. They had a special ceremony in the fall (10th month) which was characterized by drinking, singing, and dancing throughout both day and night. Respect for the Tiger Spirit was a notable element of their religion and they believed they could predict periods of famine through observation of the stars.

To the north of the Yemak in what is now Hamgyŏng Province lived the Okjŏ, considered by the Chinese writers as the most remote of the wild tribes. Their list of tribute comprised sables, as well as grass cloth, fish, salt, and sea products but not horses, which, together with cattle, were said to be relatively scarce. Various cereals were grown but we may assume with greater difficulty than was encountered by any of the other groups farther south. The Okjŏ fought with spears primarily and were considered particularly vindictive. This opinion may in part have resulted from their reaction to having women of their tribe requisitioned for the eastern courts. Okjŏ girls gained a great reputation for beauty and it is still a tradition in Korea that the most attractive women come from the province of Hamgyŏng. Among the Okjŏ, girls left their homes at the age of about ten to go and live with the families of their betrothed. At the time of marriage, however, they returned to their parents and the future husbands had to pay a bride price before the marriages were consummated. At death the bodies were laid out in shallow graves and after the flesh had desiccated, the bones were collected and a secondary burial was made in a hollow tree trunk which comprised the family vault. These vaults extended up to a hundred feet in length and opened at the ends. A wood image was erected beside this vault and food set out for the spirit of the deceased.

The Malgal, a loose federation of seven tribes speaking a distinct language, lived north of the Yalu River but frequently moved into the Peninsula. They raised various grains, preferring the millets and wheat, but barley is also mentioned, besides rice for making wine. We also read of numerous vegetables and sunflowers as well. The Malgal also kept many pigs but lacked cattle and sheep, seeming to depend to a considerable degree on fishing and hunting for their sustenance. Although they had some horses, they pulled ploughs by hand; likewise, they pushed their carts instead of hitching animals to them. Their houses were excavated in banks or ridges of ground (earth dikes), the entrance being made through a thatched roof. Any location high enough to protect one's house against the rain was desirable, for the country was low and damp.

Of all the tribespeople, the Malgal were reputedly the most warlike. They were dominated by powerful chiefs who were respected and feared by their followers. In fighting they used a bow made of horn and arrows less than two feet long, the points of which were dipped in a deadly poison made during the summer (7th or 8th month). The arrows of several of the eastern Malgal tribes were stone-tipped.

Commentators consider the Malgal to be the filthiest of all the groups, largely it would seem because, at least at the time of marriage, they washed their faces with urine. The bride wore a hemp skirt and the groom dressed in a pigskin with a fur hat ornamented with a tiger or leopard tail. On the evening of marriage, the bridegroom is said to have come to the bride at her home "to hold her breasts" which may be a reference to the marriage ceremony. If a husband was informed of his wife's adultery, he might kill her, then, regretting his impetuousness, kill the informer. Most incredible to those who have recorded accounts of Malgal culture is the custom of feeding the dead bodies of their parents to the sables in the fall and winter so as to make those animals easy to catch. When parents died in the spring or summer, however, they were buried at once. The Malgal, fond of liquor in a country of brackish water, chewed up rice and then allowed it to ferment into an intoxicating drink. They also had a religious regard for mountains, showing an unusual respect by not defecating on them.

East of the Malgal lived the people variously known as the Suksin or Ŭmnu (Sushen, Eumna, Yilou). Their country extended north from that of the Okjŏ, perhaps as far as the Amur River. Our information about them refers most directly to the third century A.D. They were not numerous but they were strong and brave. Like the Malgal, these people spoke a distinct language, raised some cereals, and kept pigs. They also had cattle and horses. The story is told that in winter they sat on pieces of meat in order to thaw them, which seems reasonable, and that they then fed themselves by picking up the meat with their toes. To the statement of this somewhat extraordinary behavior, it can be added that they were the only tribe without bowls with which to eat. For the sake of some "salt," they also drank water in which charcoal ashes had been placed.

The Suksin did not sit cross-legged. These people braided their hair and wore only a breechcloth in summer. In winter, in addition to their pigskin garments which probably were not very warm, they smeared their bodies with grease as a protection from the extreme cold. The Chinese say they smelled bad.

The Suksin lived in semisubterranean houses during the colder part of the year, it being noted that the greater the rank of the owner, the deeper was the excavation.* Added to this description of their shelter are the statements that there was a common cesspool in the center of each of the houses and that in summer the people lived in trees. It is easy to understand that the writers were somewhat incredulous of such behavior and gave emphasis to their own misinterpretations of primitive customs among people of the northern regions. By analogies to similar aborigines we may infer certain explanations. First, it would be logical to believe that the more important men or chiefs of the tribe presided over the larger and more elaborate dwellings, which would consequently be more deeply excavated. It is not impossible that these were communal dance houses rather than the residences of individual families. Secondly, the reference to cesspools in what would be the normal location of the fireplace is most probably an over-accentuation of the likelihood that old people or small children urinated at the edge of the fireplace during the night, behavior not offensive in an area where the acidic quality of urine makes it valuable both for washing grease from the body and as a reagent in the tanning of skins. Finally, it is not unlikely that the people lived in the open during the summer or in temporary and rather inconspicuous shelters. Possibly they occupied tree platforms part of the time but it seems highly probable that permanent structures were built high above ground at least primarily to serve as caches or repositories for food, furs, and other materials subject to the depredations of various animals. It was these latter shelters

---

* Chinese versions of this commentary state that the Suksin were usually cave dwellers, the deeper the cave the better. The most respected families occupied caves nine ladders in depth (e.g., Parker, 1890a :173).

which most likely were referred to and not fully understood by the commentators when they said that the people lived in trees.

The Suksin were illiterate and occupied a region too mountainous for roads. They responded to the authority of numerous chiefs but lacked a centralized government or supreme ruler. They were skillful sailors, using boats to make piratical raids on the Okjŏ along the seacoast to the south. For fighting they had a bow four feet long which was as strong as a crossbow, stone-tipped arrows which had been poisoned, and also armor made of hide and bone. These items, together with sables and red jade, were their most important articles of trade.

Relations between the sexes before marriage were apparently extremely free, the Chinese describing the girls as lewd. If a man wished a girl to marry him, he put a feather in her hair and if she was content with the proposal, presents were offered formally to negotiate the marriage. Once married, the woman restricted her sexual intercourse to her husband. Punishments among these people are said to have been strict, the death penalty being meted out for such unacceptable acts as thieving. On the other hand, one's word is reported to have been as good as a contract.

The reputation of the Suksin for cruelty was enhanced by their custom of not weeping on the occasion of a parent's death, behavior which they considered unmanly. The dead person was buried on the day of his decease and a food offering of butchered pigs was piled on the coffin for the departing spirit. It is an interesting historical note that envoys of these people supposedly visited the Chinese court about a thousand years before our era but did not come again until the third century A.D.

The last group which we shall mention is the Yujin, or Nuchen, who were related to the Suksin and lived around about the headwaters of the Yalu River, between the latter people and the Malgal. The Yujin are said to have been the lowest of the tribes, being composed of individuals descended from the other groups. They raised horses, oxen, and pigs, while wild oxen, donkeys, and boars are also mentioned as plentiful. Although they probably undertook limited agriculture, like their neighbors, the Yujin are noted as deer hunters, being skillful in the art of decoying the animals which they shot with bows and arrows. They are said to have eaten the venison raw, which of course includes a possible reference to dried, frozen, or slightly broiled meat. Sometimes they drank deer milk. They used their oxen as pack animals and prepared the skins as a covering against rain. Of their houses, we only know that they were roofed with bark.

It is clear that the Yujin liked liquor for they are said to have been amused by intoxicating tame deer. When they became drunk themselves, they were apt to kill people, even their own parents. Therefore drunkards were tied up and, on becoming sober, expressed gratitude for having thus been prevented from committing murder. When not drinking, the Yujin were good-natured and brave; also they could not be frightened by death.

Their officials were named after the five and the twenty-eight stars. Taxation records were kept by notching sticks and messages sent by the same means, three notches indicating the greatest urgency in the latter case. In warfare, the Yujin fought in ranks, the spear bearers first, then those with swords and clubs, finally the bowmen. When the leader of a group of five was slain, the other four were killed; when the leader of ten died, the two leaders of five were killed; so likewise the leaders of ten when the leader of a hundred fell. However weak this tribe may have been in the time we are recording, it is not altogether surprising that it was from these Yujin that Agolt'a rose to be leader of the Golden Horde and ultimately emperor of the Chin dynasty of Manchuria (and later, China) in the year 1115.

If we summarize our data on the culture of the people of the Korean area as they are thought to have existed roughly two thousand years ago, certain conclusions may be drawn. Within the purview of economics we find that all the people were agricultural, although the amount of farming depended on the potentialities of the localized culture and environment. We also see that each group except the Malgal had cattle in various quantities while horses were even more characteristic of the area. Besides these animals, it is probably safe to assume that the people in all quarters of the Peninsula raised pigs.

The distribution of semisubterranean houses is less clearly indicated but the description of those of the Suksin and Malgal in the north and of the Mahan in the south, together with no contradictory evidence elsewhere, leads us to accept tentatively that this form of shelter was the primary one at this time. Other common aspects of culture which can be inferred include the making of grass cloth, a generalized tribal organization under the leadership of chiefs with varying degrees of authority, shamanistic spirit worship, and an unusual propensity for singing, drinking, and dancing, at least on ceremonial occasions.

Regarding the several groups from the viewpoint of cultural differences it seems obvious that the Yeguk and Maguk, the Okjŏ, the Suksin, the Yujin, and the Malgal tribes must be considered collectively as less advanced than the others. The Chinhan and Mahan had a more complex social organization and were well on the way toward developing city states, following the introduction of rice culture and slavery. It is also notable that besides hemp and flax, silk production was available as a source of material for clothing in these southern areas. Finally, as a focal center for Korea, we find the ancient urban culture of P'yŏngyang a walled city such as was unknown in the south, with subsidiary fortress towns, having long received the benefits of contact with China. How much the people of the local Nangnang countryside were actually affected is not clear but the cultural contact was probably sufficient to raise them above the level of the so-called "wild tribes" if not to make them the equal of a group like the Chinhan.

13

ECONOMIC, SOCIAL, AND RELIGIOUS CULTURE

TO REVIEW the available cultural data through the epoch
of the Three Kingdoms up to the present century will be easier
if we follow the development along particular lines such as economics,
religion, and the various arts rather than to describe the culture as a
whole according to different periods or localities.

If we turn first to the subsistence problem we find little to be added
to what we have already learned as far as specific foods are concerned
except that Ma Tuan-lin states that by the third century A.D. the
people of Silla were familiar with and presumably used the cereals,
vegetables, meat, and fruits common to China. It was specifically
noted that cooking was carried on inside the house in winter and that
ice was used as a preservative in summer. We can note the absence
of sheep, which animals we know were introduced by the thirteenth
century but were not successfully adopted.

Although periodic shortages must always have occurred, the
populace seems to have fared comparatively well during the first few
hundred years of our times. One significant introduction, the ox
plough, appeared in Silla at the beginning of the sixth century. The
drinking of tea is said to have been sponsored in Korea as a substitute for intoxicating liquor by the first woman ruler, Queen Sŏn-dŏk
(632-647), but the plant was not grown at that time. Even in China,
from whence the leaves came, tea was still a rarity, having been introduced (or possibly reintroduced) there by a Buddhist missionary
from India in 543. As an exchange for fine Korean paper, tea seeds
were sent from the T'ang court in 828 and planted in the Chiri Mountains, southeast of Chŏnju. Hsü Ching (Sŏ Gŭng), the famous
Sung envoy to Korea in 1124, said that Korean tea was bitter to the
Chinese taste, but commented on the beauty of the Korean teapots,
some of which were small ones of blue ware, as well as on the teacups
decorated with gold and floral designs, or sometimes black. Tea remained a fashionable beverage of the rich until the seventeenth cen-

tury, when it is said almost to have disappeared from use in Korea at the time tobacco became popular.[1]*

By the beginning of the Koryŏ dynasty the demand for rice was apparently greater sometimes than the supply. In the year 985, the king ordered the erection of granaries at various places throughout the country as a method for famine relief. Shortly before he had adopted from China the ceremony of Royal Ploughing and soon afterwards ordered that metal weapons be converted into agricultural implements, as well as offering prizes for improved production. It is clear that food had become a national concern.

In the middle of the thirteenth century, we read of a dam being built on one of the islands to reclaim land and in the next century there is reference to the extension of cultivation up the slopes of the mountains. A famine in 1401 had the interesting result of bringing about an attempt to prohibit liquor in order to save grain. Although there is no indication that the proverbial Korean drinking was much curtailed, it can be reported in this connection that there was a more successful period of prohibition between 1726 and 1775 at which time, however, liquor was proscribed more on moral grounds than from a lack of rice with which to make it.

During the Japanese invasions of 1592-97, great suffering followed from the lack of food production but within fifty years the situation had reversed itself and Korea was enjoying a period of plenty. It is from approximately this date that we find a conflict between the extension of cultivation and the preservation of adjacent forest land serving as the source of fuel. Apparently from ancient times the Koreans have used the lower branches of pine trees and the underlying grasses to supply their fires for cooking and heating. Until this day, food and fuel remain the crux of the local economic situation. In the middle of the eighteenth century, police were used to guard the fuel supply around the capital and during recent decades the patrol has been widely extended together with considerable effort toward reforestation.

Tobacco was brought into Korea from Japan at the beginning of the seventeenth century and about 1650 we find an attempt to introduce the growing of cotton into Hamgyŏng Province, the desire being expressed that its cultivation be extended over the entire kingdom. Cotton had certainly first come into Korea long before this period,

* The references to sources for Part Four will be found on pages 273-74.

but the date is not known.   One report is that it was introduced from China at the end of the Koryŏ dynasty, along with the spinning jenny and the wool beater, but even the fourteenth century seems much too late.   It is pertinent that cotton is said to have reached Japan around the year 800.[2]

The food supply appears to have grown problematical toward the end of the seventeenth century.   The annual custom of royal prayers for successful crops was inaugurated about 1680 and some fifty years later we find reservoirs for irrigation water being built, as well as granaries in the east coast region.   These developments, together with the establishment of a government Bureau of Agriculture in 1733, indicate the increased concern with the food supply.   Once again, in 1814, we read of a severe famine and the country was plagued with epidemics and shortages for some years.   Under the Japanese rule great advances were made in agricultural practices until for a period in the second quarter of the twentieth century Korea became one of the great rice exporting countries of the world.

The earliest depiction of Korean dress comes from the tomb paintings of the Koguryŏ dynasty in the sixth century.   There we see both men and women wearing jacket coats reaching a little below the hips, with a decorated neckband which continued down the front openings as a border and encircled the bottom.   Complementary bands occurred at the ends of the sleeves.   The men had full trousers and apparently cloth shoes, while the women wore pleated skirts reaching to the ground.   A man is shown with a small close-fitting cap with a feather stuck up on each side, while a woman wears a bandeau around the hair.   Such costumes are obviously those of the upper class and probably much more elaborate than the usual dress of the common people, about which we lack information (Pl. 24, p. 175).[3]

At later periods we find Korean clothing greatly influenced by China.   Ma Tuan-lin states that the dress of the T'ang dynasty was adopted in Silla in 624.   Hsü Ching reports in 1124 that when women traveled they were veiled to the feet in a black gauze mantle, outside of which they wore a hat.[4]   Mongol styles were introduced into the Koryŏ court in the thirteenth century but not without resistance, and it is unlikely that the people were much affected.   Also the comment that women and men, including monks, adopted the same costume about 1370 is corroborated by the fact that women's skirts were ordered shortened in the latter half of the fifteenth century in order to distinguish them from men's. Probably the greatest impact for stylistic change came from the Ming dynasty soon after it came to power in the fourteenth century. The Koreans welcomed the overthrow of the Mongols and, finding revered China once again supreme, the court quickly copied its great neighbor and the style spread among the people. It is commonly stated that the pattern then set continued into the present century, not being discarded under the Manchu invasions, as was the case in China itself. According to the *Mun Hon Pi Go,* or Korean Encyclopedia, the distinctive headband worn by men was unknown until about 1380, when a Chinese Taoist priest introduced it. Nonetheless, it would seem that some sort of headband must have been worn with the topknot hairdress adopted at a much earlier time.[5] Pride in hats, presumably the distinctive black horsehair headdress of the men, is mentioned at the same period. Between 1649 and 1660, hat brims were made narrower and the crowns lower until in the latter year the size was set by royal edict. The crown was to be nine inches high with a six-inch opening and the brim nine inches wide all around making a total diameter of two feet.[6] In the sixteenth century, class distinctions in clothing were enforced, the common people being forbidden to wear the full flowing sleeves which were finally banned altogether in 1895 as a part of the effort to modernize the country.

The white color most frequently seen in adult Korean costumes was apparently taken from China, for it is written that emissaries going there in B.C. 710 dressed purposefully in the white clothes of that country, thus indicating that the Koreans themselves did not do so ordinarily. By the third century A.D., however, the official costume had become white in Silla and the use of that color apparently spread among the people up to the time of the Mongol invasions. It should be mentioned that the color referred to was not necessarily limited to the pure white of modern sheetings but probably included shades varying from that of unbleached hempen cloth to sky blue, such as appears in the tomb paintings of the sixth century.

During the Mongol conquest of the thirteenth century, official impetus was given to the adoption of their favorite blue-green color, and in the following century, black was substituted as fashionable. By the first half of the sixteenth century blue, black, and red are said to have predominated over white. The old white clothing probably never disappeared among the people, however, for as late as 1734 we find blue, black, and red being officially ordered as a substitute for white. By 1800 the white color had regained the prominent role it plays in the dress of Korean adults to this day.[7]

So far, we have been speaking of the most common dress color of the people. We can note that special colors were used to designate court rank as early as 517 in Silla when lavender, red, and blue formed a graded hierarchy. This system was apparently elaborated under the Koryŏ kings as we read that in 961 purple, red, deep red, and blue respectively represented positions of descending order. In the seventeenth century, palace hats and embroidered insignia depicting such animals as the stork and tiger were characteristic of high officials (Pl. 23, p. 174). Blue, the color of the east from the Chinese viewpoint, was worn in a very pale tint for ancestral worship while red served to designate a scholar who had passed the national examinations. It should be noted that, as in China, white is the Korean color of mourning.

Of clothing materials, grass (hemp) cloth and skins seem gradually to have been replaced by woven materials of silk and cotton. The production of silk cloth, apparently favored in the first millennium of our era, was periodically forbidden or at least discouraged in the second, for we find bans against it in 1036, 1743, and finally in 1889. For economic reasons, cotton goods have gradually become the outstanding clothing material.

The hair and headdress of Koreans have come in for considerable attention since the early days. In the third century it is reported by Ma Tuan-lin that the men of Silla shaved their heads but that the women had beautiful hair and used no cosmetics. Two hundred years later we read of particular headgear designating twelve ranks of Koguryŏ court officials and that scholars were marked by wearing two feathers in their hats. The tomb paintings of the following century show such a headdress as well as a woman with a patch of red on each cheek, which appears to indicate cosmetics (Pl. 24, p. 175).[8] Women apparently came to enlarge their coiffures by adding false hair, for in 1788 this practice became forbidden to all but a special class of females and those in mourning. The celebrated Korean topknot worn by men is said to have been introduced by Wi-man in B.C. 193, if not before, and survived the Manchu style of dressing the hair in a pigtail which the latter forced the Chinese to substitute for their topknot.[9] The Japanese started their campaign against this manner of fixing the hair in 1896 and continued it during the period of their ascendancy until the topknot has almost disappeared.

To conclude the data on dress, it may be said that the people of the Peninsula were referred to as cleanly by the Chinese, even in early days. The previously mentioned Sung envoy of 1124 recorded that Koreans took a bath the first thing in the morning and that in warm summer weather men and women freely bathed together twice a day in open streams, laughing at the Chinese as dirty. Apparently the Chinese in time influenced the Koreans towards greater modesty. The Korean passion for appearing in freshly washed clothes also attracted the attention of the envoy, as it has almost every observer since the beginning of western contact.[10]

Evidence on the historical development of general housing in Korea is conspicuously absent in occidental literature. The transition from the earliest forms, presumably semisubterranean, to the modern single-story thatched or tile-roofed homes probably attracted little attention from the Koreans themselves. The common system of heating through flues beneath the floor was invented, according to tradition, by the Koguryŏ people about 500 A.D. It is mentioned as though distinctive of Korea in the *Old T'ang History* (*Chiu T'ang Shu*) compiled by Liu Hsü about 934. A Korean poem written around the year 1200 also confirms the use of this method of heating.[11] Elaborate building constructions seem to have been confined to royalty and to the religious edifices of the Buddhist religion. Temples and monasteries began to spring up in the fourth century and certainly reached their apogee under the Koryŏ dynasty, from which a considerable number of examples remain. Mention should be made of the existence of dolmens, probably dating from prehistoric times, and of the elaborate tomb mounds constructed intermittently since the first century.

Other buildings of stone seem largely limited to shrines, pagodas, bridges, gates, and walls. For each category, Chinese examples were apparently the primary models. It is notable that in both the seventh and eleventh centuries walls are said to have been built across the whole northern part of the Peninsula as a defense against armies attacking from Manchuria. Elaborate walls were also built during the Koryŏ dynasty as protection for cities and fortress-monasteries. Extensive dikes and sea walls began to appear in the same period.

Among more singular customs, we find that in 1205, live children were buried under palace posts, apparently to insure guardian spirits for the newly constructed building. About 1340, a unique iron palace was built but it has not survived. Danger from fire existed in the cities, for we find that all roofs in P'yŏngyang from 1624 to 1905 could legally be constructed only of tile, thatch covering being a serious hazard. On the whole, Korean building customs probably changed less than any other aspect of the culture, up to the introduction of modern construction by the Japanese after 1885.

Developments pertaining to transportation and communication were also conservative. The use of horses, unquestionably introduced from the northwest in very early times, is distinctive in Korea because of the special breed of small size, although large horses were also used. Cheju Island became a famous place for horse raising under Mongol direction in the latter part of the fourteenth century and was long continued there if we can judge from references to horse taxes as late as 1722. Horses in Korea have been principally used for riding and as pack animals. In the fifth century a horse relay system was established in Silla. Donkeys and mules substituted at times for horses since early days and it is an interesting note that a gift of camels was refused in 942. No record of the adoption of the latter animals has been found.

Oxcarts are stated to have been introduced into Silla about 420. They may have been known earlier in Koguryŏ, but record of such a gift from the Chinese court in 499 implies rarity. An oxcart also appears in Koguryŏ tomb paintings of the sixth century.[12] Hsü Ching, the Chinese envoy, however, states that in 1124 women rode horseback when they went out, there being neither carts nor chairs even for queens to ride in (Pl. 26, p. 190).[13] Certainly oxen hitched to a two-wheeled cart are now one of the common sights of the Korean countryside. While referring to wheeled vehicles, mention should be made of the unicycle, a sort of carrying chair supported under the center by a single wheel. This contraption is said to have been invented in the second quarter of the eighteenth century and was granted as a privilege to officials of the third grade. It was probably always something of a curiosity and may have been adapted from the Chinese wheelbarrow, which does not seem to have been taken over in the Peninsula. Electric streetcars startled the capital in 1885 and the first railroad, from Seoul to Chemulpo in 1900, was followed a few years afterwards by a line from Pusan to the Manchurian border.

Ships, like horses, were used by Koreans from prehistoric days, but the Peninsular people were never great sea rovers. The Japanese and Chinese more often came to them in boats, and even the Arabs sailed into the southern ports by the seventh century or soon afterwards. Of fishing and coastal trading boats, however, the Koreans made great use. The earliest known replica of a vessel appears as a Silla pot. This ornament depicts a small craft perhaps about twenty feet long, but before the end of the eighth century warships probably four to five times that length were constructed, using a crew of three hundred men. It is said that horses could be ridden around the deck.[14] About 1060, we find the Koryŏ government building one hundred and six ships for transporting rice, and in the following century attention was given to clearing channels which impeded the coastal trade. Cloth was used for sails at least by 1124 and the Korean ambassador returning from China introduced the compass in the year 1525. Cannon were adapted to naval vessels in the reign of the last Koryŏ king and by the time of the Japanese invasion of 1592, Korea had developed the "Turtle" ship which was for that period unusually large, fast, and well protected from attack. It also belched smoke from its prow but there is doubt whether it was ironclad as tradition would have us believe. At the beginning of the fifteenth century, the Korean navy had 543 vessels, 538 about 1675, and 812 in 1744.[15] Periodically, one hears of voyages to China but except for the use of vessels in connection with invasions, little interest is recorded in maritime ventures. Like China, the nation was inclined to turn in upon itself.

Until the establishment of the first telegraph system in 1885, which connected Seoul with Peking, the fastest way to indicate danger on the borders was by means of an elaborate system of beacon fires of which there were five lines around the country, with 696 stations. By the use of eighty-six fires, a message could reach the capital from the most distant point, about 300 miles away, in less than four hours. The origin of the system was Chinese and it seems to have been utilized within Korean territory as early as the third century although not systematically adopted until 1151. It was greatly improved after the founding of the Yi dynasty in 1392 and was not discontinued until 1894.[16]

Before turning from the general subject of transportation and communication it may be worth while to make some comment on the historical trade of the Peninsula. It is clear that the continent, and China in particular, was the chief source of foreign materials, many of which were adapted to Korean production. Our information is still too limited to give more than an intimation of the early economics but something can be gleaned by noting the lists of goods demanded or given in tribute or payment to foreign countries. In the days of the Three Kingdoms it is clear that Silla was an important source of metals. Iron is perhaps the first to be mentioned but gold, silver, copper, and lead soon take precedence which they seem to have held at least until the end of the Koryŏ dynasty.* Pearls are another item of value with the fishery centered on Cheju Island. Sable and tiger skins were prized commodities, and possibly sea otter skins as well, although the earliest record available on tribute lists is in the thirteenth century, when the demand for this fur had begun to heighten the search for them. Also, horses should not be forgotten in considering trade. Grass (hemp) cloth, silk, and cotton fabrics seem to have been in demand in that order chronologically. Korean paper was recognized by the Chinese as early as the T'ang dynasty (618-907) to be superior to all others. This white, smooth, and tough paper manufactured from the bark of the mulberry tree was imported for the printing of the imperial records, and has been justly famous for over a thousand years. Curiously, it is stated that not until the K'ang Hsi period (1662-1723) did the Chinese discover how it was made.[17]

It is not inconsistent to mention beautiful girls, for they were a recognized commodity in the period of Mongol domination and apparently had been supplied in smaller numbers for centuries before. They have been increasingly difficult to obtain since the fall of the Koryŏ dynasty. Under the Yi kings, items such as mats with red flowers, dyewood, black pepper, and ginseng became valuable products for export. Since the opening of Korea to world trade, a major shift to food products has characterized the economy.

The local exchange of goods was encouraged through organized markets, which we know existed in Silla since at least the fifth cen-

* *The History of the Later Han Dynasty* (25-220 A.D.) states that the surrounding peoples traded with the Chinhan (i.e. early Silla) for the iron which the latter produced and that it was used for money. Parker, 1890b:221.

tury. Merchants were granted monopolies by the court as a source
of revenue. When the Koryŏ court was first established in Songdo
in 919, the king had large houses and shops specially built for
merchants in the center of the city. Interest on loans was formally
established at 10 per cent a month during that century.

Although iron blanks had been used as a kind of money at least as
early as the second century, true coins were not used until 996.
These were of solid iron, silver ones being minted in 1101 and the
circular copper cash with the square hole within a year of the same
date. Rice and cloth, however, remained the unit for trade in the
Koryŏ markets and metallic money had almost disappeared by the
end of the dynasty, although silver "bottle" money as well as "dollars" are mentioned just before the Mongols lost power. There was
also some unusual arrowhead money, with four characters on the two
sides of the tang, which was issued in 1464, but none is known to
have survived. Paper money was ordered printed by the first Yi
king in 1392 but became discredited when the Japanese invaded the
country in 1592. In 1651 metal money was again minted and the
use of cloth as a medium of exchange prohibited in order to establish
the money successfully. Nonetheless, coinage remained a serious
problem for the Koreans up to the period of recent Japanese subjugation.[18]

Taxes, from the earliest days, were collected largely in the form
of rice and cloth, and references to tax matters are frequent in the
histories. At times the rulers were generous, especially when famines
occurred; more frequently they taxed everything which could produce any revenue. In about 1690, the people of Songdo complained
that they even had to sell their children in order to meet the demands
made on them. Notable occurrences pertinent to taxation were the
first general levy in about 1275, called the "house linen" tax, then the
farming out of the tax collecting in 1593, and the plebiscite of 1750
in which the people voted for a house tax instead of land and poll
taxes. Most of all, however, they objected to paying more than three
or four times the legal rate, an abuse they long suffered because of
the rapacity of corrupt local officials dependent upon the system of
"squeeze."

In our survey of the political history of Korea we have seen how
the governmental organization shifted from tribes to federations of
local populations, then from small kingdoms into a unified nation

37. BRONZE MIRRORS

38. MEMORIAL STONE IN SŎN AM TEMPLE, SOUTH CHOLLA
PROVINCE

39. PAEKCHE CLAY TILE

40. GRAY JAR INCISED WITH HORSES, SILLA PERIOD

under a supreme dynastic ruler. It is clear that after the fifth century, when a formal relationship of vassalage to China was accepted by each of the Three Kingdoms, the political forms were taken more and more from the latter country and periodically adjusted to the changes developed in succeeding Chinese dynasties. Posthumous titles, the ordering of official rank, the system of provinces and prefectures, as well as many other devices were borrowed from the Middle Kingdom before 1000 A.D. Intermittently, the government became priest-ridden and quantitatively there was more ineffectiveness and abuse of power than there was able political leadership. The florescence of good government might roughly be attributed to two periods, one under the Koryŏ kings between about 950 and 1150, the other being that which began with the Yi dynasty, let us say from 1400 to 1550. After 1150, Buddhist priests, eunuchs, and debauched kings prepared for the political downfall over which the Mongols presided.

The establishment of the Yi dynasty in 1392 was a major event in Korean history. Politically, few changes have equaled the effect of the reforms of the first Yi kings. The development of feudalism was checked by the enforced disbanding of retainers gathered by the local lords. The rulers then avowed themselves to be the servants of the people and attempted to act accordingly, an exceptional political point of view for the fifteenth century and one which would make an interesting experiment in the present period. By the end of the sixteenth century, however, leadership failed and the government succumbed to clan political parties. Within a hundred years, nepotism was undermining the central government and the people were ruled locally by political appointees whose justice and consideration were autocratic and unevenly distributed through their surrogate ajŏn. The insecurity of the central political organization is indicated by the elaboration of the secret police system, dating from about 1733. The government was rotten at the core when it was pushed aside by the Japanese in the twentieth century.

Some special aspects of the social organization of the Korean government deserve at least brief attention. A conscious tradition of the value of justice is very old in the Peninsula. We will remember that a penal code is said to have been introduced by Ki-ja before B.C. 1000, and various revisions were made during the following centuries. It is clear, however, that by the middle of the first millennium of our era punishments had become various and severe, for we read that in Koguryŏ a person convicted of treason was tied to a pole, scorched, and then beheaded while his property was confiscated and his wife and children enslaved. From this period on, descriptions of tortures are frequent. The Koreans seem to have borrowed many of the techniques of China and applied them as rigorously, if with less subtlety. The list includes beatings on the soles of the feet, on the shin bones, on the calves, on the knees, on the buttocks, and on the back; tying the legs at the knees and ankles so that the bones could be broken with levers, tying the body into a tightly flexed position and rolling it about, searing with hot irons, burying to the shoulders, tearing apart by oxen, and many others. The treatment was probably no more various than that applied by Europeans and certainly less ingenious than the practices of the Catholic Inquisition. One does get the impression of a more general and continued recourse to torture than in other countries, however, which suggests deep-rooted repressions in the national character structure.

During the florescences of the Koryŏ and Yi dynasties many reforms were made in the criminal codes. Trial by three judges was introduced about 1040 and between 1400 and 1550 many attempts were made toward regularizing legal sanctions and reducing the severity of punishments. A notable move was the publication of a code of laws about 1469. Consideration for human suffering was more the exception than the rule, nonetheless, and barbaric practices continued into modern times, allowing the people little freedom from fear.

In Korea slavery stems from prehistoric times as it does in most parts of the world. Individuals, families, and sometimes larger groups were forced into servitude as the result of crime and particularly because of unsuccessful revolts against authority. Not infrequently, individuals sold themselves into slavery to escape the struggle for a secure subsistence. It is significant that the slave class was comprised almost entirely of native Koreans rather than having an out-group origin; also, and perhaps in consequence, slaves for the most part were relatively well treated.

By the end of the Silla Kingdom there were large numbers of slaves, and one of the first reforms of the Koryŏ kings was directed towards their liberation. Thousands were freed but, as was almost inevitable, complexities arose, one of which was the revolt of certain slave groups inspired by the freeing of others. This caused a conservative reaction but there was a second definite attempt towards emancipation about 987. Later in the Koryŏ period there were more uprisings and some reforms but the progressive movement had passed.

At the beginning of the Yi dynasty an old law that the grandson of a slave should be free was enforced. This right had been generally disregarded, as apparently it was again, for we find the effort to make it effective coming up in the second quarter of the eighteenth century. By this time, the slavery of adult males had greatly lessened as a result of the Japanese invasions ending in 1597. These left such a scarcity of Korean males that the slave servant economy was upset. It is notable that about 1650 all common prostitutes were converted into government slaves. Government slavery was abolished one hundred and fifty years later. Finally, the impact of the western world brought about the abolition of hereditary slavery in 1886 and under the Japanese all Koreans were freed to become equally subservient to the Mikado.

Differentiated from slavery was the system of serfdom, which had become the dominant class relationship after the sixteenth century. All commoners owed taxes and services to some local Yangpan (noble) and to a large degree were controlled in their movements. This serfdom was theoretically abolished about 1773 but the practice lasted long thereafter, and its spirit has been preserved under the alien rulers of the twentieth century.

The historical evidence on social classes is somewhat confusing. From the available data it would seem that there has long been a primary dual division of the society on the basis of a differentiation between nobles and commoners. At the opposing limits of these two basic classes, the royal families and the slaves can be distinguished. In late centuries, an intermediate or middle class built upon the advantages of education and wealth has been recognized.

Entangled with the presentation of the class problem are the special professional groups, regarded as somewhat outside the normal system because their activities are viewed as degrading in the hierarchy of Sino-Korean cultural values. Seven degraded professions, said to have been formally designated as such about 1450, are (1) servants of the sheriff who beat men, (2) buffoons or traveling singers, (3) butchers, (4) basket makers and bark peelers, (5) female sorcerers, (6) dancing girls, and (7) makers of leather shoes. Such a list more commonly includes the categories of boatmen and monks.[19]

The professions mentioned above are but a few of the many, most of which became incorporated into tightly organized guilds which have had the monopolistic privileges of trade unions. The pattern is almost certainly of Chinese origin, where individual guilds have been claimed to have been in existence since the Han dynasty (B.C. 206-220 A.D.). Probably cognate professions were organized a great deal later in Korea. For centuries members of the Peddler's Guild have been of political significance as special messengers and investigators, as well as night escorts.

The patrilineal family system may have been prehistoric but was certainly accentuated under Chinese influence at the time of the beginning of the Three Kingdoms. A date of B.C. 32 has been given for the adoption of Chinese surnames in Silla although we know that commoners had only personal names in third century Koguryŏ. Probably some hundreds of years passed before the system was thoroughly established. Women at no time shared this distinction and male dominance was strongly emphasized in the borrowing of Confucian values. A Japanese student of Korean cultural history lists 298 surnames in Korea, of which among the most common are Yi, Kim, Chang, Yun, Ch'oe, Yu (or Lui), Hong, Sim, Hwang, Cho, and Han.[20] With three exceptions (Han, Yu, and Hwang) these surname groups have broken down into exogamous clans designated by an additional name indicating the origin. There are, for example, 84 different Kim clans such as the Andong Kim, the Kimhae Kim, and so on. In a technical sense, these clans, of which there are 1,072, might properly be called sibs and the surname groups, phratries. The patrilineal family system has operated independently of the class system to the present day.

Pertinent to recognition of individuals within the family, mention should be made of name-tags. About 1425 a law was enacted requiring each adult male to carry on his person a small piece of wood bearing his name. This was done to prevent evasion of taxes and military service. The method was apparently not effective and the law was abrogated in 1469. There are references, however, to these identity tags about 1700 and they were used up to modern times.

Turning to customs relating to marriage, we find a gradual progression of formalization resulting from influences from China except during the period of Mongol dominance. In the earliest times, relations between the sexes were relatively free. Silla apparently responded to Chinese values first and Ma Tuan-lin states that in the third century only the rulers were marrying close relatives. In Koguryŏ, two hundred years later, the people were said to have been lewd and shameless, there being many unmarried women without fixed husbands as well as marriages contracted between couples as the result of love, all of which was something of a shocking state of immorality from the Chinese viewpoint. As mentioned in the po-

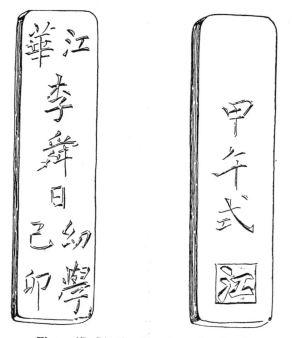

Figure 17. Identity Tag (*opposing faces*)

litical history, the Koryŏ kings established brother-sister marriage in the ruling family and after the Mongol conquest the court became dissolute relative to almost anyone's standards. Women were hardly safe from the rapacity of the courtiers anywhere, and about 1372 sodomy on the part of the king and his playmates became a public scandal.

With the establishment of the Yi dynasty, the situation changed to one of strict morality with encouragement of Chinese standards of propriety between the sexes. There were lapses, however, and in the great reforms of about 1650, the king put a stop to the practice of taking girls for the palace without their fathers' consent. He also ordered that children born of incestuous unions, formerly exposed in the streets, should be given government care and that there should be no more marriages between families of the same name. Another impetus toward formalization of interpersonal relations appears in the law forbidding the remarriage of widows, which was promulgated toward the close of the fifteenth century. This remained the ideal henceforward, if not the practice. About 1642, marriages were forbidden during the three-year period of mourning for one's parents.

A greatly accentuated regard for values connected with death and related ceremonial is clearly evidenced from early periods of the Three Kingdoms and can reasonably be attributed to the impact of Confucian doctrine. Elaborate royal tombs are characteristic of Korea, as of China, and even before the middle of the fourth century a paternal corpse was the most valuable of all hostages. Ma Tuan-lin's report on fifth century Koguryŏ tells us that the dead body was placed in a room and buried on a lucky day after three years. The three-year mourning for fathers, mothers, and husbands commenced with weeping but ended at the interment with gay gestures and dancing. Property of the deceased's family such as clothing, carts, horses, and so on were placed in front of the tomb to be taken possession of by the participants. In Silla, until 503, living persons were buried with the king. In that part of the country, we should remember as exceptional that at least some of the kings during the seventh and eighth centuries were cremated. This practice, probably resulting from Buddhistic influence, never became general outside the priesthood, as it did in Japan.

References to the extended mourning periods are frequent from the fifth century on. As early as the tenth century efforts were made to reduce the time and consequent expense which burdened the populace. Under the Mongols in 1360, so many people had been killed or driven to suicide that the period of mourning reached its shortest limit, being reduced to a few days, but it soon became extended again. The great Yi kings tried to curtail the extravagance and unreasonable practices. About 1420, massive stone tomb slabs were replaced by four cheaper ones in royal graves and geomancers all over the kingdom were forbidden to delay interments by elaborate searches for lucky ground. Some fifty years later it was ruled the graves must be placed so as not to interfere with agricultural activities. The economical viewpoint did not continue to prevail, however, for in 1575 and again in 1720, we find being introduced the custom of the whole populace undertaking mourning for royalty.

The preoccupation with death is related, in essence, to religious ideas and it may be well at this point to see what we can learn of the historical development of that aspect of culture in Korea. In recent times it has been frequently written that the Koreans have no religion, an opinion which has also been forcefully denied. It is probably safe to aver that the religious culture of the Koreans differs from that of most nations both because no one or two religions are outstandingly dominant and because there is a greater formalization of what are generally considered primitive religious elements. Certainly, however, the Korean pattern is related to those of China and Japan.

Historically, the earliest religion of Korea is spirit worship or Shamanism. Known to the people as Sinkyo, it remains the most general one to this day, even if not so apparent to those who customarily conceive of religions as belonging on a more developed plane of theology. The essentials of the belief were probably held by the people before they migrated to the Peninsula from northeast Asia, the geographic center for Shamanism. This religion postulates a universe in which not only human beings have souls or spirits, but lower animals and inanimate things have them as well. The problems of life are adjusted by having a proper relationship with the world of spirits. Each person can do this to a limited degree himself, but in cases of special difficulties one goes to an individual who has attained through religious experience an unusual intimacy with one or more spirits and is thus in a position to explain and sometimes influence the course of events.

In Korea, this religion has developed so that the dominant class of shamans are women known as mutang, although there are also other classes of which the best known are the p'ansu, a group composed of men who are blind. Taking the complex as a whole—the mutang priesthood with their supporting musicians and other assistants, the elaboration of their places of communion with the spirits into small temples sometimes artistically decorated through Buddhistic borrowings, and the subsidiary detachments of professional supporters—it seems safe to say that in no other country has Shamanism reached such a high development. On the other hand, since Shamanism stems from preliterate societies and has lacked a systematically expressed doctrine, it therefore has had little resistance to borrowing and has tended to vary in time and place, adopting superstitions, ideas, practices, and paraphernalia where it found them. Shamanism is consequently not only difficult to comprehend in and of itself but it is also difficult to isolate historically in order to make comparative studies. What appears as the obvious common origin of Shamanism and Shintoism, for example, is not easy to define. It is interesting to speculate whether or not the impact of Confucianism on primitive Shamanism was not largely responsible for the concentration of power in the female mutang whereas Japan, lacking this influence, developed primitive Shamanism into Shintoism.

Treating of the old spirit worship, Ma Tuan-lin records that in third century Silla there were religious services for mountain spirits as well as for those of the sun and moon. Sun worship did not die out, for we find reference to the Koryŏ king paying obeisance to the solar deity on Kanghwa Island in 1233. Actually the Koguryŏ and Paekche kings had, potentially, a mythological basis for claiming descent from the sun not unlike that of the Japanese Mikado.

The advent of both Confucianism and Buddhism brought about periodic official repressions of Shamanism but the latter also left its mark on both. The animal festivals reported in connection with Buddhism in the tenth century are one of the possible influences. Buddhism was tolerant, too much so for its own purity. The intelligent early Yi kings attacked religious superstitions of all faiths and we find various occasions when shamanistic practitioners were prohibited from the capital. In 1413, for example, all the practitioners of Shamanism were ordered to deliver up their books, which were then burned. Even as late as 1893, however, the Korean queen was so respectful of the mutang that she elevated one to the rank of princess, at the same time banishing a man to Cheju Island for protesting.

Confucianism comes next to Shamanism in terms of long-range influence on Korean religious life and has had an overwhelming effect on the social and political aspects of the culture.[21] Its introduction from China preceded the period of the Three Kingdoms and became stronger in Silla than in either of the other two. Its great appeal has been essentially to men, a factor which, as has been suggested, probably contributed to the predominant role assumed by women in

Shamanism.   As a state religion, its position can best be shown by a comparison with the historical progression of Buddhism in the discussion which follows.   In general, one feels that Confucianism, except for periodic pulsations, claimed a fairly even and gradually strengthening hold on Koreans from its inception to the time of European contact.

Buddhism, as the first of the great world religions, reached the Peninsula from China in the fourth century, being introduced into Koguryŏ in 372, then into Paekche about 384, and finally into Silla approximately fifty years later.   Paekche and Koguryŏ both apparently accepted Buddhism with immediate enthusiasm, two large monasteries being established in the latter kingdom within a few years. By 392, seven more had been built and Buddhism became the religion of the country by decree.

In Silla, on the other hand, the acceptance of Buddhism was slower and not until 524 did it assume a dominant role.   From that date, however, its ascendancy was rapid.   By the middle of the century the teaching of Buddhism was decreed by the ruler and it is said that he received from the emperor of the Ch'i dynasty in China as many as 1,700 religious books at one time.   The result of such enthusiasm was that the succeeding king became a monk when he took the throne in 576 and his queen became a nun.   This high-water mark for Buddhism during the era of the Three Kingdoms lasted until about 664, when the then ruling king attempted to stifle it by forbidding anyone to give the monks support.   Inevitably, the political influence of the Confucianists had been minimized but with the repression of Buddhism it began to rise, even the queen giving support at the beginning of the eighth century.   A hundred years later the building of monasteries and the manufacture of gold and silver Buddhas were prohibited.

With the political unification of Korea under the Koryŏ dynasty, the latent strength of Buddhism showed itself.   Buddhism, although under restraint, was recognized as the state religion and gradually grew in power with monks periodically dominating the rulers.   For a period from 969 to 1036, Confucianism gained the upper hand in the court, then lost it to the Buddhists who skyrocketed to control, which they held practically to the end of the dynasty.   The edicts of 1036 fired the fuse.   It was decreed that if a man had four sons one must become a monk and the death penalty was banished in deference to

the religious ban on bloodshed. Boys went along the street with open
Buddhist books on their packboards so that the priests could read
aloud as they walked behind. In 1048, the king fed and housed ten
thousand monks in the palace—or at least more than one could
readily count. A decade later he decreed that one of every three sons
must become a monk and had nails made for monastery construction
from metal intended for arms. He thus initiated the period of great
religious building. He also took many of the best lay homes and
gave them to the priests. About 1140 we read of a Buddhist ceremony at which thirty thousand monks were present.

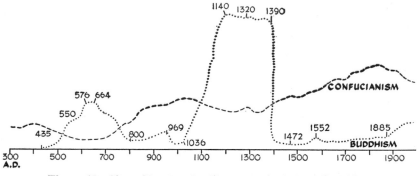

Figure 18. Chart Showing the Florescent Periods of Buddhism

After the Mongol invasion in the twelfth century, the whole country suffered and there was less wealth for priests. There was some
reaction in favor of Confucianism in the fourteenth century but
Buddhism held its sway over the rulers until the dynasty fell in 1392.

With the resurgence of Korea under the early Yi kings, backed by
the power of the newly established Ming dynasty in China, the Peninsula entered on a period of enlightenment. The Yi kings were not so
much pro-Confucianist as they were anti-Buddhist, and the power of
the latter religion crashed even more rapidly than it had risen. The
debauchery of certain court monks had reached an all-time high and
the new rulers showed their contempt for the decadence into which
Buddhism had fallen. In quick succession, laws were made prohibiting women from visiting monasteries, monks were stopped from con-
gregating to pray for rain, and land was taken from them and restored to the people.

The personal attitude of the rulers was shown in a number of instances during the florescence of the Yi dynasty. In 1406, the

Chinese emperor asked that a famous copper Buddha on Cheju Island be brought to Seoul from which place the king could forward it after the proper ceremonies, but the king refused to bow to it. When the queen mother had a Buddha built in 1489 for the monastery outside the East Gate of Seoul, an irate subject broke it to pieces. When the queen mother urged his death, the king replied that the man deserved a gift. Again about 1512, the king ordered a great copper Buddha in the ancient Silla capital of Kyŏngju broken up for the metal. The apogee of the intellectual attitude is illustrated by the Yi king who, desiring to do away with a convent about the year 1650, was faced with the objections that it served as a storehouse for royal ancestral tablets, is reported to have said, "Well, dig a hole and bury the whole lot."

Besides these personal instances of disdain toward religion we find a ban effective about 1420 on the custom of building monasteries at the graves of kings, and in the last half of that century, an edict against monks attending or praying at funerals. Antagonism reached a high point in 1472 when all monks were finally driven out of the capital and the city prohibited to them. With the exception of a few intervals, this rule seems to have remained in effect until 1895. The twenty-three convents existing in Seoul were likewise removed about 1477.

Despite these attacks, the influence of Buddhism was still strong among the people and there were intervals of royal support. One king is said to have been responsible for the erection of a standing Buddha in the capital in 1465 but it is unclear whether this form, unusual in Korea, was meant as support for the orthodox religion or the contrary. In 1552, the queen mother, who had become a devout Buddhist, was active in a reform movement. Buddhism never returned to a vigorous stage, however, although it has been liberated and helped by Japanese influence for the past fifty years. In 1947, it was estimated that there were only seven thousand monks in all of Korea. Apart from other contributions, Buddhism at its heights carried with it the greatest development of the arts in Korean history, a subject which will be reviewed in the following pages.

The next great religion to influence the Peninsula was Christianity. The first contact apparently came with the advent of Hideyoshi's armies in the invasions of 1592-97. Konishi, one of the two commanders, was a Christian as were many of his troops, and at one period both a European and a Japanese priest were ministering to them. This in itself hardly suggests much contact with Koreans but it must be remembered that a certain number of Japanese soldiers married native women and settled in the Peninsula. Also, many Koreans were kept prisoners in Japan for a long period before return-ing to their homeland. Both circumstances at least created the pos-sibility for conversions. In any event, it is certain that Christianity did not take hold at that time. Christianity, however, became popu-lar with a certain class of young Korean men who learned of it from books brought from Peking in 1603 and 1604.[22] We may note further that a Korean envoy to China in 1631 had some contact with a priest in Nanking who had been a companion of the famous Père Ricci. Korean documents also assert that foreign Roman Catholic priests, possibly Chinese, entered the Peninsula in 1686. The ex-pected confirmation seems to be lacking, however, and the report may be erroneous.

After the middle of the eighteenth century, it is said that the Christian doctrine was spreading among individuals of Hwanghae and Kangwŏn provinces, and that this brought about the censure of persons who had destroyed their ancestor tablets. About 1783, a Christian convert was baptized in Peking and returned to Seoul, giv-ing new impetus to the religion which spread southwards. Needing a priest to instruct them properly, the Koreans sent to China for one in 1791, the first year in which Koreans were killed for avowing Christianity. A Chinese priest crossed the Yalu River border with great secrecy in 1794. At that time it was estimated that there were some five hundred believers. The number rapidly increased and in 1801 persecutions began, in which the Chinese priest was decapitated. Thirty years later Korea was made a bishopric and, after much fruit-less effort, one French priest crossed the frozen Yalu in the winter of 1835, his head hidden under a large mourning hat. Two more followed by 1838, when the Christian population is said to have reached 9,000. The following year all three foreign priests were killed in an outburst of persecutions.

By 1844, two more French priests entered in disguise. At the middle of the century it was estimated that there were eleven thou-sand Christians and that this number had doubled before 1866, when they had the leadership of twelve foreigners. That fateful year saw the martyrdom of nine of these, only three escaping to China. Active persecution continued for years and thousands of converts were destroyed. It was not until 1881, the year before the first treaties with the western powers, that the persecutions were finally to end. Whatever else may be said of the first hundred years of Christianity in Korea, it was certainly a period of extraordinary martyrdom. The Roman Catholic priests chose to die rather than abandon their followers when the Korean government gave them the opportunity to do so. Their courage contributes one of the most amazing chapters in the history of missions, and the steadfastness of the Korean converts parallels the faith of the early Christians subjected to the persecutions of Roman emperors.

Two Protestant missionaries made brief visits to Korea before the country was opened to foreigners. The Reverend Charles Gutzlaff distributed religious literature in Chŏlla Province during two months in 1832, as has been previously mentioned. Also, in 1865, R. J. Thomas, serving the London Missionary Society, went to the Peninsula with some Roman Catholic Koreans returning from Shantung. He stayed on the coast for two and a half months, disposing of some copies of the Bible printed in Chinese. The next year he tried to enter Korea again but lost his life on the *General Sherman* when it was burned in the Taedong River.[23] Protestant missionaries entered Korea as permanent residents in 1884, first a Presbyterian and then Methodists the following year, the English Church adding to the number in 1890 and the Canadians in 1898. The Russians sent priests around the turn of the century. By the time of the Japanese annexation in 1910, it is estimated that there were two hundred thousand converts under the guidance of about four hundred and fifty foreign leaders, of which some fifty were Roman Catholic priests, four Russians, and the remainder Protestants. It is notable that of the latter over three hundred were Americans. The success of these missions in Korea was phenomenal, bringing Christianity into a position of importance unequaled in any other oriental country of high indigenous civilization. Although Christianity suffered a setback during the period of Japanese control, it has been estimated as late as 1944 that there were some seven hundred thousand Christian Koreans of which somewhat more than half were Protestants.*

* Oliver, 1944:68. The figure given by Oliver may be slightly high; also one might profitably distinguish between adherents and full members of the churches. Van Buskirk, 1931:167; 172. For a summary of the spread of Christianity in Korea, see Latourette, 1944.

Ch'ŏndokyo, the last important religion to be treated historically is, like Shamanism, of native origin, but is less than one hundred years old. It started as a Messianic cult in 1859 in the south of Korea. Its founder was a man named Ch'oe, who was born in 1824. After considering Catholicism, he rejected it and in a following state of religious ecstasy received divine guidance for the establishing of the new religion which was called Tonghak, or Eastern Sect, in contrast to Sŏhak, or Western Sect, the name given to Catholicism. The doctrine which developed, viewed objectively, appears to have been compounded from features selected from other religions. Certain basic elements seem to be shamanistic, the five relations and disregard of immortality appear to come from Confucianism, the law of the heart cleansing came from Buddhism, and monotheism from Christianity. Also, such elements of worship as the use of candles and prayer beads, the ceremonial eating of food and wine, purification with water, as well as other behavior, suggest obvious religious parallels.

Acceptance of the new religion took hold vigorously and, as might be expected, gained strength from the martyrdom of its founder in 1865 who was caught in the general persecution of Christians with whom he was reasonably enough confused. A strong nationalistic element was logically associated with the indigenous quality of this religion, and it became a factor in the opposition to foreign influences. In 1893 it was rumored that great numbers of the Tonghak were coming from the south to drive the Japanese and other aliens out of the capital. The resulting insecurity was a factor leading to an occupation by Chinese troops, which in turn brought about the Sino-Japanese war of 1894. It was supposed that the attacks on the Tonghak army and the execution of their general in the following year gave the coup de grâce to this group, but it was not so.[24]

With the greater religious toleration resulting from world impact on Korea, the Tonghak flourished and in 1905 took the name of Ch'ŏndokyo, or Society of the Heavenly Way. Their new leader died in prison as a martyr to the independence movement of 1919, and once again the increment of the followers greatly increased. Communicants to the number of two million have been estimated by an outside source for the year 1930.[25] If this figure is even approximately correct, the importance of the Ch'ŏndokyo cannot be overlooked.

Concluding our discussion on religion, Shintoism should be mentioned as gaining a few thousand Korean followers during the period of annexation, a historical trend which is possibly of more political than religious significance. It is also important to record that, in the long years of Chinese contact, there is no evidence that Mohammedanism ever affected Korea. Taoism is occasionally referred to, for example, in the seventh century Koguryŏ, but its influence seems to have been on the philosophical level except for elements which have become an indistinguishable part of Shamanism. The cult of Tan-gun, the mythological ancestor of the Koreans, is obviously old in the Peninsula. The altar to him on Mari Mountain is periodically repaired by official order, reference to this practice being recorded at least as early as about 1639. Again, in 1786, we find a great mound in P'yŏngan Province recognized as the grave of Tan-gun, a seemingly gratuitous attribution. Since the Japanese occupation, recognition of Tan-gun has been on the increase. quite reasonably as a reflection of intensified nationalism.

Finally, a word should be said about the annual cycle of monthly ceremonies in Korea. These holidays of religious origin, in general, parallel those of China although as in the latter country, they vary considerably according to time and the propensities of local custom. Most, if not all, of the ceremonies are very old and those of greatest importance have strong Confucian elements, as seen in the emphasis on ancestor worship. The most notable festivals have been those of the New Year culminating, one might say, in the ceremony of the fifteenth of the first month, then the celebrations on the third of the third month, on the fifth of the fifth month, and on the fifteenth of the eighth month.

As described for the village of Sŏndup'o, the celebration of the New Year was preceded by a period of special preparations of food and clothing. Then on the first day of the first month, the feast to the ancestors was held. The following two weeks provided a holiday period when everyone had as good a time as possible. The men and boys played yut and flew kites while the girls and young women jumped up and down at the ends of teeter-totters. On the fifteenth day of the first month, the celebration reached its peak and close. Kites were cut loose in the belief that they would carry off any sickness which threatened the community, after which kite flying became taboo for the remainder of the year. This was also a day on which men engaged in fighting with stones. Although this last activity gives a Korean emphasis to the occasion, the chronological correlation with the Chinese Festival of the Lanterns, which supposedly originated in the Han dynasty, indicates the source of this holiday.

The sixth day of the second month is mentioned in the historical literature as a night when the relation of the Pleiades to the moon was observed in order to predict whether or not the crops would be plentiful. Early in the third month, or sometimes late in the second, since the date was determined by the position of the sun rather than of the moon, the Koreans celebrated "Cold Food" day, offering to their ancestors special cakes baked with azalea flowers on them, afterwards eating these delicacies and drinking wine. The following day was that of the Chinese Ch'ing Ming Festival, also known in Korea. On the eighth day of the fourth moon, the birthday of Buddha was celebrated in the glow of innumerable lanterns of many shapes hung from tall poles. One of the most popular feast days was that of the fifth of the fifth month when women, girls, and boys indulged in swinging. This festival, and its Chinese counterpart, stems from a midsummer celebration of great antiquity. The sixth moon was characterized by the hot "dog days" on which Koreans drank dog soup and ate red bean porridge as a tonic against the extreme heat. On the seventh of the seventh moon, as for centuries in China, Koreans have looked toward the Milky Way to see whether, as the old story goes, the magpies have formed a bridge for the Oxherd (Aquilla) to join his love, the Weaving Girl (Lyra). In Korea and in China, the fifteenth of the eighth month signified the Harvest Festival, which was combined in the long-distant past with a sacrifice to the moon. During the Yi dynasty the festival became important for ancestral worship. The ninth day of the ninth month was recognized in Korea by the drinking of chrysanthemum wine. The fifth of the tenth month has also been noted in the historical sources as a day when offerings have been made to the spirit of the house. Finally, in the annual round, at the winter solstice, red bean porridge was offered to the spirits, some of it being thrown outside the gates, as a method of warding off disease.[26]

The historical references give altogether inadequate descriptions, but it is notable that the post-harvest festival of the tenth month, not uncommonly referred to from the first to the fifth centuries, seems to have given way to those mentioned.[27] Correlations are difficult, however, if only because of the shifts in the calendrical system. During the twentieth century, emphasis on all festivals, with the possible exception of that of the New Year, has been greatly muted and some have practically disappeared.

14

THE ARTISTIC AND INTELLECTUAL ASPECTS OF CULTURE

TO GIVE a historical survey of the arts in Korea we can most reasonably begin with music, singing, and dancing, as it is of these that the people have been extraordinarily fond. In the Three Kingdoms period, the Koreans requested musical instruments from the Chinese to add to those that they had already obtained. By the fifth century, according to Ma Tuan-lin, the five-string lute (ch'in), the twelve-brass-string harp (cheng), the flageolet (p'ili), the flute (ti), the orphic pipe (hsiao), as well as drums and other percussion implements were used in Koguryŏ. In Silla we find the interesting account of a king sending three men to Kaya (the dependencies of Karak) in 552 in order to learn music from a master there who played on a twelve-string harp which he is credited with inventing, but almost certainly by elaboration from a Chinese model. It seems clear that by this period music had reached a sophisticated plane in the cultural centers of all of the Three Kingdoms.[28]

One exceptional development of this time related to music was bell-casting, a special facet of Korean art in which the Peninsula people excelled. The first technical instruction undoubtedly came from China, and production prospered along with Buddhism. Bell-making centered in the Silla country, partly we presume because of the supply of metal there and the familiarity of artisans in the use of it. At least we do not find that any bells were cast in Koguryŏ. Bell metal normally consists of copper and tin in the ratio of four to one.

The oldest extant specimen was cast in 726 and weighs 3,300 pounds (Pl. 22, p. 159). This is a midget, however, compared to the second earliest, the Kyŏngju bell, cast in 773 and estimated to weigh 79 tons. This great weight, if correct, probably makes it the third largest functioning bell in existence, being exceeded in size only by those of Moscow and of Mandalay. Some twenty-three of these Korean bells are preserved, the last having been made in 1727. The large Korean bells, it may be noted, are not rung by a clapper but are struck externally by the end of a swinging beam.[29]

Although the popular interest in music continued through the Koryŏ period, the height of development was not reached until the Yi dynasty, when the art was intelligently fostered. At one time in the latter part of the fifteenth century there were more than eight hundred musicians attached to the court. Original composition was encouraged as well as new arrangements of old pieces. As the Yi dynasty declined, however, so did this interest. With the opening of Korea a new impetus was given by the importation of western music introduced initially by the missionaries. The Koreans seem to have responded more generally than other Asiatics and in a way which to some degree has also stimulated a revival of interest in the classical forms. It must be said that Sino-Korean music was not a cultural development which ever reached the complex of perfection attained in other arts, a judgment clarified by comparisons with the West where symphonic music has flourished during the last few centuries. Nonetheless, native Korean music should not be abruptly dismissed for it still holds possibilities for significant expression from so musical a people.

To sing is a definite part of the Korean national character. Farmers like to go to the fields in singing groups and may have done so from time beyond record. Songs from various regions have been handed down for over a thousand years. Obscenity is a notable trait in some. According to one story, the old Kaya music master mentioned above as the inventor of a twelve-string harp objected at the court of Silla when his students proposed to expurgate his verses. In the thirteenth century, one of the Koryŏ kings is specifically mentioned as spending his time singing obscene songs. There are other songs which tell of the beauty of a place or refer to some dramatic event in the history of the country. Love was not excluded, and one of the most famous of all Korean songs, "Arirang," is said to have been first sung by a man on his way to the place of execution. Singing occurred with or without musical accompaniment and has been institutionalized particularly by the girl entertainers known in Korea as kisaeng.

Dancing, the third of the related arts, may be the oldest of all and is certainly as deeply rooted in the hearts of the Koreans as are music and singing. Except, however, for its anciently established popularity, little detailed historical information is available. We read of clouds of dancing girls in the twelfth century when the Koryŏ court was at its peak of splendor. Even then the tradition of trained dancers was old. One king, about 1180, is recorded as himself dancing for the entertainment of his guests, a pattern which can still be found in the simplest farmer's house. Both men and women, dance, but not together. After the advent of the Yi dynasty and its moral restraints, a law was made about 1477 to suppress the kisaeng, the plan being to train boys as professional dancers in their place.

An interesting account of dancing in the fifteenth century is given by Nam Hyo-ŭn, who died in 1492. He says,

> We Koreans have learned the dances of the barbarian in which we bob our heads, and roll our eyes, hump our backs and work our bodies, legs, arms and finger-tips. We shut them up and shoot them out, bound after bound like to a twanging bow. Then, bouncing forth like dogs, we run. Upright, bear-like, we stand and then like birds with outstretched wing, we swoop.
>
> From highest lords of state down to the lowest music-girl all have learned these dances and take delight therein. They are called the *Ho-moo, the Wild Man's Dance,* and are accompanied by instruments of music. At first I rather favoured them myself, though my dead friend, An Cha-jung, was much opposed. Said he, "Man's attempt thus to show himself off is unworthy the part of a human being. Such actions lower him to the level of the beast. Why should I take my body and put it through the motions of an animal?" I thought this remark somewhat extreme until I read Prince Hap-cha's comment on seeing the dance called *Tan-chang Kyung* or *Monkey's Bath.*[30]

The suppression of the kisaeng failed and in the beginning of the sixteenth century there was a great revival of their dancing. The kisaeng were a professional group, undoubtedly originating with the girl entertainers of ancient China, where they came into prominence during the T'ang dynasty. The institution flourished among the dance-loving Koreans, and, it would seem, was then passed on to the Japanese who developed it into its best-known form where the performers are called geisha or "accomplished persons." These girls, chosen for their charm and beauty, were trained from childhood to sing and to play musical instruments as well as to dance while in fact becoming the most highly educated women of the East, the companions of artists and scholars as well as of the rulers of the land. In social freedom they were the most privileged group in oriental civilization and the most loved. They were not prostitutes and did not suffer the disrespect that women of the latter class have so generally been accorded. The profession has no exact analogy in western cultures, the closest approximation probably being the hetaeri of ancient Greece.

The kisaeng entertainments seem to have started as a court institution which was firmly established by the time of the Koryŏ dynasty, and remained under the patronage and protection of the crown until the overthrow of the last kingdom. In its most complex form, the kisaeng dances approached allegorical or semireligious plays, but at least by later years the emphasis was laid on stylized gestures appreciated for their rhythmic perfection and grace. The major movements of the kisaeng are so much a part of Korean personality that they can frequently be seen in the gestures of a country girl. One of the most memorable is a head turned sideways and hung pensively beside an outstretched arm, the hand limp, the whole symmetry reflecting the role of shy submission in the Korean female.

The kisaeng reach out to the small country towns, where they may still be found as purveyors of wine and food and pleasure. But the dancing does not stop with them. In the smallest village farm girls will dance on every suitable occasion and it also takes little urging to find a man who will perform after the wine has been passed at a small and intimate gathering of men. The indescribable individual movements vary like spring clouds or bending reeds when sometimes blown before a storm, but the collective behavior is inimitably Korean. There are those among alien observers who see nothing of beauty in these dances, but no Korean fails to respond for he has the spirit of the dance within him.

In the fine arts as well as the subsidiary techniques, the Koreans have achieved a distinguished place among world civilizations. Painting was appreciated at an early date but little of it has survived the forces of destruction, largely, we may assume, because of the relative lack of stone or brick structures with which the preservation of ancient painting is generally associated. The most notable exceptions, only brought to light in recent years, are the mural paintings of the stone tombs of third to sixth century Koguryŏ. In them we find examples of a highly developed pictorial art in a distinctive style, creations which equal if they do not surpass anything known elsewhere in the Far East for the period. There are polychrome representations of important personages, officers on horseback, people moving in carts, and various other activities

(Pl. 24, p. 175). Wild beasts and spirits are also portrayed which, together with ornamental designs, often fill every available space of the enclosure. Stem, leaf, and flower motives, either individual or spread out in scroll-like borders, are superbly drawn. Geometric designs also occur. The colors vary from pastel ochers and pale blues, now perhaps faded, to deep red, green, and black.

Commentators on these murals have mentioned Chinese and Mongolian influences as well as comparisons with early art of the Mediterranean cultures. Similarities to the cave painting of Tun-Huang on the northwestern border of China are unmistakable, but the style must in fairness be credited as Korean until future discoveries prove it merely peripheral to some other center.* It should be stated that at least one other example of this type of art has been discovered elsewhere in Korea. A fresco of floating clouds and flowering lotus appears on a royal grave in Puyŏ, the Paekche capital from 538 to 660.

There are no early examples of painting from Silla but the histories report that in 552 an artist there had such genius that when he painted a tree on a monastery wall birds attempted to perch in its branches. We also read that Chinese artists came to the Silla court during the T'ang dynasty (618-907). The names of numerous painters are recorded from the Koryŏ period, but it is not until about the fourteenth century that we have examples of their skill. Ever since that time, painting has held its recognized place in Korean culture and it is today one of the enthusiasms of the people, although a contribution relatively overlooked in the world of art (Pls. 23–29, pp. 174–75, 190–91, 206).[31]

Stone sculpture may be regarded as even outranking painting in the Peninsula. It flourished along with Buddhism, becoming almost completely a religious art appearing in the statues, pagodas (dating from as early as 635), stupas, lanterns, and various ornaments appurtenant to the shrines and monasteries (Pl. 34, p. 222). First among Korean treasures stands the Stone Cave Shrine or Sŏkkulam built in 752 on the top of a hill facing the Japan Sea (Pl. 30, p. 206). The site is about twenty miles from the Silla capital and has been made pleasantly accessible by the Japanese if one does

---

* Pelliot, 1914-21. Particularly notable are the likenesses that occur in the designs in Cave 120N illustrated in Vol. 5, Pls. 247, 257, and 258. This cave of 538-9 A.D happens to be one of the few definitely dated. For the Korean murals see Eckardt, 1921, and the *Chŏsen Koseki Zufu*, 1915: Vol. 2.

not mind the last hour-long climb from Pulkuk temple, itself a monument of no mean order (Pl. 33, p. 222). The cave is an artificial dome-like structure of granite blocks which was later covered with earth. The entrance is an uncovered passage over five meters long through which the rising sun shines on the Buddha's face. In the center of the cave an enormous figure of Sakyamuni sits in peaceful contemplation, a smooth simple mass of cool gray granite. Even more remarkable than this statue are twenty-seven slabs placed in the surrounding walls and entryway, each 1.92 meters high. Each bears in bas-relief a figure of an Arhat, a Bodhisattva, or other member of the Buddhist pantheon (Pl. 31, p. 206). Behind the Sakya is the Kwannon with eleven heads, while above the slabs are niches containing smaller sculptures (Pl. 32, p. 207). It is perhaps the Arhats who strike one's attention particularly because of the restrained simplicity with which their robes are cut, by their natural poise, and by their powerful faces, some of which have strikingly Armenoid features. If Korea had contributed nothing more to art, the Sŏkkulam might alone outshine all comparable jewels of eastern civilization.*

Besides the many other religious sculptures worthy of description, mention must be made in passing of the memorial stones and tomb figures in the Chinese tradition which, although semireligious in nature, are at least not Buddhistic in origin. These are common enough and except for certain turtle-based memorials are perhaps less distinguished than their continental prototypes (Pl. 38, p. 238). Besides sculpture in stone, there are also many beautiful examples of Buddhas in clay, wood, and gilt bronze, some of which date from the advent of the Indian religion into the Peninsula (Pl. 35, p. 222).

Of the special and minor arts of Korea, the manufacture of lacquer ware is one of the oldest. Specimens of plates and boxes have been found in the tombs near P'yŏngyang, which date back nearly two thousand years, and excellent pieces have survived from various periods since that time. Mother-of-pearl inlay with both red and black lacquer was characteristic of the Yi dynasty but degenerated in quality towards the end of the kingdom. The restraint

---

* Excellent photographs of Sŏkkulam are available in Eckardt, 1929, but for the best see the magnificent collection of plates published by the Japanese (*Bukkoku-ji*, 1938). These shrine sculptures show similarities to work outside Korea as do the cave paintings, and there is a tradition that they are the work of a Chinese artist. Even if this should prove true, the Koreans should gain the credit by giving him such an opportunity to express himself.

of design in the earliest lacquer pieces shows the distinctive artistic feeling which is characteristic of the finest Korean art. It is unfortunate that lacquer ware does not often survive the centuries as well as do artistic creations in stone or pottery. If it did, we might discover that during the first millennium of our era the Koreans had brought this form of craftsmanship to great perfection, one which the Japanese in the centuries following were to elaborate to its supreme expression.

The Koreans also created ornaments from various semiprecious stones as well as of gold, silver, and bronze (Pl. 36, p. 223). These pieces, however, although frequently of superior quality as exemplified by mirrors, do not seem in the aggregate to place the Peninsula on an artistic level with either China or Japan (Pl. 37, p. 238). The same may be said of the wood carving, although, as in the case of lacquer, the period of greatest accomplishment may have been one from which the destruction of years has deprived us of examples on which to judge. Wood engraving we know since the time of the Koryŏ dynasty, particularly as the result of the extensive manufacture of wood blocks used in printing books. These included illustration as well as text. Achievement in this direction, however, apparently never developed into the multicolor productions characteristic of Japan, although the black and white prints had become common enough by the seventeenth century.

Finally we must consider ceramics, in which field Koreans need offer apologies to none. Unfortunately, archeological work, lagging behind that in both China and Japan, has not furnished us with much information on the historical sequence of pottery development before the period of Chinese colonization contemporary with the formative period of the Three Kingdoms. Nor has there been much application of scientific method to the excavation of later ceramic sites. The high points have been made clear for the past two thousand years, however, and the material proves more than adequate for esthetic judgment by the time Korean potters reached a controlled mastery of their medium.

For general orientation, the ceramics of Korea can be classified into three major groups, each associated with a familiar dynasty or kingdom. These are (1) Silla, (2) Koryŏ, and (3) Yi. This grouping may somewhat over-simplify the situation but it nonetheless represents the logical reduction to the least number of the artistically important categories of Korean pottery. By introducing the subject, with a comment or two on the earlier ceramics, and by also indicating certain varieties of the Koryŏ wares, the outline should be sufficiently simple to retain easily in mind.

It seems more than probable that Koreans have been making pottery for many thousands of years, sharing in the techniques which we find spread over much of northeast Asia in prehistoric times. Remnants of such pottery are found from time to time although they are too seldom appreciated as the tokens of material from which one day will be rendered the early story of a nation now lost in mythical accounts.

During the time of the conquest of the Ki-ja dynasty by the Chinese Han dynasty considerable impact must have been given to the potter's art, for ornamental tiles showing ceremonial scenes were being used. This specialty, elaborating with time into architectural elements including pictorial panels, has continued to the present day as a notable facet of Korean ceramics (Pl. 39, p. 238).[32] From the same period we find clay vessels, the surface decoration of which has been incised with complex geometrical designs. Quite likely, a similar development of ceramic material was going on contemporaneously in south Korea.

In Silla, between the third and seventh centuries, a very distinctive type of pottery had become characteristic (Pl. 40, p. 239). These pieces were of gray to black earthenware in complex forms varying from shallow dishes with openwork pedestal bases to ornate representations of mounted horsemen with full paraphernalia (Pl. 41, p. 270). The cutout portions of the bases or decorative parts usually had the form of triangles or rectangles. Although the Silla pottery has not gained the wide appreciation accorded to the Koryŏ celadons, a few connoisseurs regard these creations as superb examples of the primitive quality in ceramic art.

Before the close of the Silla dynasty, technical skill in the potting of wheel-thrown vessels had been completely mastered. The Peninsula proved rich in the plastic clays required for the finest ceramics. Glaze had been applied to the surface. All that was needed for perfection was to achieve the exact oxidizing temperatures in the sausage-like kilns stretching up the hill slopes (Pl. 44,

p. 271). This last requirement was obtained approximately at the beginning of the Koryŏ dynasty and Korean ceramics entered the great age of celadons.

The first variety of Koryŏ celadons to appear had clear surfaces in a translucent green somewhat lighter in color than their almost identical counterparts produced contemporaneously by the Chinese of the Sung dynasty. The Korean work can also be distinguished by the marks on the bottom surface left by three pellets of clay on which the piece rested in the kiln and not infrequently by the six-fold indentation of the rim.

A second variety of celadon soon followed and may be recognized by a design in slight relief which was impressed into the unfired clay with the aid of a wooden mould. So delicate and restrained are the patterns, usually copied from some element of the landscape, that at first glance the eye is scarcely aware of them. But pour a clear liquid into such a dish and the decoration will stand out with amazing subtlety. It is this variety of Koryŏ celadon which is the prize of the sophisticated collector. It is uniquely Korean and to those who appreciate it, without peer in the world.

Having achieved the perfection of simplicity, the Koryŏ potters began to experiment with their technique. By incising their designs more deeply, they produced various shadings under the glaze, thus bringing about a third recognizable variety of ware.

By the twelfth century, a fourth variety of Koryŏ celadon had been developed, one which is the best known of all Korean ceramics (Pl. 42, p. 270). In these pieces elaborate designs were finely cut, the incisions being then filled with white kaolin or black clay. The whole vessel was afterwards carefully smoothed. When the piece had been finally glazed and fired, the white and black figures loomed mistily under the transparent green. Certainly some of the vases of this variety, especially when not over-ornamented, are masterpieces which have been quite understandably prized by American and European collectors. It should be mentioned that the Koryŏ celadons and particularly the later ones appear in an infinite variety of forms, ranging from the simplest bowls and vases to complex bottles, wine jugs, teapots, and headrests (Pl. 43, p. 270).

Toward the end of the Koryŏ dynasty, two other varieties of Korean ceramics began to displace the celadons. The first of these wares has its parallel, and probably its antecedents, in the Tz'ŭ

Chou pottery of China. Such vessels characteristically have a gray, brown, or cream background with simple but bold ornament of brown to black flower petal designs. The commonest form is a tall vase widening from the base to shoulders and then curving in to constrict the opening with a stubby rim. Glazing has been made subsidiary to the painted design by reduced firing temperature and sometimes does not even cover the lower portions of the vessel. The effects are often strikingly beautiful in their simplicity.

In the last century of the Koryŏ dynasty, a ware widely known as Mishima had gained popularity. These pieces, mostly plates and bowls, have designs punched into them, the holes then being filled with white kaolin or some contrasting clay, after which the ware was glazed and fired. One may interpret such workmanship as a technical degeneration of that done in the creation of the celadons. The designs, geometric or floral, have lost the delicacy of the earlier Koryŏ period and the gray to white finish seems almost dirty in contrast to the pale green surfaces previously admired. The Koreans, unlike the Chinese, rarely if ever used a seal impression on the base of a vessel to denote the maker. With the advent of the Mishima pottery, however, the chronologically minded makers frequently imprinted the year for the future delight of antiquarians. Qualitatively this ware might be better classed with that of the following dynasty, especially as it continued in production for several hundred years (Pls. 45 to 47, p. 286).

The Yi group of ceramics was so much more variable than those of the preceding periods that no attempt will be made to classify them as a whole. Blue and white porcelain, as in China, became popular and the plain white variety also, although the latter never equaled in color quality the long tradition of the Ting ware. One variety of Chien ware, later famous in Japan under the name Temmoku, was developed in Korea.

Pottery making in Korea suffered a severe blow in the invasions at the end of the sixteenth century and numerous masters were sought out and sent to Japan. The Peninsula's loss was the Islands' gain, for in no aspect of culture is Korea's contribution to Japan more obvious than in ceramics. In the Land of the Rising Sun they found in that time an appreciation probably even greater than at home and they succeeded in creating an impact which is esthetically alive to the present day.

A résumé of the Korean ceramic tradition shows that, sensitive to their natural opportunities, the Peninsular people developed a tradition of fine potting in the first millennium, a manifold of skills which by the twelfth century brought them such fame that even the Chinese paid respect to their genius. Then invasions and degeneration, followed by a shift from esthetic-religious values to an emphasis on moral and intellectual aspects of the culture, blocked the truly great creativeness of the pottery families. Some found opportunity in Japan, the others carried on in quiet sadness, their descendants throwing long rolls of clay upon the wheel to make the massive jars which give Korea today its impression as the land of the multiple million pots.*

In concluding our historical survey of Korean culture we shall need to consider the intellectual activities of the people of the Peninsula. First we might note, as has been mentioned before, that from early times there was a high regard for astronomy and calendrical reckonings. It is said that a permanent record of eclipses was kept since B.C. 57, these giving authenticity to the historical sources in which they were used for dating the reigns of kings.† Registering the fact that an expected eclipse did not occur, as was done for example in the eleventh century, points to a knowledge of the mathematical computations necessary for predicting such natural phenomena, even though in this case an error seems to have been cited.

A stone observatory built in 647 still stands on the outskirts of Kyŏngju, the Silla capital (Pl. 48, p. 287).‡ Shortly afterwards, the kingdom adopted the latest Chinese calendar out of deference to her powerful neighbor, and in 718 the first water clock in Korea was constructed. The Chinese calendar was probably known in several parts

* The statement on Korean ceramics combines the personal prejudices of a long appreciation of this oriental art with some study of present-day Korean kilns, fine collections both in Korea and other countries, as well as perusal of many oriental art publications. Conversations with an expert potter and connoisseur such as Warren A. Gilbertson have been most pleasant and helpful. For illustrated works on Korean pottery, the following are suggested as relatively available: Eckardt, 1929; Honey, 1947. For the more elaborate presentations, see *Chōsen Koseki Zufu*, 1916: Vol. 3; 1928: Vol. 8; 1935: Vol. 15; *Museum Exhibits Illustrated*, 1918-43; and especially *Ri Oka Hakubutsukan*, 1932: Vol. 2.

† The first eclipse actually recorded in Silla is stated to have taken place in B.C. 54 (Rufus, 1936:16), or B.C. 53 (Hulbert, 1905: Vol. 1:ii, 35). There is also said to be an unaccounted-for break in the Silla eclipse records between 256 and 787 A.D., although notices of other celestial phenomena are available from that kingdom (Rufus, 1936:16).

‡ The date is sometimes given as 640 (e.g., Eckardt, 1929: Figure 21) but Rufus has been followed as the more pertinent reference (Rufus, 1936:13).

of the Peninsula before the rise of the Three Kingdoms and it became a custom to accept revisions at irregular intervals, those from the Ming in 1370 and from the Manchu in 1627 being specifically mentioned.

During the Koryŏ dynasty, the astronomers observed 128 solar eclipses and 70 comets. More remarkable, they recorded 34 sunspots with the naked eye—an old Chinese custom, although credited in the West to Galileo with his newly invented telescope so late as 1609.

The central planisphere of King Yi T'ae-jo in 1395 has been judged one of the outstanding scientific achievements of the Yi dynasty, and records of the making of astronomical instruments are frequent thereafter. Rain gauges, for example, were distributed to every province in 1442, some two hundred years before data on rainfall were kept in Europe.[33] About 1653, the astronomical learning of the Jesuits in Peking diffused to Korea and in the middle of the eighteenth century, a new model of the solar system was set up to take the place of one destroyed in the Japanese invasions. In 1886, the Gregorian calendar was accepted as official, but the lunar calendar also continued in use.

Although a knowledge of medicine must have been ancient in Korea the first clear available reference pertains to the sending of Chinese physicians and drugs to the Koryŏ court in the year 1079. Possibly this stimulus led to an interest in natural plants, for by 1115 a Koryŏ king had become an enthusiastic botanist. He established a royal garden with rare and beautiful species which his agents discovered in various parts of the Peninsula. Not being content with this, he proceeded to exchange specimens in China for exotic flora not represented in Korea. This botanical garden seems to have continued in existence until 1419 when it was given up by an early Yi king in an effort to economize.

In the third quarter of the fifteenth century, a hospital was founded to care for those suffering from indigestion, a medical bureau was established, and Korean treatises on medicine were published.* Previous to that time it would seem that the only authoritative medical works were the traditional Chinese texts, of which the first is attributed to the legendary Emperor Shên Nung in the third

---

* Of these, at least one general work on medicine published in twenty-five volumes during the late sixteenth century is known to have been appreciated even in China (Courant, 1936:89).

millennium B.C. With the advent of the Yi dynasty, however, the accumulated experience of Korean practitioners began to be recognized although laymen still distinguished between the doctors who could read classical Chinese and those who could not.

Treatment consisted mainly of prescribing drugs, most of which were concocted from medicinal herbs and a touch of flavoring, but sometimes ingredients were added which strikes one as strange indeed from the standards of an empirical pharmacopoeia. Surgery was comprised almost wholly of acupuncture undertaken after the examination of the pulse. Then, following various theories and charts, the needle or other sharp instrument was inserted at some point of the body and withdrawn. Instead of this method, surgeons on occasion substituted an application of heat, either by employing a hot poultice or by burning one or more cones, usually made of the crushed stalk of mugwort (Artemesia), at certain places on the body. Needless to say, lacking anesthetics, this type of surgery, like any other, was not pleasant.[34]

Mention should be made of the special attempts, beginning in 1786, to deal with cholera which in that year is said to have caused some 370,000 Korean deaths including that of the infant crown prince. Serious cholera epidemics occurred throughout the nineteenth century and made an American hospital, established in 1885, greatly appreciated. The Japanese also founded hospitals following the annexation and in 1914 licensed native doctors in a move both to control the ancient practices and prevent their perpetuation. Nonetheless, even educated Koreans worried with illness still commonly revert to the drug merchants who purvey miraculous cures under signboards bearing the legend "Inherited Medicine."

We should remember that, according to tradition, Ki-ja introduced Chinese writing into northwest Korea over three thousand years ago. Certainly it was no mysterious medium in his capital in the days following the Han invasion. Whether it survived between the two periods in Korea is a question and it was clearly an accomplishment restricted to a very few individuals for long afterwards. According to Ma Tuan-lin, writing was unknown in Silla in the third century, notations being made by marking wood. This is partly borne out in the Korean histories by the statement that before the end of the fifth century in Silla, although many Chinese words had been introduced into the language, the use of written characters had not become general. From that time on, however, there was a great rise in learning. About 540, requests were made by the court of Paekche to the capital of the Liang dynasty in China for books and teachers. Probably the advent of Buddhism a hundred and fifty years earlier had created the initial impact.

A major date in the history of Korean culture is the year 543, when the king of Silla brought together the leading scholars of the time to compile the history of that country from the available materials. In due time they produced the *Historical Records,* which were to become one of the principal sources of the later *History of the Three Kingdoms.* Koguryŏ followed in 600 with a comparable history in a hundred volumes known as the *Record of Remembrance.*

The last few centuries of the Silla dynasty produced several noteworthy developments. One was the invention of Yidu, a system by which certain of the Chinese characters were used to indicate the suffixes of Korean. These notations were written into the margins of Chinese texts, greatly facilitating the reader who had to translate the characters into spoken Korean. The Chinese system of writing, difficult in not being phonetic, at least conforms in its isolating structure to Chinese speech. The linguistic structure of spoken Korean is entirely different and shares no common origin with the Chinese, thus making the correlation of characters with Korean phonemes a special problem.

About 789, the Chinese examination system, one of the most remarkable educational devices of all time, was introduced into Korea as a permanent part of the culture.[35] This meant that, henceforth, public recognition and reward would be given avowedly to the most learned of the nation. Even though the system too frequently failed in practice, the theory was upheld as a constant ideal and became for the people, as in China, not only the greatest symbol of the democratic principle but a constant reinforcement of the value of knowledge.

In the middle of the tenth century, soon after the Koryŏ dynasty had established control over the whole Peninsula, these examinations were put on a competitive basis for the entire nation. The subjects dealt with were heptameter and hexameter verse, commentary, historic citation, medicine, and divination. Twenty-five years later, it is noted that the study of the classics was stressed and the king himself judged the papers. By 1024, several examinations were held in succession in order that candidates might compete from any village, three contestants being permitted from a community of a thousand houses, two from a settlement of half that number, and one from smaller places. Degrees were commonly given in three grades after 993, but others were added periodically. From early in the Koryŏ dynasty there were also special competitions in military and naval science as well as in instrumental music, languages (Chinese, Mongolian, Yujin, Japanese), besides others in miscellaneous subjects.

At times the examination system suffered, as in 1084, when the king, during the great rise in enthusiasm for Buddhism, substituted a test based on knowledge of that religious doctrine. This was a passing aberration and the study of the classics again became of paramount importance. About the middle of the fourteenth century a concluding essay was required on whatever the candidate considered the most important question of the time.

At the close of the Koryŏ period, the system fell to its lowest ebb and for the year 1368 was actually abandoned. Educational values deteriorated so much that for a time scholars had to take their final examinations in Nanking. The dissolute court was not above conferring the Korean award upon infants in arms, thus earning for it the popular term "Pink Baby Powder Degree."

The advent of the Yi dynasty soon restored the examination system to its former high status. King Sŏng-jong gave it particular attention and during his reign, beginning in 1470, three preliminary examination winners from each province except Kyŏngsang, Chŏlla, and Ch'ungch'ŏng, which were allowed five each, had the opportunity to compete in the capital twice a year on the third day of the third month and on the ninth of the ninth month for the final degrees. By the middle of the seventeenth century, nepotism had become common and thereafter intellectual values suffered with the weakening monarchy.

To return to the training of which the examination system was the symbol, we know that by the ninth century it was customary for some Silla scholars to study abroad. In 840, over a hundred such men are recorded as returning to Silla. Obviously, the sophisticated T'ang court must have had a great influence on Korea. One of the outstanding literary figures of Korea, Ch'oe Ch'i-won, who lived at the close of the Silla dynasty, was an example of the educated group. At twelve he went to China to study and obtained a literary degree

41. POTTERY HORSE AND RIDER FROM KYŎNGJU, SILLA PERIOD

42. KORYŎ CELADON WITH INLAID CHRYSANTHEMUM AND
PEONY DESIGNS

43. KORYŎ CELADON WATER PITCHER WITH INLAID PEONY
DESIGNS

44. FIRING POTTERY IN KILN NEAR SAMKU LI

there at eighteen (in the year 874). On his return he held a high position in the court but soon retired to the quiet of the mountains in order to write in peace.

Ma Tuan-lin observes that even in the beginning of the Koryŏ dynasty the Koreans were celebrated for their literacy in respect to the Chinese classics. Many Koryŏ editions of the famous work on filial piety were actually sent to the Middle Kingdom. There were schools in all neighborhoods, which even the poor could attend. In P'yŏngyang, the first Koryŏ king had established a more advanced institution for the study of literature and medicine, as well as religious rituals. The most notable intellectual achievement of the dynasty was probably the great compilation known as the *History of the Three Kingdoms (Sam Guk Sa Ki)* which appeared about the year 1145 from the hands of Kim Pu-sik. This work, still extant, is the base on which all later histories rest.

For the remainder of the Koryŏ dynasty, intellectual life waned. The great florescence was past and although there are records of schools being founded and of thousands of books being purchased in China, the country suffered from the overwhelming effects of Buddhism and foreign invasions.

Then, with the advent of the Yi dynasty, came the greatest intellectual period in Korean history. In 1403, the Chinese characters were cast in metal and numerous books were printed in movable type, decades before the publication of the Gutenberg Bible. In fact, there is important evidence that movable metallic type existed in Korea as early as the period between 1232 and 1241, the basic idea having come from China, where the invention of individual clay types has been credited with certainty to Pi Shêng in the first half of the eleventh century.[36] If, however, metallic type were cast in the thirteenth century, its adoption did not become significant until the advent of the Yi dynasty, although the process was almost certainly known in the days of the last Koryŏ kings. The first Yi type is stated to be of copper, but within fifty years a double size font was cast in lead, as well as others in bell metal, a variety of bronze.[37]

In 1443, an equally significant development occurred when Chŏng In-ji, the compiler of the *Koryŏ Sa,* together with several contemporaries under orders from King Se-jong, originated ŏnmun, a highly efficient phonetic alphabet which put the writing of everyday Korean speech within the easy possibility of everyone's learning.

Because of the prestige of the Chinese character, its long scholarly tradition, and the mass of literature already available, ŏnmun did not displace it, but became in theory the written language of women. Actually, although to this day any man of educational pretensions prefers the Chinese character, ŏnmun is the more certain means of conveying ideas to all Koreans.

Volumes on many subjects appeared during the first hundred and fifty years of the Yi dynasty. Books on history, military science, medicine, agriculture, weaving, geology, music, arithmetic, astronomy, social customs, as well as dictionaries, indicate the variety. Actually the number of books published was not great. Printing was almost a royal prerogative because of the expense, and editions were small, some amounting to only twenty copies or less. Thus a valuable Korean book became a rare item on its date of publication. Written manuscripts, in consequence, remained relatively more common than they did in either Japan or China. According to Courant, who compiled a magnificent bibliography of over 3,200 books printed in Korea before 1895, the works on history are outstanding for their scholarly quality. While he consistently emphasizes the influence of China, Courant singles out the fields of military science, medicine, and languages as showing the originality of Korean research.[38]

In the first half of the sixteenth century a central repository for books was established in the capital, and shortly thereafter various works planned for the education of the common people were distributed over the Peninsula. The Japanese invasions were, of course, a serious blow to intellectual endeavors. The great fonts, consisting of innumerable pieces of type, were destroyed and were not replaced until about fifty years later. The last great spurt in publication came in 1796, under a king who was devoted to books. He had several hundred thousand more pieces of copper type cast and personally fostered the printing of fine volumes.

The development of schools had continued along with the increase in book publication. In 1420, a royal college of literature was established and, in the middle of the same century, an institution for the study of the Chinese vernacular. At the opposite social extreme we find that teachers were sent during the middle of the seventeenth century to found schools along the Tumen River which forms the northernmost boundary of the nation, the least cultivated region of the whole Peninsula.

The vigor of the dynasty had passed, however, and shut off from all outside influence, Korean education began to lag. By the time of European contact, the western world had progressed so far that Korean learning seemed primitive. In 1883, Americans started an agricultural school near the capital and three years later another for the teaching of western languages and sciences. By 1895, over a hundred young men were sent to study in Japan. Other attempts followed but the procedures of education had to be completely modernized, a movement which met with much resistance from conservative scholars. The process is not yet complete, but it is greatly significant today that the force of the ancient cultural tradition is so strong that when the average Korean is asked what he wishes most for his country, he unhesitatingly answers that it is schools.

REFERENCES TO SOURCES FOR PART FOUR

[1] Ludlow, 1923:36-37; Gale, 1925:184-85; Gale, 1926:257.

[2] Parker, 1890b:242; Gale, 1926:122-23.

[3] Eckardt, 1929:Pl. 1.

[4] Gale, 1925:263.

[5] Gale, 1924:246; Gale, 1926:122.

[6] Gale, 1927:58.

[7] Gale, 1927:57-58.

[8] Eckardt, 1929:Pl. 1.

[9] Gale, 1900:2; Hulbert, 1900:26, 45; Gale, 1924:246.

[10] Gale, 1925:263.

[11] Gale, 1925:233.

[12] Eckardt, 1929: Fig. 252.

[13] Gale, 1925:263.

[14] Chōsen Sotokufu, 1916-33: Vol. 5: Pls. 87-90; Underwood, 1934:40-41; Fig. 38.

[15] Gale, 1926:239; Underwood, 1934:51-52, 65, 74-84.

[16] Koons, 1925:46-52.

[17] Gale, 1925:183-84.

[18] Ichihara, 1913:45-74; also see Gardner, 1895.

[19] Moore, 1898:129.

[20] Aoyanagi, 1924.

[21] For a recent study of Confucianism in Korea, see Youn, 1939.

[22] Gale, 1927:82-83.

[23] Latourette, 1944:419-20.

[24] Junkin, 1895:56-61.

[25] Wagner, 1931:150.

[26] Morse, 1897:9-11; Gale, 1900:17-18; Gale, 1927:79-80.

[27] For a special mention of the post-harvest feast, see Gale, 1925:7.

[28] For a classified list of Korean musical instruments, with some comments on the history of Korean music, see Boots, 1940:1-32.

[29] Cable, 1925:1-54; Chōsen Koseki Zufu, 1916:Vol. 4: Pls. 505ff.

[30] Gale, 1926:143.

[31] For a list of Korean painters, see Hunt, 1930, and for excellent illustrations, the Chōsen Koseki Zufu, 1934:Vol. 14 and Eckardt, 1929.

[32] Hamada, 1934.

[33] Rufus, 1936:30-31.

[34] For a bibliography of native works on medicine as well as for examples of remedies and treatment, see Bowman, 1915; also see Busteed, 1895 and Gale, 1899:34-36.

[35] For an interesting résumé of data on the examination system from Korean sources, see Hulbert, 1923.

[36] Carter, 1931:159-79, 251-59; Trollope, 1936:106.

[37] Courant, 1936:15-16.

[38] Courant, 1895; Courant, 1931:19-25, 80-97.

Part Five

MODERN KOREA

15

THE PERIOD OF JAPANESE ANNEXATION

THE RELATIONSHIP of Japan and Korea in the twentieth century is an extraordinary segment of human history and one which, to comprehend objectively, requires emotional restraint on the part of those who have been involved intimately with either of the two peoples. Certainly the quality of evil is no more reserved for one nation than are the manifestations of good will. Misery as often results from a dominance motivated by a sincere desire to bestow blessings on others as it does when self-interest leads to actions devoid of sympathy for one's fellow men, especially when the latter are ignorant and weak. In any event, it is more intelligent to seek an understanding of human beings than to pronounce judgments upon them.

In the decade preceding the opening of the twentieth century, and in that following, the Peninsula, after long isolation, suddenly became part of the international world. Many Korean customs and institutions were by then not only medieval in character but were also functionally degenerate. In the long view it would appear that the people were happier and more productive in the first part of the Yi dynasty than during the last.

Foreign contacts at their beginning were investigatory and experimental. Frustrations in establishing friendly relations sometimes led to extreme aggression followed by pity or contempt. On one thing the alien powers involved seemed to agree. Korea should be modernized at least to the point of developing a responsible government which could guarantee internal security and the opportunities for economic and religious activities which the several powers considered as the basis for modern civilization. Not to develop Korean markets and resources or not to improve the Korean mind was unthinkable. Unfortunately, the acceptance of such an attitude is simple only to the sophisticated, and Korean officials were not. Most of all, they wished to be left alone.

When the incapacities of the Korean government became obvious, the foreign powers shifted their focus of attention to each other as potential dominators of the Peninsula. As the primary investments of the English, French, and Americans had been directed toward saving souls, physical force was not a constant complement of their actions. China, Russia, and Japan, however, were juxtaposed to Korea with armies close at hand. Each considered that the subjection of the Peninsula by either of the others would be not only an economic loss but a vital threat to its national security. And since none trusted another, Korea became from that time on, a pawn in an international conflict for power.

Japan, by her military defeat of China in 1895, and of Russia ten years later, gained the controlling position. These successes, following their own remarkable absorption of western technology, seemed to fill the Japanese with a spiritual sense of obligation to save the world, and more immediately their nearest neighbor. Unconquered throughout history, and inculcated with the belief that through superior mental and physical self-control they were the children of destiny, these islanders planned to spread beauty and order under the divine direction of the descendants of the Sun Goddess. For the less spiritual Japanese, the movement proved equally satisfying for more mundane motives.

With this rationale, the Japanese attempted a truly unusual political move, that of absorbing another great nation with an ancient civilization. Korea was not to become a subjugated territory, not a colony, not a dominated ally in some political axis, but an inherent part of a New Order. The Koreans as younger brothers were to learn to labor and live so as ultimately to share equally in an expanded and unified culture. From the first success they would go on together to enfold Manchuria, China, and eventually the world. This was a magnificent inspiration but it had crucial weaknesses.

From the Koreans' point of view, there was more than a doubt of the God-given superiority which the Japanese assumed. The theory did not account for a thousand years of piracy, the invasions of Hideyoshi, or the alien origins of so many Japanese technical skills. Furthermore, the Koreans did not want to be younger brothers of a people for whom they had been the historical teachers. They did not want to give up their own language and to learn Japanese, and, for better or worse, they preferred to determine their own destiny.

Men of courage can lead the masses when fortune is in their favor and the same men will struggle to the death for their individual liberty when fate opposes. Thus the great Koreans fought and still fight on.

To return to an objective account of events, we find the Japanese shifting from their sixth guarantee of Korea's independence as late as 1904 to complete political absorption of that country six years later.[1]* Japan had secured herself from outside interference first by her defeat of China, then by a military alliance with the British, who wanted a counterbalance against Russia in the East, and lastly by a stinging victory over the latter nation. The United States, on whom the Koreans depended most, was blocked from giving any diplomatic aid by the personal prejudice of President Theodore Roosevelt. This the Japanese knew.[2] The major moves in the Peninsula consisted of forcing the Korean emperor to relinquish his authority to Marquis Ito as Resident-General on November 17, 1905, and finally to abdicate in favor of his feeble-minded son on July 19, 1907. This child of tragedy approved the annexation of his country to Japan, which was proclaimed August 29, 1910. For the ten years following 1905, the Korean people carried on armed resistance while the Japanese used military force to suppress the patriots. They called them bandits and, in so far as possible, hid all accounts of unrest from the world at large.

In the official reports on the administration, reforms, and progress in Chosen which were published in English after 1907, the Japanese presented to the western nations an outline of their imposing accomplishments in Korea. In one of these, Count Terauchi, who was Governor-General from 1910 to 1916 states:

I think further that though it was undoubtedly a great cause of felicitation to the State that the annexation was accomplished in peace, the ultimate end is by no means realized. There is no gainsaying that the final aim with which Japan has placed Korea under her rule is the transformation of a decayed kingdom into a prosperous and rich country, and the gift of good administration and peace to the new subjects of the Empire.[3]

According to Terauchi, at the beginning not many changes were introduced into the Korean political system beyond the elimination of the emperor, the cabinet, and a few boards. The retrenchment of expense, particularly by the reduction in the number of Korean officeholders, seems to have been an important policy. As an example,

* The references to sources for Part Five will be found on pages 346-48.

the judicial system with Supreme, Appeal, District, and Local courts was streamlined by eliminating the District Courts, while hearings in Local Courts were placed under a single judge. Also, the Government-General "was obliged to effect a great economy in salaries" throughout the administration.[4]

Provincial rule was likewise kept largely to the old form but experienced Japanese were appointed to local offices and that of the myŏn or township, the lowest in the hierarchy, was given special attention in order to expand its activities beyond tax collecting for "the encouragement of productive industry, education, hygiene, civil engineering and other public works."[5] Later, in 1917, village councils as an administrative subdivision of the myŏn were authorized. Village headmen had previously conducted their affairs under the guidance and control of the district magistrate. This responsibility was shifted to the myŏn heads and, thereafter, Japanese became potential appointees to the latter positions.[6]

Even more significant was the matter of police power, still in Korean hands until 1910, which "left much to be desired in the maintenance of peace and order." During the previous year the police and Japanese gendarmes had "more than 780 encounters with insurgents and brigands, who numbered in all more than 34,400." It was therefore decided that the gendarmerie and police be amalgamated and that their direction be entrusted to the Japanese, with the result that after the annexation "only small bands of brigands remained in remote places." By 1913, "the administration of police affairs was made all but satisfactory."[7] In the matter of punishments, "it was arranged that the Penal Code and other laws obtaining in the mother country should be applied alike to Koreans and Japanese. In consideration of the present condition of Koreans, however, flogging was retained as a measure of punishment for trifling offenses."[8] Although Governor Terauchi sometimes lacked the time which he regarded necessary for attention to prison matters, his concern with them is clear as shown in his "Instruction to Prison Governors" given in 1912. He wished the inmates to be given work, not only for the benefit of their health, but to increase the income of the institutions in a time of economy. He particularly emphasized the importance of only certain types of lectures and books reaching the prisoners, pointing out that "a prison is not a place where ordinary education is given." He also warned: "It is not good to try to make prison equipments too good. If prisoners are fed too well in comparison with the living of lower class people, it may lead some people to regard prisons as places of refuge from starvation and hardship." [9] Terauchi publicly asserted that he wanted only to make those punished, penitent and good men.

Great attention was given to the financial structure of the country, and its currency was established on a stable basis. The small national income rose by leaps and bounds under careful Japanese supervision and hitherto unheard-of sums were expended in the modernization of Chosen. Everything possible was done to further industry and trade. Japanese industrialists were encouraged to develop the country, fishermen were invited into Korean waters to teach the local people by both precept and example, and tens of thousands of lower-class Japanese immigrants arrived to take up the wasteland and turn it into thriving farms. Railroads and highways were extended and improved in all directions, while aids to navigation of every kind including major harbor constructions revolutionized transportation. When the express ferries arrived from Japan, some of the finest trains in the world left the docks of Pusan (Fusan) and traveled at high speed northward, only pausing at Seoul (Keijo), before racing on into Manchuria for connections with the lines leading across Siberia to Europe. The capital became a modern city with multistoried government buildings and widened streets.

The rural regions were not forgotten. At a cost of about twenty million yen, over a period of eight years, excellent land surveys were made of the entire country.[10] Special attention was given to the individual ownership of agricultural tracts and to their registration.[11] Advisory groups and experimental stations were set up to increase not only the quantity but the quality of farm products. Efforts were devoted to the improvement of everything from livestock to fruit trees. Another major field of activity attracting Japanese attention was that of forestry. The government undertook to supply seedlings and a nation-wide campaign impressed on the people the desirability of replanting the denuded hillsides. There was also the question of the investigation and disposal of state forests, enterprising individuals and corporations being given the opportunity of developing these national resources.[12]

The need for expansion of the school system was also recognized by the Japanese, who considered it so important that over a year was spent in special study before adopting a plan of reorganization. The new scheme enforced from November, 1911, had "as its chief aim the education of Koreans on the basis of the Imperial Rescript on Education, so that they may become good and loyal subjects of the Empire," while the greatest stress "was laid on common and industrial education and it was arranged that higher education should gradually be given." [13] The importance of emphasizing industrial training in Korean schooling was not wholly a Japanese idea, for Yun Tchi Ho (Yun Ch'i-ho), probably the most influential Christian in Korea of his day, held that opinion and gave money for the explicit purpose as early as 1893 while still a student in the United States. [14] Terauchi expressed the view that

. . . in order to remedy the chronic evil inherent in Koreans of being addicted to empty talking and idleness, it is necessary to inspire in them the love of active and painstaking work. For this reason Koreans must be guided in the habit of industry and the appreciation of the pleasure of work. Accordingly, I, the Governor-General sought by all means to make the avoidance of empty theories and the respect of practical knowledge the guiding spirit of the education of Koreans. . . . [15]

The teaching of Japanese was especially encouraged in the schools in order that the children might acquire one of the most essential qualifications as subjects of the Empire. It should be pointed out that the sons and daughters of the large number of Japanese immigrants in Korea attended special schools particularly adapted to their needs and background. As regards private schools and village schools, the administration paid great attention to their supervision. Mission schools were allowed to continue their services to the Korean people although the Japanese government leaned heavily towards the separation of church and state in the matter of common education. The viewpoint is perhaps of such significance that it deserves to be stated in the words of Governor Terauchi.

A number of theological schools have been established by the missions for training workers for the propagation of the religion, besides many schools of the elementary and intermediate classes for giving common education to Korean children as a means of converting them. The total number of pupils attending these schools is about 40,000. These schools were mostly founded when educational work was still very poor under the Korean Government and on account of their being affiliated with the Christian churches it is but natural that the Bible should be, as it is, used as the foundation of moral teaching and religious principles of the churches [and] be inculcated in the pupils. In consequence there cannot but be something desirable left untouched in the education undertaken in these schools as viewed from the point of the national education. After annexation accordingly the educational authorities of the Government-General took pains to explain to leading missionaries the educational policy of the Government and made them aware that no matter whether undertaking propaganda or educational work they should be careful to pursue the course taken by the State and strictly avoid deviating from it. On the other hand in consideration of their work being philanthropic, the Government took measures to give them due protection and facility. As the result of these measures taken, most of the foreign missionaries now appreciate the motive of the Government-General and seem to endeavor to act in conformity with its administrative policy. In many of the schools managed by them they have reformed the curriculums and adopted new textbooks in pursuance of the directions given by the authorities. Some have engaged Japanese as teachers of the national language and some asked the Government to furnish them with designs for new school buildings and their equipments. The relation of foreign missionaries with Japanese Christian pastors has become very smooth and efforts have been put forth by some of them to establish close relations between Japanese and Korean churches by means of an occasional exchange of pastors. The attitude of Korean converts towards the Government has also greatly changed for the better and now it is very rare that men indulging in seditious utterances and acts appear among them. As a matter of fact, of private schools in Chosen giving common education, those in a comparatively good condition are mostly those established by foreign missions. Under the circumstances if the separation of education and religion be enforced all at once, those mission schools will be obliged to close their doors and there being a dearth in the Government and public schools able to take their place their closure will leave a great gap in the educational work in Chosen. For this reason, for the time being, the authorities concerned pay attention only to the prevention of evil that may occur on account of the presence of these schools, intending later to enforce the principle of education standing aloof from religion.[16]

With respect to higher education, it is said that some Koreans proceeded to Japan in pursuit of knowledge. Before 1912, fifty were appointed to study at government expense but it was "found that not a few erred in their career, either showing themselves weak in their determination, or neglecting their work or obtaining mistaken ideas." Thereafter, not so many but more carefully selected students were sent to be placed under supervision in Tokyo as there was fear that they might "be spoiled by a frivolous city life." [17] By 1917, there were seventeen such government scholars but the number studying at their own expense had increased to 623.[18]

Freedom of religion was clearly enunciated by the new regime as stemming from the guarantees of the Japanese constitution. The center for Confucian studies in the capital was fostered by a gift of a quarter of a million yen from the Imperial Donation Fund. Buddhism was relieved of many restrictions which had developed under the Yi dynasty and provisions were made for its revival and propagation under orderly regulations so that "more than 20,000 priests and nuns living in about 1,400 temples and monasteries were able to engage in their work, being given due protection and raised to the same position as other religious workers." The strength of Christianity being recognized, no particular assistance seems to have been accorded this religious group which, according to the Government's report, numbered at the beginning of the annexation period, some 80,000 Catholics and 360,000 Protestants. According to Terauchi:

Not a few people formerly embraced the religion more with political and other mundane purposes so as to derive benefit from the influence enjoyed by missionaries than actuated by real faith in it. Sincere and zealous converts, however, are also found in no small number.[19]

The Japanese, as might be expected of a people who long have laid emphasis on cleanliness in their culture, paid considerable attention to sanitary and medical problems. The Hansŏng Hygienic Association, for instance, which does scavenger work for the city of Seoul, was founded with funds given by the imperial crown prince on his visit in 1907. The Taehan Hospital, established in the capital the same year and which became the Government-General Hospital, treated 810,000 patients in the three years following annexation; of these patients 201,000 were Japanese and 609,000 Koreans. It was difficult to procure trained physicians as directors of provincial hospitals because of the salaries demanded, so military surgeons were appointed with excellent results, these men, it being said, becoming very popular among the local inhabitants. Although ultimate goals could be reached only through a long-term program, effective prevention of general epidemics became immediately noticeable.[20]

In 1916, Count Hasegawa succeeded Terauchi as Governor-General and developments went on apace. With the change previously mentioned in the myŏn administration, there were some fears that there might be difficulty in raising the expected revenue but these proved groundless. This was attributed not only to the improved efficiency and prosperous economic conditions "but to the gradual increase in willingness on the part of the taxpayers to comply with the requirements of the times." [21]   In short, from the published reports, the progress of the Japanese government in carrying out the successful annexation of Korea was, if anything, more than satisfactory and deserving of commendation from the observing world.

Then suddenly and without warning an extraordinary thing occurred. On the afternoon of March 1, 1919, thirty of the most prominent Koreans in the country, having signed a proclamation of independence, sent a copy to the Governor-General with their compliments. After this the Central Police Station was called, the action explained, and the men awaited arrest which followed as soon as the astounded officers could arrive. While being driven to prison, great crowds cheered them from the streets. The people by this time were fully aware of the nature of the occasion for at two o'clock special copies of the proclamation had been read by appointed delegates in public places over the country. Kil Sŏn-ju (Kil Sun Chu), pastor of the largest Christian church in Korea and one of the thirty-three who affixed their names to the proclamation, was delayed a few hours in coming from P'yŏngyang but he immediately went to the police and asked to join the others. The movement was by no means wholly led by Christians, for the first signer was Son Pyong-hi, the leader of the Ch'ŏndokyo, or Society of the Heavenly Way, the powerful nationalist sect which the Japanese had encouraged, it has been said, to counteract Christianity. Of the thirty-three signers, fifteen were members of this group, fifteen were Christians, and three were Buddhists. The two other signers not at the reading had been sent to Shanghai to represent the group abroad.[22]

The immediate spread of peaceful demonstrations over Korea was phenomenal and clearly the result of a carefully planned program. How such organization was achieved unseen by the hawklike eyes of the Japanese secret police soon became one of the most incredible aspects of the whole situation. Particular effort apparently had been made to keep any information from foreign missionaries so as not to involve them. A mimeographed sheet called "The Independence News" appeared on the day of the proclamation and daily for months thereafter. It is reported that the Governor-General found two copies on his desk every morning and that the Japanese were completely baffled by their almost spontaneous and universal appearance.[23]

The popular action consisted primarily in meeting at a predetermined point, sometimes the Christians convening at one place and the non-Christians at another, then joining to march down the streets shouting "Manse," the ancient national cheer, until dispersed by the police. Bands playing music led some groups. The completely national character of the demonstrations was shown by the fact that coolies, nobles, scholars and preachers, children and aged, male and female, walked side by side. Some policemen who worked for the Japanese changed into civilian clothes and joined the crowd, stores and schools closed, and economic life came almost to a standstill. There was no rioting. With rare exceptions, the Koreans did not even indulge in their national pastime of throwing stones, so carefully had they been instructed in avoiding all possible signs of physical violence. There is reason to believe that the Koreans gave one of the most extraordinary examples of passive resistance to foreign domination that the world has ever seen.*

Once recovered from their original surprise, there is no question that the Japanese were not only shocked but truly frightened. It was not that the officials lacked personal courage or that the Japanese numbered but a few hundred thousand in a country of millions, a large part of whom were roaming the streets and shouting for independence. The Japanese possessed guns and an army while the Koreans had neither. The principal reaction seems to have been born of frustration and a feeling of outrage that these subjugated people should dare so boldly to ask for liberty from the God-given imperial plan for their political and social salvation. No conciliation or sympathy was offered. All the organized power under the Governor's direction was turned towards controlling the populace by force.

The Koreans would not give in, however. When the police raced to one place to suppress a demonstration, they then discovered that the real center of activity was in the opposite quarter of the city. On March 5, shops and schools were ordered to open again but the shutters remained up and the children stayed away. By April, soldiers forced the merchants to receive customers but some who came were

---

* McKenzie, 1920:251-52. Although the demonstrations were nonviolent, in a few cases individual Koreans reacted spontaneously against the cruelty of the repression. In one such instance on the fourth day of the demonstration, a college student thrashed a Japanese civilian who was pulling a Korean girl by the hair through the streets and beating her. The gendarmes cut off both his arms and took him to prison. Chung, 1921:223-24.

45. KORYŎ VASE WITH RED TINTED FLOWERS ON WHITE
BACKGROUND

46. MISHIMA VASE OF EARLY YI PERIOD

47. MISHIMA VASE OF EARLY YI PERIOD

48. STONE OBSERVATORY NEAR KYŎNGJU (647 A.D.)

told that what they wanted was not available. In one school the children were persuaded to come back to receive their promised certificates at a formal ceremony which had been scheduled. The Japanese officials were delighted when a boy of about twelve made a beautifully proper speech of appreciation on behalf of the class for the awards received. But he closed by pulling out the banned Korean flag hidden under his jacket and shouting "Manse!" Then all his classmates whipped out flags and cried "Manse!" after which they tore up their hard-earned certificates in front of the horrified guests and marched out.[24]

Although the Japanese clamped down a tight censorship, word spread to various parts of the world and particularly to America that what was happening in Korea was almost too shocking to relate. Hundreds had been arrested at first, then thousands and tens of thousands. There was not even standing room left in the jails of Korea. Unresisting demonstrators were attacked with clubs, with swords, with bayonets, and even firemen were brought into the struggle, using hooked poles to tear the human beings apart. Old men, women, and children were whipped thirty times each day for three days. Of this punishment legally given for "trifling offenses" some died. Badly wounded persons were hauled out of hospitals and flogged. It became a national police pastime to strip school girls naked and make them stand around before slapping and beating them. This was considered particularly effective as Korean girls, unlike the Japanese, are extremely modest about exposing themselves. It must be remembered, of course, that to the Japanese such attitudes seemed silly and consequently the treatment does not reflect quite the same psychological state of mind as it would were it performed by Koreans or Americans. Less common but frequent are reports of more barbaric tortures such as the pulling out of toenails, searing with hot irons, and other even more sadistic refinements in causing pain to the human male and female.

The situation became so horrible that two famous Korean scholars, long friends of Japan and ennobled by the emperor, sent a dignified appeal for independence to the Governor-General, deploring the severe measures taken to suppress the demonstrations. The two were immediately arrested with other members of their families. Viscount Kim, who had been head of the Confucian College, was sentenced to two years' penal servitude and his elderly companion for eighteen months. The sentences were both stayed for three years, however, presumably in consideration for their age. Kim himself was eighty-five. Their younger relatives were given sentences to be worked out at hard labor.[25]

The fanatical terror continued, with the Japanese burning entire villages in the provinces. Unquestionably, the Christianized natives were singled out for attention, not it would seem directly because of their religion but because of their western democratic ideas and attitudes, presumably resulting from the educational influences of mission schools. The members of the Ch'ŏndokyo were also not neglected. In one celebrated case, adherents of the Christian and Ch'ŏndokyo religions were cornered in a church, subjected to a fusillade of shots, and then the building was fired.[26]

It is not the purpose here to elaborate on the atrocities following the Korean independence movement of 1919. What has been stated is perhaps a too brief summary. The accounts are plentiful and from independent sources which sufficiently confirm the facts. To these the interested reader can find reference in the works of Chung, Cynn, and McKenzie.

The impact of these events did not fail to reach the United States, and considerable protest was raised in the public press. In August, 1919, Count Hasegawa was replaced as Governor-General by Viscount Saito. It seems true, whether or not the latter said as he is reported to have, that by that time all Koreans of sufficient intelligence or force of character to lead their countrymen to higher things were either in prison or in exile.[27]

To understand the effect of the first ten years of the Japanese annexation on Koreans it is obvious that one cannot limit one's self to the official reports of the government. The timing of the proclamation of independence, it is clear, was immediately influenced by the death of the last free emperor of Korea, whose public funeral was scheduled for the third of March. He had died in January and, it was rumored, by poison. Thousands of people had been allowed to come to Seoul on special trains for the final rites. The demonstration of nationalism was moved up two days for fear that the plans might be anticipated by the police. Also having an impact in bringing about a public expression of the independence movement was the current of idealism which swept the world at the end of the First World War, largely as a consequence of the utterances of President Woodrow Wilson.[28]

Of much deeper significance, however, was the long-term Korean reaction to the Japanese control of the Peninsula. In the first place, the assertion by Governor Terauchi published in 1914, that the annexation of Korea had been accomplished in peace seems to have been so contradictory to the facts that it is not possible to conclude that he believed it himself. The conflict with the "Righteous Army" of Koreans who fought from the hills with antiquated firearms after the deposition of the emperor can hardly be justified from any unbiased point of view as the suppression of "bandits." Men do not sacrifice their lives so cheaply for material gains. The so-called "conspiracy case" of 1911-12 was also no peaceful gesture. In it one hundred and five Koreans, including some of great prominence such as Baron Yun Tchi Ho, were sentenced to from five to ten years in prison for allegedly plotting to kill Governor Terauchi soon after his arrival in Korea. The reviews of the case, the later commutations and imperial pardons, all contribute to an appreciation of the real injustices perpetrated by the secret police. As for the public statements of the Japanese, they leave no doubt that they were all part of a highly organized program of propaganda which became increasingly effective with the passing of time.[29]

The changes made in the administration of Korea for the sake of efficiency and economy seem to have had the common objective of placing power in Japanese hands. Once gained, this power was wielded with extraordinary rigor. The police in particular, having been given the privilege of summary judgments on minor offenders, with the support of an elaborate spy system and control over the movement of persons, apparently developed a tendency toward sadistic brutality. The old Korean punishment of flogging with a paddle acquired a new meaning when applied with a pair of bamboo rods in the hands of a foreigner. Torture unquestionably took place in some of the prisons and it was almost impossible for Koreans to obtain justice. The number of summary police judgments went on increasing, so that by 1917 they involved 93,575 offenders. The official report states that "of the persons implicated in these cases 92,808 were found guilty, 23 proved their innocence, and the remaining 744 were pardoned."[30] In short, to be apprehended by the police was practically the same as to be convicted. In 1913, the government reported that two thirds of the persons given police trial were flogged but omitted the percentage in later accounts. If this ratio continued, it has been estimated that 294,000 individuals were whipped between 1913 and 1918 alone, or about one out of every fifty-nine Koreans in the country including men, women, and children.[31] The desire for independence would seem comprehensible for this reason alone.

The Japanese introduced a modern monetary system which created benefits for all concerned, but many aspects of the new financial control did not. Rich Koreans, for example, were required to have Japanese stewards who functioned as household accountants and advisors without whose approval any expenditure might cause the confiscation of the families' fortunes. Inevitably, Japanese businessmen were favored over Koreans and the latter found it difficult to compete in the processes of national industrial development.[32] Lumbering in Korea's great northern forests also became an exploitative activity of outsiders, with little benefit to the people. Actually, the local price of wood went up. Licensed monopolies on such things as cotton and fertilizers created even greater hardships on the natives. Much progress is claimed by the Japanese in improving the country's system of transportation and communication, but the Korean comment that most of this effort was impelled either by military expediency or economic exploitation rather than from consideration for helping the native population cannot be disregarded as wholly prejudiced. In any event, these expensive changes created an enormous Korean national debt where practically none had existed before.

One of the principal causes of Korean complaint during the first decade of Japanese control was the confiscation of land by the latter for the advantage of their immigrant nationals. This was done by arbitrarily taking over the public domain or crown lands, municipal holdings, and land belonging to the Buddhist temples. The highways and railroads are said to have been built on ground likewise taken without payment. There is also reason to believe that the careful surveys of the country and registration of agricultural fields were not done without appreciation of the advantages which might be gained through such knowledge by those interested in acquiring valuable property. The Oriental Development Company, organized by the Japanese to develop unused parts of the country and to promote

Japanese immigration, at times showed little mercy in advancing what seemed so good a cause. Diverting essential water is reported as one method which was used in forcing Koreans to sell valuable fields. As a result of such abuses, thousands of Koreans were obliged to seek a poor livelihood in unproductive sections of Manchuria.[33]

Despite the apparent emphasis on the expansion of education under the Japanese, the methods and restrictions created bitter resentment. Koreans have described the situation as intellectual strangulation. It is stated that soon after the annexation all the Korean histories and biographies of eminent national figures were collected from schools and libraries, as well as from some private homes, and burned.[34] This does not seem inconsistent with the avowed purposes of making Koreans standardized subjects of the Japanese empire, but it might not simultaneously make them good and loyal ones. The processes of denationalization were certainly not liked. To add insult to other deprivations, the differentiations between the schooling offered to Japanese and to Koreans placed the latter at a disadvantage in competing for positions in business, the professions, and in government. Higher education or study abroad was almost impossible to obtain except by a few sons of wealthy parents who had allied themselves with the new government. Worst of all, to the minds of the Koreans, were the attempts at "thought control." Nothing like free speech or debate was legally possible. The people had no right of assembly and no press, free or otherwise. In 1916, there were twenty newspapers, eighteen in Japanese and one each in Korean and in English. Three, including the last two, were government publications.[35] Obviously, the only source of reasonably unbiased information on many subjects came through the missionary schools taught largely by Americans. In the flow of knowledge this was a difficult leak for the Japanese to plug. Christianity as a religion they would tolerate with oriental charity toward alien beliefs but free thought and democratic ideals they could not accept as consistent with the plan for the New Order in East Asia.

Lastly, to record the contributions not generally publicized by Japan, one must mention the introduction of morphine and organized prostitution into Korea.[36] The latter came naturally as an intrinsic part of the island culture and needs no explanation to account for its presence. An unrestricted sale of morphine, banned in Japan itself, can hardly have resulted from the economic motivation alone, by which the English merchants tried to justify their opium trade with China a century before. The charge that the Japanese consciously encouraged the sale of drugs in order to demoralize the Koreans hangs like a dirty cloud over the Mikado's administration.

One of the results of the independence movement and its repression was a meeting in Seoul on April 23, 1919, of delegates from each of the thirteen provinces of Korea to frame a constitution for a Provisional Republic. This group composed themselves into a National Council and elected officers including Dr. Syngman Rhee as president. Concurrently, exiled Koreans met in Siberia and Manchuria for the same purpose, naming Rhee president and premier respectively. The three organizations merged and the first National Assembly was held in Shanghai. Their attempts to present their case at the Peace Conference in Paris following the First World War ended in failure, however, as a result of Japan's influence when the Japanese delegates threatened to withdraw if this were done.[37]

As indicated by the leadership, the liberation movement previous to 1920 had stemmed from certain religious groups. One official report on the beliefs professed by 15,224 of those arrested for taking part in the demonstrations of 1919 showed 14.89 per cent were members of the Ch'ŏndokyo, 14.80 per cent were Presbyterians, 3.40 per cent were Methodists, 0.35 per cent were Roman Catholics, whereas 5.74 per cent gave allegiance to various other denominations or religions and 60.79 per cent disclaimed any affiliation.[38] Even without allowing for the possibility that a reasonable number of prisoners hid their church connections, it is clear that, proportionate to their respective populations, the members of the Ch'ŏndokyo and the Christians (with the conspicuous exception of the Roman Catholics) bore the brunt of the action as well as the punishments. In consequence, through sheer annihilation, these organizations began to lose their dominant position in the struggle for independence and when the movement went underground a new power, that of the communists, appeared. The intellectual stimulus of the Russian revolution, which was influencing the world, particularly affected Korea from which country hundreds of thousands of refugees had already fled into Manchuria and the adjoining Russian territory. Henceforth it became fashionable for the Japanese to refer to small armies of fighting nationalists as "bolsheviks" rather than simply as "bandits," knowing that this designation would attract the sympathy of western governments.[39]

To some degree, the advent of communism, with its militant atheism, tended to split the independence movement. Many of the Christian revolutionary leaders who escaped the Japanese purge of 1919 had fled to the United States, Hawaii, or China where they were helped by democratic sympathizers. Refugees in Manchuria or Russia, on the other hand, were brought into contact with the Marx-Lenin philosophy which had a tremendous appeal to people overwhelmed by economic and political imperialism. Moreover, many of the Korean patriots were discouraged with the Christian alignment as such, for it seemed historically that the promised and expected support from the Christian democratic countries of the West always faded away in the light of political expediency. In time, with assistance from the Soviet Union, a new revolutionary organization developed inside Korea, bringing with it reborn hope for the underprivileged. From this communist influence, known in the Peninsula as the "northwind," the Church turned to defend itself.[40] Although still primarily devoted to the goal of national freedom, the independence movement thereafter had a dual approach which was ultimately to result in two major political groups aligned with the conflicting ideals and power of Russia and the United States.[41]

Following Viscount Saito's accession to the Governor-Generalship in August, 1919, a plan of wholesale reform in the administration was inaugurated. The Japanese stated that this program was being contemplated, but that the sudden disturbances had forced a delay in accomplishing the desired changes. It seems obvious that this explanation was offered only to save face and that the independence movement, with the international reaction to its suppression, was directly responsible for the shift in governmental attitudes. The new policy included the rescinding of the restriction of the choice of Governor-General to military men only, the substitution of an ordinary police system like that in Japan proper in place of one acting independently of the local civil administration, and the abolition of flogging (March, 1920). Besides these specific changes, various goals were expressed among which was the intention to eliminate discrimination between Japanese and Koreans, to bring about an abatement of formalism (e.g., school teachers were no longer to wear swords), to decentralize administrative authority, to allow freedom of speech, assembly, and press, to develop respect for native culture and customs, and to promote friendly feeling between Japanese and Koreans.[42]

Although most of these reforms had only nominal value, the treatment of the people as a whole from that time forward seems to have improved. But from the Korean viewpoint the treatment left a great deal to be asked and, for those bent on freedom nothing short of independence would suffice. From an external examination and particularly to one prejudiced in favor of technological advances, the changes in the country from 1920 to 1945 were considerable. It would also be unjust to overlook the efforts of many able Japanese in the administration who, within the limits of their understanding and ability, individually devoted themselves to the welfare of Korea.[43]

Perhaps one of the most valuable changes was the great expansion of the school system. Despite the extremely pro-Japanese bias of the curriculum the organizational plan involving the setting up of at least one common school in each of the 2,493 myŏn in the country was efficient. Between 1912 and 1919, the number of common schools had gradually risen from about 350 to around 500, but with the accelerated effort over 800 had been established by 1922, 1,500 by 1929, and 2,600 by 1937.[44] To have over nine hundred thousand children in common schools by the latter year, when only some twenty thousand had been in schools in 1910, is not an achievement to be overlooked, however unfavorable the ratio may appear when compared to that for Japanese or Americans. Unfortunately the same consideration was not shown in providing opportunities for higher education, secondary schools remaining wholly insufficient to meet the demand, and university training, as previously, being almost impossible to obtain.[45] One of the problems with which the administrators were faced in all except the common schools was the regular recurrence of student strikes, generally in protest against some aspect of the inadequacy of the system, but often coupled with a political purpose.[46] The annexing power obviously linked the extension of Korean education with a threat to the national security.

Another significant effort of the Japanese was shown in their interest in the classification and preservation of the ancient treasures of the country. Probably no cultural group excels these island people in their general appreciation of esthetic values directed towards things perceived. From the beginning of the occupation a real effort was made to discover, record, and publish the distinguished artistic productions of ancient Korea. In the capital, several of the royal palaces were converted to museum use and a new imposing edifice was built as well. Supplementary museums were fostered in other parts of the country and various undertakings carried out not only to preserve monumental works but also to make them easier of access. In this the Japanese seem to have done their best in a manner consistent with their efforts at home.[47]

Since most Koreans engage in agriculture, farmers and their land form the base on which Korean culture is built. With respect to this primary occupation, Japanese influence was mixed in value. Certainly the islanders tried diligently for many reasons to pass on their own highly developed farming skills to the natives, for the need to increase production became great, especially during the regime of Governor-General Ugaki, in the thirties. This man, together with his predecessor, Viscount Saito, was much more humane and helpful than either of the early appointees or the extreme militarist, General Minami who took over control with an iron hand in August, 1936. A serious problem existed, however, in that Korea was Japan's rice basket and the demands for grain were increasing as the Empire became more and more involved in military "incidents." Complicating the situation was the extraordinary rise in Korean population which is estimated to have grown from about thirteen million in 1909 to twenty-four million in 1940. As a result of export and the expanding demand, according to Grajdanzev, the per capita consumption of rice, which is the Korean's principal food, dropped almost fifty per cent between 1915 and 1938.[48]

The plight of the farmers in many parts of the country had been desperate, particularly since the late twenties. The pattern seems to have been for landowners to fail to make ends meet, to go into debt, and finally to lose their land, thus becoming tenants with a bare subsistence. For those who were tenants in the first place, things proved even worse and enormous numbers were forced to emigrate or become wanderers trying to grow enough on which to live in unprofitable forest areas. As one correlate of this process, nonfarming landlords increased their holdings one hundred per cent between 1918 and 1932. It has been estimated by Grajdanzev that less than 3 per cent of the total agricultural families owned about two thirds of the cultivated area and, furthermore, that less than 20 per cent of such families brought the amount controlled by the few to approximately 80 per cent.[49]

The aspect of this situation which particularly embittered the Koreans was that the land passed into the hands of Japanese investors who not only prospered from the crushing economic conditions but manipulated them to their advantage. Although the government stopped publishing statistics on Japanese ownership, estimates indicate that it reached 68 per cent in some of the most fertile areas and that before 1928, about one fourth of the land in south Korea was already in Japanese hands.[50]

The growth of industrialism under Japanese influence offered some assistance in absorbing the population. At the time of the annexation probably over 90 per cent of the people of Korea could be considered agricultural by occupation. In 1920, the figure given was 87.1 per cent; by 1929, the number had dropped to 81.8 per cent, and in 1938, to 75.7 per cent. Concomitant with this was a shift from rural life to urbanization, but even by 1938 only about 14 per cent of Koreans lived in cities of over 15,000 population, compared to 40 to 50 per cent in Japan or the United States.[51]

Grajdanzev who devoted himself to interpreting Japanese economic data on Korea in a manner which would reveal the truth behind highly prejudiced reports perhaps shows some bias natural to one resentful not only of injustice but of its meticulous concealment. For him, industry in Korea was little more than the domination of foreign capital in the interests of Japan. The same was true for the tremendously expanded fishing trade, in which natives were effectively reduced to a dependent labor force. He points out that even in the development of forestry the Japanese themselves admitted a destructive course, since the yearly planting did not equal the felling of trees. Relative to the extension of transportation and communications, he affirms that the great harbor improvements were built to aid only Japanese shipping and that they offered little advantage to Korean vessels. On the much-touted mail and telegraph system he comments that the average Korean sends only one letter every two years and one telegram in eight. Whatever may be said of these technological achievements and motivations for them, they were expensive. Not counting the cost of "military and naval protection for Korea," with internal revenue reaching over three hundred million yen, it was still necessary to borrow almost two thirds of that amount to meet current expenditures. By 1940 the Korean national debt amounted to over a billion yen. Some authorities even claimed the Peninsula to be a financial burden to Japan.[52]

During the years after 1941, when Japan attacked Pearl Harbor and entered into military conflict with the United States, every effort was made to force Korean production for the war effort without allowing a situation which could result in internal revolt. The country was also stripped of metal, ranging from the farmers' musical instruments to the iron water mains of the capital, for which concrete pipes were substituted. The modern heating plants, plumbing fixtures, and metal railings of many houses went the same way.[53] Strict censorship, plus the stoppage in any ordinary contacts with the outside world, kept most of the people ignorant or misled in terms of the detailed course of events but for every Korean the basic significance of a defeat of the Japanese could hardly be overlooked. Resistance to change is so great, however, that after forty years of political domination it is uncertain how large a majority actively wished for a revolutionary shift in the political order. Fear of the uncertain and unknown, as for most people, was a dominant emotion.

For the revolutionary Koreans outside the country, the outcome of the war was all-important and the different groups were marshaled under Russian or American guidance to aid in the victory over Japan. The United States, thrown suddenly into the direction of world affairs on a new level of power, proved to be at a disadvantage in the Far East. Despite their long-standing sympathies, Americans had been given only a provincial education in the world sense and were thus extremely ignorant of the Orient relative to their knowledge of Europe, which in a western nation comes as a part of the cultural heritage. It consequently proved difficult to make decisions about a Korea which was hardly more than a name.

One of the results of the Cairo Conference between the governmental heads of China, Great Britain, and the United States was a statement issued on December 1, 1943, containing the sentence: "The aforesaid three great powers, mindful of the enslavement of the people of Korea, are determined that in due course Korea shall become free and independent." The phrase "in due course" proved extremely disturbing to the Koreans and on its face value it remains hard to interpret the inclusion of the phrase as being consistent with thoughtful diplomacy. More important for the future of Korea was the secret agreement made at Yalta during February, 1945, which allowed the Russians to occupy one half of the Peninsula and the American forces the other. Some representative of the United States accepted a decision which prevented the settlement of Korean affairs for years to come. This tragedy was discovered soon after the Japanese surrendered on August 14, 1945, thereby ending their thirty-five years of formal rule over the Peninsula.

16

THE MILITARY OCCUPATION OF KOREA BY RUSSIA AND THE UNITED STATES

ANY ATTEMPT to present a résumé of the Korean situation since 1945, when the country was occupied by armed forces of Russia and the United States, will suffer because there has not been time for individuals to achieve the adequate perspective necessary to produce unbiased analyses of events. Furthermore, the requirements of military expediency, carried over from the war years, have prevented a free access to and distribution of information with the consequence that many of the reports have been written under stress of emotion and with a large measure of prejudice. In these circumstances, a critique of the sources must necessarily be more subjective than would otherwise be desirable for the marshaling of facts. Cognizant of the situation, one seeks to present the picture fairly, facing the truth as it will be some day clearly seen.

The problem begins with the complicated situation of having three nations engaged not only in local political rivalries but also in those which involved world powers on the broadest level of international diplomacy. First in number were the nearly thirty million Koreans spread over the Peninsula who, liberated after forty years, were suddenly presented with the responsibilities of free men but at the same time were encumbered with entertaining two large groups of highly armed and well-meaning strangers. Next were the Russians, of whom it has been estimated some two hundred thousand crossed the northern border beginning August 13, 1945. We can presume that they were greeted cordially at first meeting, since they arrived under auspicious circumstances. Smallest of the three groups, probably never totaling eighty thousand, were the Americans who began to debark at Inch'ŏn, the port of Seoul, on September 8, 1945.* The reception from the native populace was all that could be expected

* According to the *New York Times* of May 29, 1949, the maximum number of United States troops serving in Korea was 77,643 in October, 1945.

of a grateful people. From that time on, more and more Koreans became less and less happy. Having made their hospitable gestures, it is clear that they would have greatly preferred that their visitors go home.

Why the Russians wanted to continue the occupation of Korea is a question to which it is easy to find answers. It has been said that in the latter part of the nineteenth century the 38th parallel had been considered a possible line on which to divide influence on the Asiatic continent with Japan. Although this arrangement was not consummated, it is presumed that Soviet officials were aware of it when the question of military responsibilities for the defeat of the Japanese in Korea was brought up at Yalta. If so, it explains the manner of splitting the country between two occupying forces decided upon at the Potsdam Conference in July, 1945, assuming that the Americans were expected to reach the Peninsula in the course of actual fighting.[54] It would be unjust, however, to conclude that the same type of expansion desired by the imperial czars was motivating the Politburo in Moscow. In fact it should be sufficient reason, apart from all others, that the Soviet Union wanted a sympathetic government in the Korea which touched her southeastern borders. The men in the Kremlin assumed that if the United States was to occupy a part of the country something would have to be done to counteract, from the Russian viewpoint, such reactionary influence on the new republic.

The Americans moved into Korea according to the military plan stated above, but why they remained is something of a puzzle. Presumably, once arrived, there was neither time nor understanding sufficient to change the direction of events before involvements were so great that withdrawal would have proved embarrassing. We might also recognize that, in 1945, Americans were still naïve in their expectation of creating a brave new world on the ideal basis of international cooperation. From a purely military outlook, it is exceedingly doubtful that the Army would have chosen to place three divisions in near isolation on that difficult terrain of the Asiatic mainland, in juxtaposition to the Soviet Union's overwhelming Siberian armies. To consider even the possibilities of a real conflict with the latter must have given so experienced an officer as Lt. Gen. John R. Hodge uneasy moments. It could also be that some decision makers thought that Korea would become an excellent outpost in which to inculcate American values or, at worst, that the occupation would prove valuable in restricting Russian influence.

Between the time of the Japanese surrender and the arrival of American troops, Korean leaders headed by Lyuh Woon-heung (Yŏ Un-hyŏng) set up the Preparatory Association for Establishing the Nation, of which he was president and An Chae-hong vice-president. This organization, which contained men of all shades of political opinion including communists, formed local committees throughout the country for the preservation of order and convened a national congress in Seoul. In this action they were given cooperation and facilities by the retiring Japanese authorities, while their committees were sanctioned in the north by the Russians. Lyuh Woon-heung had been one of the Shanghai exiles participating in the prewar Provisional Republic, and at that time was regarded as a rightist. About 1937 he was arrested in the Japanese Concession but was not convicted and later edited the *Central Daily News,* one of the papers published in Seoul which was shut down in 1938 for printing a picture of a famous Korean Olympic champion marathon runner with the Japanese flag on his shirt blocked out. Lyuh kept quiet until the liberation, but did organize a small underground party. The Japanese invited him to act as the Korean most likely to keep peace in the country, and many have wondered if he would not have done so had he been given the opportunity. To their surprise, the Koreans discovered that the phrase "in due course" implied a longer residence of foreign troops than one required simply to dispossess the Japanese of their control.

When Lyuh's Preparatory Association for Establishing the Nation proclaimed the Korean People's Republic on September 6, 1945, and proceeded to assume governmental authority, it met resistance from the Americans almost at once and by December such activities were declared unlawful.[55] Lt. Gen. Hodge's orders were to set up the United States Army Military Government in Korea (USAMGIK) south of the 38th parallel rather than to enter into diplomatic negotiations with any local administration, and he followed them. Ill-adapted for civilian rule as military organizations may be, they face the same problems. In the case of Korea, a more difficult locale for experimentation could hardly have been selected. Here was a country of great population and long civilization, ground under the heel of conquerors for two generations and left in dire economic straits which even the Japanese could not resolve, suddenly cut in two with the major portion depending on guidance from an occupying force few of whom had any meaningful preparation for the task or any wish to undertake it. It is a tribute to the American character that some tried so hard to meet the challenge and the responsibility.

The first few months of the occupation were ones of relative freedom and excitement for the allied forces, helped by the air of expectancy on the part of the natives. Lt. Gen. Hodge, at first, and it would seem logically, tried to retain trained Japanese in their posts until an effective replacement could be made by Americans or Koreans. The local protest proved so great, however, that this policy was changed to one of complete repatriation of the Japanese which was achieved with amazing rapidity, affording the first American personnel some opportunity to acquire souvenirs from the homes of the departing islanders. Considering the attitudes engendered by the warfare with the Japanese, the program was carried out with as little personal abuse as could be expected and it may be added that the subjects of the Emperor were particularly courteous in their cooperation.

On December 27, 1945, a major diplomatic move occurred when by the Moscow Agreement provisions were made to establish a four-power trusteeship of Korea for a period of up to five years, as well as a Joint U.S.-U.S.S.R. Commission to assist in the formation of a provisional Korean government.[56] When this news was announced in Seoul on the next day it was followed by a work stoppage and a mass demonstration which brought the public to a stage of hysteria in opposition to the trusteeship. This uproar was directed by Kim Koo as chairman of the Korean Provisional Government which had come over from Chungking on November 23 and had been competing with the moderate leftist People's Republic for popular support. With the news of the Moscow Agreement, his cabinet had gathered, some arguing that they should all die together if necessary in throwing the Americans out of the country. One member, on his own authority, had posters distributed over the capital to that effect. This suggestion to the milling thousands of aroused Koreans left the American command with a new sense of insecurity.[57] Fortunately one Korean, Chough Pyong-ok, came out in support of USAMGIK and carried the day, thus becoming thereafter what one informant described as "a tin god to the generals." Chough, who had at one time been a teacher in Chosen Christian College was later, logically enough, appointed as Head of the Department of National Police, with which organization he had had no previous connection.

For some time forward, the American official policy seemed to swing more to the right. This was partly a reaction to the incomprehensible Korean political confusion and partly the result of the influence of the relatively few English-speaking Korean leaders educated as Christians in the United States, themselves out of touch with those indigenous independence groups ranging from moderates to extreme left-wing revolutionaries. Military Government was in an effective sense cut off from these latter parties because of the language barrier, since the principal Korean interpreters and most of the Korean-speaking Americans, largely from missionary backgrounds, were prejudiced against them. USAMGIK was caught in a political rut from which it was impossible to extricate itself and there was nothing to do but drive on.

With the ideals of liberty sweeping the country and no native government officially sponsored in the southern zone, it was inevitable that political coteries blossomed in profusion and of every color and fragrance. It was a common joke among the people that whenever five persons came together to discuss the future government of Korea they formed a political party. At least fifty-four of these factions were in existence shortly after the liberation. With the requirement of registration as a party for political recognition, the number increased to one hundred and thirty-four by March, 1946. Soon afterwards these organizations were divided into two classes, so that by the following June there were one hundred and seven national and seventy provincial parties.[58] As would be expected, most of them had little influence or consistency except to add to the confusion. One, called the Old Patriotic Man's Society, was reported to have actually but five members, all of whom were over seventy years of age. This group made frequent broadcasts, always criticizing the left wing and the manners of young people, deprecating such radical behavior on the part of girls as indulgence in lipstick and permanent waves. Any summary presentation of the Korean parties is especially subject to confusion because most of the groups suddenly appear, divide, amalgamate, disappear, or at least change their names, while their leaders create them, are elected or appointed, retire or resign, reinstate themselves, and in some cases are assassinated.

To consider briefly the more important of the parties and their alignments which confronted Military Government by 1946, we can begin with the communists, who seem to have had a definite organization operating within Korea by 1924.[59] Soon after its formation, however, Japanese attacks resulted in the members spreading out around the country. About 1936, the Communist Party was revived and went underground, where its personnel worked in cooperation with the two Korean communist parties of Manchuria, the Kando and the M(arx)-L(enin) Party, supported partially by funds from the Comintern.

Another left-wing group called the New People's Party was organized immediately after the liberation by Koreans. Most of its members came from the Chinese communist center in Yenan but were under the leadership of Paik Nam-un (Paek Nam-un).* The latter had been a professor of social science at Chosen Christian College in Seoul, was imprisoned by the Japanese, and then kept under close surveillance after being set free about 1938.

Third was the moderate-to-left People's Republican Party (or People's Party), which name was given to the supporters of Lyuh Woon-heung's People's Republic after Lt. Gen. Hodge had opposed his assuming governmental authority.[60]

In August, 1946, a conference of these left-wing groups was held with the hope of establishing unity among them, but this goal was not achieved. Part of the communist faction decided to continue to operate by itself, while the members of the People's Republican Party who did not wish unification, led by Lyuh Woon-heung's brother, Lyuh Woon-hong, split off to form the Social Democratic Party.[61] The great majority, however, realigned themselves into two organizations, the South Korean Labor Party and the more moderate Social Labor Party. In time, the latter association lost part of its membership by defection and the name was changed to the Diligent Laboring People's Party.[62]

Of these left-of-center parties, the largest numerically was the South Korean Labor Party headed by the elderly Huh Hun (Hŏ Hŏn), a lawyer famous for defending political cases under the Japanese and for an equally extraordinary disregard of personal

---

* The New People's Party seems to be the same as that called the Korean New Democratic Party, which is reported to have changed its name from Yenan Independence Alliance in March, 1946. *Summation*, February, 1946:283; *Ibid.,* March, 1946:9.

financial success. The second largest membership was probably in Lyuh's Diligent Laboring People's Party, with his brother's Social Democratic Party running third.

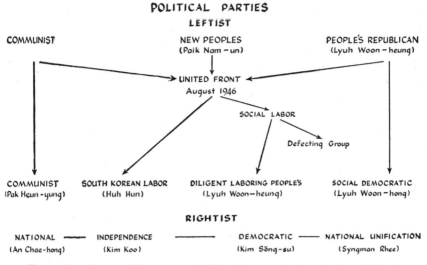

POLITICAL PARTIES

Figure 19. Chart of Important Political Parties in the Period 1945-47

Not long after the unification meeting, Huh Hun was arrested by the police and beaten, but was later released. The leader of the Communist Party escaped and was last reported to be in north Korea. Lyuh Woon-heung survived until August 19, 1947, when he was assassinated by parties unknown. According to gossip, he was one of five left-wing Korean leaders for whose death an enormous price had been offered by certain rich Koreans. On the other hand, a moderate leader so tremendously popular could have as well been considered the greatest threat to the success of the extreme radicals.*

Moving to the right-of-center, we also find four predominant factions functioning soon after the liberation. Of these the National Party was comprised largely of local Koreans in contrast to the dominance of returned refugees in certain other alliances. The leader of this group was An Chae-hong who had been vice-president of Lyuh's "Preparatory Association for Establishing the Nation." An, who had been graduated from Waseda University and was imprisoned nine times by the Japanese, had like Lyuh been a newspaper

---

* In November, 1947, one Han Chi-kŭn was convicted of the assassination and sentenced to life imprisonment. *Summation,* November, 1947:200.

man in Seoul.[63] He differed with the latter on policy and ultimately won the support of the American Command.

In some ways, perhaps the most significant of the right-of-center coalitions was the Korean Independence Party, which developed under the leadership of Kim Koo from his following in the Korean Provisional Government which had moved over from China. The latter had included factions of the Korean Revolutionary Party and the Korean Anarchist Party, as well as others. During the previously mentioned difficulties with Lt. Gen. Hodge in December, 1945, over the attempted assumption of governmental authority, various left-wing elements retired from the Provisional Government, leaving Kim Koo's followers to carry on as the Independence Party. Kim Koo, was an internationally known revolutionary figure for having directed the assassination of General Shinegawa in Shanghai in 1932, the same occasion on which Admiral Nomura lost an eye. He had further touched Korean hearts when his son married the daughter of An Chung-kǔn, who killed Prince Ito at Harbin in 1909.*

Further to the right stood the Korean Democratic Party, in which the dominant figure was Kim Sŏng-su, the former president of Korea University, who at the same time had successfully operated a cotton spinning mill during the Japanese administration.

Almost as a third major group in the party system of Korea were the organizations of Syngman Rhee (Yi Sung-man). This extraordinary person has been probably the outstanding international figure in Korean politics. Born in 1875, he began his political career at the age of twenty by championing liberal reforms in the old kingdom. For these activities he spent the years from 1897 to 1904 in prison. Released, he went to the United States to study, finally earning postgraduate degrees from Harvard and Princeton. Returning to Korea in 1910, he started the Korean Christian Student Movement but escaped to Hawaii two years later to avoid arrest by the Japanese. Following the independence movement of 1919, he was elected president of the Provisional Republic and for the years thereafter devoted himself to the cause of Korean freedom.[64] Like some other leaders in 1945, he at first suffered a disadvantage from having been exiled from the country so long. Also, his nineteenth-century Christian radicalism had tended to become the right-wing conserv-

* *Summation,* May, 1946:16. Kim Koo was assassinated by An Do-hi on June 26, 1949.

atism of the twentieth, thereby—from some quarters—bringing down upon his illustrious head the charge of being a fascist reactionary. Directly after the liberation he organized the Headquarters for the National Unification and almost at the same time, the National Society for Rapid Realization of Korean Independence.

Aligned with left- or right-wing political parties, but of a somewhat different character, were a number of youth organizations sometimes hiding under the guise of representing the Boy Scout movement. Certain bands of these young men gained an infamous reputation for violence. Some did not stop short of blackmail, torture, and murder in their supposedly anti-communist campaigns. Support was provided by men who had either grown wealthy by cooperating with the Japanese or through graft since the liberation. The latter group felt that radical factions were getting out of hand and that some active opposition would greatly assist in preserving what seemed to be worth-while values, a judgment which apparently came to be viewed sympathetically by a large number of the Korean police.

In January, 1946, the Korean Boy Scouts were disbanded by Military Government for having two thirds of their membership over eighteen years old and for terroristic activities. Near the middle of 1947, two other youth associations were dissolved for similar reasons. Presumably to offset these evils, USAMGIK officially sponsored one group known as the Korean National Youth which was initiated in August, 1946, and led by Lee Bum-suk (Yi Pŏm-sŏk), a former military commander of the Korean forces in China. This organization grew in numbers during 1947 from twenty thousand to almost half a million. Although not as rightist as several of the youth groups, according to some opinion, even this movement was modeled after the Hitler Jugend.[65]

South Korea also contained two large labor unions, the Great Korean General Labor Union, supported by the right-wing powers, and the Nationwide Discussing Labor Union, tied to the left. Complementary to the latter and reaching out to the smallest village was the National Farmers' Committee. Since the latter could potentially become one of the most powerful organizations in the country, some of the information not generally available concerning it may not only be intrinsically interesting but may also serve to illuminate the structure and operations of left-wing Korean organizations in general.

First of all, reasonably objective and unprejudiced observers may
state that the Farmers' Committee (actually an association, not
simply a committee in the American sense of the word) is a communist organization and that it is controlled from Russia. Like so
many judgments, such an honest opinion may be the truth but neither
the whole truth nor nothing but the truth. What can be more just
than to present a sample of the data from a typical area which the
aforementioned observers would accept and let the reader draw
conclusions for himself?

The propagation of the Farmers' association was undertaken soon
after the liberation on August 15, 1945. Organizers were sent out
from Seoul to select local representatives for the various myŏn. It is
fair to assume that the majority of these organizers were relatively
sophisticated politically and members of extreme left-wing parties,
the policies of which would be hard to prove were not dictated by
Russians. In short, we can presume most of these men to have been
communists.

Of the local representatives chosen, some were certainly old-time
underground members of the Communist Party. Others, however,
were simply individuals persuaded to act on the basis of their liberal
ideas, men of better than average education who favored a fundamental change in the conservative political and social pattern enforced
by the Japanese. Many of these Koreans were influenced less by
their knowledge of communism as a political philosophy than by their
positive dislike for the existing situation which they knew very well.
The program submitted as a basis for membership in the Committee
consisted of three essential points. First, all farmers should belong
to an association as the only effective means to protect their interest;
second, there should be equality of opportunity; and third, the farm
land of absentee landlords should be confiscated and distributed to
actual farmers without charge. Obviously, only the last of these
goals showed the clear mark of communism.

In the first months after the liberation, membership in the association remained small in areas where the majority of the farmers owned
some land of their own. Whereas the Japanese had been taking
50 per cent of the principal crops, USAMGIK had cut this levy to
30 per cent and the people were pleased. The idea of belonging
to an organization which would promote their interests appealed to
many, but the farmers, being conservative and individualistic, were

somewhat disturbed by the actualities of confiscation. Unquestionably, the majority wanted redistribution of the land but were not agreed on the method of achieving this reform.

The association grew considerably in membership with the passing of time, as the initial enthusiasm over the liberation faded. The uncertainty of governmental authority, the inefficiency of the unexperienced Korean officials, the depressed economic conditions with inflated prices, and the restoration of the national police system, combined to heighten insecurity. Mutual discussion among the farmers became a matter of greater significance. When a group of the leaders went to the police to ask for permission to hold a meeting, they were arrested. The reaction to this renewal of the old Japanese methods of dominance swept through the countryside like a violent windstorm, blowing bitterness up and down the valleys. Membership in the Farmers' Committee shot up like a star shell and burst into a white light over the pine-topped hills. The direct repression of the Korean populace by the highly skilled and powerful military administration of the Japanese was one thing; the attempt by a native political group quite another. Even the despotic Korean kings carefully cushioned their subjugation of the peasants with an ancient descending order of authority. The modern young Korean farmer had been to school and he did not want to be arrested simply on suspicion by a stranger.

Just previous to the second anniversary of the liberation, the national police were alerted against the possibility of mass demonstrations of the populace. The members of the force were nervous and uncomfortable. Then an interesting thing took place, which can be exemplified by a specific instance. A message was sent around to the villages that a signboard of the Farmers' Committee was to be put up at their headquarters in the town on market day. The increase in attendance at the market was barely noticeable but there were a few more young men than usual. The signboard was fastened against the front of a store and the people looked at it and sauntered along. The less than half a dozen local members of the national police force, without waiting to see more, retired to their headquarters from which place they could observe nothing and telephoned for reinforcements. The latter arrived in an open truck almost an hour later. About a score of men armed with carbines jumped down and were joined by the local members of the force who came out to the road. By this time what there had been of a normal crowd in the market had thinned out. Others, seeing the truck, came up to discover what the excitement was about. The police looked and acted rather sheepish. They were persuaded to start making arrests by the local officer in charge, who was greatly excited. Young men among the onlookers were grabbed and pulled to the truck. Some protested and some tried to pull away; some even laughed. One boy was hauled out of a barber shop where he had just finished having his hair cut. Tension began to rise among the people, first showing itself in shrieks of laughter as a boy would break loose. Then came a strange stillness and a gradual receding into doorways and down the road. Most of the onlookers could have run but they did not. They remained as though held by surprise or by shock but without showing any sign of aggression. When the open truck was filled to capacity, it drove off over the hill.

That night there was more quiet in the villages than the usual stillness of the evening brings. Each community missed one or more of the young married men who had been carried away on that truck. Those who remained gathered on a matang in the moonlight. Bitter words were said but most were spoken softly. Much of the time the men sat near each other, silently, like frightened animals.

The next day the local police remained in their police box as though in a state of siege. They had brought in their wives and children for protection. With their guns and ammunition close at hand, they sat drinking. The chief was violently excited and loquacious. It was no easy thing to suppress a riot. They had confiscated thirty sickles and twenty pitchfork heads. But there was only one rusty pitchfork head to show as evidence. The twenty and thirty weapons were not taken from the men but were in a store. He knew the guilty, however, by the look on their faces. They were all communists. And the leaders who had not been caught? He was hunting them. This would be difficult as he did not know the country, having recently come from north Korea. But he would catch them if he had to arrest every man in the district.

In the days that followed the police trucks drove down the road with their loads of prisoners. In some villages not a young man was left. Although few of them had ever heard of Marx or Lenin, the Farmers' Committee easily enrolled the wives and the old men and everyone who escaped. It may be true when one says that the Farmers' Committee is a communist organization but the statement is neither the whole truth nor nothing but the truth. One approaches the whole truth only when one comprehends the significance of sign-boards.*

To return to the earlier American endeavors to preserve order in the midst of this political maelstrom, on February 14, 1946, the U. S. Commanding General set up the Representative Democratic Council of Koreans as an advisory group, with Syngman Rhee as chairman. This effort only antagonized the left-wing organizations which, not being satisfactorily represented, refused to cooperate. Without re-solving the problem of political coalition, which was perhaps im-possible, the American authorities proceeded in the direction of gradually turning over the government to Koreans. Consequently, in September, 1946, the United States personnel became nominally advisors to Korean heads of the various departments.† Since the latter men neither enjoyed the morale-building cohesion of belonging to an officially supported political party nor could consider them-selves truly democratically designated representatives of the majority of the populace, the situation proved somewhat quixotic. Curiously, the attitudes of the American advisors and assistants towards their somewhat inexperienced superiors evolved into friendly, humorous, if periodically naïve, relationships which could hardly be credited to the citizens of any other nation. Genuine respect and affection for individual Koreans were offset only by the administrative indigestion from which the American Army sometimes suffers when it comes into contact with civilians. Considering the defects, the progress was remarkable.

Concurrent with the shift in formal administrations, USAMGIK proceeded with the establishment of a Korean Interim Legislative Assembly to comprise a membership of ninety, one half elected by the populace and one half appointed by the American command. The elections carried out in the fall of 1946 returned almost no one except

---

* These wholesale arrests caused a protest by the Soviet delegation of the U.S.-U.S.S.R. Joint Commission meeting in Seoul. Lt. Gen. Hodge replied that the arrests were necessary to control seditious activities and that the Russians were abusing their role as guests in the American zone by making statements to the press on the matter. *Summation,* August, 1947:185-93. Later, official mention was made that these arrests were started on August 9, 1947, to avoid riots planned, according to the police, by the South Korean Labor Party to take place on the second anni-versary of the liberation. *Ibid.,* October, 1947:134.

† *Summation,* August, 1946:99; *Ibid.,* September, 1946:11. Actually, there was a Korean serving as Director of Education as early as December, 1945. *Ibid.,* December, 1945:201.

right-wing candidates, a result so obviously not a free expression of
the people that the vote was annulled in Seoul and in Kangwŏn
Province; a second attempt, however, did not change matters. With
the exception of excluding communists, Lt. Gen. Hodge clearly attempted to make the appointed half of the assembly more representative of the political leanings of the Korean populace. Among his
selections were Lyuh Woon-heung, An Chae-hong, and Kimm Kiusic
(Kim Kyu-sik). The last, a moderate rightist, was graduated from
Roanoke College, Virginia, in 1903 and had been a minister in the
Provisional Republic set up in Shanghai following the independence
movement of 1919. He became chairman of the Korean Legislative
Assembly which first met on December 12, 1946.* The Assembly,
once the members agreed to sit down with each other, turned into a
lively body with the left wing fighting the right and the right concentrating its attacks on Lt. Gen. Hodge for supporting the trusteeship provision of the Moscow Agreement. The process of creating
self-government continued, however. In February, 1947, An Chae-
hong was appointed Civil Administrator and on May 17 the Military
Command took the formal position of being an Interim Government.

In September, the Korean problem was introduced in the General
Assembly of the United Nations, with the result that a resolution
was passed on November 14 stating that "the Korean people themselves should create a provisional government through free and secret election of representatives and that subsequently foreign troops
should be withdrawn."[66] The Commission appointed by the United
Nations to supervise the elections arrived in south Korea in January, 1948, but was barred from the Russian zone. Despite this re-
buff, elections were held in the area of American occupation on May
10, 1948, the Commission somewhat curiously "having satisfied itself as a result of its extensive field observations in various key districts of south Korea that there exists in south Korea in a reasonable
degree a free atmosphere wherein the democratic rights of freedom
of speech, press and assembly are recognized and respected."[67] The
National Assembly convened on May 31, and on July 12 adopted the
constitution of the new Democratic Republic of Korea, which was
proclaimed on July 17, 1948. On July 20, Syngman Rhee was

---

* Kimm Kiusic has been reported variously as Minister of Communications and
Minister of Education. Oliver, 1944:46; *Summation,* October, 1946:18; Chenery,
1947:79. For statements on election annulments and a list of the personnel of the
Assembly, see *Ibid.,* November, 1946:13, 17-18, and *Ibid.,* December, 1946:13-14.

elected President of the Republic by this right-wing Assembly and proceeded to take over his duties in what has been called a strong-executive system of democratic government. One of his first moves was to nominate Lee Bum-suk, the leader of the Korean National Youth association, for the position of Prime Minister, an appointment which was approved by the Assembly on August 3. The formal termination of the United States Army Military Government in Korea took place on August 15, 1948, and action was directed toward the final withdrawal of troops, which Rhee repeatedly stated in his inaugural address would be undertaken as soon as his government requested it.

To turn to the Russian occupation in the northern zone of Korea, we find that skilled Japanese were retained at their technical posts, as the American Command at first attempted to do. The Russians followed their original policy to its logical conclusion, however. Other Japanese, instead of being repatriated, were forced into labor battalions where their polite behavior did not always save them from such desperate conditions that Koreans expressed pity for them. Even to the liberated populace the Russians were not restrained in their behavior and Chung states that during the first few months "the Soviet soldiers were engaged in an orgy of robbery, rape and murder."[68] Robbery, rape, and murder undoubtedly occurred in the northern zone as they did in the southern, and probably to a greater extent. An occupying army is difficult to restrain and the Russian temperament is more volatile than the American. Also, the Soviet Army had fewer candy bars. Such behavior was a problem to both commands and it cannot be accepted on available evidence that uncontrolled attacks on the Korean people were approved, much less desired, by the Russian government.

In their approach to the local political situation it is clear that the Soviet officials did not insist on formally asserting their authority. On the contrary, they realistically reinforced the provisional people's committees, which were largely led by Korean communists and resistance leaders released from Japanese imprisonment. Elections to expand these committees in rural areas took place in the fall of 1945. As in south Korea, various political parties sprung up which, in so far as possible, were purged of any leadership which might be considered either pro-Japanese or antagonistic toward basic Soviet values. Since holding an official position under the Japanese or remaining rich during their regime was generally considered tantamount to being pro-Japanese, such individuals suffered hardships and many migrated southwards. A united front of all political and social organizations was thus achieved early in 1946, while on February 9 of that year the Provisional People's Committee of Northern Korea came into being and unanimously elected Kim Il-sŏng as Chairman.

With the political situation well in hand, an election was held on November 3, 1946. This was of the typical Soviet variety, in which voting is a public approval of victorious candidates, who, since they have no competitors, have obviously been selected by other means. In any event, over four and a half million people, comprising within a few tenths of 100 per cent of the registered voters in northern Korea, are stated to have participated. It is also interesting and indicative of their selection that of the total of 3,459 deputies elected, of whom 453 were women, approximately 51 per cent were nonparty members, 32 per cent belonged to the Labor Party (a combination of the Communist and New People's parties), 10 per cent to the Democratic Party, and 7 per cent to the Ch'ŏndokyo Party.[69]

The representatives of the People's Committee met in February, 1947 and voted unanimous approval of all the legislation previously put into effect, established a National Assembly which in turn elected a Presidium of eleven persons. The following year, on August 25, another election was held for delegates to the Supreme People's Council which shortly afterwards (on September 9, 1948) proclaimed the establishment of the Democratic People's Republic of Korea. This move was obviously a reaction to the inauguration of the Democratic Republic of Korea in the southern zone. The claim was made for the People's Republic that, in accord with a proper representation of the population of the whole country over which it claimed jurisdiction, 360 of 572 seats in the Supreme People's Council were occupied by vote of south Koreans. This was a counter to the southerners' gesture of leaving vacant about one third of the seats in their legislative assembly for future members to be elected in the north. On September 19, 1948 the Soviet Foreign Ministry informed the United States that, in response to a request from the Supreme National Assembly in north Korea, all her troops would be withdrawn from the country by the end of 1948.[70]

After this résumé of activities on the part of Koreans in relation to the occupation authorities in their respective zones, we can briefly survey the interaction of the two military commands and, following this, the policies they inaugurated apart from those which were primarily political. As previously stated, provision was made in the Moscow Agreement of December, 1945, for a Joint U.S.-U.S.S.R. Commission. A preliminary conference held between the Russians and Americans from January 16 to February 5, 1946, unfortunately developed a major point of conflict which was never to be resolved. To the important question of what political parties and social organizations should be consulted in preparation for the establishment of a provisional Korean government, the Russian answer insisted upon exclusion of all groups which had opposed the Moscow Agreement. Since these included those led by Kim Koo and Syngman Rhee, it was concomitant to placing a ban against right-wing elements, a condition unacceptable to the American delegation. On the other hand, the Russians claimed that the Americans denied recognition to certain organizations of their preference.

When the Joint Commission itself convened between March 20 and April 8, 1946, the arguments on this issue led to a stalemate and what little there had been of the spirit of cooperation between the two zones practically disappeared. Unable to resolve the problem locally, the matter became the basis of an exchange of letters between the U. S. Secretary of State, G. C. Marshall, and the Soviet Foreign Minister, V. M. Molotov, with the result that the Joint Commission was at last directed to reconvene, which it did from May 21 to October 18, 1947. Starting with the hope of resolving the primary disagreement, the representatives of the two governments once again became deadlocked and would not even agree on a joint report. The United States then suggested a four-power conference to include China and the United Kingdom but the Soviet Union, apparently regarding such an aggregate as somewhat prejudiced, refused to accept the proposal. The matter was finally brought before the United Nations by the United States, with the results previously described.

Before going on to economic and other cultural problems of the two military governments, some explanation of the police and security systems of liberated Korea should be given. Under the Japanese administration, no aspect of the imperial rule was more hated by the people, and for obvious reasons. Removing the Korean members of the force from their position of power was probably as immediately satisfying as any other aspect of the Japanese surrender. The populace despised as renegades these men who, perhaps because of the nature of their work, had developed what has been one of the most sadistic organizations of modern times, as conquered people came to know to their sorrow wherever the Japanese were victorious.* Attacks on the police during the first month of liberation, needless to say, greatly heightened the existing antipathy.

In the northern zone there is adequate evidence that the former police personnel was permanently eliminated. The development of political control was such that it left little possibility for anyone to disguise his former affiliations and those who escaped headed southwards as rapidly as possible.

The problem of policing the American zone was more complex, however. In contrast to the Russians, who had given refuge to thousands of Koreans for many decades and consequently had a large body of trustworthy agents and interpreters, the United States army landed with practically none. Not only was contact with the masses of the people minimal, but for various reasons—economic, medical, and social—restrictions were also placed upon interpersonal relations between Koreans and Americans soon after the liberation which left most of the latter in an intellectual vacuum with respect to native life. The necessity for a strong police force grew upon the occupation authorities from the time when mass disturbances began in late 1945. Mobs composed of a strange and exotic populace inspire much more fear than those made up of a group of one's countrymen, and although Korean gatherings may appear from the center as no more than carnivals, from a distance the potential power of the surging multitude can seem to justify calling out tanks.

In the beginning, the American command attempted to use Japanese police to keep order but immediately met with passive resistance from the Korean populace. In establishing a new force, it would appear that the symbolic significance of disavowing the old one was not adequately realized. In any event, a nucleus of technically experienced men was retained. As pressure for security officers grew, no American was in the position to determine the previous status or

---

* A simple indication of this is the statement made by a group of Philippine naval officers two years after the surrender, that no Korean would dare to set foot on their islands because of the atrocities committed by the Korean police whom the Japanese armies brought with them.

loyalties of the thousands of men in the reconstituted organization. Under the circumstances the personnel was almost inevitably not only infiltrated by former members, of whom an indeterminate number had fled from the northern zone, but also by outright criminals as well.* It is reported that between September, 1946, and July, 1947, south Korean police arrested 113,447 persons of whom 96,670 were convicted, confessions being obtained in some cases by torture.† In the bloody Taegu conflicts, variously charged to communism and administrative injustice, forty-four or more policemen were killed by the maddened citizens in that city alone.[71] Whatever the reasons, it is certain that the national police had become once again a group hated by myriads of the populace.[72]

The Russians, immediately after their occupation of the country, began the creation of a people's militia, arming the men with captured Japanese weapons. This group, indoctrinated with communist values, not only functioned as a reinforcement to the regular police force but was also clearly aimed at protecting the political organization of north Korea from any development on a national scale which might undermine its power. By January, 1947, this program was expanded by a plan to draft and train all able-bodied males from the age of seventeen to twenty-five, thereby ultimately to provide a militia of approximately half a million men. The implications of such a proceeding are clear. Should the intended withdrawal of foreign troops from Korea take place, the northern administration set up with Russian guidance over approximately one third of the population would thus be in a position to dominate the whole of the country by military power if necessary.[73]

No effective countering move seems to have been made in the south until after the establishment of the Democratic Republic of Korea, although it is difficult to assess the real strength of the national police from a military point of view. Since that time, however, there are indications that with American advice and assistance

* In June, 1947, of 25,356 Korean police, over 4,100 or about 16 per cent had pre-liberation experience which could rarely have been achieved except as employees of the Japanese. *Summation*, June, 1947:31-32. A statement of the USAMGIK position defending this situation was made by the U. S. Military Governor. *Ibid.*, October, 1946:26.

† The official reports mention warnings to the police on third-degree methods and also the discharge of officers for undemocratic practices. *Summation*, March, 1946:7; *Ibid.*, May, 1946:6; *Ibid.*, May, 1947:25; *Ibid.*, July-August, 1948:213-14. For a more descriptive statement of "undemocratic practices," see Kang, 1948:20.

a considerable strengthening of security forces has taken place.* Whether these developments will lead to civil war when foreign controls have been removed and with what effect are questions so soon to be answered that there is no longer much significance in making predictions. It is noteworthy, however, that even before the end of 1948, antigovernment uprisings of considerable proportions occurred in the southern provinces of the country and on Cheju Island. These were reported as effectively suppressed within a reasonably short time.[74]

Economically, the problems of the two zones also stem from different conditions. Whereas, the Russians had to deal with a population estimated for 1948 to be from nine to ten millions, the American zone contained double this number of people in an area of about 37,000 square miles out of the total 85,602 comprising Korea. Furthermore, some two million of the population of south Korea represented recent Korean immigrants, of whom roughly one half had been repatriated from Japan and most of the remainder had escaped across the border from the north. Thus over 10 per cent of the people in southern Korea were practically in the position of refugees, whose presence created the necessity of their being productively integrated into the economy.[75]

Although the southern provinces are famous as food-producing areas, the harvest proved inadequate, requiring grain collections and rationing to achieve a reasonable distribution, as well as large imports to offset the shortage. Not only were both natural and extraordinary increases in the population responsible for this condition but production of food had fallen off as well. The Japanese had deprived the farmers of the output of Korean fertilizer plants in order to make explosives from it, and the main source of this needed material was in the hands of the Russians, who were not overgenerous in shipping it south. Important livestock such as cattle, hogs, and chickens had also fallen off about 50 per cent between 1942 and 1948. Further, the wartime deforestation to obtain household fuel caused flooding which likewise decreased crop yields. This complicated series of factors was just too much for the Korean farmers to comprehend so they deduced that the Americans had followed the Japanese

---

* On April 30, 1949, the *New York Times* reported that President Syngman Rhee had decided to double the defense forces in south Korea, increasing the standing army to 100,000 and establishing a reserve of 200,000 men. To train these troops he said that he would ask the United States government for 500 officers.

pattern of exporting Korean food. Consequently, they were not completely cooperative.*

The Russians, on the other hand, could supply fertilizer and developed morale by an almost immediate redistribution of the agricultural land confiscated from nonfarming landlords. Agrarian reform represented one of the most important goals desired by the great majority of the Korean people. The satisfaction from this situation was considerably offset, however, by the imposition of taxes and contributions equivalent to about 50 per cent of the crops.[76] The Russian troops depended upon local produce, so the natural food shortage of the northern zone remained a serious problem.[77]

The Russian procedure of reallocating private property conflicts with the American tradition, and the United States authorities, although desirous of at least dividing up great areas taken from the defeated Japanese, could not decide for more than two years on a satisfactory method. Finally, by an ordinance issued on March 22, 1948, the organization of the New Korean Company (which had been set up in March, 1946, to manage the farm holdings of the Japanese Oriental Development Company) was designated the National Land Administration and given the purpose of assisting landless tenants to become farm owners. The plan consisted of selling the Japanese holdings to those farmers who actually cultivated them, providing the fields in one man's possession were not in excess of two chŏngbo.† To prevent speculation, special restrictions were placed on resale. The price consisted of annual payments of 20 per cent of the major crop over a period of fifteen years. Slightly over 15 per cent of the agricultural land of south Korea was thus made available for distribution and it was reported that within a few months, the number of owner-operators had risen by 126 per cent over the totals for 1944, while the number of tenants had been decreased by 56 per cent during the same period.[78]

As might be expected, the financial structure of Korea, based on the yen, went to pieces after the surrender. But the debacle was particularly assisted by the Japanese, who had more than doubled the amount of currency in circulation, in anticipation of defeat.[79] The Americans fixed an exchange rate for paying Korean employees at fifteen wŏn to the dollar, whereas by January, 1946, about one

---

* It is ridiculous to attribute this idea of the farmers simply to communist propaganda. Very few Americans could understand the situation themselves.

† A chŏngbo equals 2.45 acres.

hundred were offered on the black market and on March 11, 1947, when the official exchange rose to fifty wŏn to the dollar, the black market value moved to about three hundred. A highly paid Korean USAMGIK employee could hardly be expected to survive on his salary alone and consequently theft, graft, and other corruption flourished in a fashion which would have brought respect and admiration from the most proficient courtiers in the lush days of the Yi dynasty. This seemingly unsurmountable situation disgusted most Americans as well as Koreans.[80]

Under the Japanese, only about 25 per cent of the government's income in Korea was derived from taxes, most of the remainder resulting from state-owned public utilities and monopolies. After 1945, the yield from these latter sources, except for those from the salt and tobacco monopolies, practically disappeared in deficit operations. At the same time, direct taxes fell off appreciably through evasion and inefficient administration. To meet the costs of government, the Bank of Chosen had doubled the amount of paper money in circulation by the beginning of 1947, bringing the total to over eighteen billion wŏn. Inflated prices were the inevitable concomitant. In the Russian zone, special occupation currency was issued but a lack of data, together with the special character of Soviet economics, makes the results difficult to appraise.[81]

The industry of Korea, largely centered in the northern zone, had been fostered as an integral part of Japanese economy, not as a self-sufficient indigenous development keyed to the requirements of the country itself. The Russians promptly nationalized their holdings, sent in Soviet engineers to work with what skilled Japanese technicians were available, and organized Korean labor into cooperative groups. Some machinery was apparently removed by the Russians, who considered it more useful elsewhere. Such action should not be judged offhand as unreasonable since we know that some heavy industry in the south was closed down because it could not be operated locally on a sound economic basis.*

* Shoemaker, 1947:15. It is interesting in this connection that Ambassador Edwin W. Pauley, U. S. Reparations Commissioner, toured northern Korea and reported on June 4, 1946, that the Russian commander, General Chistiakov stated that there were no removals of industrial equipment of any kind to the Soviet Union. Pauley adds that after being particularly observant "only on two or three occasions did we view anything that would indicate that such removals had taken place, and those only to a minor extent . . . which could well have been for intra-Korean movement." *Summation,* June, 1946:17-18.

Although of less magnitude, industry created greater problems in the American zone. The repatriation of all the Japanese left inadequate and unskilled staffs. The willing and enthusiastic Korean replacements proved sometimes unintentionally destructive as substitutes for the machinery-minded foreigners. The labor corps, which had fared badly under the former owners, was not inspired by any signs of a revolutionary change in their status and consequently remained particularly subject to communist influences. Finally, a lack of raw materials, together with the breakdown of transportation, made many of the plants inactive.

One of the first enterprises undertaken by the Americans was to restore the railroads and in this project they worked with a zest reminiscent of a father who sets up a toy train for his son. Scores of much-needed locomotives were imported from the United States and soon, as by a miracle, traffic was moving all around the country, with express service again connecting Pusan and Seoul. Nevertheless the equipment, including most of the roadbeds, remained in a dangerous state of disrepair. Sometimes a long iron bar on a switch engine would be lashed with a heavy bamboo reinforcement. The Korean personnel showed obvious delight in running their trains (most of which were restricted to native passengers) and welcomed the rare American rider with a combination of courtesy and pride.

Other forms of transportation fared less well. Many of the automobile roads became periodically impassable and such buses as remained verged on disintegration. Road traffic, which is said originally to have passed to the right and to have been shifted to the left by the Japanese, was changed back on April 1, 1946 to conform to the old Korean custom.* Nowhere was the collapse of the local systems more obvious than in Seoul which in June, 1947, had only forty electric streetcars still moving to serve a population estimated at a million.† As a result, the people exhausted themselves in traveling to and from their work. Other utilities fared somewhat better but were sadly in need of repair. Many mines had been depleted by the Japanese but a few in the south producing gold, graphite, lead, and tungsten

---

* *Summation,* March, 1946:7. Confirmation of an original Korean custom of passing to the right has not been found. One of the earliest foreign residents specifically mentions that the law of the road was to turn to the left. Gilmore, 1892:132.

† USAMGIK reported only 30 streetcars operating the following month, but the number was brought up to 130 by September, 1946, through import of much-needed repair parts. *Summation,* July, 1947:66; *Ibid.,* October, 1947:97.

indicated profitable futures. Most important, the coal supply was inadequate. The highly organized fishing industry broke apart after the surrender, as it had been controlled by Japanese and coordinated with their own. This forced a return to the technically less proficient methods of local Korean villagers. Commercial shipping also reverted to an almost primitive level since the major coastwise trade had been carried in Japanese vessels.[82]

A staggering blow to the economy of south Korea was delivered when the electric power supply from the Russian zone was cut off on May 14, 1948. South Korea could then have produced only about one third of the 200,000 kilowatts required if its economy had been fully functioning. Before the division of the country, however, Korea had adequate resources from fine modern hydroelectric plants which the Japanese had constructed in the northern provinces. The Russians first claimed that the American Command had not paid for power received and then demanded that negotiations be conducted with the Korean People's Democratic Republic, which was not acceptable, the whole proceeding being considered a political maneuver.[83]

On some social aspects of culture, the policies of the occupation authorities in the two zones may also be compared. The Russians, for example, although nominally tolerant of religion, probably showed neither special respect for the Christian churches nor offered them protection from the attacks of militant Korean opponents. It must be remembered, however, that the Protestant sects would come under the suspicion of being pro-American, while the reported slaying of a Roman Catholic priest by Soviet soldiers may possibly have been influenced by his German nationality.[84] The Americans, on the other hand, although realistically tolerant of religion, certainly started no campaign in propagation of the Christian faith. In fact, some of the missionaries objected to a lack of official support.

In the field of public health, the contributions of the Russians are unknown. The disease-conscious Americans naturally emphasized efforts in this field if only for their own protection. With some problems such as sanitation they found the Koreans peculiarly unappreciative, but in dealing with epidemics quite the contrary. It has been said that the prompt control of the cholera outbreak under the difficult conditions that followed the Japanese surrender was the outstanding contribution of the occupation. In November, 1946, when the epidemic was considered officially over, 15,615 cases had been reported with 10,191 deaths.[85]

In both zones, the educational systems were fostered. The Russian program may have been effective if only because of the opportunities it offered for cooperation with the mass of the people. In the American zone, a great effort was made to supply millions of new textbooks which would provide for teaching in the Korean language without the heavy restrictions and bias enforced by the Japanese administration. The books were printed in the native alphabet, ŏnmun (or hangŭl), with the innovation of having the characters run horizontally from left to right instead of vertically.* More difficulty was encountered at higher levels of education because of the lack of teachers, the low salaries offered, the tendency of older Korean students to marry politics and education, as well as the inevitable deficiencies of equipment. One can believe, however, that there was freedom of information to the degree to which it was possible to communicate it.[86] Considering all students, Lt. Gen. Hodge, speaking for the American administration, claimed that there were 50 per cent more Korean children in school during 1947 than there had been before the liberation.†

For the adult population, verbal and pictorial propaganda in favor of American ideals was almost nonexistent, at least relative to the extensive dissemination of pro-Russian values. The notion seemed to be current that the Americans could best represent their way of life through simply living it; if so, the majority created a strange and misleading spectacle by their enforced isolation and superior attitudes. The Russians, on the other hand, organized tours in the Soviet Union for the benefit of north Korean cultural leaders, an undertaking facilitated by the juxtaposition of the two countries. They also may have had the advantage in promoting artistic activities to which the Americans were slow in giving effective support. Despite difficulties, the Americans did seem to make realistic contributions in the realm of sports, an aspect of life for which Koreans have showed tremendous enthusiasm.

* *Summation,* April, 1946:31-32. By the beginning of 1948, some 12,702,129 textbooks are reported to have been published since the liberation. *Ibid.,* January, 1948:205.

† Hodge, 1947:831; McCune, 1947a:13. The school population for 1939 was 998,455 (including Japanese); for 1944 it was 1,555,336 (including Japanese); for 1945 (December), 1,722,938; and for 1947 (October), 2,388,463 (excluding folk schools); *Summation,* February, 1946:297; *Ibid.,* October, 1947:154.

If USAMGIK, partly because of language and communication difficulties, proved less generous of cultural gifts than people might have preferred, the policy was clearly directed toward allowing freedom of Korean self-expression within limits short of physical violence. Free speech was held up as an ideal, and except for occasionally suppressing a newspaper under charge of publishing false statements and inciting riots, the freedom of the press was fostered. By 1947, there were some eighty-five daily newspapers appearing in south Korea, of all shades of political opinion. Also, over a quarter of a million radio sets were in use, receiving a wide variety of programs.[87] It is a striking fact that although the American regime appears to have leaned well to the right, almost constant verbal abuse and vituperation were accepted with reasonable equanimity from sources which might have been expected to be most sympathetic.[88] The inevitable conclusion must be drawn that, for better or for worse, the Koreans as a whole would have preferred to determine the course of events by themselves.

17

KOREA IN RETROSPECT

PROBABLY the most interesting books ever written present an individual's solutions to the problems of the people with whom he happens to have been associated. Such accounts are inevitably exciting because everyone living in a social world reacts more or less acutely to the surrounding human beings who so much control his own life and happiness. It is natural to identify one's self with a writer and to see and believe with him. Unfortunately, an author may have strange eyes and a perverse understanding which prejudices those he informs, themselves unable to gauge the truth of his statements. Contrariwise, a man may set down his thoughts with such amazing comprehension of human joys and sorrows that time will attribute his knowledge to divine inspiration. The value of revelation, however, proves difficult to assay, whether offered as philosophy, science, or religion, and the death of countless millions may result from these gospels before their influence burns away, leaving, as with *Mein Kampf,* cold gray ashes on a dusty shelf.

In this study of the Koreans, the purpose has been to present first that which any objective observer might see of the life of the people, and then to distill the essence of simple facts from the writings of hundreds who have added to the record and gone their way. Where the spirit has not aged, the biases have been blended, but not so subtly that the component flow of sweet and dry cannot be distinguished. No hidden wormwood has been added to confuse the mind and no aphrodisiac to excite the passions. The reader has had a drink of such truth as can honestly be served and, if yet unsatisfied, has been guided to the sources from which it springs. Thinkers will be pleased that it has thus been made possible for them to form their own opinions and, if slightly wearied, may on sober reflection even remember with some affection the bottle they have shared.

With this introduction, a summary and evaluation of the data on Korean culture from the writer's viewpoint may now be safely given.

Indeed, it may by some few be considered most desirable that one who has long studied the evidence should present a personal opinion of its meaning and thus purvey that promised inkling of the *why*.

It is certain that most of the ancestors of the Koreans were migrants from the northland and came down into the Peninsula at least four thousand years ago, many of them perhaps long before that time. Their Korean language is a branch of that Altaic stock to which Finnish, Turkish, Mongol, and Tungus-Manchu belong.[89] Judging also from their physical type, the Koreans might well have originated in northeast Asia and not unlikely with some early admixture of white-skinned peoples from the West.* In the south of the Peninsula there was probably an increment of voyagers from Japan or even of those who followed the sea lanes northwards directly from more distant lands. Chinese immigration, we can assume, began to be significant in the twelfth or eleventh centuries B.C. and reached its greatest proportions in the first three hundred years before our era. Ever since that time, there has been periodic absorption from surrounding areas. From the mingling of these peoples the present-day Koreans are descended.

In comprehending the origin and development of Korean culture we encounter difficulties not only through the lack of accurate records on the genesis of customs, but also in distinguishing those traits which since time beyond memory were shared with other people from those which were borrowed, and from those which, although stimulated by diffusion, resulted in significant achievements properly credited to the Koreans themselves. Can we be sure, for example, that the Koreans' ancestors did not invent the hunter's bow or tailored clothing? Did they borrow the method of heating whole rooms in their houses? And has their technical gift for making fine paper been intrinsically Korean? An exacting search for the answers to such questions, if important, proves pedantic. What becomes vital to recognize is that all human accomplishment results from the accumulated labor and thinking of an interminable line of predecessors, individuals whose national and racial allegiances are largely fictional.

---

* As we know them today, the Koreans range in stature from 162 to 167 cm. (5 ft. 4 in. to 5 ft. 6 in.) which is near the general average of human beings (165 cm.). This is about two inches taller than the Japanese and slightly less than that of the northern Chinese. Their heads are broader than those of either and also high. Dark eyes peer from folded Mongoloid lids, their hair often appears in shades of brown, and skin varies from a yellowish cast to almost white. Hrdlička. 1945-46 :33-43.

Korean culture, taken as a whole, is as distinctive as any other, not-withstanding the tremendous influence of China which Koreans them-selves would be the first to insist upon recognizing. Chopsticks and agriculture, clothing styles, tile roofs, oxcarts, sedan chairs, suspen-sion bridges, metal casting and glazed ceramics, lacquer work, musi-cal instruments, books and writing, are just a few of the material things and techniques contributed by the Middle Kingdom. Even more important are the formalized patterns of political and social organization, the scientific observations, the Confucian values per-meating the ceremonial crises of an individual's life. And yet each act and almost every object has an indigenous touch, a distinction which marks it for the sensitive observer as Korean rather than Chinese.

Although the methods of growing and cooking rice closely parallel those of China, when Korean meals and eating habits are considered as a whole, the difference is enormous. The emphasis on pickled food and pepper seasoning provides a cuisine as contrasting as would that of Syria. Likewise, although the style and color in costume came from the Yellow River in centuries past, who has ever seen a Chinese dressed in a starch-slick bulging white coat and pantaloons, with wrist and ankle bands, and a fancifully delicate black broad-brimmed hat to top his dignity? Where else will one find women in such full flowing skirts and breast-revealing little jackets? Taken in its en-tirety, the old Korean costume is unmistakably unique.

The Korean houses differ from their western neighbors' even more than the food and dress. In the village, each is an isolated dwelling with glistening bedroom floors of heavy brown paper as smooth and trim as linoleum, besides being equipped beneath with a system of flues which foreshadowed modern radiant heating. In these rooms and in those with floors of polished wood, the people wear no shoes, keeping the surfaces clean and clear. Such orderli-ness is indicated even by the frequently swept clay matang over which one approaches the house. The similarity in dwellings is obviously closer to the Japanese. Perhaps the cleanliness value came from these water-washed neighbors of warm southern origin. The Ko-reans may have combined Chinese clay walls and tile roofs, too dan-gerous for the earthquake-shaken islands, with the Japanese mat and pole house, then added paper floors with an improved heating system.

From early times, the Koreans have been noted as travelers. Men tended to trot rather than walk if there was any reason for speed, and it is not surprising that this long tradition has found modern expression in successful Olympic marathon champions. The men are also celebrated carriers of heavy loads by means of a special packboard. These traits more suggest a northern complex than any other, one of cold forested country where men moved quickly to be warm and had to carry burdens on their backs because of lack of roads in a rough terrain. We should also remember the native Korean pony with the savage temper, a little beast unlikely of either Chinese or Japanese ancestry. If the early people coming south did not bring this pony with them, they must have acquired it long ago from horse-using tribes roaming eastward over the steppes from Central Asia.

In their technical skills and artistic productions, the Koreans have perhaps showed less originality than an ability to adopt, encourage, and sometimes improve on Chinese contributions. Casting of metal serves as an example. The people in the south of the Peninsula worked with iron from an early date and it is at least questionable, considering both size and artistic perfection, whether any nation has ever produced the equal of the bells of Silla. We should not, of course, forget the creation of metallic type, but there is even a Korean mold for the most common things such as the sickle with its right-angle blade, which every farmer uses. Perhaps this latter tool is simply a conservative ancient trait that successfully resisted replacement by the curved cutting edge which in surrounding areas has understandably become the symbol of agrarian labor.

Fine Korean ceramics will seldom be confused with those from any other source, nor will most of the common pieces. At what date pottery was first made in the Peninsula is still unknown, but that time lies surely in the prehistoric past. We can assume that the potter's wheel and the art of glazing came from China but the final products of the hot kilns had the peculiar Korean touch burned into their fragile bodies.

A most extraordinary feature of Korean culture has been the practice of large groups of men or boys gathering on opposing sides to hurl stones at each other, with expected fatal consequences. Throwing stones is a trait which has certainly not been limited by ethnic boundaries but certainly no other people ever encouraged it over so long a period as a national pastime. Such violence is clearly neither consistent with Chinese values nor compatible with the manners of the Japanese. Here again, the links lie northward to individuals more unrestrained in temperament. Living Russians tell of similar stone fights taking place on the newly frozen river ice in country as far west as the Bug River of southeastern Europe.

In singing, drinking, and dancing we find a complex which the Chinese commentators emphasized as distinguishing the Koreans from the earliest days. Again, it is not a case of unique behavior but the quality of general participation in it that makes the impression on the observer, and again one turns to Russians in the north to find a parallel.* Clearly, both Chinese and Japanese singing and dancing are more restrained and formalized, while intoxicated persons are seldom seen in those countries. Although China's impact in developing classical music and the ritual dancing of the kisaeng is unmistakable, the widespread participation of the villagers in these arts is indigenous like the hills.

Hospitality is not in itself a rare trait but the degree to which the Koreans have traditionally carried it has been realistically exaggerated. It has frequently been recorded that a traveler could wander from one end of the kingdom to the other, depending daily on some village stranger to supply him with a roof and meal. For the rich man, a coterie of guests was the necessary and inevitable mark of his position, causing an almost constant competition between his resources and his reputation. This is a frontier pattern, and particularly in the north where the rigors of physical existence habitually demanded the privilege of one man depending upon another when emergency arose. If a stranger was not killed, he was fed and sheltered. The Koreans developed into a civilized nation without losing their hospitableness toward human beings and made a social fetish of this attitude.

One peculiar quality of the Korean social organization which is more difficult to understand historically is the sharp dichotomy of the two-class social structure, which at times seems to have developed into an almost rigid separation of the nobles and the commoners. Such social cleavage has not been typical of China and if more suggestive of Japan, still seems extreme. Offhand, one finds a

---

* In speaking of Russians, here as elsewhere, the reference is to the collective Euro-Asiatic culture group occupying a vast national area, not to the limited pre-revolutionary dominant class or culture with strong Byzantine influences which so often blind the eyes of western historians to the total, significantly oriental, culture complex of Russia as a whole.

similarity to the relation between the Chinese and the peoples who ruled over them during conquest dynasties. One likewise thinks of Russia under the czars. It is possible, if this overemphasis of class consciousness was not culturally inherited, that the influx of foreigners as such—Chinese, Mongols, and others—may have been deviously responsible.

The behavior of Korean men in their social relationships to women, excepting kisaeng, has been marked by an aloofness possibly unsurpassed by any other people in the world. Whereas men's avoidance of females not belonging to the household, or even of particular relatives within it, occurs—and sometimes assumes a major importance—in various societies, Koreans have tended on both sociological and psychological levels to carry the ideal of male superiority to a point of pseudo-isolation even from their wives. The explanation seems apparent. The Koreans, with a suggestion of unconscious embarrassment, have naïvely carried their conception of Confucian ideals to a heroic level which would surprise the Chinese and astound Confucius himself.

Finally, our attention is drawn to the extremely important role of Shamanism, or spirit worship, as it has developed in the Peninsula. As has been stated in the special discussion of this subject, the ancient roots of the religion are buried beyond our view in the northern forests from which the Koreans came. The reason that Buddhism did not clear the ground after its introduction during the fourth century can perhaps be explained only through an understanding of Korean personality. Buddhism fell a degenerate victim to the onslaught of rational Confucianism and left Korean women free to institutionalize primitive superstitions. Their success has been underestimated only by those whose bias prevents recognition of strong religious feeling unhallowed by orthodox conventions. Sometimes called a nation without religion, it is probably more accurate to describe the Koreans as intrinsically the most deeply religious people of the Far East.

Our review of things outstandingly Korean leads us inevitably to the concept of personality and its meaning as a historical determinant of cultural trends. We cannot know empirically, of course, the personality of the distant ancestors of the Koreans. Early Chinese descriptions are helpful, however, and so are what we judge to be the essential aspects of the modern character. To these we can add some intuitions, dangerous though they be, based on our knowledge of northern neighbors who less long have been exposed to civilization.

All in all, we reconstruct a picture of a people with some smouldering violence in their nature, struggling against an environment in which for each brief victory there was a period of severe constraint. The cycle of the seasons brought its turn of hot summer, with sudden need for an intense spending of energy in the accumulation of food, and afterwards the snow of frozen winter to seal the people into the silence of their valley settlements. First rest, then exuberance, followed by the compression of long nights, the load of pent-up emotions, fears, speculations, and anxiety. This is the aboriginal calendar of cold for northern latitudes. The imagined prototype of the Korean personality is an introverted individual with considerable emotional instability, capable of the sustained quiescence of the hibernating bear and of the fury of the goaded tiger.

People of the rich Korean temperament could not have accepted Chinese culture with natural ease. The latter was too rational, too formal, and emotionally too cold. The Koreans wanted pepper and pickle with their rice, if they were to sit quietly and eat. They were probably accustomed to even stronger smells and flavors in their food. How they became so content with a colorless black and white costume may seem surprising—until we remember ancient chroniclers repeating that the delicate hat was forced on the Koreans to calm them down. It is probably even more important to recall that such dress has been characteristic only of the Yangpan who became masters of restraint in idleness, thus emphasizing one aspect of the national character. The Koreans are very frequently damned as the laziest people on earth and in the next breath praised as miraculous workers, runners, burden bearers, and displayers of superhuman sources of energy. And if the latter, how not the former? These are compensatory qualities, not alternatives, as one should know from personal experience.

Abandon from restraint also marks their drinking and dancing, while stone-throwing epitomizes their violence. Even their singing suggests an irresistible need for emotional expression, the same quality one finds among the Russians. Perhaps there is something in it of reaction to the long winter nights, for music has a strange beauty in its power to dispel the pervading silence of the arctic snows. Percussion instruments achieved a particular popularity and their throb, clang, or boom seemed to invoke the spirits. The Korean passion for casting big bells may be more than happy coincidence. However this may be, the periodic excitation of Shamanism, the musical crescendos of the performance alternating with an eerie stillness, the terrific anxiety leading to immediate contact with the spirits in a highly animatistic universe, cohered so closely with the Korean personality that it seems the natural counterpart.

So far we have been considering the effect on society of the Korean personality, albeit one so tenuous and hypothetically conceived. It follows logically, since the interactions are reciprocal, to think of the impact on the personality of the growing culture. First, let us remember that the major foreign cultural influence came from China, a land of very different environment producing a people of contrasting national character—mature, highly rational, emotionally restrained, and effectively productive. The Koreans were almost overcome by their admiration for Chinese civilization and attempted to carry its ideals into practice with a fervor and literalness that were almost pathetic. At certain periods, in some aspects of culture, one might say that the Koreans out-Chinesed their teachers. This reaction appears most conspicuously in their application of Confucian values to the family system. The patriarchal head of the Chinese household became in Korea a tyrant and an unnatural symbol of superiority; the inferior social status of women was emphasized to such an illogical conclusion that it was no longer easily possible for a man to enjoy a conversation with his wife; and ceremonialism connected with ancestor worship was elaborated to a degree that made death almost more important than life. Koreans are known even to have complained of shortcomings in the manners of the Chinese and they developed a labyrinth of verbal expression, based on degrees of politeness, that frequently interfered with more significant matters of communication. All this proliferation of formalism necessarily proved a strain on the personality. The innately emotional Korean thus often becomes repressed to the point of explosion, and then bursts but with much more noise than effect.

The typical Korean baby seems happy enough, obviously finding gratification in nursing at will. Generally, competition from a younger brother or sister forces the small child to seek other forms of satisfaction but he is restricted to spending much of his time strapped to some older person's back. He can look or listen or sleep but, like a convalescent in a hospital bed, the most exciting periods of his day are his meals. Growing older, he meets responsibilities, particularly in the deference of his behavior to the older males around him. The adventurous escape of American children from parental control, their direct and indirect attacks on adults, adventures so exciting that they cannot possibly remember to return home at mealtime, are satisfactions which are normally denied the Korean child. His father is typically stern and somewhat distant and only the women of his household will grant him much physical affection. If he feels particularly alone he may seek the food and warmth of his mother's breasts years after the period of normal weaning. The concern with food is also indicated by the frequency with which one sees Korean children standing with their mouths open, or often sucking on their fingers. The tremendous interest in drinking and eating is never lost. Adult Koreans are notoriously heavy consumers of rice if it is available and will spend many hours in feasting with as many guests as possible. We should remember the rich fisherman who struts down to his vessel, protruding his bare belly over his rolled-down trousers as a symbol of success. Food is more than life to Koreans and unfortunately a disproportionately large cause of their illnesses and death.

To return to the Korean youth, we find that at puberty he is cut off from most of the few sources of manifest affection which had been available. Typically, and not always unconsciously, he hates his dominating father. He is deprived of intimacy with the female sex since he cannot even approach the girls who might normally attract and absorb his energy. Physical satisfactions and ego gratification are both lacking. Without them one finds violence and sadistic tendencies rising, while rioting and torture seem consistent with this cultural inadequacy for the opportunity to love. With such a background for marriage one would expect sadistic elements in the sexual relations of Koreans. It is almost amusing, therefore, to have had the first informant questioned reply that his sister had left her husband because he pinched her too painfully during intercourse.

The lack of ego gratification shows itself in the frequency with which Koreans demonstrate or verbalize their desire to undertake actions of heroic proportions. They will risk the most cruel punishments for the sake of a religious belief or a political cause. The evidence for this is clear if one only takes into consideration the per-

secution of Christians or of the supporters of the independence movement. The young Korean approach to the field of finance or art is
typically the same. His talk and expectations, irrespective of any
evidence of either hard work or genius, set a standard which would
be satisfied only by his becoming a Rockefeller or Rachmaninoff.
However he may achieve it, the Korean goal is to be a hero.

All this is very frustrating and rarely results in expression which
is adequately satisfying to the ego. The Koreans quarrel intermin-
ably without decision, the men will battle physically for hours and in
the end one can seldom ascertain who defeated whom. Riots frequently cause no more damage than carnivals. Socially or politically,
action is seldom brought to a sharp conclusion. Even in extreme
drinking, the Korean staggers to his bed rather than reaches the extreme culmination of alcoholic excess by collapsing unconscious on
the social scene.

Without trespassing too far into the sometimes mysterious by-
ways of the seven magic systems of psychoanalysis, it seems safe to
characterize the Korean personality as one emphasizing oral-sadistic
components in Freudian terms, and as also illustrating clearly the exploitative orientation, more often in its negative aspect, described by
Eric Fromm. The foreigner may remain uncertain whether he likes
Koreans, but in his personal contacts he will seldom have felt such
powerful impulses to love a people or to hate them.

Before attempting to evaluate Korean culture as that of one nation
among many, something should be said about its influence on surrounding countries. Although it is improbable that there could be
such large-scale gifts from China without some return, Korean contributions are not easy to perceive. There is a possibility that painters in the Peninsula may have added some freedom to the brushwork
in the great mural painting of fifteen hundred years ago which critics
so quickly attribute to the Chinese, despite the peripheral distribution
of the evidence. In general, the Koreans were not always as much the
slaves to previous art forms as the Chinese were themselves and some
reflection of this freedom may yet be found in further study of the
Middle Kingdom. The civilization of the Peninsula unquestionably
had a great impact upon the more primitive nations to the north but
since the latter likewise reacted to Chinese contact, it will require
more detailed studies than are now available to weigh and measure
the increment of years.

For the Japanese, however, Korean cultural gifts were large. Interestingly enough, the pattern of selection has been focused on the two fields of art and religion, the former of Chinese origin but touched by Korean genius, and the latter not fundamentally Chinese at all. Shamanism, or spirit worship, may well have reached Japan with the earliest settler but was undoubtedly reinforced by Korean contact as occasion offered in later times. Buddhism, on the other hand, strongly infiltrated the islands during the middle centuries of the first millennium of our era. The Japanese wove this religion more intimately into the texture of their life than did either the Koreans or the Chinese. The latter were perhaps too rational for its ultimate acceptance and the Koreans not rational enough.

The great transfer of artistic techniques from Korea to Japan took place almost immediately after the acceptance of Buddhism, that great promulgator of the arts and international agent. Fine metal work, the making of paper, the introduction of the potter's wheel, lacquer, and wood block printing were probably all adopted in Japan during the years roughly between 500 A.D. and 800 A.D.* The same is true of temple architecture, of which the earliest surviving example in the Far East, that of Hōriuji near Nara, is traditionally attributed to Korean workmen of whom there was a large colony in Japan. Nara, still bearing its Korean name, is said to have been originally a Korean settlement. The Japanese enthusiasm for Korean potters long continued, notably kindling Hideyoshi's interest about 1570. Following his invasions of the Peninsula, large numbers of skilled craftsmen were brought back to Japan, thus creating a local renaissance in the ceramic industry. The Japanese also took much of their intellectual learning from Korea but again it becomes difficult to distinguish what is Korean, what Chinese, especially as direct influence from China increased as time went on. To each and every gift Japan added its special touch, even as Korea has done.

Summarizing the similarities and differences of Korean culture with respect to the neighboring areas, the kinship with China appears most obvious as one runs through the long list of material, social, and intellectual traits. Despite the historic connections, Korea and Japan are less alike. There is resemblance in their terraced rice

* Rein gives the date for the introduction of papermaking into Japan as 610 A.D., of the potter's wheel as 724 A.D. Rein, 1889:392, 457. The date of the Japanese acceptance of Buddhism is commonly stated to be 552 A.D., but the first influences may have been somewhat earlier.

fields but it arises from the coincidence of their somewhat similar mountainous terrain. Perhaps in some intangible way the Koreans are closer to the Japanese in their pure esthetic values, but this feeling might be difficult to defend. More significant is the similarity of Koreans in personality and temperament to the peoples of the north. The motions and movement, the fast and the fierce, are paralleled there. And behind it all is a deep religiosity which merges Korean humanity with the natural environment in a union more intimate and elemental than one would expect of a society so civilized. As for the differences, Chinese culture is more intellectual, Japanese more esthetic, and the northerners more unconstrained.

A personal evaluation of the cultures of all nations does not place the Korean in the first rank of ten or probably even in the second. Distinguished by long duration in time, Korean culture may be held as one of the twenty-five great developments in the history of civilization which, if true, constitutes an impressive human achievement. It will not be possible to review world culture here, but a few critical comments may indicate a method for drawing such conclusions. As we have seen, at various florescent periods, some superlative artistic objects were created in Korea. In the field of visual arts—painting, sculpture, architecture, and ceramics—all reached the level where comparisons in terms of merit demand the ultimate sophistication. Intrinsically, the Koreans are probably more musical than either the Chinese or Japanese, but in this aspect of culture the whole Far East lags noticeably behind the West. Considering the more abstract quality of esthetics, the Koreans do not seem greatly differentiated from the Chinese, but both fall short of that exquisite sensitivity for physical beauty which, in the opinion of many, places the Japanese without equal.

In food production, the Koreans have been consistently self-sustaining over thousands of years, most of the time not only avoiding starvation but eating extraordinarily well. Unfortunately, to the gourmet's taste their cooking ranks far below the peak set by the neighboring Chinese or distant French. It might be regarded as on the level of the Japanese cuisine, or quite superior to that of the English peasant. The Korean dress is clean and simple but a little impractical in the demands it makes for care. The Koreans seem to wash to please their vanity, the English to please their conscience, and the Japanese for physical satisfaction. Korean housing deserves a superior rating. In an environment of uneven temperatures and considerable rainfall they have devised comfortable homes which are well arranged, dry in summer and warm in winter. Furthermore, the standard of cleanliness in their homes is high. The well-swept ma-tang, the climbing gourd vines, and the kitchen garden form a little jewel in an exquisite valley setting. Over the ages, the Koreans have proved themselves to be excellent defensive fighters. They have shown little of that spirit of military conquest that has marked the Japanese or Mongols, the French or Germans. It is a singular fact that a thousand years of national unity passed unblemished by civil wars.

As previously emphasized, Korean productive energy tends to be intermittent rather than sustained. In consequence, the people have not shared the reputation for industriousness given to both Japanese and Chinese, or Germans in the West. Also, the Korean mind does not have the intellectual turn, that quality of constant willingness to reason, which, for example, distinguishes the Chinese or the Jews. Mentally the Koreans seem more akin to the imaginative Irish or smart peasants of sunny Spain. In the adjustment between the sexes, the Koreans fall very low relative to world values, and in the whole field of social relations, their development has been inadequate compared to their material and artistic achievements. To put it bluntly, they fail to provide for really satisfying self-expression.

The class system and slavery also have stultified Korean national life and at times a sense of individual human justice seems almost to have disappeared. Admittedly, this quality of respect for all persons within a group has always been rare, appearing strongly only during recent times in certain north European countries such as Sweden. In fact, the whole Korean political system rarely rose above its archaic form and in the last centuries became noticeably decadent.

So much for suggestions towards a comparative and historical evaluation of Korean culture, inadequate as the ideas have been. We must now turn to the place of Korea in the contemporary international scene, for whatever the limitations of this people during their long isolation, the future looms pregnant with possibilities for a far-reaching effect on the destinies of eastern Asia and ultimately the world.

In times past, Korea has enjoyed periods of efficient administration. At the beginning of the nineteenth century, however, the country suffered not only from a weak and ignorant, if well-intentioned, king, who was plagued by the inheritance of deep corruption in the established political system. The official group in Korea, with rare exceptions, seemed to have lost all interest in the people at large except in so far as they might be considered a source of the wealth which could be squeezed from their collective labor. In the Ministry of the Interior, the examination system as a measure of competence for governmental office had become a transparent farce. Political preferment was purchased and the new incumbent usually hastened to regain his financial investment along with a profit as large as possible before the office was resold behind his back. The Law Ministry presided over a dispensation of justice for which it is difficult to find instances to support the name. A member of the official group could have an ordinary person jailed by simple complaint and if the latter could not buy his freedom, he would probably suffer barbarous physical punishment and remain indefinitely in prison. A court was the last place to which equals would resort for the settlement of interpersonal disputes. Even a witness might be tortured on the chance of extracting information. Graft permeated the other departments on a scale commensurate with the potentialities. The result of this situation was that few sincere men could survive an honest attempt to work for the welfare of the country. To do so threatened the security of the official group as a whole and marked one out for political disaster. The profitable course was to spend one's time in the right company so as to protect one's income, if not to increase it. This was an official's duty to his family and to the miscellaneous congeries of hangers-on towards whom hospitality became the hallmark of success.

That Korean officials were so distinctively set apart from the people as a whole may have been an advantage, for it tended to confine the behavior pattern within the group, just as infectious cases are isolated in one ward of a hospital. The majority of the nonofficial population appeared uncontaminated and the question may be asked how this could be. The answer lies in the understanding of the peculiar role of the ajŏn who filled the lowest rural offices. Although they followed the group pattern of increasing their income as the opportunities offered, they alone among the officials personally knew the people and, knowing them, respected them because they realized their power. It was the ajŏn who kept peace by warning their superiors of the point beyond which the harvest of the farmers' labor could not be taken without revolt. When abuse became intolerable, the people could turn on the officials and drive them out and this they sometimes did. Generally they remained quiet, bearing the burdens of their life with that equanimity which may make one marvel at the tolerance and the courage of simple human beings. The attitude towards the Yangpan class was one of mingled respect and fear, becoming warmly responsive on the rare occasion when a man in authority showed an understanding sympathy and consideration for their problems and equally bitter and vindictive towards the sadistic despot. The difference between the two groups was partly one of degree reflecting the great disparity of wealth, but in some aspects of life the basic principles and behavior were fundamentally opposed.

With the opening of the country, the westerners who flowed in were largely dedicated to the propagation of Christianity. The common people and these English-speaking strangers liked each other extraordinarily well. The success with which the new doctrines permeated the populace may be attributed not only to the religious nature of the Koreans, but to the fact that Protestant Christian ethics happened to supply those gifts of greatest cultural need, particularly in championing the personal dignity of the individual—of a woman as well as of a man. In theory, the religion placed great emphasis on love, justice, and personal freedom, irrespective of age or position, while in practice the missionaries stressed modern education and medical care for each and all. These were the very things the people lacked, and the downtrodden Koreans responded by the tens of thousands in a heroic revolt against habitual restrictions. The bonds between the missionaries and the common people proved strong and good but their friendship ran afoul of a contrary set of alien influences.

Dominant among other foreigners were the Japanese, the great majority of whom were concerned with diplomacy or economics. Their contacts concentrated on the ruling class, and they came not bearing gifts but with a sword. After a short period of orientation and mild persuasions, they viewed their Yangpan acquaintances as hopelessly unregenerate, and where they could not bribe them, cut them down. Since international politicians share more interests in common than they do with the peoples to whom they dictate, Japan gained approval for the military subjugation of Korea. Naturally, the Koreans did not like this rape of freedom, but the Japanese warlords showed them nothing but contempt and ruthless suppression. The Americans and the British who lived among the common people begged in their homelands for assistance to Korea, but their pleas were muffled by the cleverest propaganda ever to drip from lying tongues. And so for thirty-five years the Koreans worked in bondage with humbled pride, but still appreciative of whatever learning their masters could be persuaded to purvey.

The Japanese regime was not inefficient, but it worked towards evil ends. Relative to certain criteria, good government may be achieved without a foundation of democratic principles, provided those who rule recognize and demonstrate a responsibility *for* the people. The Japanese avowed good intentions but were too unenlightened to carry them out and rationalized the costs of their extravagant national ambition as contributions to human welfare. The passing of time produced an unexpected result. The leaders of the Japanese government so successfully confused the world with illusions of their superiority that they finally fooled themselves, spreading their undeclared wars and suffering everywhere, until the Mikado's vainglorious empire collapsed in absolute defeat.

The years following 1945, when Korea became free of the Japanese, are the most difficult to analyze, and constitute a period in which it requires courage to trespass beyond the descriptive facts. From the Korean point of view, the division of the country at the 38th parallel and the consequent occupation of the two parts by Soviet and United States military forces proved a disastrous development of inconsiderate diplomacy. The Koreans wished to handle their own affairs and it cannot be demonstrated that they could not have done so creditably with a minimum of assistance. Instead, the Peninsula became a field of contest on which Koreans were virtually forced to side with one of the great powers.

If the victorious allied command insisted upon guidance for Korea, then it was a responsibility that Russia might have reasonably undertaken alone. The positive reasons for this belief, based on the assumption of sharing the rights and duties of a successful ally in a long and expensive war, were the juxtaposition of the Soviet Union and Korea, the century of experience with Koreans as refugees, and the appreciation of the social and economic problems of a people long dominated by a grasping and corrupt minority. On the negative side, it would seem somewhat unreasonable to the Soviet Union that the military power of the United States should be extended beyond the Pacific to within a few miles of her own territory while presuming to assist Koreans, about whom Americans knew little with respect to their language, customs, or social and political requirements. To those with eyes focused on larger issues, such prejudices of the Russians, of course, will seem trivial.

In the occupation, Soviet favoritism for the industrial laborers and the masses of the agrarian population was inevitable. The members of the wealthy ruling class, and particularly those surviving by co-operation with the Japanese, received little support in the problems of readjustment. The limitations of the Russian system of government were equally apparent.

The American attitude was one of tremendous good will towards Koreans, tempered by some anxiety and fear of the exotic. Unprepared to make effective contacts with the ordinary villagers, and indeed going to the extremes of prohibiting any sharing of basic human activities, they proceeded to give advice, sometimes dictatorially, but more often in a democratic spirit naïve only in assuming implicit political values which Koreans, lacking education and experience, could not even understand. The reaction of the American staff in the resulting confusion was frequently that of sympathy, but unfortunately too often summed up by shouting some personal opinion of "these god damn Gooks!"

Confounded by the Korean personality, which expressed itself in political cliques marked by both verbal and physical violence, and affected by the rising antagonism toward Russia in the western world, the United States policy fostered an orderly assumption of power by some group of Koreans who could be depended upon to oppose Soviet domination of the Peninsula. Given this premise, which for purposes of real influence was practically limited to English-speaking Koreans, the military advisors could neither control nor keep abreast of the political maneuvering of their Korean protagonists who operated with the intuitive astuteness of years of practice. Facing an agreement to withdraw their troops the American command retired with a measure of obligation to support an extreme right-wing government representing something far from the ideals of western democracy. The United States had again been caught in the position of aligning its power with the reactionaries of a minority class and of allowing Russian prestige to rise over Asia as the champion of the people. An occupation justified to liberate a great nation and to promote therein a free and democratic government was concluded with two Korean armies firing at one another over an arbitrary boundary, each under the guidance of the paid military advisors of the liberating powers. Thus was an unaggressive Korea brought to the verge of civil war for the first time in a thousand years.

The future of Korea is uncertain. Left alone, the people might be expected to resolve their internal difficulties without protracted battles. The Koreans want self-determined national unity above all else and it is highly dubious that any leader whose authority has been dependent upon foreign patronage can long survive without it. Should the United States and the Soviet Union continue to reinforce the military strength in their zones of former occupation, the resultant Korean fighting may launch the final conflict of the world. If now, when whipped by alien antagonism, the heroic Koreans refuse to destroy each other, their culture may once again become a light towards which all men turn in admiration, a symbol of that universal hope that simple people have for peace.

POSTSCRIPT
November, 1950

Most unfortunately, Koreans with the power to make decisions did not realize that an appeal to arms would bring down a terrible rain of destruction upon their country. Since August, 1949, when the manuscript of this book was completed, events have turned the attention of the whole world towards the Korean Peninsula. On June 25, 1950, the armed forces of the Democratic People's Republic of Korea surged southward in a sudden onslaught with the purpose of uniting the country.

It can be said with certainty that the basic cause of the war lay in the partition of Korea. All Koreans have wanted unity. They love their country. Both of their governments have consistently claimed jurisdiction over the entire nation; each has promised that it would join together what Russia and the United States had put asunder. But each group of leaders insisted that it be done in its own way.

To summarize recent events, we should first recall that the Soviet Union withdrew its troops from north Korea by the end of 1948. leaving a well-armed people's militia behind and a plan to provide a force of half a million men (p. 317). Six months later the United

States had withdrawn its troops, leaving little more than a much hated police force to defend the Republic of Korea.

Syngman Rhee, a president with dictatorial powers, was inaugurated on August 15, 1948. His government was in trouble from its inception. The north Korean radio broadcast threats to destroy the new south Korean officials as treacherous traitors. On his return to America, Lt. Gen. Hodge prophesied that guerrilla warfare would commence as soon as United States troops were ordered out of Korea, if not sooner.[90] At the beginning of October, a widespread plot to assassinate Rhee and other government officials was revealed by the Minister of Home Affairs. Then a rebellion broke out in the port of Yŏsu on October 19; shortly thereafter, Sunch'ŏn was captured. The insurgents were estimated in numbers up to 12,000. At least 400 police were reported killed and countless soldiers and civilians died. The southern forces finally succeeded in suppressing the revolt, and their revenge was barbaric.[91] President Rhee implored the United States to keep its troops in Korea. In December, insurgent guerrillas were still active in the area of the uprising. Significantly, one hundred and eighty-five flags of the Democratic People's Republic were captured. By the end of that winter, 15,000 Cheju islanders are said to have died as the result of revolts against the Rhee government. In 1949, northern forces increased their intermittent firing over the border along the 38th parallel, and hundreds of south Korean troops deserted to the People's Republic.[92] As the last United States soldiers departed on June 28, 1949, the north Koreans invaded the Onjin Peninsula.

Internally, Rhee's government was filled with dissensions. On June 26, 1949, Kim Koo, one of the most prominent rightist leaders, was killed by a member of his own party. The insecurity which this circumstance aroused undoubtedly contributed to an increased control of the country by the south Korean army and its military police. Civilian agencies were dominated and these police even took over traffic direction in the city of Seoul. During the months of July and August, newspaper reporters were so blatantly arrested that the United Nations Commission on Korea suspended all press conferences.[93] By the end of 1949, the south Korean army was estimated at 100,000 and its military police at 50,000.[94] The police publicized murder and brutality by depositing the dead bodies of their prisoners on the doorsteps of civilians as a warning, and the Home Minister of the Republic of Korea stated that "the torturing of communists by the police is not to be criticized".[95] Some members of the National Assembly, however, had the courage to protest publicly. By March, large parts of south Korea were in the grasp of a terror unparalleled in the world. Everyone was afraid.[96]

In 1950, a bill was introduced into the National Assembly to amend the constitution and thereby make the cabinet responsible to the Assembly rather than to the president. A dispute followed on the method of voting. The month of May, however, brought the new elections for the National Assembly which were desired by the Rhee opposition and helped, it is reported, by the United States State Department.[97] The voting for 210 seats, contested by 2,144 candidates, apparently was carried out with surprising freedom from restraint. Chough Pyong-ok, former head of the national police was defeated in Seoul, as were other Rhee supporters. It appeared that Rhee might become a figurehead president when the Assembly met and voted again on the proposed constitutional amendment.[98] The north Koreans, however, interrupted this democratic procedure by taking things into their own hands.

The position of the United States, after the withdrawal of its troops, was extraordinarily complex. It had sponsored the government of the Republic of Korea and had finally seen it recognized in Paris on December 12, 1948, by the United Nations General Assembly. Therefore, the support of the United States could be expected On June 8, 1949, President Truman recommended to the Congress that it authorize 150 million dollars for continuing economic assistance to Korea. Secretary of State Acheson, in support of the request, stated that without assistance the government of south Korea would fall in a matter of months.[99] Congressional opposition to Korean aid stemmed from the political antagonisms of Republican leaders, a general movement toward economy, and, perhaps most important, from a less verbalized feeling that Rhee and his government were only a small edition of the obviously unsuccessful General Chiang and his Kuomintang. The aid bill failed of passing by two votes when it came up on January 19, 1950. Sending "money down the Korean rat hole" was the opinion of a leading Republican congressman, and Democrats agreed.[100] On February 9, however, the House of Representatives reversed itself to the extent of authorizing 60 million dollars for Korea in a bill which also carried aid to the

Chinese Nationalists beleaguered on Formosa. On June 10, 1950, the Moscow newspaper *Izvestia* published the hope of the north Korean government to unite Korea by August 15, 1950, the fifth anniversary of liberation from the Japanese.[101] Not many Americans read *Izvestia,* and few were excited by the possibilities of an attack.

Americans were electrified, however, when, following the invasion, President Truman ordered the armed forces of the United States to the defense of the Republic of Korea. Clearly, the Soviet Union was sponsoring armed aggression, and aggression against a government recognized by the United Nations. The latter body, on June 27, recommended that its members support the Republic of Korea.

The course of the war followed a definite pattern. The northern forces, excellently armed by the Russians with rifles, tanks, and artillery, moved southward rapidly. Seoul was occupied within four days, and the southern army became largely demoralized. There seems little doubt that had not American ground troops been sent in to fight a delaying action, the north Koreans would have reached Pusan quickly. The tide was stayed at Taejon by the hand-to-hand fighting of Maj. Gen. William F. Dean and a few thousand American soldiers with outmoded equipment, but it was not until August 5 that the thrust of the north Koreans, attacked as they were by overwhelming air power, was stopped along the Naktong River.

There a period of bitter fighting set in which was to last without major gains on either side until September 15. Then the troops fighting under the flag of the United Nations achieved the initiative on the ground. Marines, backed by the Navy, landed at Inch'ŏn and rushed to recapture Seoul. By September 26, the soldiers on the Pusan beachhead, holding what once had been the old Silla Kingdom, had broken through the Naktong line and joined forces with those from Inch'ŏn. Seoul was liberated in flames. Gen. Douglas Mac-Arthur and Syngman Rhee made their triumphal entry into the city on September 29. Although south Korean troops crossed the 38th parallel along the east coast on October 1, foreign units waited for United Nations authorization which was given October 7. The following day large numbers of American soldiers rushed toward P'yŏngyang, the northern capital, which capitulated readily on October 20. Six days later the troops reached the Korean-Manchurian border and it seemed that open warfare was soon to come to an end.

It remained only for the United Nations to carry out their plan to give the Korean people the opportunity to elect a democratic and free government. In the relaxation of victory, when the United Nations soldiers from overseas were beginning to hope that they would soon be returning home, a new foe unexpectedly appeared to block the mountain passes. Tens of thousands of Chinese troops crossed the Yalu River from Manchuria while guerrillas, inspired by these communist allies, attacked from the hills. Swiftly a new battle line was formed across the Peninsula, now white from winter snow. There, suffering from bitter cold, the armies of the western world moved cautiously toward the might of Asia.

REFERENCES TO SOURCES FOR PART FIVE

[1] For a list of Japan's treaty promises see Chung, 1921:339.
[2] Harrington, 1944:302-18; Nelson, 1945:258.
[3] *Results of Three Years* . . ., 1914:1.
[4] *Ibid.* . . ., 1914:4.
[5] *Ibid.* . . ., 1914:5.
[6] *Annual Report* . . ., 1920:153; also see Noble, 1941.
[7] *Results of Three Years* . . ., 1914:7-9.
[8] *Ibid.* . . ., 1914:50.
[9] *Ibid.* . . ., 1914:91-95.
[10] *Annual Report* . . ., 1920:146-47.
[11] *Results of Three Years* . . ., 1914:47.
[12] *Ibid.* . . ., 1914:26-28; *Annual Report* . . ., 1920:98-101.
[13] *Results of Three Years* . . ., 1914:52.
[14] Van Buskirk, 1931:179-81.
[15] *Results of Three Years* . . ., 1914:54.
[16] *Ibid.* . . ., 1914:58-60.
[17] *Ibid.* . . ., 1914:55.
[18] *Annual Report* . . ., 1920:121.
[19] *Results of Three Years* . . ., 1914:57-58, 60-61.
[20] *Ibid.* . . ., 1914:61-63.
[21] *Annual Report* . . ., 1920:10-11.
[22] Cynn, 1920:25-26; McKenzie, 1920:245-46; Chung, 1921:197-99, 205; Keith and Scott, 1946:33-35. One statement describes sixteen of the signers of the proclamation to have been Christians: Van Buskirk, 1931:54.
[23] Cynn, 1920:47-49; Chung, 1921:208, 214-15.
[24] Cynn, 1920:49-55; McKenzie, 1920:255-56.
[25] Cynn, 1920:56-60; McKenzie, 1920:257-58; Chung, 1921:210-11; Keith and Scott, 1946:39-42.
[26] Cynn, 1920:66-71; Chung, 1921:233-35; Keith and Scott, 1946:48-54.
[27] Chung, 1921:208.
[28] Cynn, 1920:16-18; Chung, 1921:191-92.
[29] Brown, 1912; Brown, 1921:344-52, 571-72; Chung, 1919:144-66; Chung, 1921:243ff.
[30] *Annual Report* . . ., 1920:128-29.
[31] Chung, 1921:82.
[32] Barstow and Greenbie. 1919:922; Chung, 1921:117-24.

[33] Chung, 1921:108-17.

[34] Chung, 1921:125ff.

[35] Cynn, 1920:117-25.

[36] McKenzie, 1920:84; Chung, 1921:145-54.

[37] Chung, 1921:211; Oliver, 1944:45-48.

[38] *Annual Report . . .,* 1921:159.

[39] Chung, 1921:188-90.

[40] Van Buskirk, 1931:56-58, 147-51.

[41] For an interesting review of anti-Japanese activities after 1919, see Wales, 1942.

[42] *Annual Report . . .,* 1921:6-11, 151-53, 171-72; *Annual Report . . .,* 1937:7-8.

[43] For an early somewhat prejudiced and naïve account of Japanese accomplishments, see Ireland, 1926.

[44] *Annual Report . . .,* 1921:74-84; Van Buskirk, 1931:123; *Thriving Chosen,* 1935:13; *Annual Report . . .,* 1937:81.

[45] Grajdanzev, 1944:261-76.

[46] Van Buskirk, 1931:131-33.

[47] *Thriving Chosen . . .,* 1935:25-28; *Annual Report . . .,* 1937:92-94; for reference to Japanese archeological publications see, for example, Hewes, 1947.

[48] Grajdanzev, 1944:72-73, 118; for data on population also see McCune, 1946:281-85.

[49] Van Buskirk, 1931:68-71; Grajdanzev, 1944:107-13.

[50] Brunner, 1928:126-27; Van Buskirk, 1931:71-73; Grajdanzev, 1944:106.

[51] Grajdanzev, 1944:79-80.

[52] Grajdanzev, 1944:126, 130, 147, 193, 200, 210-11.

[53] Fisher, 1946:263.

[54] McCune, 1946:285-88; Chung, 1947:41-42.

[55] McCune, 1947b:11-14.

[56] *Korea's Independence,* 1947:18-19.

[57] For another interpretation of this situation, see Izard, 1947:9-11.

[58] *Summation,* October, 1945:163-65; *Ibid.,* February, 1946:281-83; *Ibid.,* March, 1946:2; *Ibid.,* June, 1946:16; *Ibid.,* August, 1946:15; *Ibid.,* October, 1946:18; *Ibid.,* September, 1947:118-19.

[59] Wales, 1942:40-42.

[60] *Summation,* November, 1945:182-83; *Ibid.,* December, 1945:188.

[61] *Ibid.,* May, 1946:15.

[62] *Ibid.,* October, 1946:19; *Ibid.,* May, 1947:16.

[63] *Ibid.,* February, 1947:11.

[64] Oliver, 1944:49.

[65] *Summation,* January, 1946:285; *Ibid.,* January, 1947:85-86; *Ibid.,* May, 1947:25; *Ibid.,* October, 1947:165; *Ibid.,* January, 1948:235. For general references to these youth organizations, also see Kang, 1948:20 and Martin, 1948:53, 55.

[66] *Korea,* 1948:122.

[67] *Ibid.,* 72.

[68] Chung, 1947:43.

[69] For more detailed summaries of such data on north Korea, see McCune, 1947b:24-27; Washburn, 1947:152-60.

[70] *Korea,* 1948:124.

[71] *Summation,* October, 1946:23-26; McCune, 1947b:17; Martin, 1948:46.

[72] For an understanding of the administrative organization of the Korean national police, both before and after the liberation, see *Summation,* July, 1946:14-21; *Ibid.,* November, 1947:201-04, and *Ibid.,* December, 1947:167-69.

[73] Chung, 1947:60-63; Washburn, 1947:153.

[74] *New York Times,* October 21-27, 1948; April 10, 1949.

[75] For an important recent summary of Korean economics, see Shoemaker, 1947.

[76] Martin, 1948:49.

[77] Kang, 1948:19.

[78] *Korea,* 1948:30-31; Weinert, 1948.

[79] Fisher, 1946:265-66.

[80] For a colorful statement on graft in Korea, see Kang, 1948:19-21.

[81] McCune, 1947a:12; Shoemaker, 1947:12-13.

[82] For a summary of the Korean fishing industry, together with a list of the types of fish which are caught, see *Summation,* May, 1946:37-38 and *Ibid.,* June, 1946: 26-33.

[83] *Korea,* 1948:34-37.

[84] Chung, 1947:77-78.

[85] *Summation,* November, 1946:74.

[86] *Ibid.,* November, 1945:193; *Ibid.,* August, 1946:80-81; *Ibid.,* December, 1947: 71; *Ibid.,* October, 1947:156-57. For lists of south Korean colleges and universities, with the number of their students, see *Ibid.,* November, 1946:76 and *Ibid.,* November, 1947:226-27. It is interesting to note that the three major libraries in Seoul possess 442,979 volumes, mostly in Japanese, Korean, and Chinese. *Ibid.,* June, 1947:87.

[87] *Summation,* May, 1946:91; *Ibid.,* May, 1947:78; *Ibid.,* July, 1947:99-100; *Ibid.,* September, 1947:128-29.

[88] For a famous, if restrained, example of this criticism see the editorial published in the *Korean Daily News (Chosun Ilbo). Summation,* August, 1946:89-90. For an example of less restrained criticism, see *Ibid.,* December, 1947:162.

[89] Ramstedt, 1939:iv.

[90] *New York Times,* August 31, 1948.

[91] *Life,* November 15, 1948:55-58.

[92] *New York Times,* February 4, 1949; May 7, 1949.

[93] *Ibid.,* July 23, 1949.

[94] *Ibid.,* February 1, 1950.

[95] *Ibid.,* February 1, 1950.

[96] *Ibid.,* March 6, 1950.

[97] *Ibid.,* May 31, 1950.

[98] *Ibid.,* May 31, 1950.

[99] *Ibid.,* July 2, 1949.

[100] *Ibid.,* January 20, 1950.

[101] *Ibid.,* June 27, 1950; For a fuller treatment of political events in Korea since 1945, the recently published work of the late George M. McCune is highly recommended (George M. McCune, *Korea Today,* Harvard University Press, 1950).

A LIST OF KOREAN WORDS IN THE TEXT

Ajŏn [Adjun] 아젼 (衙前)

An Chae-hong [Ahn Chai-hong] 安在鴻

An Chung-kŭn [An Chung-kuen] 安重根

An Do-hi [An Tu-hi] 安斗熙

Andong 安東

Angul, see Wanggul

Anpang 안 뺭

Arirang [Ariran] 아리랑

Asan 牙山

Ch'ae Nam-sun 崔南善

Chang 張

Changgi [Changi] 將碁

Changsŭng [Chang-sung] 長丞

Chang Tong 쟝동

Changu 長皷

Chaohsien, see Chosŏn

Ch'apssal [Ch'apsal] 찹쌀

Cheju 濟州

Chemulpo 濟物浦

Chênfan, see Chinpun

Chichang 지장

Chiksan 櫻山

Chin 津

Ch'in 琴

349

Chingang [Chin-gang] 鎮江

Chinhan 辰韓

Chinju 晉州

Chinpun [Chinbun] 眞番

Chiri 智利

Ch'itan, *see* Kitan

Cho 趙

Ch'oe [Choi] 崔

Ch'oe Ch'i-won 崔致遠

Ch'oji 草芝

Cholbon [Chulbon] 卒本

Chŏlla 全羅

Ch'ŏndokyo [Chundokyo] 天道教

Chŏndung Sa [Chondongsa] 傳燈寺

Chŏngbo [Chungbo] 町步

Chŏng In-ji [Chung In-chi] 鄭麟趾

Chŏngjok [Chonjok] 骿足

Chŏng-jong [Chung-jong] 正宗

Chŏngju 定州

Ch'ŏngju 淸州

Chŏnju [Chon-ju] 全州

Ch'osan 楚山

Chosŏn [Chosen, Chosun] 朝鮮

Chosun Ilbo 朝鮮日報

Chough Pyong-ok (Cho Pyŏng-ok) 趙炳玉

Ch'ul-jong [Ch'uljong] 哲宗

Chu-mong 朱蒙

Ch'unch'ŏn 春川

Ch'ungch'ŏng 忠清

Chungin 中人

Chun Hun 田壎

Eumna, *see* Ŭmnu

Fusan, *see* Pusan

Ha-bu-ru 解夫婁

Hado Myŏn [Hwado Myun] 下道面

Haegu [Ha-gu] 海口

Hamgyŏng 咸鏡

Han (river) 漢江

Han 韓

Han Chi-kŭn [Han Chi-keun] 韓致根

Hangŭl [Hangul] 한글

Han P'yo-kyu 韓浦奎

Hansŏng 漢城

Hanyang 漢陽

Hong 洪

Hong Yeu-ha 洪宥河

Hop 合

Hsüant'u, *see* Hyundo

Huh Hun (Ho Hon) 許憲

Hwang 黄

Hwanghae 黄海

Hyŏlgu [Hyul-ku] 穴口

Hyŏn [Hyun] 縣

Hyundo 玄菟

Iksan 益山

Imdun 臨屯

Imjin 臨津

Inch'ŏn 仁川

Jang 長

Kaesŏng 開城

Kan 間

Kang Do [Kangdo] 江島

Kanggye 江界

Kanghwa 江華

Kanghwa Chi 江華誌

Kangnŭng 江陵

Kangwŏn 江原

Kang, Younghill 姜鏞訖

Kapkan Ri [Kapkan-ri] 甲串里

Kappikoch'a 갑피고차

Karak 駕洛

Kaya 伽倻

Keijo, *see* Seoul

Kiesang, *see* Kisaeng

Ki-hak 기학

Ki-ja 箕子

Ki-jun 箕準

Kilsang 吉祥

Kil Sŏn-ju [Kil Sun Chu]   吉善宙

Kim   金

Kim Che-won (Kim Che-wŏn)   金載元

Kimch'i [Kimche]   김치 (沈菜)

Kim Chung-sŏp [Kim Chung-sup]   金正

Kimhae   金海

Kim Il-sŏng [Kim Il-sung]   金日成

Kim Koo (Kim Ku)   金九

Kim Kyŏn-myŏng (Il Yŏn)   金見明 (一然)

Kimm Kiusic (Kim Kyu-sik)   金奎植

Kim Pu-sik   金富軾

Kim Sŏng-su [Kim Sung-su]   金性洙

Kim Woo-sik (Kim U-sik)   金于植

Kisaeng [Kiesang]   妓生

Kitan (Kedan) [Ch'itan]   契丹

Ko   高

Koguryŏ [Koguryu]   高句麗

Kongju   公州

Koni   꼬니

Koryŏ [Koryŭ]   高麗

Ku   區

Ku Jang [Kuchang]   區長

Kum   錦

Kumhae   金海

Kun   郡

Kung-ye   弓裔

Kwagŏ [Kwaga, Quaga]   科擧

Kyodong 喬洞

Kyŏnggi [Kyonggi] 京畿

Kyŏngju [Kyongju] 慶州

Kyŏngsang [Kyongsang] 慶尚

Kyŏn-hwŏn [Kyun-whun] 甄萱

Lee Bum-suk (Yi Pŏm-sŏk) 李範奭

Li (area) 里

Li (Yi) 李

Lint'un, see Imdun

Li Sung-man (Yi Sŭng-man) 李承晚

Lolang, see Nangnang

Lui, see Yu

Lyuh Woon-heung (Yŏ Un-hyŏng) 呂運亨

Lyuh Woon-hong (Yŏ Un-hong) 呂運弘

Ma 馬

Madang, see Matang

Mahan 馬韓

Majin 馬津

Mal 맠

Malgal 靺鞨

Manse [Mansei] 萬歲

Mari San 摩尼山

Maru 마루

Matang [Madang] 마당

Ma Won 馬援

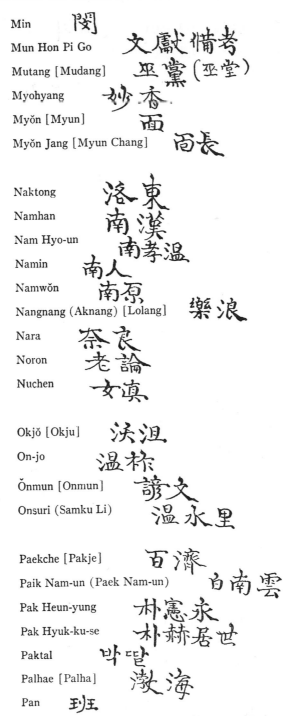

Min　閔

Mun Hon Pi Go　文獻備考

Mutang [Mudang]　巫黨 (巫堂)

Myohyang　妙香

Myŏn [Myun]　面

Myŏn Jang [Myun Chang]　面長

Naktong　洛東

Namhan　南漢

Nam Hyo-un　南孝溫

Namin　南人

Namwŏn　南原

Nangnang (Aknang) [Lolang]　樂浪

Nara　奈良

Noron　老論

Nuchen　女眞

Okjŏ [Okju]　沃沮

On-jo　溫柞

Ŏnmun [Onmun]　諺文

Onsuri (Samku Li)　溫水里

Paekche [Pakje]　百濟

Paik Nam-un (Paek Nam-un)　白南雲

Pak Heun-yung　朴憲永

Pak Hyuk-ku-se　朴赫居世

Paktal　밝달

Palhae [Palha]　渤海

Pan　班

Pan Jang [Pan Chang] 班長

P'ansu 判數

Pi-ryu 沸流

Pongch'ŏn San [Pongch'on San] 奉天山

Pudul 부들

Pukhan 北漢

Pulkuk 佛國

Purak [Pulak] 部落

Pusan [Fusan] 釜山

Puyŏ [Puyo] 扶餘 (夫餘)

Puyu (Puyŏ) 扶餘

P'yong [Pyun] 坪

P'yŏngan 平安

P'yŏngyang 平壤

Pyŏnhan [Pyonhan] 弁韓

Quaga, *see* Kwagŏ

Ri 里

Sam Guk Sa Ki 三國史記

Sam Guk Yu Sa 三國遺事

Samku Li [Samgoli] 三巨里

Samnang [Sam-lang] 三郎

Sangge [Sang-ke] 契

Sangnŏm [Sangnom] 裳님

Sarang 사랑

Se-jong 世宗

Seoul (Sŏul) 서울

Silla 新羅

Sim 沈

Sinkyo (Singyo) 教神

Sŏbuk [Subuk] 西北

Sŏch'ŏn 舒川

Sŏhak [Suhak] 西學

Soju [So-ju] 소주

Sŏk [Suk] 石

Sŏkkulam 石窟菴

Sŏm [Som] 섬

Sŏmjin [Somjin] 蟾津

Sŏn-dŏk [Son-duk] 善德

Sŏndu Ku [Sŏndoku] 船頭區

Sŏndup'o [Sondopo] 船頭浦

Sŏndu Ri [Sondoli] 船頭里

Sŏngch'ŏn 成川

Songdo (Kaesŏng) 松都 (開城)

Sŏng-jong [Sung-jong] 成宗

Son Pyong-hi [Son Byung Hi] 孫秉熙

Soron 少論

Suk 石

Suksin 肅愼

Sungyung [Sung yung] 숭용

Sushen 肅愼

Sut'u 蘇塗

Syngman Rhee (Yi Sung-man) 李承晚

T'aean 春安

Taedong (river) 大同江

Taegu 大邱

Taehan [Taihan] 大韓

Tae-jong [T'a-jong] 大宗

Tae-wŏn [Tai-wun] 大院君

T'akju [Tak-ju] 濁酒

T'amna 耽羅

Tan-chang Kyung 단챵경

Tan-gun [Tangun] 檀君

Toe [Toi] 되

Tong Guk T'ong Gam 東國通鑑

Tonghak [Tong-hak] 東學

Tongni [Tong-ne] 洞里

Tong Sa Kang Yo [Tong-sa Kang-yo] 東史網要

Ugu 右渠

Ullŭng 欝陵

Ulsan 蔚山

Ŭmnu [Eumna] 挹婁

Wang 王

Wang-gŏn [Wang-gon] 王建

Wanggul [Wangul] 왕읍

Whanto 丸都

Wi-man 衛滿

Wŏn [Won] 圓

Wŏnsan 元山

Yakju [Yak-Ju] 樂酒

Yangpan [Yangban] 兩班

Ye 穢

Yeguk 濊國

Ye-jong 睿宗

Yemak 穢貊

Yi [Li] 李

Yidu 吏讀

Yilou 挹婁

Yi Sun-sin 李舜臣

Yi T'ae-jo [Yi T'a-jo] 李太祖

Yŏng-jong [Yung-jong] 英宗

Yŏt 엿

Yu [Lui] 柳 (兪. 劉)

Yujin 女真

Yun 尹

Yun Tchi Ho (Yun Ch'i-ho) 尹致昊

Yut 윷

BIBLIOGRAPHY

The books and articles on Korea listed below have been limited to those specifically mentioned in the text. Many others read in the process of preparing this work may be found in the standard bibliographies of Underwood (1931) and Gompertz (1935), which list over 3,000 titles in Indo-European languages. For early works in Chinese published in Korea, the *Bibliographie Coréenne* (1894-96 and 1901) is invaluable. Lautensach (1945) also has an important bibliography, especially for recent articles in foreign languages. The names of the principal periodicals published in Seoul in English have been abbreviated as follows: *Korean Repository*, Vols. 1-5, 1892, 1895-98 [*K. Rep.*]; *Korea Review*, Vols. 1-6, 1901-06 [*K. Rev.*]; *Transactions of the Korea Branch of the Royal Asiatic Society*, Vols. 1-30, 1900-1940 [*Trans. R.A.S.-K.B.*].

ALLEN, HORACE N. "Some Korean Customs: Dancing Girls," *K. Rep.*, Vol. 3, pp. 383-86. Seoul, 1896.
————. *Things Korean: A Collection of Sketches and Anecdotes, Missionary and Diplomatic.* New York, 1908.
Annual Report of Reforms and Progress in Korea (1907). Seoul, 1908. [These "Reports" continued to be published with slight changes in the title. Those in 1909 and 1910 bore the initial word "Second" and "Third," respectively. From 1911 to 1936 the words "Chosen" and "Keijo" were substituted for "Korea" and "Seoul," although the latter terms were added in parentheses from 1911 through 1920. From 1937, conforming with the revised system of alphabetizing Japanese, "Chosen" and "Keijo" were spelled "Tyosen" and "Keizyo."]
AOYANAGI, TSUNATARO. *Chosen Bunka Shi (Cultural History of Korea)* [Text in Japanese]. Seoul, 1924.
BARSTOW, MARJORIE, and GREENBIE, SYDNEY. "Korea Asserts Herself," *Asia*, Vol. 19, No. 9, pp. 921-26. New York, 1919. [Also reprinted in *The Culture of Korea*, 1945-46, pp. 294-309.]
BERGMAN, STEN. *In Korean Wilds and Villages.* London, 1938.
BISHOP, ISABELLA BIRD. *Korea and Her Neighbours.* 2 vols. London, 1905 [1st ed. 1898].
BOOTS, J. L. "Korean Musical Instruments and an Introduction to Korean Music," *Trans. R.A.S.-K.B.*, Vol. 30, pp. 1-32. Seoul, 1940.
BOWMAN, N. H. "The History of Korean Medicine," *Trans. R.A.S.-K.B.*, Vol. 6, Pt. 1, pp. 1-34. Seoul, 1915.
BROUGHTON, W. ROBERT. *A Voyage of Discovery to the N. Pacific Ocean.* London, 1804.
BROWN, ARTHUR JUDSON. *"The Korean Conspiracy Case."* New York, 1912.
————. *The Mastery of the Far East.* New York, 1921 [1st ed. 1919].
BRUNNER, EDMUND DE SCHWEINITZ. "Rural Korea: A Preliminary Survey of Economic, Social and Religious Conditions." In *The Christian Mission in Relation to Rural Problems Report of the Jerusalem Meeting of the International Missionary Council*, March 24th-April 8th, 1928, Vol. 6. London, 1928. [Another edition with different pagination, New York, 1928; also a preliminary draft with different pagination, New York, 1928.]
Bukkoku-ji Temple and Sekkutsu-an Cave in Keishu, Chosen (Bukkoku zhi to Seki-kutsu an) [Text in Japanese]. Keijo [Seoul], 1938.
BUSTEED, J. B. "The Korean Doctor and His Methods," *K. Rep.*, Vol. 2, pp. 188-93. Seoul, 1895.

CABLE, E. M. "Old Korean Bells," *Trans. R.A.S.-K.B.,* Vol. 16, pp. i, 1-45, 53. Seoul, 1925.

CARLES, W. R. *Life in Corea.* London, 1888.

CARTER, THOMAS FRANCIS. *The Invention of Printing and Its Spread Westward.* New York, 1931.

CAVENDISH, A. E. J. *Korea and the Sacred White Mountain.* London, 1894.

CHANG TONG, see *Tong Sa Kang Yo.*

CHENERY, WILLIAM L. "Stalemate in Korea," *Collier's,* Vol. 120, No. 16, pp. 76-85. New York, 1947.

CHŎNG IN-JI, see *Koryŏ Sa.*

Chōsen Koseki Zufu (Album of Ancient Remains of Korea) [Text in Japanese], 15 vols. Seoul, 1915-35.

Chōsen Sōtokufu Koseki Chosa Hokoku (Annual Reports of the Archaeological Survey of Korea) [Text in Japanese], 17 vols. Seoul, 1916-33.

CHUN HUN. *Kanghwa Chi (History of Kanghwa)* [Text in Chinese], 2 vols. Seoul, 1931.

CHUNG, HENRY. *The Case of Korea.* New York, 1921.

——. *The Russians Came to Korea.* Seoul and Washington, D. C., 1947.

CLARK, CHARLES ALLEN. *Religions of Old Korea.* New York, 1932.

COURANT, MAURICE. *Bibliographie Coréenne. Tableau littéraire de la Corée contenant la nomenclature des ouvrages publiés dans ce pays jusqu'en 1890, ainsi que la description et l'analyse detaillées des principaux d'entre ces ouvrages.* 3 vols. Publications de l'école des langues orientales vivantes, 3d series, Vols. 18-20. Paris, 1894-96.

——. *Introduction to the "Bibliographie Coréenne"* (Translated from the French by Mrs. W. Massy Royds), *Trans. R.A.S.-K.B.,* Vol. 25, pp. ii, 1-99. Seoul, 1936.

——. *Supplément à la Bibliographie Coréenne (Jusqu'en 1899).* Publications de l'école des langues orientales vivantes, 3d series, Vol. 21. Paris, 1901.

CULIN, STEWART. *Korean Games with Notes on the Corresponding Games of China and Japan.* Philadelphia, 1895.

The Culture of Korea (Edited by Changsoon Kim). [Washington, D. C.?], 1945-46.

CYNN, HUGH HUENG-WO. *The Rebirth of Korea: The Reawakening of the People, Its Causes, and the Outlook.* London, 1920.

DALLET, CHARLES. *Histoire de l'Eglise de Corée.* 2 vols. Paris, 1874. [The culturally important introductory section of this work has been reprinted almost in its entirety in Adrien Launay, *La Corée, les missionnaires français.* Tours, c. 1895.]

ECKARDT, ANDREAS. *A History of Korean Art* (Translated from the German by J. M. Kindersley). London, 1929.

FISHER, J. EARNEST. "Korea Today," *The Far Eastern Quarterly,* Vol. 5, No. 3, pp. 261-71. New York, 1946.

GALE, JAMES S. "A History of the Korean People," *The Korea Mission Field,* Vol. 20 (1924), pp. 134-36, 156-59, 179-82, 201-4, 223-25, 244-47; Vol. 21 (1925), pp. 3-7, 25-29, 47-51, 73-77, 95-99, 115-20, 139-44, 176-80, 181-85, 229-33, 235-39, 261-65; Vol. 22 (1926), pp. 6-10, 26-30, 49-53, 77-81, 107-11, 122-27, 139-43, 159-64, 188-92, 220-24, 235-39, 255-59; Vol. 23 (1927), pp. 5-10, 56-60, 79-83, 105-8, 123-27, 147-51, 165-69, 193-97. Seoul, 1924-27. [Each chapter, 1 through 38 inclusive, corresponds with one set of page numbers, i.e., Chapter 1 is pp. 134-36, etc. An undated, partly unpaged reprint of this work was also published in Seoul.]

——. "The Influence of China upon Korea," *Trans. R.A.S.-K.B.,* Vol. 1, pp. 1-24. Seoul, 1900.

——. *Korean Sketches.* New York, 1899.

GARDNER, C. T. "The Coinage of Corea," *Journal of the China Branch of the Royal Asiatic Society,* New Series, Vols. 27-28, pp. 71-130, 1892-93. Shanghai, 1895.

GILMORE, GEORGE W. *Korea from Its Capital.* Philadelphia, 1892.

GOMPERTZ, E. and G. "Supplement to 'A Partial Bibliography of Occidental Literature on Korea' by H. H. Underwood, Ph.D., 1931," *Trans. R.A.S.-K.B.,* Vol. 24, pp. 21-48. Seoul, 1935.

GRAJDANZEV, ANDREW J. *Modern Korea.* New York, 1944.

GRIFFIS, WILLIAM ELLIOT. *Corea: The Hermit Nation.* 4th ed. New York, 1894 [1st ed. 1882].

HALL, BASIL. *Account of a Voyage of Discovery to the West Coast of Corea and the Great Loo-choo Island.* London, 1818. [Sections dealing with Korea have been reprinted in the *Trans. R.A.S.-K.B.,* Vol. 11, pp. 3-37. Seoul, 1920.]

HAMADA, KŌSAKI (with SUEJI UMEHARA). *Shiragi Koga no Kenkyu (A Study of the Ancient Tiles of Silla)* [Text in Japanese with English summary], Tokyo Imperial University, Dept. of Literature, Reports on Archaeological Studies, 13. Tokyo, 1934.

HAMEL, HENDRIK. "An Account of the Shipwreck of a Dutch Vessel on the Coast of the Isle of Quelpaert, Together with a Description of the Kingdom of Corea," *Trans. R.A.S.-K.B.,* Vol. 9, pp. 93-148. Seoul, 1918.

HAMILTON, ANGUS. *Korea.* New York, 1904.

HARADA, YOSHITO. *Lo-Lang: A Report on the Excavation of Wang Hsü's Tomb in the "Lo-Lang" Province, an Ancient Chinese Colony in Korea* [Text in Japanese and English]. Tokyo, 1930.

HARRINGTON, FRED HARVEY. *God, Mammon, and the Japanese.* Madison, Wis., 1944.

HEWES, GORDON W. *Archaeology of Korea: A Selected Bibliography.* Research Monographs on Korea, Series F, No. 1. [Hamilton, N. Y.?], 1947.

HODGE, JOHN R. "With the U. S. Army in Korea," *The National Geographic Magazine,* Vol. 91, No. 6, pp. 829-40. Washington, D. C., 1947.

HONEY, W. B. *Corean Pottery.* London, 1947.

HONG YEU-HA, see *Tong Guk T'ong Gam.*

HOUGH, WALTER. "The Bernadou, Allen, and Jouy Korean Collections in the U. S. National Museum," *Annual Report of the Board of Regents of the Smithsonian Institution . . . for the Year Ending June 30, 1891, Report of the U. S. National Museum,* pp. 429-88. Washington, D. C., 1892.

HRDLIČKA, ALEŠ. "The Koreans." (In *The Culture of Korea,* pp. 33-43, 1945-46.)

HSÜ CHING. *Hsüan Ho Fêng Shih Kao Li T'u Ching (Hsüan Ho's Embassy: A Book on Korea)* [Text in Chinese]. Seoul, 1911. [Hsü Ching (1091-1158), pronounced in Korean, Sŏ Kŭng, visited Korea for about five weeks in 1124. The preface of his book is dated in the month after he left Korea. The manuscript was apparently written during the voyage home which, because of storms, required forty-two days. Hsü Ching's book was first printed in 1163.]

HULBERT, HOMER B. *The History of Korea.* 2 vols. Seoul, 1905.

———. "Korean Survivals," *Trans. R.A.S.-K.B.,* Vol. 1, pp. 25-50. Seoul, 1900.

———. "National Examination in Korea," *Trans. R.A.S.-K.B.,* Vol. 14, pp. 9-32. Seoul, 1923.

———. *The Passing of Korea.* New York, 1906.

HUNT, CHARLES. "Some Pictures and Painters of Corea," *Trans. R.A.S.-K.B.,* Vol. 19, pp. 1-34. Seoul, 1930.

HUNT, J. H. "Land Tenure and the Price of Land," *K. Rep.,* Vol. 3, pp. 317-19. Seoul, 1896.

ICHIHARA, M. "Coinage of Old Korea," *Trans. R.A.S.-K.B.,* Vol. 4, Pt. 2, pp. 45-74. Seoul, 1913.

IRELAND, ALLEYNE. *The New Korea.* New York, 1926.

IZARD, RALPH. "Close-Up of Korea," *New Masses,* Vol. 63, No. 9, pp. 8-11. New York, 1947.

JENNINGS, FOSTER H. "Korean Headdresses in the National Museum," *Smithsonian Miscellaneous Collections,* Vol. 45, pp. 149-67. Washington, D. C., 1904.

JUNKIN, WILLIAM M. "The Tong Hak," *K. Rep.,* Vol. 2, pp. 56-61. Seoul, 1895.

KANG, YOUNGHILL. *The Grass Roof.* New York, 1931.

――――. "How It Feels To Be a Korean in Korea," *United Nations World,* Vol. 2, No. 4, pp. 18-21. New York, 1948.

KEITH, ELIZABETH, and SCOTT, E. K. R *Old Korea: The Land of Morning Calm.* London, 1946.

KIM KYŎN-MYŎNG (IL YŎN), see *Sam Guk Yu Sa.*

KIM PU-SIK, see *Sam Guk Sa Ki.*

KIM SAN and WALES, NYM. *Song of Ariran.* New York, 1941.

KOIDZUMI, A. and SAWA, S. *The Tomb of Painted Basket of Lo-Lang.* Detailed Report of Archaeological Research, Vol. 1. Chôsen-Koseki-Kenkyû-Kwai (Society of the Study of Korean Antiquities). Keijo (Seoul), 1934.

KOONS, E. W. "Beacon-Fires of Old Korea," *Trans. R.A.S.-K.B.,* Vol. 16, pp. 46-52. Seoul, 1925.

Korea, 1945 to 1948: A Report on Political Developments and Economic Resources, with Selected Documents. Department of State, Publication 3305, Far Eastern Series 28. Washington, D. C., 1948.

Korea Review, Vols. 1-6. Seoul, 1901-06.

Korean Repository, Vols. 1-5. Seoul, 1892, 1895-98.

Korea's Independence. Department of State, Publication 2933, Far Eastern Series 18. Washington, D. C., 1947.

Koryŏ Sa (Annals of Koryŏ) [Text in Chinese], by CHŎNG IN-JI. 100 vols. 1454.

LANDIS, E. B. "Notable Dates of Kang-wha," *K. Rep.,* Vol. 4, pp. 245-48. Seoul, 1897.

LATOURETTE, KENNETH SCOTT. *A History of the Expansion of Christianity,* Vol. 6. New York, 1944.

LAUTENSACH, HERMANN. *Korea: Eine Landeskunde auf Grund Eigener Reisen und der Literatur.* Leipzig, 1945.

LEE, HOON K. *Land Utilization and Rural Economy in Korea.* Chicago, 1936.

LONGFORD, JOSEPH H. *The Story of Korea.* London, 1911.

LOWELL, PERCIVAL. *Chosön: The Land of the Morning Calm: A Sketch of Korea.* Boston, 1886. [Although this book bears the imprint 1886, it actually appeared in 1885.]

LUDLOW, A. I. "Pottery of the Korai Dynasty (924-1392 A.D.)," *Trans. R.A.S.-K.B.,* Vol. 14, pp. 33-62. Seoul, 1923.

MA TUAN-LIN. *Wen Hsien T'ung K'ao* (Korean: *Mun Hon T'ong Go*) (*Institutional History*) [Text in Chinese]. Presented to the Mongol emperor in 1319 [MSS translation, in part, by Li An-che, 1947].

McCUNE, GEORGE M. "Korea: The First Year of Liberation," *Pacific Affairs,* Vol. 20, No. 1, pp. 3-17. New York, 1947 [cited in footnotes as McCune, 1947a].

――――. *Korea's Postwar Political Problems* [Mimeographed]. Secretariat Paper No. 2, Institute of Pacific Relations. New York, 1947 [cited in footnotes as McCune, 1947b].

McCUNE, SHANNON. "Physical Basis for Korean Boundaries," *The Far Eastern Quarterly,* Vol. 5, No. 3, pp. 272-88. New York, 1946.

McKENZIE, F. A. *The Tragedy of Korea.* London, 1908.

――――. *Korea's Fight for Freedom.* New York, 1920.

McLEOD, JOHN. *Narrative of a Voyage in His Majesty's Late Ship Alceste, to the Yellow Sea, along the Coast of Corea.* London, 1817.

MARTIN, ROBERT P. "Korea: The Country Nobody Knows," *'48:The Magazine of the Year,* Vol. 2, No. 4, pp. 42-56. New York, 1948.

MILLER, HUGH. "A Royal Funeral in Korea," *Trans. R.A.S.-K.B.,* Vol. 17, pp. 15-35. Seoul, 1927.

MILN, LOUISE JORDAN. *Quaint Korea.* London, 1895.

MOORE, S. F. "The Butchers of Korea," *K. Rep.,* Vol. 5, pp. 127-32. Seoul, 1898.

MOOSE, J. ROBERT. *Village Life in Korea.* Nashville, 1911.

MORSE, EDWARD S. "Korean Interviews," *Appletons' Popular Science Monthly.* Vol. 51, pp. 1-17. New York, 1897.

Mun Hon Pi Go (Korean Encyclopedia) [Text in Chinese], 100 vols. Seoul, 1908.

Museum Exhibits Illustrated [Text in Japanese with titles of illustrations of earlier volumes also in English], Government-General of Chosen, Vols. 1-17. Seoul, 1918-43.

NELSON, M. FREDERICK. *Korea and the Old Orders in Eastern Asia.* Baton Rouge, La., 1945.

NOBLE, H. J. "Recent Administration in Korea," *Amerasia,* Vol. 5, No. 2, pp. 84-90. New York, 1941.

An Official Guide to Eastern Asia: Trans-Continental Connections between Europe and Asia: Vol. 1, Manchuria and Chōsen. Tokyo, 1913.

OLIVER, ROBERT T. *Korea: Forgotten Nation.* Washington, D. C., 1944.

OPPERT, ERNEST. *A Forbidden Land: Voyages to the Corea, with an Account of its Geography, History, Productions, and Commercial Capabilities, &c., &c.* New York, 1880.

PARKER, E. H. "Early Japanese History," *The China Review,* Vol. 18, July 1889, to June, 1890, pp. 212-48. Hong Kong [cited in footnotes as Parker, 1890b].

———. "On Race Struggles in Corea," *Transactions of the Asiatic Society of Japan,* Vol. 18, Pt. 2, pp. 157-228. Tokyo, 1890 [cited in footnotes as Parker, 1890a].

PELLIOT, PAUL. *Les Grottes de Touen-Houng,* 6 vols. Paris, 1914-21.

RAMSTEDT, G. J. *A Korean Grammar.* Suomalais-Ugrilaisen Seuran Toimituksia [Memoir of the Finno-Ugrian Society], Vol. 82. Helsinki, 1939.

REIN, J. J. *The Industries of Japan.* London, 1889.

Results of Three Years' Administration of Chosen Since Annexation. Government-General of Chosen. [Seoul?], 1914.

Ri Oka Hakubutsukan, Shozohin Shashin Cho, To-ji-ki No Bu (Yi Household Museum, Picture Album of the Collections, [Vol. 2] *Ceramics).* [Text in Japanese], 3d ed. [Seoul ?], 1932 [1st ed. 1912].

ROSS, JOHN. *History of Corea, Ancient and Modern with Description of Manners and Customs, Language and Geography.* London, 1891 [1st ed. 1880].

RUFUS, W. CARL. "Astronomy in Korea," *Trans. R.A.S.-K.B.,* Vol. 26, pp. 1-52. Seoul, 1936.

Sam Guk Sa Ki (History of the Three Kingdoms) [Text in Chinese], by Kim Pu-sik, 10 vols., [Edition of 1393-94 extant]. ca. 1145.

Sam Guk Yu Sa (Records Remaining of the Three Kingdoms) [Text in Chinese], by Kim Kyŏn-myŏng (Il Yŏn). ca. 1925.

SANDS, WILLIAM FRANKLIN. *Undiplomatic Memories.* New York, 1930.

SAVAGE-LANDOR, A. HENRY. *Corea or Cho-sen: The Land of the Morning Calm.* London, 1895.

SHOEMAKER, JAMES. *Notes on Korea's Postwar Economic Position* [Mimeographed]. Secretariat Paper No. 4, Institute of Pacific Relations. New York, 1947.

SLAWIK, ALEXANDER. "Die Chinesischen Präfekturen (Kün) in Korea zur Han-, Wei- und Tsin-Zeit." *Wiener Beiträge zur Kunst- und Kultur-Geschichte Asiens,* Vol. 7, pp. 5-13. Vienna, 1933.

Summation of Non-Military Activities in Japan and Korea, Supreme Commander for the Allied Powers, September-October, 1945. [Following the first five numbers, the reports on Korea, originally appended to those on Japan, appeared separately with the imprint *Summation of U.S. Army Military Government Activities in Korea, Commander-in-Chief U.S. Army Forces, Pacific,* No. 6, March, 1946 to No. 22, July, 1947. No. 23 of the series appeared with the imprint *South Korea Interim Government Activities, United States Army Forces in Korea,* No. 1. August, 1947. Then followed twelve more volumes, Nos. 24 to 35, September, 1947 to September-October, 1948, with the added line "Prepared by National Economic Board." One more volume for November-December, 1948, was expected to be issued, but if so, it has not been seen. The first five numbers were apparently mimeographed in Tokyo, the last thirty in Seoul.]

TAYLER, CONSTANCE. *Koreans at Home,* 2nd ed. London, 1904.

Thriving Chosen: A Survey of Twenty-Five Years' Administration. Compiled by Government-General of Chosen. [Seoul ?], 1935.

Tong Guk T'ong Gam (The Complete Mirror of the Eastern Kingdom) [Text in Chinese], by Hong Yeu-ha, 7 vols., ca. 1654. [This work is a textbook edition of the *Tong Guk T'ong Gam* by Sŏ Kŏ-chŏng and Chung Hyo-hang, published in 28 vols. in 1485.]

Tong Sa Kang Yo (Summary of Korean History) [Text in Chinese], by Chang Tong, 9 vols. ca. 1884.

Transactions of the Korea Branch of the Royal Asiatic Society, Vols. 1-30. Seoul, 1900-40.

TROLLOPE, M. N. "Book Production and Printing in Corea," *Trans. R.A.S.-K.B.,* Vol. 25, pp. 101-7. Seoul, 1936.

——. "Kang-Wha," *Trans. R.A.S.-K.B.,* Vol. 2, Pt. 1, pp. 1-36. Seoul, 1901.

UNDERWOOD, HORACE G. *The Call of Korea: Political, Social, Religious.* New York, 1908.

UNDERWOOD, HORACE H. "Korean Boats and Ships," *Trans. R.A.S.-K.B.,* Vol. 23, pp. viii, 1-99. Seoul, 1934.

——. "A Partial Bibliography of Occidental Literature on Korea; From Early Times to 1930," *Trans. R.A.S.-K.B.,* Vol. 22, pp. 17-186. Seoul, 1931.

UNDERWOOD, L. H. *Fifteen Years Among the Top-Knots or Life in Korea.* New York, 1904.

VAN BUSKIRK, JAMES DALE. *Korea: Land of the Dawn.* New York, 1931.

WAGNER, ELLASUE. *Korea: The Old and the New.* New York, 1931.

WALES, NYM. "Rebel Korea," *Pacific Affairs,* Vol. 15, No. 1, pp. 25-43. New York, 1942.

WASHBURN, JOHN N. "Russia Looks at Northern Korea," *Pacific Affairs,* Vol. 20, No. 2, pp. 152-60. New York, 1947.

WEINERT, OLGA. "The Korean Land Reform," *Military Government Journal,* Vol. 1, No. 8, pp. 1-5, 24. Washington, D. C., 1948.

YOUN, L. EUL SOU. *Le Confucianism en Corée.* Paris, 1939.

INDEX

Abortion, 113
Acheson, Dean, 344
Address, terms of, 50-51
Administrator, Korean Civil, 20
Adoption, 40, 147
Adultery, 216, 221, 224
Affection, sources of, 333
Afterbirth, disposal of, 93
Age, comparative figures, 42-43; headband as a symbol of, 139; system of counting, 43, 104; veneration of, 50, 52, 61, 62, 114, 124
Agent, absentee landlord, 70, 71
Agolt'a, 227
Agriculture, 6, 17, 61-63, 229, 295; among tribespeople, 218, 219, 221, 222, 223-24, 226, 227; Department of, 23, 231; implements, 19, 64, 65, 67-73; influence of China, 215, 229, 327; influence of Japan, 67, 231, 295; introduction of, 214; products raised in Söndup'o, 62-63, 90; teaching of, 102, 160, 281
Ainu, 160
Ajön, description of, 135; role of, 338
Alceste, ship, 204
Alcoholism. See Drinking
Alphabet, phonetic (önmun), 271
Altaic, language, 326
Altars, 16, 152, 160
Americans, attitudes toward Koreans, 303, 341; establish agricultural school, 273; ignorance of Koreans, 302, 341; Korean attitudes toward, 12, 59, 206, 302, 323; medical aid, 268, 322; policy of, 303, 341; schools taught by, 291. See also United States
American zone, 299-324; area, 318; currency, 319-20; effect of repatriation, 321; elections, 312; exchange rate, 319-20; heavy industry closed down, 320-21; Korean People's Republic declared unlawful, 301; number of troops, 299, 299f; population, 318; power cut off, 322; restrictions on troops, 316; treatment of Japanese, 302; U. N. Commission, 312; withdrawal of troops, 313, 342-43. See also United States
Amur River, 171, 224
Amusements, children, 96
Ancestors, worship of, 38, 108, 114, 119-20, 121-22, 233, 332
Ancestor tablets, 30, 99, 117, 119, 120, 128, 249, 250

An Chae-hong, 301, 305-306, 312
An Cha-jung, 258
An Chung-kŭn, 306
An Do-hi, 306
Andong Kim, clan, 242
Anesthetics, lack of, 268
Animals, wild, 15, 260
Animism. See Spirits
Ankle bands, 327
Annexation, Japanese, 9, 10, 22, 277-98; effects of, 23, 44, 50, 57, 58, 60, 72, 88, 90, 114; Korean acceptance, 279; propaganda of, 285
Anniversaries. See Ceremonies
Anpang (women's quarters), 136-37
Aphrodisiac, 325
Apiaries, 88
Appearance, physical, 6, 33, 326
Arborvitae, 14
Arch, memorial, 152
Archery, 141
Architecture, 24-31, 135-37, 234-35, 263, 335, 336
Arirang, song, 257
Armor, of Suksin, 226
Army, American, 311, 345-46; north Korean, 317; south Korean, 318f, 343; Yi dynasty, 195
Arrests. See Police
Arrowroot, 119
Arts, historical survey, 256-66; influence of Buddhism, 249
Asan, 208
Ashshovel, iron, 28
Ashtrays, 30
Assassination, 303, 305, 305f, 306, 306f, 343. See also Murder
Assembly, freedom of, 291, 293-94, 312
Assembly, South Korea Interim Legislative, 311-12
Association, School Support, 103
Astrology, 223, 254
Astronomy, 216-17, 266-67
Atrocities, 286f, 287-88, 289-90, 316f, 343
Automobiles. See Transportation
Awards, royal, 141
Ax, 126
Azaleas, 15

Backgammon, 142
Badgers, 15, 78
Bag, mesh, 78; rice straw, 62, 65, 74, 116
Ball, rice straw, 97; rubber, 96
Balloon flower, 86

367

VERMONT COLLEGE
MONTPELIER, VERMONT

WITHDRAWN